Wives Not Slaves

Wives Not Slaves

Patriarchy and Modernity in the Age of Revolutions

KIRSTEN SWORD

The University of Chicago Press

Chicago and London

PUBLICATION OF THIS BOOK HAS BEEN AIDED BY A GRANT FROM THE
BEVINGTON FUND.

The University of Chicago Press, Chicago 60637
The University of Chicago Press, Ltd., London
© 2021 by The University of Chicago
Published 2021
Printed in the United States of America

30 29 28 27 26 25 24 23 22 21   1 2 3 4 5

ISBN-13: 978-0-226-75748-3 (cloth)
ISBN-13: 978-0-226-75751-3 (e-book)
DOI: https://doi.org/10.7208/chicago/9780226757513.001.0001

Library of Congress Cataloging-in-Publication Data

Names: Sword, Kirsten, author.
Title: Wives not slaves : patriarchy and modernity in the age of revolutions /
    Kirsten Sword.
Other titles: American beginnings, 1500–1900.
Description: Chicago : The University of Chicago Press, 2021. | Series: American
    beginnings, 1500–1900 | Includes bibliographical references and index.
Identifiers: LCCN 2020029630 | ISBN 9780226757483 (cloth) | ISBN 9780226757513 (ebook)
Subjects: LCSH: Marriage law—United States—History. | Equality before the law—
    United States—History. | Equality—United States—History. | Sex role—
    United States—History. | Sex discrimination—Law and legislation—United States—
    History. | Women's rights—United States—History. | Patriarchy—United States—
    History. | Male domination (Social structure)—United States—History.
Classification: LCC KF510 .S96 2021 | DDC 346.7301/63—dc23
LC record available at https://lccn.loc.gov/2020029630

♾ This paper meets the requirements of ANSI/NISO Z39.48–1992 (Permanence of Paper).

To my households
Bryan, Phyllis, and Eric Sword
Elena and Rowan and, especially, Aaron Stalnaker
Thank you for teaching me the virtues of dependence and love.

Contents

WHEREAS *Eunice Davis,* Wife of me *John Davis* of Portfmouth, Taylor, has abfented herfelf from me, without juft Caufe, and refufes to live with me, tho' often requefted, and has left three fmall Children in a very unnatural Manner:

THIS is therefore to forbid any Perfon entertaining or harbouring her on my Account, or giving her Credit for Money or any Thing whatfoever. And yet notwithftanding this Conduct, I promife, in Cafe fhe will foon return to her Duty, and the Care of her Children, as a Mother ought to do, fhe fhall be kindly received, provided her future Conduct is agreeable to Reafon.

                                        his
                        JOHN † DAVIS,
                                      Mark.

FIGURE 0.1 John Davis advertisement, *New-Hampshire Gazette,* July 30, 1762
Courtesy of the American Antiquarian Society

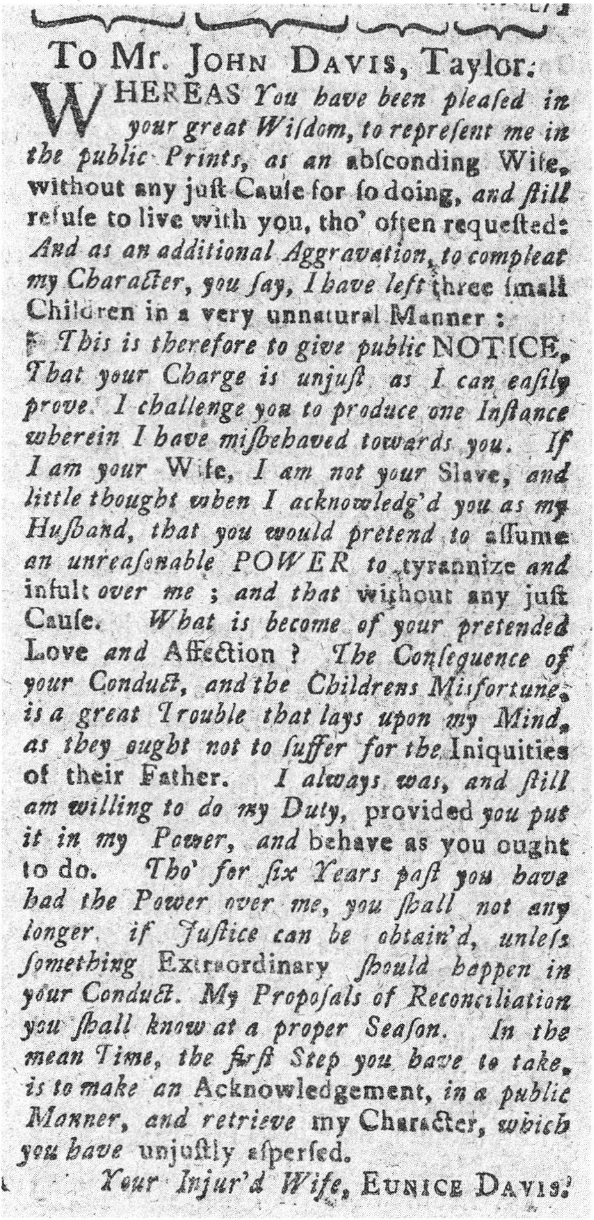

To Mr. JOHN DAVIS, Taylor:

WHEREAS *You have been pleased in your great Wisdom, to represent me in the public Prints, as an absconding Wife, without any just Cause for so doing, and still refuse to live with you, tho' often requested: And as an additional Aggravation, to compleat my Character, you say, I have left* three small Children in a very unnatural Manner :

This is therefore to give public NOTICE, That your Charge is unjust, as I can easily prove. I challenge you to produce one Instance wherein I have misbehaved towards you. If I am your Wife, *I am not your* Slave, *and little thought when I acknowledg'd you as my Husband, that you would pretend to assume an unreasonable POWER to tyrannize and* insult *over me ; and that without any just* Cause. *What is become of your pretended* Love *and* Affection ? *The Consequence of your Conduct, and the Childrens Misfortune, is a great Trouble that lays upon my Mind, as they ought not to suffer for the Iniquities of their Father. I always was, and still am willing to do my Duty,* provided you put *it in my* Power, *and* behave as you ought to do. *Tho' for six Years past you have had the Power over me, you shall not any longer, if Justice can be obtain'd, unless something* Extraordinary *should happen in your Conduct. My Proposals of Reconciliation you shall know at a proper Season. In the mean Time, the first Step you have to take, is to make an* Acknowledgement, *in a public Manner, and retrieve my Character, which you have* unjustly *aspersed.*

       Your Injur'd Wife, EUNICE DAVIS.

FIGURE 0.2 Eunice Davis advertisement, *New-Hampshire Gazette*, August 6, 1762
Courtesy of the American Antiquarian Society

Introduction
"If I am your *Wife*, I am not your *Slave*"

"If I am your *Wife*, I am not your *Slave*," Eunice Davis reminded her husband in the pages of the 1762 *New-Hampshire Gazette*. When she agreed to marry him, Davis continued, "[I] little thought . . . that you would pretend to *assume* an unreasonable POWER to *tyrannize* and *insult* over me; and that *without any just Cause*. What is become of your pretended *Love* and *Affection*?" Eunice Davis's impassioned protest reads like the climax of a novel. She deftly employed the language of revolutionary politics. And she marshaled arguments suited to a court of law. Yet Davis was neither a novelist, nor a political theorist, nor a lawyer. She was the wife of a debt-ridden, semiliterate tailor, and she matters historically precisely because she was so ordinary.[1] This book reconstructs the history of similar female grievances from the mid-seventeenth-century British Atlantic to the early nineteenth-century United States. Stories like Eunice Davis's were always present, usually silenced, and profoundly revealing of fundamental assumptions about the bases for political and legal power.

Newspaper advertisements like Eunice Davis's have much in common with the viral stories of misogyny and abuse that define the historical moment at which this book goes to press. Like the women who have shared their "#MeToo" stories, or like Chanel Miller, whose victim statement captured the grief and rage of millions of sexual assault survivors, Eunice Davis turned to "new media" with her grievances because institutions of justice failed her. The chapters that follow are anchored by accounts showing how people disadvantaged by the law sought remedies in and outside the courts. Such small-scale stories offer larger historical lessons. First, they illuminate how inescapable reliance on legal sources shapes and distorts historical narratives, both at the level of surviving evidence and through the disproportionate role that legal authorities have played in crafting foundational theories of social development. Second, case studies of "eloping" wives like Eunice Davis and of the runaway slaves and servants that appeared alongside them in the eighteenth-century press offer a window on how marriage law developed in dialogue with laws defining colonial slavery and servitude. Collectively, they highlight connections between the distress of ordinary households, domestic unrest, and political unrest. They invite reexamination of sweeping histories of revolutionary change, in which the emergence of a modern social order grounded in egalitarian domestic relations displaced older patriarchy thanks to the political revolutions of the late eighteenth century. The history told here is one in which radical change and revolutionary backlash amplify each other, furthering what the historian Judith Bennett has termed "patriarchal equilibrium." Revolutions run in circles, not straight lines.[2]

In researching this book, I pulled thousands of elopement and runaway advertisements from colonial and English newspapers and tracked hundreds of cases into local archives. Such sources allow examination of the local dynamics of household justice on both sides of the Atlantic, from the English Revolution through the American Revolution. The repetitive processes by which ordinary people learned to name and challenge injustice do not conform to tidy timelines or the regional divisions one would expect based on formal legal rules. I argue that the variable patterns in local norms should be the transatlantic baseline against which we assess the prescriptive claims of legislatures, legal treatises, religious moralists, and novelists. Histories framed by assertions in prescriptive texts and easily identifiable legal landmarks too often mistake rhetoric for reality.[3]

Analogies between wives and slaves highlight that confusion, especially when the comparison is used to distinguish enlightened present from ancient past. The notion that a well-ordered society builds on well-ordered families and households, and that marriage is a means to secure that order, has a very long history. Analogies between marriage and slavery hearken back to Aristotle, whose *Politics* made the domestic government that male householders exercised over their dependent wives, children, and slaves the foundation for complex political structures. Such ideas are not timeless, but repeatedly timely. They recur as part of the processes by which gendered hierarchies defy radical transformation, despite otherwise significant cultural and economic change.[4]

The Political Uses of Ancient Patriarchy

Aristotelian and Roman arguments about household patriarchy endure because European colonial powers revived them to support new forms of government and new forms of slavery between the sixteenth and nineteenth centuries. These colonial and revolutionary undertakings established the jurisdictional framework and argumentative terms of our contemporary debates about marriage: Is it a privilege or a right? A sacrament or a contract? Is it a public or a private matter, and what might that mean? Amid the competing claims of localities, states, national governments, courts, legislatures, religious institutions, families, and married couples themselves, where does ultimate jurisdiction over marriage lie? Should marriage mediate the relationship between individuals and the state, and if so, how?

These questions are still with us today because they defy easy, concrete answers. Historically, the very attempt to decisively settle them has rekindled uncertainty. As we shall see, the pithy summaries of marriage law that generations of historians have used to frame discussion of past norms—particularly the ubiquitous explanation of married women's status under the law of coverture supplied by the eighteenth-century jurist Sir William Blackstone—should not be taken at face value. These were position statements in now-forgotten legal contests, not disinterested records of historical precedent. In his enormously influential *Commentaries on the Laws of England* (1765–69), Blackstone rehabilitated classical parallels between the law of master and slave, husband and wife, and parent and child to give deceptive coherence to a particularly piecemeal and conflicted aspect of legal practice. (His schema hinted at the variability of domestic order with the substitution of "master and servant" for "master and slave.") Blackstone's account of coverture helped turn contradictory assumptions about marital unity, masculine power, and women's subordination into fixed legal doctrine. "By marriage," Blackstone explained, "the husband and wife are one person in law: that is, the very being or legal existence of the woman is suspended during the marriage, or at least is incorporated and consolidated into that of the husband: under whose wing, protection, and *cover*, she performs everything." His definition hardened the edges of legal patriarchy while insisting he was doing the opposite. The "old common law," he assured his readers, was much more rigid than his "modern" interpretation of it.[5]

Whether in runaway ads or legal treatises, appeals to timeless patriarchal order alert us to social and political *disorder*. The legal treatises, history, and philosophy written by Blackstone and his Scottish Enlightenment contemporaries (most of whom were also lawyers by training) not only interpreted but also channeled the social and economic upheaval of the mid-eighteenth century. Their legal declarations about the "settled law" of domestic relations fit into a long-term pattern in which authoritative pronouncements about household order signaled larger conflicts over both household and political sovereignty. They assumed the mantle of antiquity in order to claim legitimacy for their own patriarchal innovations.

Public marital conflicts like Davis's were at once symptoms and sources of the disorder that characterized the eighteenth-century "age of revolutions." Eunice Davis's challenge to her husband's tyranny anticipated the language later used by political revolutionaries. In retrospect, the Davis marital conflict exposed the roots of colonists' political discontent. The crisis in the Davis marriage grew out of the economic crisis created by the Great War for Empire, begun in North America in 1754. Great Britain emerged victorious in 1763, but the costs and responsibilities of that victory fueled, in turn, the political turmoil that culminated in the American Revolution. These same decades saw massive growth and painful contractions in local and international credit networks, a dramatic expansion in the volume and variety of printed media, the emergence of an organized movement against slavery, and an upswing in popular demand for legal divorce. Historians have examined these developments separately; this book explains how they are connected.

In the Scottish Enlightenment's stage-driven accounts of the rise of modern civilizations, marriage and slavery became parallel indices of social progress. Divorce and emancipation in particular served to define modernity against a patriarchal past.[6] Ambitious historical syntheses still invoke them as evidence that American revolutionary radicalism extended beyond the ranks of white men, or as signs of broader eighteenth-century "expansion of self-determination" that enabled the concept of individual rights to triumph over "traditional" communal authority. However, as the historian Norma Basch has noted, it is easier to trace "connections between revolution and divorce at a high level of abstraction than it is to understand their influence on ordinary people."[7]

Household conflicts like the Davises' bridge the gap between the abstractions of social theorists and the experiences of "ordinary people." Such conflicts were fundamental to political debates about divorce and revolution, rather than simply influenced by them. This history seems "muddled" to us because eighteenth-century legal and social theorists established misleading expectations with accounts of social change that stressed the ways in which wives were *like* slaves. Nineteenth-century reformers, in turn, used the analogy to challenge both institutions, but on terms that allowed little room for historical complexity or dependents' agency. The American feminist icon Elizabeth Cady Stanton, for example, argued in her 1854 address to the New York legislature that the typical wife "holds about the same legal position that does the slave of the Southern plantations. She can own nothing, sell nothing.

She has no right even to the wages she earns; her person, her time, her services are the property of another." Stanton's controversial premise was that the legal emancipation of married women and slaves were equivalent steps toward social progress. When the influential English jurist and historian Henry Sumner Maine declared in 1861 that the demise of slavery and the end of women's "tutelage" in the family were key markers of the inevitable progress from "status to contract" that defined modern societies, he echoed Stanton's logic and also sought to contain it. Evolutionary progress required no radical interventions.[8]

In the early twentieth century, Virginia Woolf captured problems with the analogy between wives and slaves that still vex historians. When Woolf read literature from virtually any historical period, she could imagine women as "of the utmost importance; very various; heroic and mean; splendid and sordid; infinitely beautiful and hideous in the extreme; as great as a man" or in some accounts even greater. When Woolf read history, however, she found that these fictional women sat uncomfortably alongside their "factual" sisters. From the historians, Woolf learned that in most places and times and especially in early modern England, a woman was "the slave of any boy whose parents forced a ring upon her finger. . . . She could scarcely read, could hardly spell, and was the property of her husband."[9]

The "fact" of women's legal subordination justified historical assumptions about their insignificance and historians' lack of curiosity about their experiences. In the popular imagination, comparisons of wives and slaves still serve as a convenient way to contrast women's status in the "bad old days" with the supposedly more enlightened present. "Under the patriarchal system of values," wrote the historian Lawrence Stone of the *Road to Divorce*, "a married woman was the nearest approximation in a free society to a slave. . . . The subsequent revolution in marriage was mainly a long battle for the liberation of wives from this position of total legal subordination." According to a popular Ken Burns documentary, wives were "in fact . . . the property of their husbands." Before Stanton and Susan B. Anthony's efforts to "overthrow the customs and laws that had kept women powerless," the film concluded, "there is no women's history."[10] This form of wife/slave analogy condemns what we now see as an unjust social order, but it has the ironic effect of obscuring the history that made this condemnation possible. It perpetuates the dangerous illusion that that past is no longer with us. And it renders it very difficult to make sense of the lives of women who came before the organized reform movements of the nineteenth century, particularly the experiences of women who were, in fact, slaves.

Virginia Woolf's summary of historical "fact," in contrast, expressed frustration with histories that took legal conventions dictating women's "total . . . subordination" as the sum of their experiences. In 1929, Woolf challenged the rising generation of college-educated women to "write a supplement to history" that drew on the "mass of information" scattered about in "parish records and account books" to bring to life the ordinary women she missed in both history and literature. Almost a century later, persistent popular claims that women—or any subordinate group—had "no history" before nineteenth- and twentieth-century movements for political rights inspire the collective pulling of hair and gnashing of teeth among scholars familiar with the "mass of information" now available. Study of "ordinary" and oppressed people—male and female—has produced much more than a "supplement" to history or marginal stories driven by "identity politics." Yet social historians have not extricated themselves from the stories about legal patriarchy generated by eighteenth-century theorists. The past two generations of scholarship in women's history have inundated us with examples of "exceptions" to coverture's rules. Only very recently have we begun to recognize that legal variety may in fact be the rule.[11]

Wives Not Slaves seeks to understand the paradoxes of dependents' legal subordination and practical human agency through careful attention to how household hierarchies worked on a day-to-day basis. In the seventeenth- and eighteenth-century Anglophone world, patriarchal household order sustained itself by administering adequate justice to free household dependents as well as household heads. This was not equal justice. It was often brutal justice. But it was justice sufficiently inclusive to preserve communal investment in household hierarchy. Eunice Davis was, in all likelihood, "beaten and flung about the room." But, as she adamantly insisted, she was *not* a slave. Neither she nor her community thought she should be without recourse against her husband's tyranny. In the colonial world, her invocation of slavery was not simply abstract; such comparisons at once normalized and raised doubts about the mistreatment of enslaved people. To be a slave was to be abused, but was domestic "tyranny" acceptable in any context?

The routine violence of the slave system simultaneously threatened and reinforced patriarchal equilibrium. Slaves ran away and revolted, despite dire consequences. White colonists lived in fear of such revolts and took increasingly brutal steps to deter them. Both actions leave no doubt that the enslaved and slaveholders alike sensed the injustice and instability inherent in the system. Its fragility increased pressure on other household relationships to model sustainable hierarchy. Stories about the historical "total subordination" of household dependents, whether wives or slaves, were authoritarian fantasies designed to make such hierarchies seem less oppressive through comparison; they used claims of progress to defend stasis.[12]

Domestic violence—with or without redress—was no less possible in the nineteenth century than it had been in the seventeenth, and it does not easily fit into linear narratives about the decline of "ancient" authoritarian forms of household government. If anything, such narratives intensified legal patriarchy in the late eighteenth and early nineteenth centuries. When jurists like Blackstone framed patriarchal absolutism as the "ancient" norm and characterized equally ancient checks on householders' authority as novel "modern" exceptions, they reified patriarchal power. Such arguments were readily adopted by those who framed colonial slavery as an extension of ancient precedent, rather than a novel system of economic exploitation.

Stories about domestic conflict—about sex, money, power, and the mundane question of who gets to sleep in a warm bed—are stunningly repetitive across time and place. Elements of Eunice and John Davis's story were very old and remain very familiar. In medieval and early modern church and court records and literature, aggrieved wives who left their husbands to take refuge with family, friends, and neighbors were a constant, if not a common, presence. So too were husbands who denounced the "evil minded People" who aided their wives and passed judgment on their household affairs. If we are to understand these continuities, we need histories that explain not only how gendered hierarchies change, but also how—through such changes—they resist fundamental transformation. The politics behind claims about timeless patriarchy is an important place to start.[13]

Divorce, Jurisdiction, and the Location of Law

Seemingly arcane jurisdictional conflicts between branches of England's legal system—as well as among England, the rest of Great Britain, and her colonies—fundamentally shaped our inherited storylines of liberal progress. A brief introduction to early modern marriage law and legal terminology is consequently in order if readers are to understand the ways in which couples like Eunice and John Davis and legal authorities like Blackstone engaged with debates about what was and was not "law."

Casual invocation of "the law" as something concrete and enforceable comes easily to people who have not been entangled in the system. Even experts in the complexity of the modern American legal system are often unfamiliar with its markedly different seventeenth-century antecedents. We take for granted a system grounded in texts, including founding constitutional documents, legislative acts, and layers of published precedents. Judges in this "common law" system have considerable leeway to apply those precedents in their interpretation of codes or the circumstances of particular cases, in contrast with continental Europe's "civil law" traditions, where judicial interpretation is expected to follow written codes more strictly. The American system is also geographically organized and hierarchically nested, with lower-level local and state courts operating fairly autonomously, but with plaintiffs assuming the right to appeal to higher levels of judicial authority, ending with a final, central jurisdiction vested in a supreme court.

In seventeenth-century England, the "common law" referred not to the entire legal system, but to one branch of a multipartite system with overlapping jurisdictions. "Common law" courts dealt primarily with property and criminal disputes using a highly technical system of writs, and judges decided cases based on their understanding of this system, Crown statutes, and local custom. Textual precedent as we now understand it emerged later, in the eighteenth century and with the codification movement of the nineteenth century. At the outset of the period covered by this study, precedent was a malleable function of institutional memory, and not bound by public records of earlier decisions. To the contrary, jurists and legislators alike sought to limit access to records of their deliberations for fear that general access would limit their interpretive discretion, and they consequently distrusted the publishing industry that emerged in the middle of the 1600s.

Courts of equity constituted the second branch of the centralized legal system in seventeenth-century England. As a legal term, *equity* can be confusing because it refers both to a general principle in which authorities administer justice in ways that privilege fair—or "equitable"—outcomes over formal legal rules, and also to a specific English legal tradition that held broad jurisdiction over matters not fairly handled within the limits of the common law. England's Court of Chancery, headed by the lord chancellor, was the institutional home of equitable justice and developed the tradition's procedures and rules. The Court of the Exchequer heard both equitable and common-law matters. In general, courts of equity could prevent and even punish common-law action that equitable jurists deemed unjust. This fundamental opposition between common law and equity accounts for somewhat confusing terminology: *law* in English legal usage is assumed to refer to the common law, and the legal tradition of equity is therefore called *equitable jurisprudence* or just *equity*, never *equity law*.[14]

Finally, ecclesiastical courts made up the third branch of the centralized English legal system. Church courts had been preserved under Anglican control after the Reformation and carried on many of the traditions of Catholic canon law. Their extensive local presence and involvement with births, marriages, and deaths made them the branch of the legal system that ordinary people were most likely to encounter in daily life.[15]

By the seventeenth century, these three branches of the legal system had national reach and a hierarchy centered in London, along with other functions of the Crown. They were not, however, the full extent of the judicial system. Maritime courts drew on civil law traditions to regulate crimes and commerce at sea. Manor courts under the control of local lords and other special jurisdictions granted by Parliament, including newly founded colonies and corporations, also preserved semiautonomous courts and legal powers. Each of these had its own distinctive set of practices and rules, which drew on common law and equity but were not exclusively dependent on them. Their place in the jurisdictional hierarchy was not clear. There was no universally accepted "supreme court" to resolve conflicts among them. The modern system of judicial appeal emerged over the period of this study, in response to the conflicts generated by the expanding colonial system, which never fully replicated England's tripartite system.[16]

Marital matters almost inevitably highlighted tension between these competing jurisdictions. Marriage was a concern of common law insofar as it organized the intergenerational transmission of property. Common-law procedures relied heavily on the fiction of marital unity, the significance of which was open to contest. To counterbalance formal limitations on married women's legal agency, women and their families invoked alternative legal fictions within the common law, as well as trusts and other devices available through courts of equity.

Conflict within marriage was traditionally a matter for the ecclesiastical courts. Religious jurisdiction over marriage had provided the Catholic Church with much of its power over Europe's hereditary rulers. Under Catholic canon law, divorce as we now know it did not exist. Instead, complex rules regarding the legitimate formation of marriages allowed considerable wiggle room for those seeking annulments—a form of marital exit that had the disadvantage of bastardizing any children. Dispensation to separate but not remarry (known as bed and board divorce, or divorce *a mensa et thoro*) could be obtained in cases of abuse. Protestant reformers began reevaluating Catholic prohibitions on divorce during the 1500s, and in English politics these debates played out in the still-familiar story of Henry VIII and his many wives. Henry's unsuccessful effort to have his first marriage annulled led him to separate the English church from Roman Catholic authority. All told, Henry obtained two Anglican annulments, put two wives to death for adultery and treason, and had two marriages that ended in natural death. His shifting marital alliances produced political instability and prompted subsequent generations of Anglican religious authorities to remain more conservative on the question of divorce than their Protestant counterparts elsewhere in Europe.

This book begins a century after Henry VIII's contentious marriages, with colonial and English debates over marriage law and practice that spanned England's mid-seventeenth-century civil wars and the restoration of the monarchy in the 1660s. These seventeenth-century conflicts set the parameters for the next two centuries of debate about the relationship between authority in households and authority in politics. While the legal language about marriage remained remarkably consistent during this period, practical options for addressing marital conflict changed dramatically. The ecclesiastical courts lost power in England and were never established in most of her colonies, which adopted English institutions and rules in a piecemeal fashion. Equity expanded as a powerful albeit cumbersome tool for wealthy elites, and inspired a backlash by common lawyers and the wealthy creditors who found them useful. The resulting ascent of the common law had wide-ranging repercussions in a world in which even impoverished householders found themselves entangled in increasingly complex webs of credit and debt. International credit networks were enmeshed with the emerging system of racial slavery in ways that shaped domestic law in Britain and all her colonies, regardless of the degree to which the institution was a local presence. And finally, the dramatic growth of the press gave ordinary people power to draw on a transatlantic repertoire of debates about household order, and to make legal and moral arguments independent of the claims of local legal authorities.

In light of this context, this book considers a range of marital disputes, rather than divorce specifically. Historians focus on divorce cases because their records are often unusually rich. However, the cases here emerged in a world in which divorce was not necessarily an option or even an aim, and the more common scenario was litigation intended to force negotiation, and perhaps achieve "narrative vindication" through the public airing of grievances. Frustratingly, the most engaging stories often left no clear resolution in the records.[17] Charles Dickens's *Bleak House* illustrated the perils and inconclusiveness of familial legal conflict with a fictional equitable dispute in Chancery that lasted several generations, ending not with a decision but when the money to pay the legal fees ran out. The frequently unanswerable question of whether couples "divorced or not" is less significant than what family disputes tell us about how conflicts could be negotiated, and about the expectations and power of householders and dependents, men and women. Such patterns remain with us and are taking new forms with the advent of our own era's digital media revolution.

Debt and the Paradox of Masculine Possessory
Rights in the Age of Revolutions

The newspapers that spread throughout the British Empire during the eighteenth century became a convenient new means of asserting masculine authority. Individual husbands and masters used the press to perform disciplinary work that they could not do alone, but which established institutions were unable or unwilling to do. Political and religious authorities had distrusted print media from the time it emerged as important fuel for the Protestant Reformation in the 1500s. English authorities tightly controlled the press until 1641, when politics and the press simultaneously spun out of control; the English Civil Wars and English newspapers emerged together. The restored monarchy imposed new restrictions on the press in the 1660s, but newspapers persisted and spread from London to other English cities in the late seventeenth century, and then gradually through the colonies. Colonial papers were less noteworthy for their news, which typically reprinted English or continental sources, than for their advertising, which contained a hodgepodge of commercial and legal—and sometimes extralegal—notices.

Ads of runaway slaves and servants, as well as the lesser-known ads of wayward wives, became self-perpetuating phenomena as the press expanded, largely independent of the wishes of formal legal authorities. Ads about wayward wives, unlike those for other runaways, generated controversy. Wives repeatedly protested publicly that their husbands' advertisements were "unjust." Eunice Davis's rebuttal was one of many that spurred debate about the relationship between different kinds of dependent status and about the nature of householders' power. From the perspective of local communities, ads about wives (henceforth *elopement* or *desertion notices*) were almost as likely to indicate a rogue husband as an unruly woman. The Davis case followed a pattern that recurred for a century, as newspapers sprouted up in new communities in England and her colonies. John Davis was one of the first husbands to use the recently founded *New-Hampshire Gazette* to denounce his wife, and Eunice was not alone in thinking that he had assumed an "unreasonable POWER."[18]

Despite community and legal skepticism, husbands' advertisements became commonplace after 1750. The phenomenon encapsulated tensions that gave rise to late eighteenth-century revolutionary unrest. Husbands' advertisements were foremost a symptom of masculine economic vulnerability. By the mid-eighteenth century, even ordinary householders of modest means depended on far-reaching credit networks. War-related economic volatility and stepped-up imperial efforts to collect colonial debts amplified economic anxiety. Common-law treatises such as Blackstone's *Commentaries* emphasized masculine responsibility for dependents because this served the interests of creditors. A stringent view of coverture made it harder to shield wives' property from husbands' creditors, and conversely made it possible for an angry woman to ruin her husband, who could find himself imprisoned for debt.

Imagined threats to household integrity fueled political unrest. Possessory rights to dependents became the basis for expansive claims to masculine political rights, even as they made men vulnerable. Scottish Enlightenment and American revolutionary advocates of universal male suffrage argued, "Every man has what may be called property, and unalienable property. . . . Even men, who are in a state of dependence upon others, and who receive charity, have wives and children, in whom they have a right."[19] Exaggerated claims about a husband's "right" to the person and labor of his wife had gained traction as a means to enforce liability; they were reified by men's efforts to escape it, in a self-perpetuating cycle that grounded masculine independence in feminine dependence. This rhetorical struggle gave life to analogies between wives and slaves, eliding social hierarchies that had once given some women considerable power.

Masculine possessory rights and wife/slave comparisons took yet another ironic turn in revolutionary debates about marriage and household justice spurred by women who were actual, rather than metaphorical, slaves. Where Eunice Davis used analogies between marriage and slavery to challenge her husband's authority, enslaved men and women, in contrast, might invoke husbands' legal authority to *preserve* the "endearing ties of husband and wife." The denial of legal protection for slaves' marriages was a defining feature of colonial slavery. During a wave of activism in the 1760s and 1770s, people of color on both sides of the Atlantic pushed back, claiming marriage as a right. Paradoxically, their freedom suits turned the aspects of marriage that made it analogous to slavery into the key to enslaved women's freedom. Efforts by same-sex couples to uphold marriage as a right rather than a privilege have precedent not only in the twentieth-century civil rights movement, but in slaves' suits for freedom begun before the American Revolution. These freedom suits, moreover, pioneered the political strategies that allowed localized, individual demands for legal justice to become tests of national principles. The jurisdictional politics that make contemporary debates about marriage especially complex reflect the legacy of past debates about slavery.[20]

Past debates about marriage and household justice will not settle present ones, but they can help us understand them. In 1776, the US Congress declared, and in 1848 the women's rights convention at Seneca Falls repeated the claim, that "mankind are more disposed to suffer, while evils are sufferable, than to right themselves by abolishing the forms to which they are accustomed."[21] *Wives Not Slaves* turns this premise into a series of questions: In debates over household justice, what distinguished "sufferable" and insufferable evils? When and how did grievances generate demands for redress? And under what circumstances did the complaints of wives and slaves become issues that required the "abolition" of old forms and customs, rather than case-specific remedies?

Nineteenth-century reformers supplied misleading answers to these questions. When they imitated the Declaration of Independence in their own Declaration of Sentiments, the women at Seneca Falls strategically positioned their humanitarian demands as part of the natural legacy of the American Revolution. Political rights for women, they contended, were a natural extension of an American revolutionary political agenda grounded in the abolition of old patriarchal forms and customs. American advocates of women's rights, like the antislavery activists they imitated, had compelling political reasons to attach their agendas to the American revolutionary legacy inscribed in the Declaration of Independence.

These nineteenth-century stories obscure earlier history. The connections of both antislavery and women's rights activism to American revolutionary politics, and to each other, were circuitous rather than straightforward. There were many people in the revolutionary generations of the late eighteenth-century British Empire who imagined the abolition of slavery and the reordering of marriage as real possibilities. Both causes remained live issues in the nineteenth century, however, because they did *not* become part of the American revolutionary political agenda. *Wives Not Slaves* reexamines those revolutionary possibilities and draws new connections between the local and transatlantic jurisdictional politics that determined which patriarchal forms and customs the new nation would—and would not—abolish.

The Trials of Christopher and Elizabeth Lawson: An Introduction to Post-Reformation Debates about Marriage

Historians acknowledge the transatlantic roots of "Anglo-American" marriage law and culture, but most tell stories that accentuate contrasts. Colonial practices are measured on scales tuned to their divergence from one another and from artificially stable English norms. Contrasts between divorcing Puritan New England and aristocratic, divorceless old England are particularly common. The cases examined in this chapter and the next—the Lawsons (New England) and the Scotts (England)—at once embody and undermine such distinctions. These parallel case studies recapture the intertwined political stories and contingent nature of changes in marriage law on both sides of the Atlantic.[1]

The Scotts' story amply documents the political stakes in the making and breaking of aristocratic marriages. *Manby v. Scott* (1663), one of several legal disputes that emerged out of decades of marital conflict, entered the legal canon and helped define the next two centuries of marriage law. The Lawsons, in contrast, occupied a more modest rung on the social ladder and at the opposite end of seventeenth-century England's political and religious spectrum. Their story features somberly dressed Puritans whispering about shipboard witchcraft, shady lawyers paid with otter skins, and challenges to established legal, social, and household order rooted in radical religion and in cross-cultural encounters on the Maine frontier.

The Lawsons' and Scotts' marital disputes occurred almost simultaneously. Both couples married in the 1630s, came into significant conflict starting in the 1640s, and left records in multiple legal cases during the 1650s and 1660s; the climactic moment in the Scotts' case came in 1663, while the Lawsons' conflict persisted into the 1670s. Both of these marriages ultimately failed, in that the couples ended their lives separately, and both involved unsuccessful suits for full divorce. However, to speak of them solely as "divorce cases" distracts from a wider context in which divorce was not the primary way of settling marital conflict. The cases are historically interesting both as evidence of lively transatlantic debates about legal jurisdiction over marriage and the legitimacy of divorce, and as windows into alternative means of negotiating marital breakdown. In particular, Christopher Lawson and Edward Scott both posted public notices declaring that they would not be held liable for their wives' debts, and the cases are thus rare, early examples of a controversial practice that became common during the eighteenth century, and which later chapters of this book analyze in detail.

Taken together, the Lawsons' and Scotts' cases establish a seventeenth-century baseline for analysis of subsequent continuity in legal practice, as well as for important changes in tone. The cases illustrate the legal parameters we will see recurring in marital disputes in various places across the nearly two centuries covered in the remainder of this book. Despite the continuity in formal legal arguments, their argumentative tone and content contrasts with norms that emerged in the eighteenth century. None of the parties in these seventeenth-century disputes presents as an injured innocent. While adversarial marital conflicts in every era feature spouses who portray their partners in a negative light, seventeenth-century litigants seemed more concerned with proving their partners' faults than with vindicating themselves. They readily acknowledged themselves as sinners and framed their pursuit of legal remedies as efforts at redemption and justice for all concerned. This framework was patriarchal: male sexual misbehavior weighed more lightly on the legal scales than did female infidelity, and male violence was more easily excused. Nevertheless, Elizabeth Lawson and Catherine Scott remained entitled to legal redress in spite of their own violence and reputed indiscretions, and their misbehavior as wives did not prevent Christopher and Edward from being called to account for their failings as husbands. By the late eighteenth century, courts had become less tolerant of such moral ambiguity, especially on the part of female litigants.

This book opens with analysis of the Lawsons' dispute because it can help us see beyond the long legal shadow cast by the more prominent Scotts' case. Unlike *Manby v. Scott*, the Lawson conflict did not leave a significant textual legacy. Colonial Americans generated no law reports and left very few indications of judicial reasoning in their court records. We know the Lawsons' story primarily from a bundle of documents saved by a nineteenth-century archivist in a file on the colonial law of domestic relations.[2] While the Lawsons' case did not become a clear precedent, it does offer evidence of the unusual and misleading nature of *Manby*'s influential pronouncements about settled law. *Manby* declaimed how the law ought to work in principle; the Lawsons' case, in most respects, modeled how it continued to work in practice. Despite their stark differences, the Lawsons' and Scotts' cases drew on a common repertoire of legal and extralegal means for negotiating marital conflict. They introduce the overlapping range of communal and individual expectations about the purposes marriage served. Together they remind us, moreover, that imperial law was not simply prior to colonial law, but developed alongside and in dialogue with it. This forces a rethinking of the established historical narrative in which marital rules emanated from the imperial Anglican center. Rather, New England's Puritan divorce policy and English Anglican opposition to it emerged together from a context in which the full range of Reformation arguments about marriage and divorce were very much in play.

The Lawsons' story offers a useful introduction to this book's larger themes. First, their dispute documents the complex jurisdictional landscape in which arguments about marriage took place—a debate shaped by competing religious and civil authorities, colonial powers, and implicitly by the presence of indigenous peoples with different practices.

Second, it illustrates the repertoire of post-Reformation arguments about marriage formation, marital obligations, and divorce circulating in the seventeenth-century Atlantic world. The Lawsons' dispute drew on debates that presumed primacy of European traditions and masculine authority, but also stressed the mutual obligations of householders and their dependents. Seventeenth-century communities were far from egalitarian, but they did place checks on men who exploited their wives, children, servants, or outsiders. Such limits on male authority have been obscured by later, post-Restoration authoritarian defenses of monarchy and racial slavery, which deceptively portrayed absolutist patriarchy as an ancient and transcendent historical norm. I selected this case from among other New England disputes because it explicitly invoked the protected and privileged status of white wives; the more vulnerable status of servants, slaves, and indigenous women; and the problem presented by men who abused their power over their subordinates.

And finally, the Lawsons' story serves as a reminder that the cultural and legal development of England's colonial system occurred through multidirectional conversation. England's power gave it a very loud voice in that conversation, and has generated historical narratives that contrast colonial "experiments" with a seemingly fixed body of English law. From the perspective of participants in the revolutions of the mid-seventeenth century, however, English law in general and "domestic law" in particular were contested and in flux. In the early colonies, competing claims to authority opened the door to broad-ranging debate about the religious and secular bases for political power. Provincialism expanded rather than narrowed the scope for arguments about household justice.

The Puritan Context of the Lawson Marriage

Christopher and Elizabeth Lawson married in the midst of a religious schism in Puritan Massachusetts in 1638, and they proceeded to spend more of their married lives apart than together. Christopher lived mostly on the New England frontier in New Hampshire and Maine. Elizabeth lived primarily in Boston, with a sojourn in Cromwell's England from roughly 1648 to 1656, from which Christopher forcibly returned her to New England. After their final legal battle in 1670, Elizabeth "shipped herself" back to England and Christopher settled in Boston. The tale of their marital conflict illuminates the larger history of religious and political debates behind England's Civil Wars and the founding of New England. The Lawsons' relationship collapsed at least in part because they represented different strands of that founding moment: Christopher was an economic opportunist prone to moral lapses and too much religious and political flexibility for the taste of New England's leaders; Elizabeth erred in the other direction, and seems to have been inclined toward zealotry and the fringes of religious reform. They became thorns in the side of authorities on both sides of the Atlantic.

Christopher and Elizabeth came to New England in the Puritan "great migration" of the 1630s, in which some twenty thousand Protestant dissenters fled the religious, political, and economic tensions that led to the outbreak of England's Civil Wars. King Charles I had married a devout French Catholic princess and had given control of the Anglican Church—and the ecclesiastical court system that regulated marriage—to leaders intent on suppressing reform, and possibly sympathetic to Catholicism. Protestant losses in the continental Wars of Religion in the same period made it seem possible that England might also reestablish Catholic authority.

Puritan migrants established the Massachusetts Bay Colony in opposition to the Catholic and High Anglican stance that vested religious—and by extension earthly—authority in established institutions. The Puritans believed in the primacy of scripture and that individuals could experience God's grace directly, without the intervention of religious institutions; sanctification by direct experience of grace, rather than works, was a central Calvinist tenet. They also allowed that divine inspiration might help believers challenge corrupt authorities and laws, but they split repeatedly over how to distinguish such inspiration from heretical challenges to authority. Christopher and

Elizabeth were both tied to Puritan factions that took the idea of "free grace" and direct revelation to extremes. The couple met sometime during the famed "antinomian" or "free grace" crisis of 1636–38, in which the prayer-and-study leader Anne Hutchinson and the minister John Wheelwright were tried and banished for theology that threatened to undermine institutional authority in Massachusetts Bay. As a woman and layperson, Hutchinson was an easier target than the prominent minister John Cotton, to whom Hutchinson attributed the origin of her heretical views and who also served as Elizabeth's mentor. Hutchinson, Wheelwright, and their followers created multiple new, competing jurisdictions just outside Massachusetts borders, including the new colonies of New Hampshire and Rhode Island, as well as settlements with multiple allegiances in what is now Maine.[3]

The breakup of households related to the antinomian exodus likely explains the timing of the Lawsons' wedding. Christopher and Elizabeth Lawson were both young, single, and attached to the households of socially prominent settlers; their associates included some of the most zealous participants in the Antinomian Controversy. Christopher was a kinsman of Anne Hutchinson. He reportedly "married Elizabeth, a serving maid out of the house of Mrs. Scott," in Boston in 1638. If Mrs. Scott was Katherine Marbury Scott, the younger sister of Anne Hutchinson, Elizabeth faced uncertain prospects; her mistress was one of the exiles who founded the colony of Rhode Island that year.[4] A proposal would have seemed a timely offer of security when she found herself with few connections or "Friends" to advise her—a point that would prove critical to her later legal arguments. Christopher and Elizabeth's controversial but nonetheless influential connections might also help explain the extensive legal attention given to their later marital conflicts, even after local authorities appeared disgusted with both of them.

Most of what we know about the Lawson marriage comes from court records collected between 1668 and 1670, when Christopher Lawson aggressively petitioned the Massachusetts Bay authorities for a full divorce from Elizabeth. The case compiled testimony and old correspondence detailing decades of discord, and which can be corroborated in part by miscellaneous official sources, including birth records, deeds, and financial transactions and disputes. The outlines of the history found in those records are as follows:

Christopher and Elizabeth married around the time of Anne Hutchinson's banishment from the Bay Colony in 1638, and became part of the ensuing diaspora of her followers. Together with other kinfolk, Christopher joined the Reverend John Wheelwright (Hutchinson's brother-in-law) in founding Exeter, New Hampshire, in 1639, where he and Elizabeth presumably began their married life as refugees on the frontier. Christopher appears to have remained in exile in New Hampshire from 1639 to 1643, while the upheaval over the Antinomian Controversy worked itself out. By the early 1640s, however, Elizabeth and their three young children were back in Boston. Meanwhile, Christopher claimed multiple residences in Exeter and in Wenham, Massachusetts. He also staked one of several competing claims to territory along the Kennebec River in Maine, for which he successfully negotiated purchase from the Abenaki sachem Abagadusset in 1653. Between the late 1640s and the early 1660s, he set up household there as possibly the first—and certainly one of very few—English settlers in territory still practically controlled by the Abenaki, although it was also claimed by the Massachusetts Bay Colony, Plymouth Colony, proprietors in England, and French Acadians. Despite Christopher's prominent religious family, his commercial ambitions determined his connections more clearly than theological concerns. He spent more than thirty years "vibrating" between his family's nominal home in Boston and these outlying settlements in New Hampshire and Maine.[5]

From the perspective of authorities in Boston who would later review the Lawsons' legal complaints, Christopher's associations were not only theologically dubious but morally and politically suspect. At the same time, they bespoke status and wealth that meant he could not simply be dismissed when legal disputes arose. Christopher reputedly began his colonial career in the service of Thomas Purchase, a genteel adventurer whose 1631 marriage to the mistress of a Catholic spy for the Crown proved an enduring source of scandal. Christopher's association with Wheelwright, on the other hand, suggested an interlude of conscientious Puritan piety, albeit not of a sort favored by the leaders of Massachusetts Bay. His negotiations with tribal leaders and extended sojourns on the frontier placed him in intimate contact with people who disregarded Massachusetts's laws and moral aims; Indians fell into this category simply by virtue of cultural difference, but the outlying settlements also harbored English colonists who had been banished by Puritan authorities for crimes that included heresy and rape. By the 1660s, with the Restoration of Charles II, Christopher was working as an agent for a noble family who had long sought to overturn the Massachusetts charter from the Crown in favor of their own, competing proprietary claim. At various points in Christopher's career, fellow settlers accused him of theft, extortion, and exploitation; yet he was also allowed to secure debts and stand on juries, and he even served briefly as a deputy constable in Maine.[6] Lawson might not have come for the fish like the impious settlers of Marblehead, but he was certainly an opportunist. His insistence on pursuing business in the remote and unsettled peripheries of the New England colonies, even after it again became possible for him to live comfortably in Boston, was a major source of conflict with Elizabeth.

Elizabeth wanted nothing to do with frontier settlement. During the early 1640s, she occupied a Boston house with a wharf, gave birth to the couple's three children, and remained a parishioner of the charismatic John Cotton. Civil war broke out in England in 1642, and in 1648 Parliament and dissenting Protestant allies appeared victorious. During this peaceful interlude, Elizabeth returned home to England with Christopher's permission and legal documents granting her authority to conduct business on his behalf. Christopher claimed to have sent for her in 1651, by which time the second Civil War was underway and England had beheaded Charles I and come under Oliver Cromwell's Protectorate. In 1656, Christopher came to England himself and forced Elizabeth to sail with him back to Massachusetts.

Their first formal legal (as well as extralegal) dispute occurred shortly thereafter in 1657, when Elizabeth refused to follow Christopher back to his frontier properties in New Hampshire and Maine. At this point, their dispute did not register among the handful of formal divorce petitions that had come before the Massachusetts Court of Assistants; there are records of a dozen such petitions between 1639 and 1656, made mostly by women on the grounds of a husband's desertion and bigamy or adultery, and most of which were granted.[7] Their conflict appears to have given Elizabeth legal validation of her desire to live separately while remaining technically married. Authorities used Christopher's estate to purchase a house in Boston for her and her children, and the property was placed under the care of trustees, denying Christopher direct control.[8]

Christopher returned to the Maine frontier, where he was out of reach of Massachusetts authorities; the couple remained separated for most of the next decade. Christopher finally returned to Boston in 1668, just as the Crown ceded legal authority over the area where he had been living back to Massachusetts Bay. He promptly reasserted his marital rights, or at least pretended to seek a reconciliation. Elizabeth's predictable refusal to welcome him into her house and bed potentially gave him legal grounds for divorce, though the authorities rejected Christopher's petition. In 1670, he had again returned to the frontier and Elizabeth had "shipped herself" back to England. This would be their final separation, but it did not end their marriage. As late as 1678 Elizabeth was still litigating claims in the English courts as Christopher's wife.[9]

CIVIL VERSUS ECCLESIASTICAL JURISDICTION

To a nonspecialist, "radical Puritan" may sound like an oxymoron, especially when applied to sexual mores. Yet sixteenth- and seventeenth-century Protestant religious dissenters reoriented cultural ideals and institutional practices in a number of significant ways. They valued marriage over celibacy, increasing its importance as a foundation for a godly society. They celebrated the institution as a spiritual and sexual, as well as economic, partnership, and in the process raised the standards for what constituted a good marriage. At the same time, they denied that marriage was an indissoluble sacrament, challenging the authority of Anglican ecclesiastical courts and Catholic canon law.

Puritan insistence that marriage was a civil contract was a jurisdictional as well as theological matter. The Anglican Church had its origins in conflict over marriage law—namely, Henry VIII's infamous quest to annul his marriage to Catherine of Aragon. The pope and Catholic nations refused to recognize that annulment or Henry's subsequent marriage to Anne Boleyn, spurring him to establish a state-run church with himself as head. Catholic objections to these maneuvers were central to England's break from Rome. Henry's pursuit of theological guidance from Protestant leaders on the Continent helped lay the groundwork for a more permissive stance on divorce. For the next few generations, however, powerful figures in the Anglican church feared replicating the chaos produced by Henry's quest for an heir, and enforced policies that aligned closely with prior Catholic canon law rather than with more radical continental Protestantism. In the established Anglican church, marriage remained an indissoluble sacrament under the jurisdiction of the ecclesiastical courts.[10]

From the perspective of religious dissenters, Anglican adherence to Catholic marriage policy was evidence of institutional corruption in England's church and state. In contrast, Puritan New England self-consciously forbade clergy from officiating at weddings and gave the power instead to local magistrates. The dissenters' treatment of marriage as a civil contract and simultaneous emphasis on the spiritual and social importance of marital success opened the door to tolerance of divorce on terms recognizable today. The aim was not to make marriage secular, but to make the secular world more godly. In theory, religious leaders could avoid entangling the church in marital disputes, and godly lay magistrates could develop policies that better accommodated human frailty. New England authorities bristled at their critics' suggestion that their reformist agenda undermined both secular and religious authority, and lent itself to schism and separation. Divorce—of the colony from England or as a routine legal practice—was not their aim. Nevertheless, divorce did become an accepted tool by which all of New England's colonies regulated household order, with more than one hundred cases documented by the end of the seventeenth century.[11]

The marriage laws in place in Massachusetts Bay by the 1640s anticipated reforms that England enacted a few years later, after Protestant reformers gained legal ascendancy under Oliver Cromwell. In both old and New England, the jurisdictional gap created by the absence of ecclesiastical courts forced change. In the early seventeenth century, England had roughly 250 ecclesiastical courts, following a hierarchy roughly determined by diocese, but with numerous exceptions in "Peculiar" courts with spiritual jurisdiction inherited from pre-Reformation abbeys and monastic lands. In England, ordinary people were more likely to encounter the church courts rather than other branches of the legal system. The ecclesiastical courts had greater local penetration than the common-law courts of quarter sessions, and they touched nearly all people at some point in their lives. The bulk of their business was administrative. They settled estates, issued marriage licenses, arbitrated marital disputes, and heard suits for defamation. The latter practice, in particular, expanded dramatically in the wake of the Reformation, as the lower ecclesiastical courts came to be staffed by lay lawyers who lacked the support of clerical benefices and depended on fees for their livelihoods.[12]

The church courts were also responsible for prosecuting spiritual offenses, ranging from fornication and adultery to drunkenness, oath breaking, and religious heterodoxy. Catholics and dissenting Protestant were both targets. In the 1630s, Archbishop William Laud's zealous use of the church courts to enforce high Anglican orthodoxy helped spur the Puritan Great Migration to New England and cemented Puritan distrust of the courts.

When they established New England's legal system, Puritan authorities deliberately turned the responsibilities of the ecclesiastical courts over to civil magistrates, leaving no legal foothold for the Anglican church in the colony. Archbishop Laud provoked a backlash in England as well. Parliament removed him from power in 1641 and executed him in 1645. The church courts fell with him. They lost their corrective powers in 1641, were further thrown into disarray by elimination of the bishops and archbishops in 1643, and formally dissolved in 1646.[13] Demand for legal divorce emerged in England in this context, as it had in the Puritan colonies. (The next chapter examines these demands and the political contingencies that led to divergence between English and colonial practice.)

As the political tide turned in England, Massachusetts authorities made their preferred marital practices increasingly explicit. A 1639 law required the publication of banns—that is, the public posting or announcement of intent to marry at town meetings or church services—at least three times over two weeks before a marriage ceremony could be performed. The first written summary of Massachusetts distinctive approach to law, the 1641 *Body of Liberties*, forbade husbands from striking their wives and parents from unreasonably preventing the marriage of their children, and included adultery with a married or betrothed woman on its brief list of capital offenses. In 1647, another statute reinforced parental authority, forbidding marriages made without the consent of parents, guardians, or—in their stead—magistrates.[14] These measures, as well as other biblically inspired capital offenses such as blasphemy, witchcraft, and the bearing of false witness, shaped Christopher's and Elizabeth's actions and arguments.

Arguments for Separation and Divorce

The history of conflict that Christopher and Elizabeth Lawson had compiled by the late 1660s included nearly all of the more controversial post-Reformation grounds for separation and divorce, including illegitimate marriage formation, desertion, economic malfeasance, life-threatening violence, and an assortment of religious, moral, and sexual crimes. The couple used these expansive and contested arguments because their history did not allow the most widely accepted grounds: female adultery and male impotence. Female adultery held special status as the charge most likely to win clerical and legal sanction for marital separation or divorce in early modern Europe. It drew biblical authority from Matthew 19:9, which offered a wife's "fornication" as an exception to Jesus's admonition that man should not "put asunder" what God had joined together. Catholics acknowledged female adultery as grounds for separation from bed and board, divorce *a mensa et thoro* in the language of canon law. Protestant authorities were more likely to treat adultery in general and female adultery in particular as a crime warranting full divorce, or divorce *a vinculo matrimonii*, which permitted the innocent party to remarry. (As the *Body of Liberties* indicates, some Protestants thought adultery with a married woman should be a capital offense, a stance that if enforced would automatically free the injured spouse to remarry.) Under Catholic law, divorce *a vinculo matrimonii* was an annulment; it was reserved for marriages that had never been properly formed, and which could therefore be considered void from the outset. Catholics and Protestants alike agreed that a marriage which could not be consummated met this criterion, and that the sexually able partner could be freed to marry again. Neither argument was a straightforward option for the Lawsons. Elizabeth Lawson was a woman of unusual temper and independence, but all involved with the Lawsons' dispute agreed that she was sexually faithful to Christopher. The same could not be said about him. Even without allegations of philandering on Christopher's part, the birth of three children before they ended up in the courts proved the consummation of the marriage.

So Elizabeth was too chaste, and Christopher too demonstrably potent, to use common early modern arguments for legally ending a marriage. The charges and countercharges to which they turned instead demonstrate a degree of legal literacy that defies stereotypes about New England's isolation and provincialism. Elizabeth's claim that the marriage was improperly formed rested on distinctly Puritan ideas, as opposed to long-standing Catholic arguments about consanguinity and the validity of dispensations from the church, or the need for sexual consummation. Christopher, in contrast, stressed Elizabeth's abandonment of her marital obligations as understood under coverture, including religious and sexual obligations as well as the duty to labor in the households' interest. The pair concluded with miscellaneous accusations of slander, blasphemy, witchcraft, madness, life-threatening violence, venereal disease, and moral and sexual depravity. To the last point, even Christopher admitted that he was troubled by excessive sexual desire. Most of these allegations would have been germane to local courts across Protestant Europe, as well as in England through the Civil War years, Cromwell's Protectorate, and the first decade of the Restoration.[15] The case took a specifically colonial turn, however, with testimony that Christopher made sexual advances to his English servant, and had proclaimed that he would prefer an "Indian or negro woman" to his wife.[16] These racially tinged charges targeted Massachusetts Puritan leaders' anxieties about the colonial project, and appear to have helped secure Elizabeth significant legal protection for her rights as a wife.

IMPROPER MARRIAGE FORMATION

Elizabeth's grievances drew on Protestant debates about the proper forms and ends of marriage; they show how dissenting Protestant marital radicalism manifested in policies regarding who might marry and how, as well as in tolerance for divorce. We see this in Elizabeth's repeated claim that she and Christopher had never been properly married, both with regard to legal forms and because she found herself without "freinds" to advise her when Christopher came courting.[17]

As an argument for separation, improper marriage formation was a very old strategy. Catholic canon law allowed separating couples to remarry only when the union was judged invalid from the outset. The tension between doctrinal commitment to marital indissolubility and the practical need to end unworkable or impolitic marriages created a medieval legal system characterized by elaborate disputes over marriage formation.[18] The notorious "divorces" of Henry VIII, a century before the Lawson dispute, exploited this strategy to the fullest. Henry's "divorces" were technically annulments based on belated, convenient qualms about their legitimacy. His first wife, Catherine of Aragon, had briefly been married to his elder brother, necessitating a special dispensation for her marriage to Henry; second thoughts about that dispensation provided the legal loophole that Henry used to put her aside to marry Anne Boleyn. Boleyn's prior engagement to the Earl of Northumberland, intimations of witchcraft, and ultimately charges of adultery, incest, and treason ended that marriage with her execution rather than another annulment. Henry's inability to consummate his marriage with Ann of Cleves gave him an out for his fourth marriage, as did conveniently procured evidence that she had a prior marriage contract.[19] While all these machinations occurred under the auspices of the Anglican Church, the legalistic pretexts followed long-standing and much criticized Catholic practices.

Elizabeth Lawson's general claim that an improperly formed marriage justified separation was well established in English precedent, but her reference to the absence of "freinds" as the reason for improper formation held specific meaning and relevance within the New England Puritan community. Friendship, as a concept, is at least as malleable as marriage; in this early modern context it referred to the network of kin and community that supported one through life's stages: not peers, but patrons. Friends might, occasionally, be emotional intimates, but more important, they were sources of educational and economic opportunity, and insurance against misfortune.[20] With the assurance of security came the expectations that this network—and particularly those with power within it—would influence or even determine its members' decisions in matters that affected the group. Marriage was probably the most significant of these decisions because it necessarily redefined group membership and generated new obligations. The collective and individual goal was to make sure marriages also generated opportunities that counterbalanced the obligations incurred by the costs of raising children and caring for dependent relations. Primogeniture—the English inheritance pattern favoring firstborn sons—consolidated and conserved communal resources and linked them firmly to family. It contributed to conservatism in marriage patterns that meant that as much as a third of Britain's seventeenth-century population never married.[21]

This network of patrons looked different in the colonies than in England. Part of the allure of radical religious dissent was its attempt to redefine communal networks in ways that encouraged marriage. Puritan self-selected congregations of the godly provided their members with an alternative safety net, enabling them to break with unrepentant kin and established institutional supports. The ranks of dissenters swelled with younger sons and daughters for whom membership in godly communities offered opportunity for marriages that their kin could not or would not provide.[22] We do not know if

28

Christopher and Elizabeth were drawn into their religious communities by such prospects, but they certainly fit the broader demographic profile. Elizabeth came from a family of prosperous yeomen, but her own prospects appear to have been dimmed by the death of her parents.[23] She appears to have come to New England without close kin. Christopher emphasized that he had married her as a "serving maid," implying condescension and generosity on his part. However, in a context where life-cycle service was common practice, Elizabeth's place as a maid to a pious woman of the lower gentry did not necessarily mark her status as lower than Christopher's. She would later return to work as a lady's maid in England, suggesting familiarity with a less-demanding sort of labor than the grueling domestic work performed by most colonial servants and many colonial goodwives.

Elizabeth's quick transition from servant to wife reflected demographic patterns that gave white women advantages in the colonial marriage market, but which also created new demand for and expectations of female household labor. The gender ratio of migrants to New England was not as staggeringly imbalanced as that in other seventeenth-century colonies, but male migrants still outnumbered women three to two, and the ratio among the servant population was even more disproportionate. This imbalance made it relatively easy for English and European women to marry in the colonies. The same patterns, together with high birth rates and low infant mortality, created an unmet need for female domestic laborers during the mid-seventeenth century. In practice, the experience of a wife who was the sole domestic worker in her own home was potentially more grueling and demeaning than service in a larger, more prosperous household like Katherine Scott's (the sister of Anne Hutchinson, not Catherine Goring Scott of chapter 2). The acute shortage of domestic labor helped drive New England's military practice of capturing and enslaving Indian women and children. The Lawson marriage followed on a large influx of such captives after the brutal conquest of the Pequot tribe in 1637, and the introduction of new cultural norms and racialized servitude into their own household became another point of conflict.[24]

Christopher's and Elizabeth's accounts of their marriage's failures highlight, paradoxically, what they and their religious community hoped would be opportunities. The marriage was characteristically Puritan in that the promotion of spiritual development and the prevention of sexual sin appear to have outweighed rank and money, although the latter concerns were not entirely disregarded. Christopher's ties to the Puritan project required reinforcement, and Elizabeth seems to have had the spiritual authority—and certainly the willpower—required for the task. Whether due to carelessness or to the chaotic household reshuffling that followed Anne Hutchinson's trials, the Lawsons' wedding appears to have been hastily arranged.[25] This lack of protocol and of consent from Elizabeth's "freinds," in the more traditional sense of family and kin rather than an alternate religious community, might not have seemed ill advised at the time, but it gave Elizabeth legal grounds for her later qualms. The basis for her doubts, however, had at least as much to do with the extent to which the colonial experience redefined the roles of wives in relation to other household dependents, and exacerbated the tension between spiritual elevation and worldly gain.

DESERTION OF MARITAL OBLIGATIONS

Where Elizabeth's primary arguments focused on improper marital formation, Christopher's focused on her repudiation of the obligations of coverture, which subsumed wives' legal identities under those of their husbands. Christopher did not question the validity of his marriage to Elizabeth, but instead claimed that she had broken that covenant through willful desertion and misconduct.

At first glance, Christopher had the easier task. Coverture assigned wives more duties than husbands, and accordingly more ways to be deemed negligent. Moreover, a wife's fundamental duty to submit to her husband's authority meant that he could define her obligations and judge whether or not she had met them. Christopher's pleas, unsurprisingly, were rife with assertions of husbands' legal prerogatives and of God-given masculine authority. They were also fundamentally defensive. In contentious marriages, this broad masculine authority was a double-edged sword. A wife's failure to obey marked a husband's failure to govern. A man who invoked the legal powers conferred by the doctrine of marital unity necessarily testified to the doctrine's practical limits.

Christopher Lawson was at a moral disadvantage in the dispute, and he responded by asserting his legal advantages as a male head of household. His reactive invocation of male power illustrates how the legal doctrines of coverture and marital unity worked at the middle of the seventeenth century. The general notion that a married woman, or *feme covert*, fell under the cover of her husband's identity affirmed and organized patrilineal authority in both old and New England. However, at the time of the Lawsons' conflict, coverture was one of a number of mutable legal and extralegal expectations about husbands' authority that assumed male power, but also recognized and even gave primacy to competing claims of kin and community. It was a common-law legal principle that *might* be invoked, but the common law was not, as the historians Margaret Hunt and Timothy Stretton have argued, "the only law in town."[26] As the Lawsons' case demonstrates, husbands typically cited coverture defensively and retroactively. The appearance of the doctrine in court generally marked self-protective, after-the-fact attempts to deny the very real agency that their wives exercised in daily life and which their communities accepted as a matter of course.

Christopher repeatedly argued for his right to determine where Elizabeth lived, and to control their joint property and their children, while at the same time describing compromises that demonstrate that his power was never so straightforward. His invocation of coverture retroactively appealed to principles that held only limited sway in marital practice. Furthermore, reliance on principles that presumed husbands' sole decision-making power placed him in an argumentative bind. The authority he claimed for himself weakened his attempts to prove Elizabeth's fault. If she had deserted him, the logic of marital unity assumed his complicity. He was at pains to show that her disobedience was not of his design.

Christopher's formal assertion of legal power thus invited the law to judge him as well as his wife. Massachusetts colonial authorities were none too pleased with this task. The Lawsons lived together only intermittently during their nearly forty years as husband and wife. In itself, that was not unusual for a family with economic interests and kinship ties in multiple locales, particularly given the exigencies of colonial settlement and the political chaos that marked the period. But their dispute pointed out contradictions between overlapping Puritan commitments; in their conflict, the ideals of marital hierarchy and of spiritual and economic unity undermined rather than reinforced one another.

During the early 1640s, Elizabeth managed household and commercial affairs in Boston while Christopher secured trade goods and negotiated land claims on the frontier. An oblique reference in the papers of the prominent Puritan divine John Cotton documented these activities. A New Hampshire correspondent told Cotton to forward his reply "to Christopher Lawsons house, his wife can sende by boate."[27] Elizabeth Lawson, and perhaps her three young children, lived in a house on the water in Boston. She likely provided at least some of the capital to purchase it. Her labor certainly maintained it, and she oversaw the traffic in and out of the wharf in front of it. Common parlance and early modern records, however, registered it as Christopher Lawson's property. In account books, women's activities were similarly invisible. Colonial goodwives made substantial contributions to the household economy, but payment for dairying, spinning, weaving, nursing, and midwifery (to name the most common occupations) was almost always credited to the account of a husband or father.[28] The instructions to Cotton affirmed Elizabeth's "covered" status, even as they assumed her ability to carry out the household business—to send a "boate" to Exeter. This reference to her would not have been necessary at all were it not for the circumstance that Christopher was seldom at "his" Boston house.

Here lay the difficulty for Christopher's claims about desertion. The ideal of marital unity required couples to live together; life sometimes demanded that they live apart. What distinguished legitimate separations from illegitimate departures? Presumptions about marital hierarchy framed the answer through husbands' powers and obligations. A wife's home was where her husband said it was, so long as he had made suitable provision for his family's maintenance there. A wife could therefore become a deserter not only by moving, but also by staying put. Her adherence to her husband's wishes, at least theoretically, determined the matter. Husbands, on the other hand, could travel and relocate—so long as they provided for their families. Only when the money ran out or news came that they had remarried in a new locale did their departures become desertion. For New England authorities (as well as for local officials across the period of this study more generally), such irresponsible men represented a greater threat to social order than did insubordinate wives.[29]

The Lawsons' story could fit into either mold. Christopher would later portray Elizabeth's residence in Boston as the first of many instances in which she refused to live where he wished. Their Boston house, he claimed, had not been his desire but an indulgent expense undertaken so that she "might live under Mr. Cotton's ministry."[30] Elizabeth demonstrably had no desire to live on the frontier, but she framed this as a reflection of Christopher's inability to make adequate spiritual or economic provision for her there. Boston authorities apparently had sympathy for this view. The letter Elizabeth had forwarded for Cotton, for instance, alluded to ministerial doubts about whether a woman of status and piety could be expected to live in the heterodox settlement where Christopher made his other home. In fact, Cotton's correspondent had been seeking a ministerial position for a decade, but he decided against accepting a call issued by Christopher and other settlers in part because he thought it would prevent him from securing a godly wife.[31]

Elizabeth's reservations about the new world encompassed more than just its frontiers. In 1648 or 1649 she joined thousands other of New Englanders who answered the "call of home" during the brief interval between England's first and second Civil Wars. Like many of these reverse migrants, she framed her decision to return as a providential imperative, using this to sanction a range of "messy and ragged" motives. She was not the only one for whom the journey promised relief from a miserable marriage. Petitions

by deserted wives tell us of many men for whom migration provided an opportunity to start over, and for every instance of documented desertion there
were doubtless more that escaped the attention of the authorities. The matter
was enough of a concern that in 1647 Massachusetts Bay passed a law that
ordered immigrants to retrieve their spouses from England, on penalty of
forced return or fines.[32]

Elizabeth did not initially seem to intend a permanent separation. She
went to England with Christopher's consent, if not his blessing. He equipped
her for the voyage with a written power of attorney that ensured she would be
able to conduct business in his name. In London, she marketed his shipments
of staves and otter skins, established trading partners, collected debts on his
behalf, and pursued her claim to a greater share of her family's inheritance
than had been voluntarily transmitted by the executors. The formal power of
attorney that facilitated her activities reflected the constraints of coverture,
but it also acknowledged these limitations as a legal fiction.[33] The document
confounded Christopher's own later efforts to obtain an extralegal separation
and to portray Elizabeth as the deserting spouse. His arguments for divorce
thus also included a range of less legally straightforward allegations, including the suggestion that Elizabeth's journey carried her into dangerous spiritual territory.

RELIGIOUS OBLIGATIONS

Elizabeth lived in England for eight years, from roughly 1648 to 1656. Fragmentary evidence suggests that she became involved with Familist sectarian
radicals who flourished during the 1640s and 1650s. These groups extended
sixteenth-century practices in which a gathered "community of saints" exercised jurisdiction over the formation and dissolution of its members' marriages, denying the competing claims of the state, the established church, or
kin. Such beliefs (in which the gathered church became a surrogate "family")
manifested themselves in an array of experimental sexual and social arrangements, from polygamy to celibate communal life. Most famously, the Quaker
"Society of Friends" altered marital practices in ways that extended their egalitarian impulses. They did away with wifely vows of obedience, encouraged
husbands to renounce claims to their wives' property, and provided communal support for the families of women and men who were called to itinerant
ministry or religious martyrdom.[34]

Cromwell's Puritan government had such groups (as well as the suppres-
sion of the Anglican establishment) in mind in 1653, when it passed a law
placing marriage, births, and burials in the hands of civil magistrates. The

measure substantively replicated laws New England enacted in the 1640s. It went out of its way, however, to prescribe the *form* required for legitimate marriage under the new regime. This resembled Quaker practice in its simplicity, but differed pointedly in retaining the wifely pledge of obedience and requiring formal consent from the couples' "Parent or Guardians" and the sanction of a justice of the peace. Marriages sanctioned by the Society of Friends did not fall within the law.[35]

The newly formed Society of Friends was enthusiastically recruiting people like Elizabeth during the years she was in England, and her extended family lived in a part of Gloucestershire that was a hotbed of Quaker activity.[36] Anne Hutchinson's close associate Mary Dyer, who was certainly known to Elizabeth and Christopher, became a zealous Quaker during this time, and returned to New England in 1657, where she helped convert Elizabeth's former mistress (and Hutchinson's sister) Katherine Scott. Both women were imprisoned, whipped, and banished from Massachusetts in 1658. In 1660, Dyer famously defied her banishment and was hanged on the Boston Common. We do not know if Elizabeth also became a "Friend," but such a move would have put her at odds with authorities in both old and New England.[37]

Christopher's later petitions to the Massachusetts courts implied such radical religious affiliations without explicitly labeling them, probably because his own connections included too many heretics to bear close examination. In a lengthy letter purportedly sent to Elizabeth in England (but conveniently available to support Christopher's divorce petition), Christopher attributed her disobedience to religious delusion. He chastised her for calling him "Pharaoh" and herself "a saint, fitt for the Communion of saints"; she claimed the power to determine in God's time and on God's terms whether or not she was "called" to live with him. This kind of reasoning, Christopher knew all too well, was what had gotten Anne Hutchison into trouble. He refused to be "schooled" by the "freinds" who encouraged Elizabeth in this vein, and vigorously defended his own education by "good Orthodox" ministers in New England and old.[38]

The foremost duty of a "believing wife," Christopher reminded her, was to use her "good conversation" for the conversion of her "unbelieving husband." This was the "orthodox" answer to separatist arguments that godly spouses might be permitted to divorce unbelieving partners. Christopher and Elizabeth's arguments here both rested on interpretations of 1 Corinthians 7, in which Paul laid out guidelines on celibacy and marriage. While celibacy was the holiest state, it was famously better "to marry than to burn," and once married to stay married and exercise "due benevolence" toward one's spouse. Paul admonished Christian believers to "abide" with and attempt to save their

unbelieving spouses, yet he also provided a loophole in Jesus's general condemnation of divorce. The version of the "Pauline exception" in the King
James Bible stated that if "the unbelieving depart, let him depart. A brother or
a sister is not under bondage in such cases: but God hath called us to peace."[39]

Christopher used New England's merchant community and some of Elizabeth's kinsfolk to convey the message that she had a spiritual duty to return.
Elizabeth seems to have preferred a separated, celibate peace. She deferred
the messengers' admonitions to return to New England by citing the need to
free herself from legal entanglements that threatened both her and Christopher, and promising that soon "nothing would hinder her but God."[40]

God—or at least Elizabeth's conscience and desire—proved a mighty hin-
drance. Around 1654 she took a position as a lady's maid in England, telling
her mistress she had no husband. Her excuses to Christopher's messengers
suggest that she may have been emboldened by the Puritan Parliament's 1653
Marriage Act, which went a step beyond Massachusetts's measures in that it
declared improperly formed marriages invalid. Its parental consent requirements buttressed Elizabeth's claim that her own marriage was compromised
because her friends had not given their consent.

In 1656, Christopher sailed to London and stealthily tracked her down.
Using legal threats as well as persuasion, he convinced her mistress to dismiss her into his care. Elizabeth twice attempted to elude him, but he eventually brought her—scratching, spitting, and prophesying doom—onto a ship
bound for the colonies. The astonished ship captain rebuked her for misbehavior toward her husband, though he also condemned Christopher's violence. Christopher alleged that she was "mad," but witnesses judged her to be
"provoked by her husband" rather than mentally unsound.[41]

According to a deposition recorded by Massachusetts Deputy Governor
Richard Bellingham, bystanders advised Elizabeth to submit to Christopher
and let the "Good Gouverment in the Bay" colony settle her grievances.
This appears to have been a strategic invocation of Massachusetts *Body of
Liberties*, which Bellingham had shepherded into law during a brief stint as
governor in 1641. The *Body of Liberties* codified a critique of domestic violence found in the prescriptive writings of reformist ministers, and tacitly
repudiated legal sources that gave husbands the right to use force to "moderately correct" their wives as well as their servants and children. "Everie mar-
ryed woeman" was to "be free from bodilie correction or stripes by her husband," unless he acted in self-defense. In the event that there was "just cause
of correction," legal authorities "assembled in some Court," not husbands,
would decide the matter.[42]

Whatever sympathy the Lawsons' fellow passengers felt for Elizabeth was severely tested when her predictions about God's displeasure at the voyage began to come true. The ship ran off course and caught fire, and the crew and passengers feared witchcraft. Christopher claimed he rescued Elizabeth from a faction who wished to throw her overboard.[43] We can wonder, with their shipmates, why Christopher wanted Elizabeth back alive.

Weighing the Charges: Credibility, Economic Misconduct, Sexual Crime, Racial Boundaries, and Slander

The answer lies in economic liability, as well as in communal, and perhaps individual, scruples about sexual sin. Elizabeth had established herself as Christopher's agent in England, and so long as she had remained at large with his power of attorney, she could financially ruin him. Both of them were very much aware of this: "Had not God made mee faithfull," Elizabeth argued in her own defense, "I might have runn him much in debt & reason of the longnes of the time I was there haveing a letter of Atturney, which might have caused him to have layne in geoall [jail] all the dayes of his life." Christopher clearly felt she posed an economic threat in Massachusetts as well as in England, because upon their return he ordered "papers to bee set upon posts in Boston" warning that "none should trust" her on his account. Such action, Elizabeth protested, gave the lie to his promises of loving reconciliation. Christopher's efforts to retrieve her might also have been the result of pressure from Massachusetts authorities, who could have invoked the 1647 law ordering the deportation of migrants who did not bring their spouses with them. New England magistrates sometimes also ordered spouses to cohabit, adopting practices from English ecclesiastical courts. Christopher's testimony stressed his extraordinary efforts to recover the assistance and "Comfortable society of a wife," and framed them as something he did voluntarily; admitting otherwise would have undermined his efforts to place all the blame for their separations on Elizabeth.[44]

Christopher's efforts to discredit Elizabeth appear to have backfired, and Massachusetts authority's response suggests that—in the late 1650s, at least—her credibility was better than his. Her case first came before the authorities in Taunton, Massachusetts, who in 1657 were rounding up unattached "strangers" in the town in a court-ordered purge of Quaker missionaries. Christopher's hints about heretical tendencies notwithstanding, Elizabeth does not seem to have alarmed those who encountered her. She instead left a trail of depositions about Christopher's violence, his sexual crimes, his disrespect for household, racial, and political hierarchies, and his intent to "leave mee poore."[45]

As noted earlier, by 1658 Elizabeth and her children had been installed in a house in Boston. It was paid for in Christopher's name but reserved for the use of his wife and children. The trustees who secured this arrangement included a cross-section of New England's second-tier leadership, and their identities hint at how disputes could be mediated around the edges of the formal legal system. Two of the trustees were merchants, officers in Massachusetts militia, and long-standing members of Boston's First and Second Churches; the foremost of these was Christopher's onetime employer Thomas Lake, who had funded the purchase of the lands on the Kennebec River in Maine where Christopher was attempting to settle. The other two trustees were described as the "Ruling Elders" of the First Church of Boston (Elizabeth's home church) and the First Church of Taunton, in Plymouth Colony. Between them, these four men had formidable moral authority and considerable control over Christopher's access to money in cash-strapped New England. They appear to have established a separation agreement akin to what an English ecclesiastical court might have sanctioned, achieving a divorce from bed and board without formal legal proceedings and probably without Christopher's full consent. The absence of evidence about the arrangement seems more than a matter of spotty record keeping, because it was not included with the depositions that resurfaced in later court battles, when a signed concession from Christopher would have been very useful to Elizabeth.[46]

Christopher and Elizabeth's son was bound as a servant to Thomas Lake at around this time, further cementing Christopher's loss of household authority. There is remarkably little evidence about the impact the Lawsons' conflict had on their children. Christopher charged Elizabeth with being "unnatural" in her lack of affection for him and her "little ones." He accused her of using "immoderate correction"—that is, excessively violent discipline—before she left for England and portrayed her prolonged absence as an expression of cold indifference. He claimed that the problem of "how to dispose of" the children delayed his attempts to retrieve Elizabeth from England; it did not, however, keep him from traveling to the frontiers. The case was typical of other seventeenth- and eighteenth-century marital disputes in that children, when mentioned at all, were an economic liability to be "disposed of," with authorities aiming to keep that responsibility in private rather than community hands. By the time Christopher retrieved Elizabeth from England, their children were old enough to be sent out as servants into the households of others, much as their mother appears to have been when she was an orphaned teenager. While such life-cycle service was common in New England and in

England, it was a strategy of necessity more than of choice. Households with the means usually kept their children working at home, and servants without kin were particularly vulnerable to neglect and abuse. The Lawsons' oldest daughter left no records other than that of her birth and might not have survived childhood. The youngest married a butcher in 1657 and became a moderately prosperous Puritan goodwife. The Lawsons' son registered his opinion of his service to Thomas Lake by running away in 1661, at the age of eighteen, after which he disappeared from the records for good.[47]

FROM SEPARATION TO DIVORCE

Elizabeth's legal vindication seems to have pushed Christopher into the arms of Massachusetts Bay's political opponents. He spent most of the years between 1658 and 1668 "west of the Kennebec" in what is now Maine, and traveled to other outlying settlements, and possibly also to Barbados and Virginia. He persuaded Elizabeth to join him on the frontier for part of 1660, but she returned to Boston against his wishes. As Christopher later told the story, Elizabeth circumvented his plans to move his household from New Hampshire to Maine by fleeing with "his" goods to Boston, leaving him destitute and "distracted" in the wilderness. His plea of "distraction," implying mental illness, provided weak cover for political choices he made during this estrangement.[48] The year 1660 also saw the restoration of the monarchy in England, and by 1662 Christopher had become colonial agent for the heirs of Ferdinando Gorges, who were petitioning Charles II for the renewal of a land patent that would have given them control of Maine and much of New England. In the mid-1660s, the Gorges family briefly regained legal control of the Maine settlements, during which time Christopher swore fealty to the Crown; he was named deputy constable in 1665. Maine's jurisdictional pendulum had swung the other way by 1668, when Massachusetts Bay reclaimed control of the contested territories.[49] With this change in jurisdiction, Christopher could no longer evade Massachusetts authority, and he responded by confronting it head on.

On a Sunday morning in December 1668, after eight years of absence, Christopher turned up wet, cold, and hungry on Elizabeth's doorstep in Boston and demanded entry into "his house." She responded by violently bolting the door against him and shouting out the window that he was a "rogue and whoremaster and murtherer" who "had the French poxe" and intended to "murther her in her owne house." Christopher claimed to have civilly requested dry clothes, only to be further rebuked while bystanders "cryed out Shame on it." Elizabeth proceeded to barricade herself in the house without a fire. After four days, Christopher persuaded some of the neighbors that she might be dead in the house with starving pigs. He thus had an audience when he tore the door of the hinges and with "very Loving speech" embraced her and offered to "salute" her with kisses.[50]

Christopher's witnesses might have interpreted this as appropriate husbandly behavior, but Elizabeth understood it as a threat. It certainly appears to have been a calculated effort to set up Christopher's case for divorce by proving her hostility to reconciliation. Elizabeth greeted his embraces (and the broken door) by spitting at him and calling for a constable. When he would not leave, she went directly to the "honoured Governor" of the colony, charging Christopher with "murther, fornication and theft."[51] That afternoon the couple pleaded their case in the governor's house before three of the colony's most prominent men: Governor Richard Bellingham, Deputy Governor and Major General John Leverett, and the merchant and magistrate Edward Tyng. These men were a complicated, touchy audience for the pair: Bellingham had simultaneously implemented and personally avoided controversial Puritan marriage regulations during a prior term as governor in 1641, and as deputy governor in 1658 he had taken down the strongest witness testimony in Elizabeth's favor.[52] From the 1650s forward, Bellingham and Leverett had both been involved in witchcraft prosecutions, the persecution of Quakers, and, with the Restoration, the painstaking defense of the Bay Colony's charter against claims that such actions had placed Massachusetts Bay outside of English law.[53] Leverett and Tyng both had landholdings in Maine and at various points served among the commissioners who asserted the Bay Colony's jurisdiction over the contested territories. They almost certainly knew Christopher in that capacity.

According to Christopher, this first hearing did not go well for Elizabeth, despite her prior success. She pleaded that Christopher was a criminal who deserved to be put to death, but was unable to provide evidence for her charges. The authorities instead entreated her to reconcile with him and threatened her with prison if she refused. Christopher briefly gained possession of her Boston house in the wake of this hearing, but within the month Elizabeth had enlisted the help of her surviving trustee and obtained a power of attorney affirming her ability to act on her own behalf in the courts, without the aid of trustees or husband. In January, the county court dismissed Christopher's plea for divorce and upheld Elizabeth's property claims. When Christopher defied an injunction ordering him to return her house and goods, he was arrested and imprisoned.[54]

Christopher filed the first of his surviving divorce petitions to the governor from prison, though his detailed story and numerous supporting witnesses suggest that he had been planning this legal strategy for some time.

He had ample proof of Elizabeth's refusal to reconcile with him. He used her allegations that he was guilty of "murther, fornication and theft" as evidence that she wished him dead. His charges suggested he felt similarly about her, despite his pretense of affection. Christopher's implication that Elizabeth was a secret Quaker whose curses had power would not have been trivial charges to men who had recently put Quakers and witches to death. Neither was the suggestion that she had falsely accused him of murder; bearing false witness in such a case was itself a capital offense. He explicitly rested his case, however, on Elizabeth's "undaunted resolution . . . to doe her utmost to blemish my name ruine my estate & to continue in nott yielding that due benevolence according to the institutions and ordinance of god and her owne solemn Covenent." "Due benevolence" was a euphemism for marital sex, the legitimate and divinely sanctioned alternative to the "abuse" and "uncleanness" of "fornication" or "adultery." Christopher's need for a legitimate outlet for his sexual desires became the final crux of his case. He begged to be relieved of the "insupportable Burthen" of his absent and "inexhortable wife," whose refusal "to come neere mee her Husband any more" left him "Exposed to many Temtations."[55]

Elizabeth came across as a violent harridan even in the testimony supplied by her supporters, and she was not prepared for a new legal assault after eight years of separation. Two of her trustees had died several years before, and her defense appears to have been cobbled together in haste and with few resources, relying heavily on copied depositions taken at earlier stages in their conflict.[56] Despite these legal disadvantages and her fiercely defiant stance toward Christopher and all who aided him, she was able to thwart his quest for a divorce. Analysis of the remaining grounds they gave for separation and divorce is thus bound up with the question of what made Elizabeth credible, and Christopher incredible, despite his more persuasive documentation.

The strength of Elizabeth's case lay in her ability to play on Puritan authorities' fears of the financial costs of abandoned dependents and also of the moral risks posed by unchecked masculine violence and lust. Such "temptations" were amplified by the exploitative cross-cultural dynamics of the colonial experiment. Elizabeth's depositions simultaneously displayed a lack of formal education and notable legal literacy. Christopher's allies and actions undermined his own, better-crafted case.

"FORNICATION AND MURTHER": SEXUAL CRIME

Elizabeth claimed that she could not live with Christopher because he endeavored to make her "deny God" to the "destruction of my soul," and that his life-threatening cruelty threatened to destroy her body as well. He had violently thrown her out of the house in the "dead of the winter in the nights," leaving her there until her hands were frostbitten and bloody. She had a credible witness: a man whose status was at least equal to Christopher's, who had seen Christopher throw her to the ground and kick her on the voyage back from England. Her witness also testified that Christopher's female servant had verified Elizabeth's most dramatic account of Christopher's sexual sins. Elizabeth told of finding Christopher lying on top of his servant in bed shortly before they left England. She had leaped onto the pair while crying "fornication and murther," only to be ignored by a household that preferred to see no evil. The servant admitted the truth of her story, but protected herself by claiming that Christopher had been too drunk to act on his desires.[57]

Elizabeth's allegations of "fornication" and "murther" captured both the severity and the ambivalence in Puritan legal policy on sexual offenses. On paper, adultery and murder were parallel capital crimes, fit to be uttered in the same breath. Massachusetts authorities punished adultery to the full extent of the law only once, in 1644. Christopher and Elizabeth were both in Boston at the time, and might well have witnessed the public hanging of a young wife who regretted her marriage to a much older man, alongside one of her penitent young lovers.[58] Cromwell's Commonwealth had enacted similar penalties for adultery in the early 1650s. These do not appear to have been enforced, possibly because dire worldly consequences prescribed for sexual sin made even the faithful reluctant to pursue charges. When Elizabeth caught Christopher *in flagrante* in England in 1656, bystanders were not eager to test the law. This was true even though fornication was a lesser offense, a fallback charge for the misbehavior of single folk and married men like Christopher, who directed their illicit sexual advances to unmarried women. The householders who ignored Elizabeth's cries did not want it to be known that such disreputable acts occurred under their roof. Christopher's servant could not acknowledge having sex with her master without risking also being charged with fornication herself, regardless of whether or not the act was consensual.

Elizabeth's allegations of violence and sexual impropriety were not sufficient to account for her credibility; in many analogous cases, communities and authorities preferred to look the other way. Christopher's drunken foray into his servant's bed certainly sounded like an assault, for instance. However, neither Elizabeth nor the servant called it rape, most likely because legal and cultural expectations made such a charge nearly impossible to prove. English and colonial legal texts defined rape as "Carnal Copulation" with a woman "by force" and "against her own will," interpreting it as one among a number of sexual crimes to which sexually frustrated men were prone. Women bore the burden of proving lack of consent with their cries and physical wounds. Failure to summon witnesses, an only slightly battered body, or a pregnancy (understood to be possible only in the event of female and well as male orgasm) were evidence that a woman had not struggled enough; forced submission was still taken as consent. Social context also mattered. Women were more likely to be believed when the men they accused of rape were outsiders who could not plausibly claim a relationship with them. In seventeenth-century Massachusetts, a supportive family network was the most important factor for women who pursued charges—something that gave white women a decided advantage, but still allowed some women of color (usually bound to white families) to gain a hearing.[59] By the eighteenth century, the sexual license of men like Christopher Lawson was more likely to be tacitly accepted and ignored at law; rape charges became a tool of free whites, and prosecutions throughout the colonies disproportionately targeted black men.[60] While seventeenth-century New England authorities condemned male sexual misbehavior, they tended to see marriage as a remedy, going so far as to assign heavier punishment to a man with "a lusty young wife" than to two co-offenders, one of whom was unmarried and the other whose wife was "scrupulous of fellowship" due to pregnancy. Such assumptions about a wife's responsibility for managing her husband's lust lay behind Christopher's attempt to blame Elizabeth for "Expos[ing him] to many temtations."[61]

HOUSEHOLD DISORDER, RACIAL SERVITUDE, AND THE PRIVILEGE OF PROTECTION

In a society that understood marriage as a bulwark against sexual "temptation," Elizabeth's defense of her right *not* to have sex with Christopher required considerable legal savvy. The assertion that Christopher had violated not only his marriage vows, but also the boundaries of status and race, helped Elizabeth demonstrate that "gross disorder" in his household justified her vehement resistance. Elizabeth signed her depositions with a mark, and her recorded speech patterns were not those of an educated woman. Yet her specific charges suggest she learned some case law while pursuing her estate dispute in the London courts. She claimed, for instance, that Christopher had held her down "while another man kist her, whether" she "would or no." The charge echoed that in the notorious trials of the Earl of Castlehaven, who had been executed in England in 1631 for sexual disorder in his household that allegedly included "holding down" his wife while a favored servant raped her, as well as sexual assaults on servants of both sexes. Stories of Castlehaven's crimes and trial circulated widely over the next decades, and for Puritans they stood as an example of the aristocratic, Catholic decadence and corruption that justified both the flight to New England and the Civil Wars.[62]

Christopher's perverse sexual appetites had led him to abuse his wife, fornicate with servants, and contract venereal disease—the "French pox"; they further crossed the boundaries of race and status in ways that New England's leadership found particularly unnerving. Christopher had taunted Elizabeth with the claim that if he needed "to have a woman hee would take an Indian or negro woman before mee." Such a cavalier attitude toward sex reinforced the impression that Christopher was an ungodly adventurer of the sort enticed by seventeenth-century travel writers, who invited colonizing men to see "Whether white or Black be best, Call your Senses to the quest." Puritan leaders chafed at such imagery, and fretted over the fragile distinctions between their holy experiment and colonies founded for "Carnall and not Religious" ends.[63] Elizabeth's charges played to fears about the "heathen" outsiders who lived alongside and within the households of godly English colonists. Christopher, she implied, represented a grave internal threat to a patriarchal order premised on the notion that righteous householders would protect their dependents and preserve New England's virtue.

The Lawsons' marital conflict coincided with the contested emergence of racially justified servitude in New England, a context in which Christopher's conflation of "Indian or negro" women as a single exploitable category was controversial. The Massachusetts *Body of Liberties* was the earliest code in English America to explicitly legalize slavery, but it did not use race or religious identity to define the institution. Slave status could be applied only to "lawfull Captives taken in just warres, and such strangers as willingly selle themselves or are sold to us," although government "Authoritie" gave considerable latitude to use servitude and slavery as a punishment. Slaves were to be subject to the "liberties and Christian usages that the law of god established in Israel," and illegal "manstealing" was a capital offense. Europeans were not exempt from enslavement, and conversion to Christianity was not grounds for freedom. Neither was slave status understood to be hereditary.[64] These vague provisions allowed Puritan authorities to define and justify slavery according to their needs. Abusive masters such as Christopher Lawson undermined the rationalizations that sustained Puritan investment in the system.

A particularly ironic rationalization recast the Puritan enslavement of Indian women as liberation. English observers of cultural contrasts in the gendered division of labor made a trope of the brutal and "slavish" treatment "squaw drudges" received at the hands of "idle" Indian men. One of the earliest voyagers to the Kennebec, where Christopher eventually made his home, described men who lived in leisure, hunting occasionally while their "wives are their slaves, and doe all their worke." When he explained that he must return to England, because his "wife would not come thither except I did fetch her," his Indian contacts advised him to beat her for disobedience. Separate observers from the 1620s through the 1640s noted that Indian women "Doe most of the labour in planting and carrying of burdens; their husbands hold them in great slavery," and that they "live a most slavish life: they carry all their burdens, set and dress their corn, gather it it . . . and have all household care lying upon them." The travel writer William Wood went so far as to portray the example of English gender parity as awakening Indian women to their "female superiority"; before, they had supposedly "rest[ed] themselves content in their helplesse condition, counting it the womans portion." In contrast, "since the *English* arrivall comparison hath made them miserable, for seeing the kind usage of the *English* to their wives, they doe as much condemne their husbands for unkindnesse, and commend the *English* for their love. As their husbands commending themselves for their wit in keeping their wives industrious, doe condemne the *English* for their folly in spoyling good working creatures." Wood told a story of a heroic English wife who wielded a "warlike Ladle" and hot cooking liquid to protect a brutalized squaw from an abusive husband. In the same passage, however, he was careful to deny the "scandalous rumour" that colonial conditions were teaching English men to "learne of the Indians" to bring their wives "to the same subjection . . . and drudgerie." He assured his readers that colonial English women found "there as much love, respect, and ease, as . . . in old England."[65]

Christopher's behavior played into fears of colonial men learning "of the Indians," both with regard to brutality and with regard to sexual practices that did not follow English rules. Most English observers overlooked the ways in which Indian communities valued women's labor and also the ways in which different kinship rules might temper women's subordination. Most New England tribes practiced serial monogamy, but unhappy couples were allowed to move on to other partners. Matrilocal residential patterns meant that women could end relationships with little disruption for themselves and their children. Men were frequently the ones pushed out. Elite Indian families sometimes cemented political alliances with polygynous marriages, which Europeans perceived as serving licentious male desire. However, such arrangements typically involved women who were sisters or other close kin, for whom sharing household and reproductive labor lightened individual burdens and increased lineage prosperity. Algonquian women also exercised hereditary land rights, something Christopher overlooked to his cost—one of the land claims he negotiated was almost overturned because he contracted with a male sachem and not the woman who had hereditary claims.[66]

Far from protecting Indian women, colonial sexual norms and marriage laws imposed new burdens, of which the public shaming of the native woman Sarah Ahhaton a few months before the Lawsons' final legal battles was a telling instance. Ahhaton had married into a family of prominent Christian converts in Punkapoag, a town not far from Boston. She grew dissatisfied with her husband's infidelity and violence and eloped with another man to Sowams, where the Pokanoket sachem Metacom was uniting southern New England's tribes to resist the English. Ahhaton change her mind and returned to her husband after a few weeks' separation. Outside of English jurisdiction, she most likely could have either remained with her lover or reconciled with her husband with little stigma. Under the new English regime, she was punished for adultery and forced to wear a noose around her neck in the stocks before being sent to prison. Symbolic hanging was better than punishment to the full extent of Puritan law, but it is doubtful that Sarah Ahhaton experienced this expanded English authority as benevolent protection.[67]

The limits of English protections for dependents were also revealed by the earliest surviving story about enslaved African women in the colony, in which two of Christopher's associates were central players. The diarist John Josselyn, en route to visit a brother who traded with Indians and negotiated land claims in Maine alongside Christopher, documented the grievances of an enslaved women owned by his host, Samuel Maverick. Maverick was an Anglican minister turned Indian trader who occupied a fortified mansion on an island in Boston Harbor from the 1620s until the mid-1640s, when conflicts with Puritan leaders pushed him out. Massachusetts authorities had valued Maverick's role in military ventures against their Indian neighbors and had eagerly traded in the captives he secured. However, Maverick opposed Puritan legal reforms and undermined Massachusetts's enforcement of its moral codes, providing refuge to at least one notoriously adulterous couple and others expelled on religious grounds. By the time of the Restoration, he had become a dangerous political opponent, lobbying in England for the overturn of the Massachusetts charter in favor of the claims of proprietors whom Christopher Lawson also served.[68]

Maverick was among the first New England colonists to own enslaved Africans, and also to understand slavery in ways that legitimized rape. Maverick desired "to have a breed of Negroes." On failing to persuade his "Negro woman" to accept a male slave as a sexual partner, he had then commanded the man "will'd she nill'd she to go to bed" with her. The woman managed to convey her distress over the rape to the visiting John Josselyn, who recorded and published her grief and defiance. The woman took the sexual violation "in high disdain beyond her slavery." Josselyn seems implicitly to have agreed, though neither he nor Massachusetts authorities provided protection in her case.[69]

"LEAVE MEE POORE"

Rhetoric about protecting women of color helped New England authorities rationalize their enslavement, but was of limited practical use to the women themselves. Elizabeth Lawson invoked Christopher's preference for an "Indian or negro woman" to remind authorities of his links to a distrusted political faction, not to solicit aid for his servants. In contrast, her legally savvy rhetoric about protecting other free white women from Christopher's depravity appears to have doomed his efforts at divorce. Elizabeth argued not only that he had forfeited his claims to *her* as a wife, but that the lingering bonds of the marriage covenant obligated her to save others like her from his sin. She claimed that Christopher had pressed her to sign a private separation agreement that would allow him to abandon her and resettle with their children and another woman in Barbados or Jamaica. He had promised her rival marriage upon Elizabeth's death. Not only was such an arrangement sinful, it would leave Elizabeth alone and "poore."[70]

Elizabeth's accusations might well have been true; Christopher acknowledged that he wanted to remarry. Yet the charges could have come directly from *The Lawes Resolutions of Womens Rights*, the first (and for the duration of the seventeenth century, the only) English handbook on marriage law. The text offered Elizabeth no direct remedy, but it thoroughly compromised Christopher's ambition to marry again. It informed readers that "if a man promise to a woman which he hath adulterously polluted that he will marry her when his wife dyeth, &c. Or if a man have sought to abridge the dayes of his lawfull wife to marry another: These villanies are such perpetuall cankers in marriage, that they doe not onely hinder it to be made, but also rend it in sunder when it is made." A "Marriage sought or made with wickedness" would not "hold." Christopher's "detestable" and illegal promises were an attempt to claim the sexual benefits of marriage without genuine commitment to its long-term obligations to either Elizabeth or her rival, both of whom might end up as communal burdens.[71]

Law's Irresolution

Massachusetts authorities appear to have agreed on the Lawsons' wickedness, but they let their marriage hold. Christopher and Elizabeth resorted instead to the time-honored search for more favorable jurisdiction. Christopher's 1669 divorce petition laid the groundwork for this approach, and likely undermined his own case in the process. Both Christopher and Elizabeth had walked a fine line between knowledge and presumption as they constructed their stories for the courts. Rhetorical convention demanded that divorce petitions be humble, apolitical, and spontaneous accounts of grievances that were by no means critical of law or established authority.[72] But disagreement over husbands' legal rights and authorities' legal actions lay at the heart of the conflict. Christopher's petitions took an obsequious and pious tone with the high court to which it was directed, while at the same time including a threatening undercurrent of challenge to the Massachusetts legal system.

Some of this challenge he placed in Elizabeth's mouth. In Christopher's account, after a magistrate ordered her to live "peaceably" with her husband or go to prison, she replied that "shee cared not for them nor their prison neither." Christopher had "broken open my house and my goods," and if the magistrates would not "do me Justice," then she would have them "before the King and tryed by the Kings lawes." As we have seen, Christopher had initially won this point by invoking coverture: because he was her husband, the house and goods were his. There could be no theft. The county court, however, had moved in Elizabeth's favor, sending Christopher to prison instead. Christopher deemed himself in "no wayes bound . . . either by the law of god or the kings or the lawes of this Jurisdiction" to abide by the lower court's orders without a proper trial. The honorable gentlemen of the superior court, he was sure, would have superior wisdom and grace. They would need it if they were to discern a way that he and Elizabeth might "live together according to the holy ordinance of God." Granting him a divorce, on the other hand, would ensure that he and Elizabeth were "no longer burdensome to each other, or . . . to any of his majesty's courts." He promised also that he would remember them in his prayers.[73]

In the context of Restoration-era threats to the Massachusetts government by Christopher's allies, the implication that Massachusetts justice did not align with that of "god or king" was unlikely to be well received. The Court of Assistants was swayed neither by his evidence nor his promised prayers. They judged both Christopher and Elizabeth to be at fault, and confined the pair to prison until they either reconciled or left New England. Christopher returned to Maine, where he was placed in the stocks for "turbulent" courtroom behavior at a summer court session and for insisting that the visiting Massachusetts circuit court jurists (at least one of whom had heard his divorce petition) "should not be his Judges." A year later, in the fall of 1670, he made a last, unanswered, appeal to the governor. He appears to have remained in Boston after this petition, living off the sale of his remaining Maine land claims and, after 1678, a small stipend that his son-in-law provided on the condition that Christopher relinquish all claims to Elizabeth's house.[74]

Elizabeth obtained release after declaring she preferred death in prison to life with Christopher. By 1670, she was back in England, where she used "the kings laws" to follow through on some of her earlier economic threats. Identifying herself as Christopher's widow, she sued two of their former associates for money due him. She claimed that they had secreted her power of attorney and promissory notes left in their care during the 1650s, and colluded to keep the revenue for themselves. Stray legal documents suggest that as late as 1678 she was still using her acquired legal savvy to try to extract money from Christopher's extended English family.[75]

The lack of clear resolution in the Lawsons' case exemplifies the administrative strategy that helped keep the empire intact for the next 150 years. As Mary Bilder has argued, colonial legal culture was marked not so much by "salutary neglect" as by studied avoidance of "irreconcilable conflicts" between English and colonial law. Authorities on both sides of the ocean allowed "the ambiguities inherent in transatlantic legal culture . . . to remain unresolved."[76] Massachusetts Bay tacitly decided to renounce jurisdiction over the Lawsons' case, rather than invite further appeals to the "kings laws" by offering either party further legal vindication. Massachusetts was willing to punish the Lawsons for refusing to exercise appropriate joint jurisdiction over their household; but if the Lawsons wished to challenge Massachusetts authority by continuing their dispute, they had to take it—and themselves—elsewhere. In the next chapter, we shall see how changes in England's understanding of marriage law contributed to this ambivalent position.

Submit or Starve:
Manby v. Scott and the Making of a Precedent

This chapter crosses the Atlantic to reconstruct the story of Sir Edward and Lady Catherine Scott, whose conflict shaped English and American legal debates about marital obligations for the next two centuries. The Scotts began separating and reconciling shortly after they wed in the 1630s, and their marital conflict spanned the decades of England's Civil Wars. Catherine Scott, like her contemporary Elizabeth Lawson, did not wish to end her marriage, though she preferred to forgo her husband's company. In most other respects, the Scotts provide a counterpoint to the Lawsons' middling status and Puritan sympathies. The Scotts' case could be a costume drama, featuring amoral courtiers and secret Catholics engaged in wartime espionage and scandalous sex. It took place under the spires of Oxford, in the palatial country houses of England's nobility, and in the courts of exiled royalty in Paris and The Hague. The couple's aristocratic status and conflicting political allegiances made their case into a matter of political concern and legal precedent. Their penultimate legal battle, *Manby v. Scott* (1663), deeply informed later treatises on marriage law, though scholars have remained unaware of the political origins of the supposed truisms traceable to the case. *Manby* continued the debate about coverture: Was a wife a *feme covert* whose weak status demanded she either submit to the will of her husband or starve? Or did coverture imply reciprocal commitments, in which a wife's weak status obligated her husband to ensure she never starved? Colonial legal authorities in the Lawsons' case avoided decisive answers to these questions in an effort to preserve both moral order and colonial jurisdiction. English authorities took a more forceful approach and attempted to use the Scotts' case to support the Crown's interest in preserving hierarchy.[1]

The Scotts' story serves three purposes in this book. First, Catherine Scott's family alliances illustrate the political stakes in the making and breaking of aristocratic marriages, and the threat to dynastic power inherent in religious ideals that diminished familial control over children's marriages. Second, the case challenges generalizations about seventeenth-century England's unrelenting opposition to legal divorce. In the 1640s and again in the 1650s, Sir Edward (or rather, his kin and "friends") petitioned various interregnum governments for a divorce from Catherine. He did not succeed, but the reasons for his failure hinged on political contingencies and maneuvering by Catherine's family more clearly than on principled opposition to divorce. The hearings his petitions received remind us that New England's Puritan divorce policy and English Anglican opposition to it emerged together from a context in which the full range of Reformation arguments about marriage and divorce were very much in play.

Finally, *Manby v. Scott* set enduring parameters for Anglo-imperial legal debates about authority and obligation in households. Upon the collapse of Cromwell's Protectorate and the 1660 restoration of the monarchy of Charles II, Catherine employed a range of legal and extralegal channels to compel Edward to fulfill his duties as her husband. Restoration England's most prominent jurists heard *Manby* in 1663 and turned it to political ends, issuing parallel rulings in which "traditional" marriage and misogyny provided common ground on which to rebuild a united England. Their arguments about marriage law recapitulated, but did not settle, broader Civil War–era debates about political authority, social obligations, and legal and religious jurisdiction.

The prevailing justices in *Manby* invoked husbands' authority in order to retroactively resolve Civil War–era contests over sovereignty. They aligned the domestic power of husbands with the political power of kings, and attempted to use *Manby* to buttress the authority of the monarch, repudiate Puritan legal reforms, deflect attention away from the question of divorce, and redraw lines of jurisdiction among England's competing courts. The justices blamed matrimonial disputes and even the presence of women in the courts on interregnum innovations that had granted wives "extravagant power." They represented their own pronouncements, in contrast, as ancient "clear and settled" law. The purported antiquity of masculine privilege masked their own legal innovations and smoothed over significant disagreements about the practical implications of such patriarchal doctrines.[2]

This rhetorical move was fairly typical of English Civil War–era political debates. Puritans also claimed to be restoring the ancient purity of state and church and overturning corrupting innovations. The story behind *Manby* demonstrates why historians need to be very careful about mistaking such rhetoric for reality. The woman who provoked *Manby*'s judicial denunciations of female power was not an unruly religious radical like Elizabeth Lawson, but a staunch Royalist. Most of Catherine Scott's legal claims, moreover, were *not* products of interregnum reforms, but rather artifacts of internal contradictions within the legal system *Manby* reinstated.[3]

Manby tried—and failed—to turn coverture into a coherent doctrine. The case instead helped entrench conflicting arguments. It served those who would invoke coverture to buttress husbands' authority and constrain wives' legal options. Yet it also allowed interpretations that turned coverture into a protective privilege for wives, and actively limited husbands' power. Both strands of argument, along with assertions about the antiquity of coverture, resurfaced in subsequent centuries. Sir William Blackstone, author of the definitive eighteenth-century *Commentaries on the Laws of England*, and his nineteenth-century American counterpart James Kent, for instance, both used *Manby* as an example of the "rigour of the old rule" governing marriage. Their own precepts regarding married women's legal and economic disabilities under coverture, they assured readers, were more liberal, enlightened, and humane. The irony here is that their examples of liberality and progress *also* harkened back to arguments made in *Manby*. If we are to disentangle the history of practices of household government from lawyerly fantasies about ancient patriarchal order, the politics and judicial ambitions behind *Manby* provide a good place to start.[4]

Dynastic Marriage and Family Politics

Catherine and Edward Scott's backstory demonstrates how political, economic, and marital fortunes rose and fell together in early modern monarchies. Catherine's father won a peerage and became one of the richest men in England in part through his deft handling of royal nuptial politics. George, Lord Goring (after 1644, Earl of Norwich), had been crucial to the complex diplomatic and logistical arrangements that brought the fifteen-year-old French princess Henrietta Maria to England to marry Charles I in 1625. His more personal diplomacy between the newlywed monarchs earned him their trust, substantial responsibility for the queen's household, and extensive patronage. It also made him wholly dependent on the Crown, and placed him firmly in the Royalist camp during the later Civil Wars.[5]

Lord Goring arranged his children's marriages to diversify his family's portfolio of patronage and of property. Despite his success at securing harmonious royal matches, his provisions for at least two his own children proved disastrous. Catherine's marriage was likely made possible—and undone—by that of her eldest brother. In 1629, the elder George Goring married his son and heir, also named George Goring, to the favorite daughter of the Earl of Cork, whose Irish land acquisitions made him the wealthiest of England's lords. If things had worked as they typically did in such aristocratic alliances, the bride's staggering ten-thousand-pound marriage portion would have helped provide her husband's sisters with their own portions. Lord Goring was likely banking on this arrangement when he promised Catherine to the Scott family in 1631.[6]

These aristocratic marriages were in effect corporate mergers, in which the marriage ceremony cemented complex legal arrangements regarding the property and patronage each family would contribute to the new household and its offspring. Unfortunately, the teenaged Catherine and Edward exchanged their marriage vows before all the merger's legal niceties were in place, and the misbehavior of Catherine's brother appears to have thrown a wrench into the ensuing negotiations. The younger George Goring rapidly gambled and drank his way through his wife's marriage portion, and rudely abandoned her at her father's house when Cork refused to loan him additional funds. In the mid-1630s, his son's debts, an ill-fated colonial venture to the Amazon, and losses from his monopolies on butter and Virginia tobacco placed the elder Lord Goring in precarious financial circumstances and at odds with multiple sets of in-laws.[7]

His efforts to resolve his children's marital difficulties highlight a key point about "ancient" marriage law: family loyalties and economic imperatives trumped legal consistency. Catherine seems to have lived with her own kin and "Friends" for most of the 1630s, awaiting agreement about how and when her father would pay her sizeable marriage portion, and over Edward's family's guarantees of property that would be reserved for her separate use. In letters to Edward, she assured him of her affection and flirtatiously begged him to send her a portrait. But she would not visit him without a satisfactory settlement between their families. Bearing him children before the negotiations were complete would place her family at a legal disadvantage.[8]

As Lord Goring pushed the Scotts to grant better security to his "Kate," he stressed the authority and especially the obligations of husbands. It was *Edward's* responsibility to make provision for Catherine suited to her status. At the same time, Goring was making excuses for his own son's refusal to maintain his daughter-in-law, and insisting on *her* father's paternal obligation to support his children. Goring's opportunistic and contradictory use of legal arguments was typical of such disputes. The cases were also settled by "traditional" means: they involved lawyers, but avoided the formal legal system. Familial pressure and bribes backed by private contracts did the trick. No one went to court.[9]

Lord Goring and the Earl of Cork jointly purchased a regimental command in the Netherlands for Goring's wayward son; the younger Goring's wife obtained relative autonomy in her soldier-husband's absences. After the newly minted Col. George Goring returned to England a war hero, the couple

more or less conformed to public expectations of their married role, though
they had no children. During the same period, Catherine intermittently returned to the Scott estates in Kent, where in the early 1640s she gave birth to
a son in what contemporary letters described as the "tender care" of her in-
laws and mother. The child's legitimacy would later be bitterly disputed, but
sources from the early 1640s suggest a personal and political rapprochement
that had not yet been torn apart by shifting political winds.[10]

Divorce in Interregnum England

With the outbreak of war in the summer of 1642, Catherine found herself
caught between male relations with conflicting political allegiances. Catherine's father helped smuggle Queen Henrietta Maria, the royal children, and
the Crown jewels out of England. He then used the jewels as collateral to
finance the Royalist armies. In 1644, Charles I made him Earl of Norwich
as a reward. Catherine's oldest brother, the younger George Goring, initially
played both sides of the conflict to his own advantage; in the early 1640s, he
accepted money and a military command from Parliament before carrying
this payment and troops into the service of the Crown.[11]

Catherine's brother, General Goring, and his friend and fellow commander
Prince Rupert (nephew to Charles I) were the men who gave the term *cavalier*
its modern meanings. Puritan critics described them as "Courtiers . . . wearing
long Haire and locks, and always Sworded" who "without having respect to the
Laws of the Land, or any fear either of God or Man, were ready to commit all
manner of Outrage and Violence." Supporters of Charles I, in turn, claimed
Cavalier as a title of honor that evoked political loyalty, bravery, gallantry,
and style, as well as disregard for conventional mores.[12] Catherine might have
shared these attributes. She did spend time in the mid-1640s with the Court and
Royalist forces at Oxford, and rumor held that she was Prince Rupert's mistress.
However, such details about her life derive from divorce petitions that accused
Catherine of adultery and turned her story into a cavalier morality tale.

Edward Scott petitioned Parliament for divorce from Catherine in the
1640s, and again in 1656. His petitions are historically interesting, first because
they demonstrate that divorce was a live topic of debate for multiple interregnum governments, thereby undermining historical paradigms that cast
seventeenth-century England as "divorceless." In the context of seventeenth-
century Protestant regimes, modest provisions for divorce such as those in
Massachusetts and Scotland were the norm, and England's prevailing policies
the exception. English commitment to marital indissolubility required effort;
it needs to be explained rather than assumed.[13]

During the Civil Wars and their aftermath, the reform of marriage and divorce law was certainly on the table. The political conversation is difficult to reconstruct, not least because the Restoration government of Charles II sought to invalidate and destroy the proceedings of the Long Parliament of the 1640s. We consequently do not have the details of the divorce petition that Edward Scott and his friends brought before that body, though the case was deemed notorious by those who heard his second petition in 1656.[14]

Sir Edward Scott was not the only parliamentary supporter abandoned by a Royalist wife. His initial suit for divorce could have been inspired by the Puritan poet and propagandist John Milton, who famously agitated for divorce reform on Parliament's ascendancy in 1643, after his own wife left him to return to her Royalist family. Milton provoked considerable controversy with his multivolume *Doctrine and Discipline of Divorce* and his translation of a defense of divorce by the radical sixteenth-century theologian Martin Bucer. Scholars recognize these works (and the reaction to them) as important to the development of Milton's political thought, but typically dismiss them as having no practical impact. The timing of Edward Scott's petition and events in New England suggest otherwise. Massachusetts granted its first divorces in May 1644. This was shortly *after* news of the parliamentary debates stirred by Milton's first divorce pamphlet had time to cross the Atlantic, but *before* momentum on English reform stalled later that year. New England authorities' willingness to grant divorces after the Long Parliament dropped the issue signaled their continuing engagement with England, rather than clear divergence.[15]

As we saw in the previous chapter, Puritan New England also anticipated reforms in marriage law that England enacted only after Protestant reformers gained legal ascendancy under Oliver Cromwell. In England, the disempowerment and dissolution of the ecclesiastical court system in the early 1640s created an administrative vacuum in the regulation of marriage and of estates, as well as for community discipline in matters such as drunkenness, oath breaking, sexual behavior, and religious heterodoxy.[16] Parliament was slow to make alternative provisions for the ecclesiastical courts' administrative work. The disruption created confusion about the process of establishing a legal marriage and eliminated the legal arena in which to pursue annulments or separations.

In the year after the beheading of Charles I, the radical Rump Parliament began to address these logistical issues with laws that followed the example of radical Protestants elsewhere, and which changed the legal stakes in the Scotts' marital dispute. The 1650 "Act for suppressing the detestable sins of Incest, Adultery and Fornication" focused on preserving marital legitimacy. The section on incest simplified the list of prohibited marriages established by the Elizabethan "Table of Kinship and Affinity," which in turn had sought to clarify the Levitical prohibitions on marriage between kin on which the medieval Catholic Church had run a brisk business in dispensations and annulments. Puritan reforms reduced the number of prohibited relationships, making dispensations less necessary. They did away with consanguinity as grounds for annulment by making a prohibited marriage into a capital offense.[17] Adultery, as was already the case in New England, also became a capital crime. Fornication, defined as "carnal knowledge" of an unmarried woman, met with more leniency—at least, on a first offense—but was still to be punished with imprisonment. These offenses were to be local, civil matters, dealt with by justices of the peace and the courts of assizes. In theory, punishing consanguineous marriages and adultery with death obviated the need for divorce. In practice, the measures proved unpopular, and evidentiary requirements made them very difficult to enforce.[18]

The most thoroughgoing piece of marital reform during the interregnum was the 1653 "Act touching Marriages and the registering thereof." The Barebones Parliament, appointed by Cromwell for its Puritan orthodoxy, used this act to place marriage, births, and burials exclusively in the hands of secular authorities. The measure substantively replicated laws New England had enacted in the 1640s. It required public announcement of a couple's intent to marry for three successive weeks prior to the ceremony, and carefully prescribed the forms required for legitimate marriage. The new ceremony resembled Quaker practice in its simplicity, but pointedly differed in retaining the wifely pledge of obedience and requiring formal consent from the couples' "Parent or Guardians" and the sanction of a justice of the peace. Neither church marriages performed by ministers nor pledges before witnesses fell within the new law.[19]

The 1653 Marriage Act was the only moral-reform measure on which Cromwell's handpicked parliament reached agreement. The body struggled to defend the new republican regime against Catholic and Anglican critics on one side and more radical Protestants on the other. On balance, fringe Protestants' creative ideas about marriage and divorce were perceived as the greater threat, and it is therefore not surprising that the measure made no explicit reference to divorce. However, by granting jurisdiction over marriage to local magistrates and declaring void all marriages that did not follow prescribed forms, it provided both means and numerous grounds for marital dissolution.

The Scotts' case demonstrates further that divorce remained on the reform agenda in England throughout the interregnum. In 1656, Sir Edward petitioned the Second Protectorate Parliament (the last of Cromwell's four Parliaments) for a divorce from Catherine. His supporters referred legislators to the divorce petition he had made to the Long Parliament in the 1640s, implying

that both Edward's own divorce and divorce reform in general were unfin-
ished business. Histories of the "road to divorce" in England mention these
multiple interregnum attempts at parliamentary divorce only obliquely, treating them as confused and futile gestures and presuming that they have little
bearing on the "secular" practice of parliamentary divorce that emerged later
in the century.[20] Yet, on the ground in the 1640s and 1650s, neither Edward
nor Catherine Scott's supporters thought his petition was likely to be a futile
gesture. Their very familiarity with the legal scripts and political theatrics of
divorce demonstrate that it was a live possibility. They had good reason to
believe that Edward would win his case.

The case of the abused Mr. Scott and his "wicked wife" seemed likely to
succeed because it relied on well-established storylines about sexual scandal,
in which Catherine filled the role of a woman whose betrayal of her husband
was also a betrayal of her country and its faith. The case provided superb
political theater. MP Thomas Burton, whose journals provide the only surviving record of Oliver Cromwell's later parliaments, was an enthusiastic observer of the 1656 parliamentary hearings on the Scotts' case. He noted that
neither he "nor nobody else" took much notice "of what other Committees
sate" while they were in session. A crowd of more than a hundred, with pick-
pockets under the tables, attended one long session; another contained "most
of the House, and abundance of gentlemen of quality," including "One young
lord, who would needs keep on his hat." As Charles II reportedly noted of a
better-known, post-Restoration attempt at parliamentary divorce, such hearings could be "better than going to a play."[21]

The little historical notice the Scotts' case has received has focused on its
theatrics at the expense of its politics, treating it as a "a good scandal," of minor
interest because it "brings colour into the lives of politicians and the public
alike, not least if the lady happens to be well-connected." The nineteenth-
century editor of MP Burton's journals helped establish this marginalizing
plot by declaring pages of testimony "sufficient to prove" Edward's charges of
adultery, but too indecent to print. Such dismissals have relegated the case to
passing mention in histories with an antiquarian bent. Clichés stand in for
interpretation: "Shrews and termagants were by no means uncommon in
seventeenth-century England," notes one recent work, before concluding that
"some marriages were probably destined to fail, either because of significant
differences in temperament or because the husband and wife were both strong-
minded individuals with a propensity for self-assertion." A biography of the
Royalist military leader Prince Rupert compartmentalizes the case in a chapter
on his "Feminine Company." The biographer uses allegations from the Scott
trial to shield his heroic subject's reputation from published (and somewhat

pornographic) accusations of sexual immorality. Where Prince Rupert is allowed a certain amount of manly sexual adventurism, Catherine is described
as corrupt: "a woman of great charm and no morals, . . . who did all she could
to enhance the morale of the Oxford garrison in her own charming way."[22]

Rumor at the time of the Scotts' first trial held that Lady Catherine was a
"very common" whore. But the case had political force because Catherine was
anything but common; if she was a whore, she was a Babylonian one. Animosity
to Royalists and Catholics, and the political demands of the Commonwealth's
war with Spain, were the glue that held this otherwise fractious Parliament together. The Scott divorce came before the body as some partisan Protestants
imagined tolerating "a Turk or a Jew" who practiced their faith privately, without disturbing the "public peace." But this Cromwellian tolerance, Frances
Dolan has perceptively argued, rested on Jews' and Turks' marked otherness.
The Catholic Church—the "*Whore of Babylon*"—represented a threat of a different order: a secretive *internal* danger, manifest in the wives and daughters
of Catholic families who privately preserved their families' allegiance to Rome
while their husbands' outward conformity protected family power.[23]

From the perspective of anti-Catholic religious reformers, this feminine
Catholic threat had made its way literally into bed with the Crown in the person of Queen Henrietta Maria. The queen's "[bed]curtain lectures" had sub-
verted her husband, Charles I, so the story went, and even after his death she
still threatened to place a Catholic king on England's throne.[24] The queen was
out of Parliament's reach, as were Catherine Scott's Royalist male relatives.
Edward Scott's supporters did their best to turn Catherine into a symbolic
stand-in, who embodied everything that gave anti-Catholicism and anti-
Royalism their imaginative, emotional, and political power.

We do not know Catherine's own religious allegiances, but as we have
seen, her father's career was built around his support of the hated Catholic
Queen. The elder Lord Goring had negotiated the marriage articles that gave
Henrietta Maria freedom of religion and control over the religious education
of her children; he had brought her to England and shepherded her back to
the Continent. Moreover, Catherine's amoral eldest brother openly served the
Spanish and Jesuit enemy, who gave him a Catholic burial in 1657. And finally,
rumor had it, Catherine intended to use the cover of marriage for other illicit
ends. "It seems," Burton reported, that Catherine had "one boy very like the
Gorings, and it is her drift that boy might inherit Scot's . . . brave estate in
Kent." The boy, said the gossips, was not simply a Goring but also a son of the
hated Cavalier General Prince Rupert.[25]

In MP Burton's jocular report of the first, parliamentary divorce trial, pru-
rient interest in Catherine's reputed sexual crimes overshadowed the trial's

political implications. However, her parliamentary audience was well aware of her birth family's political significance, and also that of the Royalist men who had supported her through the war years. Edward's supporters assumed that a reform-minded Parliament would welcome the opportunity to discredit the Royalist Gorings. Their allegations tarnished not only Catherine Scott, but also the reputations of several prominent Royalists who remained in England during the interregnum. Catherine was an attractive target both as a substitute for unreachable men, and probably also as a political agent in her own right.

COVERTURE AS A POLITICAL TOOL

Questions about Catherine's power as a woman and a wife, complicated by her family and social status, lay at the heart of her legal battles. Catherine proved adept at manipulating her *feme covert* status to achieve her own ends well before she brought this strategy to her trials. The Goring family had long used the gender conventions that placed women under the cover of their male relations to provide political cover for the family. Fragmentary evidence of Catherine's life from sources outside of her marital disputes suggests that she actively participated in these political games. Such independent sources also provide a glimpse of a woman who was neither scandalous nor trivial before the divorce trial managed to "rip up the course of her life."[26]

In a letter sent from London to her mother-in-law in 1642, for instance, Catherine described herself as a "weak instrument" and the obedient servant of her husband and his family. Despite her protestations of feminine limitations, her memo conveyed news she had learned from recent conversations with "Parliament men." She conveyed an informal offer of political office to her father-in-law, subtly inviting him to declare his explicit allegiance to the king. And she alerted her Royalist-leaning in-laws to possible betrayal by her husband Edward, who had recently "pleased to command" her (through intermediaries) to secure support for petition that smelled of Puritan radicalism.[27]

Moving forward in time to the lull between the wars, a cryptic bit of Scott family correspondence referred to a 1647 "siege" on the family's largest Kent estate. A letter from a retainer to Sir Edward Scott described efforts to scare Catherine "out of her hold" in Nettlestead Place by using armed men to cut off water and block the efforts of those who would send her supplies, among them Lord and Lady Westmorland and "divers poor women." A nineteenth-century genealogist framed this as a domestic dispute, citing an apocryphal effort by Catherine to seize the manor house and by Edward to "starve her out."[28] Yet it seems possible that this quasi-military event bore some relation to the Royalist "Kentish rising" that began England's second Civil War later that year, with Catherine's father (now the Earl of Norwich) in command. Parliament had twice ordered the Scott estates searched for Royalist caches of arms, because while Catherine's husband Edward was not a Royalist, other family members were; the 1648 uprising reflected these loyalties. Norwich's Royalist forces were defeated, and King Charles I was beheaded in 1649. Norwich kept his own head by persuading a narrow majority of his parliamentary judges that his involvement in the uprising had been accidental rather than premeditated. He claimed that family connections (i.e., Catherine) just happened to bring him to Kent at the wrong time, and he had been honor-bound by his rank and acknowledged loyalty to the Crown to answer Royalist partisans' calls for leadership. He was also helped by his numerous creditors, who aided his legal defense out of fear that his premature death would leave them impoverished. Legal technicalities stemming from questions about Parliament's jurisdiction and the application of the relevant international laws of war tipped the balance in Norwich's favor.[29] Family creditors and jurisdictional concerns would occupy a similar place in Catherine's later trials.

Norwich put conventions separating domestic and feminine affairs from "public" masculine ones to political use on numerous other occasions. Insistence that the queen's maternal assistance was needed to settle the nine-year-old Princess Mary into the household of the princess's new husband, twelve-year-old William of Orange, had provided cover when Norwich escorted the royal family and the Crown jewels to the Continent in 1644. The private letters of the wife of a French diplomat served as literal cover for his subsequent diplomatic missives to the queen and caused an international incident when Parliament discovered them. Catherine and her mother probably benefited from and helped manage the complex web of legal trusteeships that Norwich used to protect the family estates from Parliament's attempts to sequester them. And under the cover of private family business, Catherine was able to visit her father behind parliamentary battle lines when he was under siege in 1648.[30]

Similar conventions likely also explain why Catherine was able to travel openly to Paris in 1649, accompanying an "incognito" male Royalist on what the context suggests was a political mission. Catherine met the famous diarist John Evelyn on that journey, and again a year later, on the road outside of London. Catherine gave him a ride in her coach, and subsequently invited him to a dinner where they met "a gentlewoman called Everard, who was a very great chymist." Evelyn judged Catherine a "very pleasant lady." The fleeting glimpses he provided of her life show us a woman who remained engaged in court circles, court politics, and seventeenth-century intellectual life. Even in the absence of her male relations, she maintained the symbols of her status and received the credit and deference appropriate to her rank.[31]

THE SCOTTS GO TO LAW

By 1656, however, the fortunes and credit of Catherine's male relations had run dry. Her eldest brother was deeply in debt and dying in the care of Jesuits in Spain. Her family's English properties were hopelessly entangled in the claims of Parliament and her father's creditors. Her father was peripatetic on the Continent, looking for sources of income after having been pushed out of the new, still-exiled King Charles II's circle of advisors by political enemies. At this low moment, Catherine again took cover in her status as a wife rather than as a daughter, invoking the reciprocal obligations outlined in her marriage contract as a means of support for herself and possibly also for her impoverished relations. She reputedly asked Edward for reconciliation—a necessary step for any husband or wife seeking to prove their partner's neglect of their marital duties. Sir Edward's refusal to allow her to live with him gave Catherine grounds to sue for alimony in Chancery, and the lord chief justice himself had reportedly granted her plea. Edward Scott's family had no intention of honoring the judgment.[32] Given the extent to which her private affairs intermingled with political controversy, it is hardly surprising that the case generated public debate.

In response to the Chancery's ruling that he continue to support his wife, Sir Edward Scott filed suit for divorce, contending that Catherine's adultery should release him from any marital obligations. When he appeared in public, however, it became clear that Edward was a "weak" and "simple" man. Because he "could not utter his mind in a word of sense," his lawyers spoke for him. The management of his "brave estate" was likewise dependent on servants and parliamentary friends. If Catherine succeeded in her own legal effort to return to Edward's care and protection, she and her own friends would not have to wait for his death to begin to make use of his property. His performance at the trial thus made her scheme for reconciliation into a substantive political and economic threat, as well as a religious and moral one.[33]

For her part, Catherine presented a "bold face" when she appeared in answer to the petition. Her lawyer nonetheless stressed her vulnerability as he played to Parliament's jurisdictional anxieties. If the Commons insisted on hearing this case, he argued, they needed to allow Catherine a genuine opportunity "to vindicate her reputation" and defend herself against charges that "seemed to rip up the whole course of her life." How was a *feme covert* to defend herself, Catherine wondered, if her husband would not grant her alimony with which to pay lawyers and call witnesses? The issue provoked prolonged debate, finally moving onto its "substance" after Edward's lawyer made nominal concessions. The forms of justice were observed, allowing the show trial to proceed.[34]

Edward's petition followed legal scripts that were evidently familiar to its parliamentary audience, contrary to entrenched historical portraits of English divorcelessness. MP Burton knew the genre so well that he readily abridged it: Edward had "married Katherine, daughter of Lord Goring. She eloped from him, and at Oxford, and other places, had children by other men. She hath contracted great debts, &c. Desires he may be divorced from her, that those children may be declared bastards, and not inherit his estates, and that he may be relieved against those debts."[35]

Edward Scott's longtime steward opened the testimony with an effort to cast doubt on the couple's marriage contract. He contended that Catherine's father had never paid the second half of her promised three-thousand-pound marriage portion, implying that this should at least limit Edward's financial obligations. The steward also anticipated legal difficulties posed by episodic (and possibly staged) reconciliations. He claimed that Catherine deserted Edward after two years of marriage, on the pretense of leaving for a month or two to visit her family. She purportedly stayed away three years, in what was to be the first of a series of elopements punctuated by brief, strategically timed reunions. At least two of the couple's reunions, Edward's supporters charged, had been kidnappings. Most recently, Catherine hired "six lusty fellows" from a tavern to bring Edward to her in London in order to thwart his efforts to prove that she was bearing children to other men. Edward escaped her clutches only after Cromwell himself intervened.[36] Regardless of the truth of these allegations, they show legal awareness of provisions in the interregnum marriage laws that made three years' desertion the threshold for voiding a marriage, on the assumption that the absent spouse might be presumed dead.[37]

The adultery charges against Catherine followed patterns found in earlier sensational trials, which were almost certainly familiar to this parliamentary audience. The divorce of Frances Howard, Countess of Rochester, and Robert Carr, Viscount Rochester (who, like Catherine's father, had been a favorite of James I) featured prominently in a 1651 publication describing the "laciviousness" that characterized the reign of James I. Frances Howard's brother, Sir Robert Howard, was notorious as the lover of Frances Villiers, who had been forced into an unwanted marriage by her father, the jurist Sir Edward Coke, in 1617. Frances Villiers had been convicted of adultery in the 1620s, after a series of scandalous trials, but her son by Robert Howard nevertheless inherited his estate. Villiers's estranged husband was mentally unstable and genuinely fond of her; he entered the priesthood and did not actively contest his wife's new relationship. However, his elder brother deemed Frances's adultery a threat to his family's political position, and he tried unsuccessfully to secure a divorce.[38] The Scott case referred directly to these earlier failed dynastic marriages by implicating yet another Howard, a nephew of both Frances and Robert Howard, as one of Catherine's lovers.

Col. Howard and the other men named as Catherine's lovers made appealing political targets for the Puritan regime, and the identity of her lawyer and more-reluctant witnesses reinforced the partisan nature of the case. For the purposes of the suit, testimony emphasized sexual impropriety, but it can also be read as an attempt to punish Royalist collaboration. Col. Howard served under the Royalist general Prince Rupert and had siblings who were notorious spies. (Rupert's purported connection to Catherine appeared as rumor only, not sworn testimony.) A maid reported that Howard and Catherine had taken separate rooms in the same house during the late 1640s and passed themselves off as husband and wife. She could not swear that they spent nights together, though when a watchdog had awakened the house at 2 a.m., she had found Col. Howard in nightclothes in her lady's room, vowing to protect her and her father's money. Prosecutors implied that this money, as well as gifts from various men—a ring valued at twenty pounds, a gift of armor, and twenty gold coins hidden in a boot—were payment for sexual favors. Yet the testimony left room for understanding all of these items as efforts at mutual support by a beleaguered Royalist network, with Catherine operating as a conduit for both money and information.[39]

The most damning witnesses had the most to gain from their testimony. A German soldier who had served in Catherine's household during the first Civil War proved an entertaining storyteller, despite his poor English and destitute appearance. He described a visit from an unnamed "Kings Chaplain," whose actions vindicated Puritan claims about Anglican corruption. "Peeping in at a keyhole," he had watched Catherine and the chaplain "thrashing under his longe Coat" on the bed. The servant could not swear to their "nakedness," but said that Catherine Scott had turned very red when he had praised the chaplain's ability to "comfort her body and soul."[40]

"The German" went on to describe what MP Burton labeled a "comedy" set in a farmhouse near the Scott estates in Kent, where Lady Scott's party stayed the night to escape a fierce rainstorm. Her servant was relieving himself in the garden when, hearing noise from his lady's bedchamber, he stealthily went to investigate. He pulled back her bed curtains and seized a gentleman whose shirt was open and britches were around his knees, sufficient nakedness to prove adultery. Lady Scott screamed. The farmer and the farmer's wife, son, daughter, and servants came running. Everyone was distraught, but no one wanted the events "disclosed" outside their circle for fear of consequences for the gentleman and his wife, if not Lady Scott. As we saw in the previous chapter, when Elizabeth Lawson caught her husband in bed with a servant, householders did not want to call attention to sexual crimes that occurred under their roofs.

The German claimed, despite the well-rehearsed sound of his tales, that he was even now terrified to identify the gentleman he found in bed with Catherine. The man, he noted, was a former member of Parliament who still had it in his power to ruin the witness, who apparently owed him a great deal of money. Only after assurances that the present Parliament would absolve him of his debts and protect him did he make a trembling show of naming Sir Thomas Twysden as the embarrassed lover. Twysden was a neighbor of Catherine's and a former MP whom Cromwell had retained as a serjeant-at-law because his legal expertise outweighed his Royalist sympathies when it came to establishing legitimacy for the Protectorate. At the time of the divorce trial, he was a thorn in Cromwell's side, having used his position to question the Protectorate's power to issue ordinances and collect taxes in Cony's case. Cromwell had remanded him to the Tower of London for twelve days in a fit of pique, but released him on reflection that such absolutist tactics undermined his regime's authority and resembled the tactics for which Charles I had been deposed.[41]

Twysden's name and the terms under which it was "disclosed" both undermine the allegations against Catherine. This was a political hit, and the parliamentary protection offered the witness was a substantial bribe. The two maidservants who reported directly witnessing adultery were most likely also paid for their testimony. An Oxford apothecary seemed to have professional as well as political axes to grind when he swore that the past and future queen's physician, Dr. Hinton, had bragged of being paid fifty pounds to secretly deliver Lady Scott of an illegitimate child.[42]

Dr. Hinton and the householder brought in to corroborate the German's story were less cooperative witnesses who felt themselves on trial. Hinton was a committed Royalist whose elite female clientele kept him practicing and out of prison throughout the interregnum, much to the displeasure of Cromwell's regime. He admitted delivering many babies while at Oxford, including one to a masked noblewoman who was *not* Catherine Scott. Lady Scott had visited him elsewhere, for other forms of feminine distress. The farmer who was supposed to have taken part in the "comedy" with Twysden remembered the furor among servants in his main hall, but blamed it on misbehavior by the German witness. The farmer denied that his wife had even been in the house. He insisted that he had not entered Lady Scott's chamber, and that nothing immoral could have occurred under his roof, especially involving a pious man and devoted husband like Thomas Twysden.

According to MP Burton, most of those at the hearing had little doubt of Catherine Scott's guilt. Catherine's lawyer Mr. Finch (probably the future Lord Chancellor Heneage Finch) did little to counter the damning testimony, but instead delayed a decision. The case was adjourned for a few days at first, and then sent together with another divorce petition to a committee that was to decide the Scotts' fate as well as to prepare a general "Bill to this House concerning divorces and alimony, and where it is fit to place the same." No record of deliberations or decisions from the committee survives, but the matter appears to have died through deferral.[43]

Sir Edward had the sympathy of his parliamentary audience and evidence that most deemed more than sufficient to prove his case. Catherine's moral and political transgressions *together* struck such a powerful chord that Edward's supporters expected little opposition; testimony, if anything, was too effective at targeting Royalists, thereby inviting criticism as political charade. They had come ready with a bill of divorce to back up his petition, and argued that an hour or two of discussion would be sufficient to dispense with the entire matter. MP Burton thought Edward's petition likely to "prove but too true." He talked "with nobody of it, but they cry out upon the Lady Katherine Scot for a very common [whore] &c." Cromwell's attorney general declared the case "notorious" and expressed hope not only of acting quickly on Edward's behalf, but of producing "a law in general" to deal with such matters. Why, then, did he fail to obtain his divorce?[44]

The answer lies less with lingering opposition to divorce than with larger concerns about constitutional legitimacy and with the practical political challenges that ultimately brought about the Restoration. The Second Protectorate Parliament struggled to balance Puritan and republican demands for legal reform with a desire for institutional stability and postwar reconciliation. Oliver Cromwell's regime self-consciously sought to preserve the rule of law. Although it had done away with the church courts, the House of Lords, and the monarchy, it had maintained the courts of common law and Chancery through even its most recent effort at military rule. Moreover, Cromwell had explicitly charged the Second Protectorate Parliament with drafting a new, sustainable constitution—a responsibility that made the body especially sensitive to matters of procedure and precedent.

A further accident of timing heightened concerns about jurisdiction, procedure, and precedent in the Scott case. Edward Scott's petition came before the body just as it concluded the contentious blasphemy trial of James Nayler, a charismatic Quaker preacher. The Second Protectorate Parliament was particularly obsessed with the "Quaker and leveler" threat to "all Laws and Government"; for this Parliament, "religious considerations *were* worldly ones."[45] The Quakers, various MPs argued, were "daily disturbing the courts of justice" with their "persons and pamphlets."[46] Quaker claims that "the Scriptures are but ink and paper" and that "they are guided by a higher light" challenged all authority and "all ordinances, [such] as marriage, &c."[47] Merging our screens with the previous chapter, remember that Elizabeth Lawson was very likely mixed up in these circles of "Friends," and had been dragged prophesying and cursing back to New England only a few months before.

Nayler's powerful oratory and provocative pamphlets had made him a divisive figure even among the Society of Friends. His immediate followers believed that he modeled the "inner light" through which Christ became at least partially incarnate in the true believer. When Nayler and his most vocal female supporters reenacted Christ's entry into Jerusalem with Nayler in the role of Jesus, however, they went too far even for most of their fellow Friends. The jurisdictional gaps created by the demise of the ecclesiastical courts and the House of Lords landed the resulting prosecution for blasphemy in Parliament, where it created sharp divisions. It was agreed that Nayler's actions were repugnant, but the legal basis for his trial was unclear. His most vociferous opponents called for the death sentence and a general blasphemy law that specifically targeted Quakers and other radical dissenting groups. More temperate voices feared making Nayler into a martyr, and that sweeping anti-blasphemy legislation, like the "former laws against Papists," might be "turned upon the best Protestants."[48] After nearly two months of impassioned debate, Nayler was sentenced to a brutal exemplary punishment that entailed branding, whipping through the streets of London, and imprisonment in Newgate.

Sir Edward's petition arrived just as the MPs returned from witnessing the spectacle of Nayler's punishment; and, like Nayler's case, it raised concerns among the MPs most worried about jurisdiction, procedure, and precedent. Hasty action on Edward's petition, it was objected, could set a precedent that "any man that is weary of his wife may be quit of her by petition." No less than her husband, Catherine was "a person of quality," and to pass judgment "with the parties unheard" would "be very unequal." The coincidence of Edward's petition and Nayler's punishment amplified reservations. Those who feared that Nayler would become a martyr under the lash and hot iron were reluctant to hand another victory to the moral conservatives, at least one of whom had "intended to have Catherine hanged in the country," under the controversial 1650 Adultery Act.[49] Timing also worked against Edward in a more mundane fashion. His petition was read shortly before Parliament's daily dinner break, and the two hours his supporters claimed were all that would be needed to decide in his favor were not to be had.

Lack of a formal ruling in his favor might not have meant failure for Sir Edward. The historian Laura Gowing argues that the point of the early modern ecclesiastical suits was "the formal articulation of complaint and conflict, rather than a judicial decision. . . . It was the narratives of litigation themselves, rather than a final sentence decided from them, that carried the weight of dispute and that brought suits to the point at which they could be resolved or abandoned." If narrative vindication was what Edward was after, he got what he wanted. The titillating evidence of servants and soldiers who had been paid to peep through keyholes did indeed "rip up" the course of Catherine's life. Some of it might even have been true. Marital estrangement certainly forced women of all statuses to negotiate an awkward course "between sexual availability, independence, new commitments, and reconciliation with their husbands."[50]

Despite Edward's apparent narrative victory, Parliament found itself no better at resolving such matters than the despised ecclesiastical courts had been. As noted, Burton's final reference to the issue, two days after the Scott trial, assigned the "Scot's Committee" responsibility for hearing another divorce trial and preparing "a Bill concerning divorces and alimony, and where it is fit to place the same." The question of where it was "fit to place" marital disputes disappeared in a maze of other intractable questions about jurisdiction that propelled the collapse of the Commonwealth less than two years later.[51] If Parliament did act, either specifically in Edward's favor or on the question of divorce more generally, the Restoration government of Charles II obliterated the record of it. The interregnum statutes regarding marriage and adultery were repudiated and allowed to lapse when the new regime took power in 1660, but they left a legacy of confusion about marriage law that was not resolved by the reinstatement of the monarchy, House of Lords, and ecclesiastical courts.

Catherine Scott helped ensure that the new regime found the problem of jurisdiction over marital disputes every bit as intractable as had the old. Immediately upon the Restoration—or perhaps even in anticipation of it—Catherine Scott and her supporters renewed their efforts to secure her claim to Edward Scott's "brave estate." Catherine sued in the restored ecclesiastical courts for "restitution of conjugal rights," a cynical attempt to regain access to the resources and privileges that came from being Edward's wife. Failing that, Catherine's ecclesiastical suit at least gave her legal grounds to claim that she desired to be reunited with Edward, and that he was therefore in the wrong for refusing to support her. *Manby v. Scott* was a parallel suit in the courts of common law and equity, in which Catherine's creditors sought to make Edward pay her debts. The legal questions shifted from the possibility of absolute divorce to the persistence of marital obligations during separations.

Manby v. Scott and the Domestication of Politics

In its final, precedent-setting iteration, the Scotts' case was literally a drama about costumes. *Manby v. Scott* turned on an unpaid tailor's bill, which Lady Catherine—as a *feme covert*—sought to charge to her husband. The lead plaintiff, Francis Manby, was one of a number of London tradesmen to whom Catherine owed substantial sums, and who wanted Edward to pay her debts. If this does not sound like the stuff of costume drama, it is because neither Catherine Scott nor the new regime had an interest in continuing the political theater of the first, parliamentary trial. Charles II and his notoriously bawdy court were not opposed to divorce on principle, particularly in cases where an adulterous wife raised questions about the descent of a "brave estate." But Sir Edward's cavalier morality tale was not the test case they wanted. Rehearsing the household disorder caused by amoral, promiscuous Royalist courtiers would not help the legitimacy of a ruler famous for his illicit sexual exploits.[52] Nor would it help the legitimacy of the Restoration government, where Catherine's purported lover Thomas Twysden and Heneage Finch (her lawyer during the 1656 trial) were both MPs and prominent jurists.[53] The looming shadow of the Scotts' dispute might have helped reinstate opposition to divorce as official legal policy, against which Parliament would eventually claim the power to make occasional exceptions. Restoration England's leading legal authorities instead used *Manby* to make indissoluble marriage into a metaphor for the bond between the king and his subjects. They sought to resolve the jurisdictional confusion in marriage law left over from the interregnum, and to smooth over the domestic and the political divisions of the Civil Wars.

Manby v. Scott shifted the legal terrain of the Scotts' conflict yet again, taking it out of the exceptional jurisdiction of Parliament and declining to wait on an ecclesiastical verdict, which in any event would have needed to be enforced by courts of common law and equity. *Manby* first came to trial in 1661 before the justices of King's Bench, England's foremost court of common law. A divided court then promoted the case to the Chamber of the Exchequer, in an unusual procedure that created a de facto supreme court when important matters of law were at stake. The chief justices and three judges from each of the common-law Courts of King's Bench and Common Pleas and also the equitable jurisdiction of the Exchequer—twelve of England's most prominent jurists—spent numerous long days in the winter and spring of 1663 debating *Manby*.

These judges knew the Gorings and the scandalous history of Catherine and Edward's marriage; Sir Thomas Twysden, who heard *Manby* as a justice of King's Bench, had been accused of being her lover during the 1656 parliamentary trial. However, the extensive reported opinion from *Manby* thoroughly erased details of the Scotts' story and its murky political context. We would not even know the full names of the parties in the case if Sir Orlando Bridgeman, future lord chancellor and a political opponent of the Goring family, had not let them slip in an opinion that remained unpublished and accessible only to legal scholars until the nineteenth century.[54] Other reports and opinions allusively disparaged both the Scotts' particular dispute and troublesome matrimonial causes more generally, and went out of their way to declare the details irrelevant. The question of divorce disappeared along with the Scotts' identities. In *Manby*, the justices told a new story about the antiquity and inviolability of coverture, using it to uphold a generic masculine authority that they hoped would transcend and heal political divisions.

In *Manby* and in her parallel suit in the newly reinstated ecclesiastical courts, Catherine and her supporters framed coverture not as a disability but as a right (much as Elizabeth Lawson had; see chapter 1). They contended that Edward was obligated to support Catherine according to her degree and quality, and remiss in his refusal to allow her to return home to him. They argued for an expansive rather than constrained understanding of the implications of marital unity: a *feme covert* might not be able to contract independently, but a wife could be presumed to be her husband's agent in household business, which encompassed virtually everything but land sales. Exceptions to this rule required that the husband explicitly and personally direct his creditors otherwise, and also prove that he had good cause to be exempt from liability for her debts.

"Women will be more tempted by want of maintenance than by abundance," cautioned *Manby*'s advocates. Husbands consequently could not lightly—and certainly not unilaterally—exempt themselves from their obligations to provide. Marital unity unquestionably made wives subordinate to their husbands, the lawyers willingly conceded, but husbands' power in turn must be subject to oversight. If a couple separated, it was up to the community, not the husband, to decide the consequences. Moreover, because the *feme covert* was "a favourite of the law," the presumption lay in favor of her support: "Though she be an ill wife . . . she must not starve."[55]

This interpretation of marital unity echoed that of the Massachusetts authorities in the Lawsons' case. Elizabeth Lawson was certainly an "ill wife," but her husband was arguably worse. Colonial magistrates had no desire to relieve him of responsibility for her because it threatened to make both of them more burdensome to their communities. Such arguments were characteristically Puritan, but the Scotts' story makes clear that these were not exclusively Puritan concerns. They reflected the perspective of petty local officials across a wide span of time and place. As a matter of local governance, female poverty was a greater threat to social order than wifely disobedience. Coverture, in this interpretation, was primarily a protection designed to enforce male responsibility for women, rather than a mainstay of masculine power.

The majority of the learned lords appointed by Charles II to Restoration England's high courts disagreed. Their prevailing arguments in *Manby* made obedience to authority paramount: "If a woman . . . will choose to starve rather than submit . . . to her husband," they asserted, "let her take her own choice." The law was not to be faulted for failing to "provide for such a wife." Neither human nor divine law, they contended, favored prodigals: "The Scriptures say, 'He that will not work, let him not eat.'" It followed, accordingly, that an imprisoned debtor must find sustenance through his labor or charity and "a woman, who can have no goods of her own to live on" and who "will depart from her husband against his will" must also "live on charity, or starve in the name of God." "In such case the law says, her evil demeanour has brought it upon herself, and her death ought to be imputed to her own willfulness."[56]

Such claims turned the authority of husbands into a foundation for political absolutism and the legitimacy of the Restoration government. For the seventeenth-century philosopher Thomas Hobbes, masters' power over their slaves was the root of the juridical powers over life and death underpinning political sovereignty. In his controversial treatise *Patriarcha*, Sir Robert Filmer similarly aligned the power of kings and fathers.[57] *Manby* extended such arguments from masters and fathers to husbands: "The husband is the head of the wife as fully as the King is the head of the commonwealth. . . . When the wife departs from her husband against his will, she forsakes and deserts his Government; erects and sets up a new jurisdiction; and assumes to govern herself, besides at least, if not against, the law of God and the law of the land."[58] It was therefore "just, that in the law . . . this offence should put her in the same plight in the petit commonwealth of the household, that it puts the subject for the like offence in the great commonwealth of the realm."[59] Unlike the king, they conceded, a husband did not have the *right* to take his disobedient wife's life. He could nevertheless effectively render her dead to his household, acting as if she was "no part of her husband's care, charge, or family."[60]

These harsh assertions about the subordinate status of wives stood at odds with arguments framing marriage as a privileged state that set wives above other dependents. Catherine Scott's lawyers insisted that her "Quality" entitled her to support that would not only keep her from starving, but also allow her to maintain a retinue of servants. Tradesmen who helped her maintain her status could not be faulted for supposing her husband would honor her debts. In like manner, Elizabeth Lawson had adamantly defended her privileges as a wife against a husband who preferred servants, slaves, and squaws. Legal marriage was a prerogative of the free that was limited for servants and denied outright to slaves.

The judges in *Manby* dismissed such distinctions. Under the common law, they contended, wives and servants were much the same. Contracts made with wives or servants could be enforced only if a husband or master had promised to honor them. And while husbands and masters ought to protect their wives and servants from beatings or slander, the common law offered these dependents no remedy if their household head would not take action on their behalf. Even "infants" were not so thoroughly "disabled" in the law, for although their contracts could be undone, they were not automatically void.[61]

The justices acknowledged that they were drawing hard lines, and that their interpretation of the common law diverged from what had become common in legal practice. They justified their stance using dubious historical claims, bad lawyers' jokes, and a dodge of jurisdiction. Sir Orlando Bridgeman, for instance, was not to be outdone by the defendant's invocation of women's favored status in English law. He contended that the court's absolutist stance on husbands' authority followed "in the steps of our ancestors," and was consequently the safest way to guarantee wives the "provision, care, and indulgence" accorded "them by the laws, and the genius, custom, and constitution of the people." Notwithstanding his own rhetoric about submission and starvation, Bridgeman insisted that coverture guaranteed English wives "more freedom . . . than in other nations" where married women enjoyed separate property rights. Lest this inadvertent admission of the exceptional nature of England's legal understanding of marital unity raise doubts about the practical implications of his hardline decision, Bridgeman concluded his opinion with a trivializing, nationalistic salvo: England had "been called the Women's Island," and "it was no less than a proverb, that if a bridge were made over the sea, all the wives in Europe would come hither."[62]

The justices further avoided the practical implications of *Manby*'s stark pronouncements through the time-honored practice of dodging jurisdiction.

Marital disputes, Sir Orlando Bridgeman loftily declared, were beneath the "great modesty and decorum" of the common law. The common-law courts were too public and too important a forum for marital matters. To have the inner workings of a marriage "ript up" before a jury and bystanders, as the common law required, would ensure enmity between husband and wife and undermine the law's ostensible commitment to reconciliation. Should word "come abroad to all women" that "the opinion of the Judges" held this husband liable for his wife's misdeeds, all "husbands would be despised," and it would everywhere be "an encouragement to disobedience." If it were "known throughout the realm," on the other hand, "that the law doth not charge the husband in this case, all the wives shall give to their husbands honour, both great and small."[63] To preserve the honor and dignity of the common law, wives should instead seek their remedies in the ecclesiastical courts because there such matters could be settled privately. Such pronouncements ignored the fact that Catherine was pursuing ecclesiastical remedies, but they were not enough to satisfy her creditors.

The denial of common law and equitable jurisdiction nominally affirmed the power of the restored church courts. However, the judges' rhetoric simultaneously positioned the ecclesiastical jurisdictions as inferior to their own, secular bodies. They also brushed off the significant jurisdictional differences in worldly power. The ecclesiastical courts had limited means to enforce their own rulings on economic matters. They might excommunicate a husband who did not comply, but obtaining practical rather than spiritual remedies for his wife was another matter. Catherine Scott's seventeenth-century supporters rejected the attempt to deny jurisdiction as "more specious than satisfactory." The common law was responsible for "taking away all she hath," and by "sending her to another Court for relief," they insisted, it neglected to give her the protection due in exchange.[64]

Manby was thus a nominal victory for Edward Scott and a thorough rebuke to his Puritan allies. Edward was not held liable for Catherine's debts. But the reasoning behind the judgment explicitly repudiated Puritan interventions in marriage law and the dissenting Protestants' emphasis on reciprocal duties in marriage. The fact that Catherine was an object of Puritan loathing sweetened this poisoned political pill and lent the justices an air of impartiality. Insiders would have recognized the rebuke to Catherine as a savvy and relatively painless political maneuver. The justices who fulminated most extensively about the dangers posed by wayward wives were political enemies of the Goring family.[65] Whatever their personal opinions of Catherine, moreover, all the justices had reason to distance the law courts from the notoriously bawdy behavior of Charles II's royal court. When taking a moral stand on sexual misbehavior, an already discredited female cavalier made a much safer political target than the openly adulterous king and his courtiers.

Catherine's creditors might not have been pleased with the *Manby* decision, but Catherine Scott appears to have obtained most of her practical objectives by other means even before the justices reached their final verdict. In the summer of 1663, the diarists John Evelyn and Samuel Pepys both noted the sudden marriage of Sir Thomas Scott, "son to Madam Catharine Scott, that was so long in law." Sir Edward Scott had recently died, and shortly before his death he had acknowledged Thomas as his heir. Pepys's patron, "Mr. Treasurer and Vice-Chamberlain" Sir George Carteret, had "overreached" his competitors in a scramble for a marital alliance, securing the newly eligible bachelor as husband for his "little daughter Betty . . . a very little young child" of about fourteen. If the moral of the Scotts' tale was that arranged child marriages were risky, no one seems to have heeded it. Pepys sensed the irony. He praised Carteret for his dynastic achievement, but throughout the remainder of his coded diary he snidely referred to Thomas as "Mr. Scott, the bastard." Thomas's new in-laws were not thrilled with their connection to Catherine, but with a certain amount of prodding they secured her the jointure (widow's maintenance) promised in her original marriage settlement. If this was not all of what she wanted, it was certainly far more than *Manby*'s rhetoric about the fate of insufficiently submissive wives would lead one to expect. We do not know what became of her unpaid debts.[66]

Making a Precedent

In his work on nineteenth-century American divorce law, the historian Hendrik Hartog cautions against scholarship that imagines "law, and in particular the opinions of nineteenth-century appellate judges, as covert political theory." All parties in the legal process, he reminds us, "had to improvise solutions to immediate and intractable conflicts, using the imperfect materials of an inherited and changing legal order. Judges were rarely the producers of a coherent system of normative values or beliefs. That wasn't their job." The justices who decided *Manby v. Scott*, in contrast, were overt about their political theorizing, even if it served somewhat covert political ends.[67] However, they neither resolved the Scotts' immediate and intractable conflict, nor enforced their expressed normative ends. In the short term, their fulminations against litigious women and jurisdictional disorder in marriage law appear to have had relatively little impact on actual legal practice. The case assumed greater importance for later generations, but not in the ways the justices intended. Far from settling the question of whether coverture was a mark of privilege or of total subordination, *Manby* eventually became a precedent that would be used to support *both* of these lines of argument for another two centuries.

The majority opinion in *Manby* stated that the threat of starvation was a legitimate means to procure wifely submission, and that any concerns about marital injustice should be dealt with in the ecclesiastical courts. The minority view countered that wayward and insufficiently supportive husbands were a greater threat to social order than disobedient wives. By framing marital conflict in general terms that pitted husbands' autonomy against wives' submission, the justices in *Manby* ignored the powerful networks of kin, community, and faith that in practice regulated marriage and determined both men's and women's access to economic and political power. If the prevailing opinion in *Manby* had prevailed in practice, the economic effects could have been profound. Under the old understanding of coverture, wives could still carry out household business relatively independently; creditors assumed them to be acting on behalf of the marital unit unless explicitly notified otherwise. In the *Manby* ruling, a wife could be allowed to act economically only with her husband's explicit permission, making contracts and purchases on credit by married women very difficult to enforce. Husbands had the power to forbid tradesmen from giving their wives credit, though at least one version of the opinion limited such prohibitions to those made in person, and declared that printed ads placed in the "News Books" were not binding.[68]

An encounter between the decidedly unsubmissive Elizabeth Lawson and Sir Orlando Bridgeman testifies to *Manby*'s practical limits as a deterrent to prodigal wives. After Elizabeth returned to England in 1670, she followed through on her promise to seek justice from the "King's laws" after those in the Massachusetts Bay Colony disappointed her. Notwithstanding his condemnation of female litigants just a few years before in *Manby*, Bridgeman, as chief baron of the Exchequer, gave her a hearing. His assessment of her case was sympathetic—or at least inconclusive—enough to allow it to linger in the courts for several more years. If the judges in *Manby* had really thought that their decision would discourage women like Elizabeth and end jurisdictional conflicts over marriage law, this ironic encounter testifies to their failure.[69]

Manby certainly did not deter Elizabeth. She continued to exploit the fiction of marital unity and competing legal forums for her own ends. Specifically, she sued the widow of the agent with whom she had worked, in Christopher's name, during her sojourn in London in the early 1650s. She accused the couple of co-opting the power of attorney she had left behind and embezzling the funds she had been collecting in Christopher's name. The charges, like her claim to be Christopher's widow, were almost certainly fraudulent, but they were not easily disproved. Unlike the Massachusetts records, English court records do not contain the evidence of decisions in Elizabeth's favor. This does not mean the legal system in Restoration London was inherently less useful for aggrieved wives. Instead, it highlights differences drawn from practical issues of scale as much as from doctrine or judicial intent. Elizabeth's ability to use the courts at all, after she appears to have alienated the network of friends who supported her earlier legal efforts, was remarkable. In Massachusetts, the intense communal surveillance possible under the Puritan regime had worked to Elizabeth's advantage. The case she brought in London would not have borne such scrutiny, and she benefited from the fact that judges in England's central courts necessarily tolerated anonymity. London's size alone meant that jurists inevitably considered many cases in which they knew neither the parties nor their networks. Had Elizabeth genuinely expected legal vindication, better friends (and facts) would have helped. Her lawsuits appear—like Catherine Scott's—to have been used as leverage in negotiations for financial support that occurred outside the legal arena.[70]

This was how marital litigation *normally* worked. Aggrieved spouses and their allies turned to the courts for leverage, but conflict resolution usually occurred through negotiations on the part of family and friends. The justices in *Manby* did not change, but rather affirmed, that status quo with their deflection of jurisdiction to the ecclesiastical courts and, by default, to various local courts of equity. All parties in *Manby* admitted that the central courts were ill equipped to determine the facts that might settle marital disputes, even if they had been disposed to do so. Orlando Bridgeman's willingness to let Elizabeth Lawson pursue her case seems at odds with much of what he had to say in *Manby*. His actions were nevertheless consistent with an understanding of law, and particularly of equitable jurisdiction, in which the courts' role as a forum for airing arguments for narrative vindication was important in itself. While wearing his hat as an Exchequer judge, he was expected to allow equitable arguments. Given such underlying assumptions, it is not surprising that *Manby* itself resolved neither the specifics of the Scotts' case nor the jurisdictional conflicts that fueled their multiple lawsuits.

What requires explanation is how we have come to expect that it should have been otherwise. The story of *Manby*'s emergence as a precedent lies only partially in the intent of its arbiters. The remainder of this book will return to uses that later generations made of the case. Its long-term history documents the emergence of the belief that judicial pronouncements like those in *Manby* could and should end disputes, that high court precedents should have real and immediate effect on local practices, and that a centralized state authority should have final jurisdiction over marriage law. None of these beliefs were entrenched in the seventeenth century.

When they disparaged the conflicts in *Manby* as products of Puritan interregnum innovation, the justices effaced a debate with deeper roots and less
partisan lines. As Catherine Scott's advocates made clear, one did not have to
be a Puritan to find insistence on exclusive ecclesiastical jurisdiction over marriage "more specious than satisfactory," or to consider rigid adherence to the
rules of coverture "inconvenient" and impractical. Neither was divorce solely
a Puritan concern. Historians have puzzled over seventeenth-century colonial
litigants who, like Elizabeth Lawson's husband, Christopher, contended that
old England would grant full divorces where New England would not, and
over officials in other colonies who did not think it outside their authority to
grant divorce with permission to remarry.[71] The persistence of such claims
reflects continuing debate rather than defiance of settled English policy. The
eventual triumph of *Manby*'s politically motivated claims about the history of
marriage law, not colonial experiments, rendered colonial practices "repugnant" to English law.

In this, as in other areas of the law, "repugnancy" was a long time in the
making, not least because the justices in *Manby* were ambivalent about how
best to ensure their own legal authority. The Massachusetts justices who tried
the Lawson dispute might have heard gossip about the Scotts' case by 1669,
but they would not—and could not—have been expected to use it as law, because of the limits of legal communication. Sir Robert Hyde's concerns about
what would happen when word of the decision spread "abroad to all women"
notwithstanding, there were no well-established mechanisms for reporting
judicial reasoning at the time the case was heard.

The preference in all branches of government was for careful institutional
control of access to the inner workings of the law. Royalist authorities were
particularly reluctant to give the public the opportunity to directly interpret
legal texts. They felt, with some justification, that they had been on the losing end of the published political debates that had fueled the Civil War. The
inclination toward secrecy was not strictly partisan. During the Scotts' parliamentary divorce trial, a senior Cromwellian MP had chastised Thomas Burton for taking notes on the "Scot's Committee." He "fear[ed] their arguments
[would] be told abroad," curtailing "the freedom and liberty of men's speak-
ing" and impairing debate. But "without their notes," Burton replied, "how
should young men learn arguments?"[72]

Manby v. Scott's real career as precedent began in the 1680s, when young
men who had been learning law by taking notes published their records as the
first modern law reports. Anthony Colquitt's 1682 *Modern Reports* was one
of the first instances in English publishing in which a book's self-proclaimed
"modernity" figured as a title-worthy selling point. *Manby*'s preoccupation

with issues that were (and remain) central to defining modernity helps account for its prominence amid the "Select cases . . . collected" in this and similar volumes.[73]

Manby was propelled into print in the 1680s by the same forces that brought about the publication of Filmer's *Patriarcha* and John Locke's more famous answer to it in his *First Treatise on Government*. Political insiders in the 1680s would have recognized these publications as involving the same circles of actors.[74] All addressed intractable problems of authority and jurisdiction. Locke and Filmer are staple sources for historians interested in the relationship between government in households and government in states. *Manby* makes a more effective bridge between "politics defined as 'the conduct and management of affairs of state'" and the "political dimensions of everyday life."[75]

The publication of multiple versions of *Manby*'s rather incoherent attempts to put patriarchal theories into legal practice preserved the arguments the case had attempted to dismiss. Reporters repeated the judges' lofty claims about general principles that concerned "every individual person of both sexes that is, or hereafter shall be, married within this kingdom," and which made *Manby* "of as great consequence to all the King's people of this realm, as any case can be." They enshrined Matthew Hale's contention that it also raised significant legal questions about the "nature of contracts" and the meaning of "consent, which is the knot and formality of contracts."[76] They were less careful about preserving distinctions between the prevailing and dissenting views in the case.

Manby's elevated rhetoric and persistent jurisdictional conflicts over marriage together made the case difficult for later generations to avoid, regardless of whether litigants were (at least nominally) Anglican aristocrats like the Scotts, propertied dissenting tradespeople and yeomen like the Lawsons, or members of the religiously motley laboring majority classed as the "lower sort." As precedent, the case established the parameters for later debates. It did not—and could not—settle them. It survived because of the utility of its arguments rather than a consensus on its answers.

The next chapters explore the processes by which *Manby*'s seventeenth-century arguments became Sir William Blackstone's eighteenth-century answers. They focus not on legal theory but on "immediate and intractable conflicts" over household government that helped transform a defense of monarchy into a means by which ordinary husbands and fathers might place their own power on a par with that of kings.

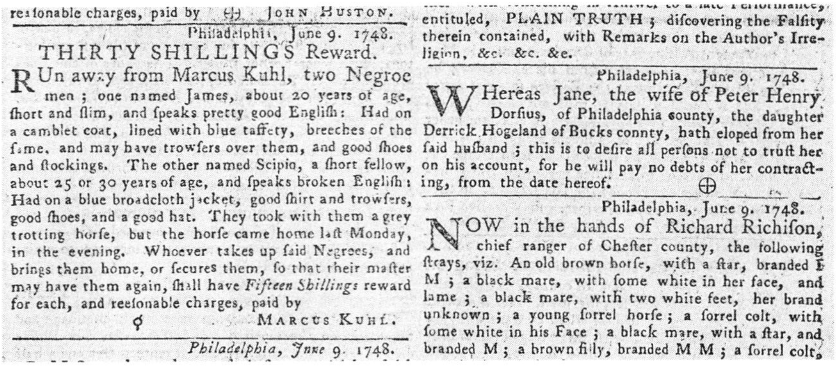

reasonable charges, paid by JOHN HUSTON.

Philadelphia, June 9. 1748.

THIRTY SHILLINGS Reward.

RUn away from Marcus Kuhl, two Negroe men; one named James, about 20 years of age, short and slim, and speaks pretty good English: Had on a camblet coat, lined with blue taffety, breeches of the same, and may have trowsers over them, and good shoes and stockings. The other named Scipio, a short fellow, about 25 or 30 years of age, and speaks broken English: Had on a blue broadcloth jacket, good shirt and trowsers, good shoes, and a good hat. They took with them a grey trotting horse, but the horse came home last Monday, in the evening. Whoever takes up said Negroes, and brings them home, or secures them, so that their master may have them again, shall have *Fifteen Shillings* reward for each, and reesonable charges, paid by

MARCUS KUHL.

Philadelphia, June 9. 1748.

entituled, PLAIN TRUTH; discovering the Falsity therein contained, with Remarks on the Author's Irreligion, &c. &c. &c.

Philadelphia, June 9. 1748.

WHereas Jane, the wife of Peter Henry Dorsius, of Philadelphia county, the daughter Derrick Hogeland of Bucks connty, hath eloped from her said husband; this is to desire all persons not to trust her on his account, for he will pay no debts of her contracting, from the date hereof.

Philadelphia, June 9. 1748.

NOW in the hands of Richard Richison, chief ranger of Chester county, the following strays, viz. An old brown horse, with a star, branded E M; a black mare, with some white in her face, and lame; a black mare, with two white feet, her brand unknown; a young sorrel horse; a sorrel colt, with some white in his Face; a black mare, with a star, and branded M; a brown filly, branded M M; a sorrel colt,

FIGURE 3.1 Marcus Kuhl/Scipio and Peter Henry Dorsius/Jane advertisements, *Pennsylvania Gazette*, June 9, 1748

Courtesy of the American Antiquarian Society

3

The Runaway Press

During the spring of 1748, in a town some distance from Philadelphia, a woman named Jane Dorsius left her husband and moved with her young children back into her father's house. At about the same time, a Pennsylvania man named Scipio left his master—twice. Scipio first claimed that he was free and sought to live and work close to home. Failing in that, he took a horse and went in search of a place his master could not reach. Had Jane and Scipio met on the road, they would have been more aware of their differences than of similarities in their situations. Yet readers of the *Pennsylvania Gazette* found them in literally parallel circumstances. In the columns of the newspaper, Peter Henry Dorsius's advertisement denouncing Jane as an eloping wife appeared immediately next to Marcus Kuhl's advertisement offering a reward for the capture and return of his "runaway Negro," Scipio.[1]

At first glance, advertisements like those for Jane Dorsius and Scipio seem to be direct extensions of the seventeenth-century patriarchal legal thought examined in the previous chapters. If dependents who would not submit might be allowed to starve, surely husbands and masters could discipline runaways. However, a seventeenth-century reader would have found the advertisements for Jane and Scipio peculiar and even problematic. Newspapers had their origins in the chaotic politics of the English Civil Wars, and such ads offered yet another example of the ways in which unregulated publication disrupted established practices of government. Recall that when Christopher Lawson had set "papers . . . upon posts in Boston" in an attempt to discredit his wife, she and Massachusetts authorities agreed that he was abusing his power. Some of the justices in *Manby v. Scott* concurred; the men who affirmed a husband's power to declare a wayward wife "dead to his household" tempered their stark pronouncements with caveats about methods. A husband might forbid a "particular tradesman" to credit his wife, but public notice to tradesmen *in general* not to trust her, and specifically notices posted in a "News-Book," overreached and would not stand. A wife who set up "a new jurisdiction" outside of her husband's "Government" was a problem. But so too were men who used the press to assert jurisdiction that ran "besides" and sometimes "against . . . the law of the land."[2]

Yet, by the mid-eighteenth century, ordinary men routinely used newspaper notices to govern their households. With their advertisements, Peter Henry Dorsius and Marcus Kuhl asserted the power to determine where and how Jane and Scipio lived and worked. They marked their legal stake in any property Jane or Scipio might claim. And they sought to judge, in place of other authorities, questions of discipline and justice raised by their dependents. The ubiquity of such notices in the press helped naturalize this extension of authority while also accentuating the parallels between the power of husbands and masters. In the papers, these parallels became norms that obscured and overrode significant differences in local and regional law and practice.

How did these genres, with their embedded assumptions about masculine household government, become generic? What was their relationship to "the law of the land"? Scipio's and Jane's cases landed side by side in the *Pennsylvania Gazette*, but they arrived there through very different trajectories. The histories of marriage and slavery underpinning these advertisements are usually told separately. Taken together, Jane's and Scipio's stories illuminate the uneven and interrelated development of both institutions, which were neither fixed in a static, patriarchal past, nor "evolving" on a linear path toward a revolutionary, egalitarian future. These case studies, in particular, demonstrate the ways that newspapers, the "new media" of the eighteenth century, reified ideas about householders' unmitigated patriarchal authority.

Within the British Empire, racial slavery, newspapers, and runaway advertisements were all new phenomena that emerged between the mid-seventeenth and mid-eighteenth centuries. This chapter examines the colonial developments that turned ads of runaway slaves and servants—and, by extension, ads of wayward wives—into a routine occurrence and a seemingly legitimate exercise of husbands' and masters' power. As we saw in the first chapter, Britain's colonies could not (and often did not want to) replicate England's complex, multilayered court system. Colonizers increasingly turned to bound labor to make their endeavors sustainable and profitable, albeit only for those deemed entitled to freedom. Both colonial trends were sustained by legal innovations, most starkly in the form of new statutes governing slaves and servants. The general inclination of these laws was toward harsh treatment of laborers and the presumption of slave status for people of color; but the lines demarcating bondage and freedom varied enough across regions to leave room for legal challenges in the unlikely event that a bondsperson had the resources. These novel colonial labor laws helped establish an authoritarian infrastructure in which it seemed natural for masters to use runaway advertisements as a means of controlling slaves or servants who crossed territory and jurisdiction.

Husbands applied similar logic when advertising wayward wives, but they found themselves on more tenuous legal footing. While colonial authorities emphatically supported masters' economic interest in their slave and servant labor, they were ambivalent about ads of eloping wives because these aimed primarily to free husbands from their obligation to support their dependents. Unlike slaves and servants, moreover, wives retained multiple avenues by which they could challenge husbands' advertisements, including the courts, their churches, their kin, and the press. As in the seventeenth century, arguing married couples continued to debate whether a *feme covert* was unequivocally entitled to her husband's financial support or whether a husband could cut her off under qualifying circumstances; ads served as a public forum for negotiating matters that marriage laws did not address with sufficient clarity. Servants and slaves received no such benefit of the doubt. Married women, slaves, and servants were indispensable participants in the colonial economy; as colonial laws defined their "disability" and dependency in ways that ensured that masters retained the wealth created by slaves, creeping authoritarianism threatened to undermine householders' obligations to other "free" dependents.

Runaway Slaves and Servants and the Development of Colonial Labor Systems

We'll begin by examining Scipio's story. To understand the context in which ads for runaway slaves developed, we must first understand the rise of slavery and distinctive slave codes in England's mainland colonies. In contrast with laws regarding marriage, colonial laws regarding slavery diverged sharply from English precedents, although we shall see in the next chapter that they—like marriage laws—emerged out of a transatlantic conversation that served imperial interests.

Racial slavery became entrenched in England's colonies with the Restoration. Even as the justices in *Manby* sought to buttress Charles II's authority in England during the 1660s, Charles's Royalist supporters, backed by English troops, sought to secure his sovereignty in the colonies. Pennsylvania came forcibly under English jurisdiction at this time. Charles II also stepped up England's investment in the slave trade during the 1660s and 1670s, thereby ensuring the presence of slavery in all of Britain's colonies. As the institution expanded, anxious colonial authorities experimented with an array of statutes designed to reinforce masters' coercive powers.[3] Runaway slave and servant advertisements, in turn, reinforced such measures. They became a means through which slave owners carried assumptions about slavery and householders' authority into places that never enacted detailed slave codes, including, beginning in the late 1660s, England itself. The variations in statute law, together with differences between emerging English and colonial conventions regarding advertisements for runaway servants, document the gradual development of racial slavery as the standard against which other dependents defined their freedom.

Runaway slaves had a far different experience than wayward wives, who were presumed to be free and who could use the variability and flexibility of marriage law to defend themselves. Scipio disputed Marcus Kuhl's legal claim to his labor, but colonial innovations in labor law ensured that his grievances did not translate into public debate about the legitimacy of Kuhl's advertisement, much less about the more general question of whether such notices gave masters unreasonable power. In contrast, ads about wayward wives inspired repeated controversy. Advertisements like Henry Dorsius's had no statutory underpinnings on either side of the Atlantic. On the few occasions when colonial legislators directly intervened in marriage law, they tended to distinguish marriage as a marker of free status. In the context of colonial bond labor, to be a wife meant that one was definitively not a slave, and usually not a servant either. *Manby*, the most directly relevant legal precedent, created room for controversy with arguments that could serve advertising husbands as well as those who wished to challenge them. In Jane Dorsius's case, such ambiguities fueled debate about the appropriate relationship between the press and the law in multiple colonies. As a wife, Jane retained the community resources needed to seek redress for the grievances that prompted her marital dispute. Scipio simply kept running.

Runaway ads are our only source of information about Scipio. Five different notices seeking his capture and return appeared in the *Pennsylvania Gazette* between 1748 and 1757. They warned readers to be on the lookout for a short man in a blue broadcloth coat, noting other details that varied with his circumstances: "a black wig"; "an old beaver hat"; a "good shirt and trowsers, good shoes and a good hat"; or "old stockings" and "old shoes." Ads of this sort are enticing yet frustrating documents. They provide the closest thing one is likely to find to a snapshot of an "ordinary" eighteenth-century person.

Non-elites did not leave portraits; they appear to us faceless in documents that took physical appearance for granted, or nameless in images constructed for other purposes. The details of a runaway's appearance, clothing, and manner can make him seem familiar, conveying the sense of shared humanity that goes along with being able to recognize a person's physical existence. But ads were mug shots, not portraits. Their fragmentary descriptions were designed to criminalize runaways, and to justify and facilitate masters' demands for their arrests. They turned skills and positive attributes into liabilities for the subject. Read against the grain, however, they can also hint at motives and ambitions, allowing us to piece together a story about Scipio's life.[4]

Scipio was born in the early 1720s, perhaps in Africa, perhaps in a non-English-speaking colony of the West Indies, or perhaps in a German household in the mid-Atlantic. His master in 1748, a Philadelphia baker named Marcus Kuhl, was of German descent. The ads do not tell us Scipio's first language, only that as an adult he was marked by his "indifferent" and "broken English." By his late twenties, Scipio was a skilled musician who sang and played "well on the banjo"; he might even have earned income for his masters (and maybe for himself) as a hired entertainer. Experience working for hire in any capacity could explain his apparent familiarity with territory outside his "home" in Philadelphia, his ability to subsist for extended periods of time outside of his masters' control, and his desire for autonomy.[5]

In 1748 and 1749, Scipio and Kuhl engaged in a protracted struggle over his status that was marked by four runaway ads in the space of eighteen months. In May 1748, Scipio had "got a pass as a free Negroe" and left Kuhl's service; Kuhl offered a reward of thirty shillings to "whoever brings him home." Kuhl suspected that Scipio was "still skulking about town," and he seems to have been correct. Less than three weeks later, Scipio had returned and run away again. This time he went on horseback with a man named James, prompting the advertisement that appeared next to Peter Henry Dorsius's notice discrediting his wife Jane.[6]

At some point in the next few months, Scipio was captured and hired out to a planter in southern Maryland—quite probably as a punitive measure. The arrangement was not to his liking. In May 1749, he turned up at a plantation on the Susquehanna River, at least eighty miles from the place he was supposed to be. If, as he told people there, he "wanted to come to Philadelphia to see his master," he was almost halfway home. However, Scipio also "had a pass with him, and pretended to be a free man." Two months later, when he had still not appeared, Kuhl and associates in Lancaster, Pennsylvania, offered a hefty three-pound reward to anyone who took up the "said slave." Their ad's wording unequivocally asserted their position on his status. Scipio and Kuhl were reunited shortly thereafter, but the homecoming must not have been very sweet—in October, Scipio ran away yet again.[7]

Scipio then disappeared from the surviving records for eight years, surfacing in 1757 in another ad that placed him in (or rather out of) the hands of a Maryland merchant. By 1757, he had acquired at least one new skill: he "pretend[ed] to be a hatter by Trade." But in most respects, the story was similar. He was still short (and now a little "thick" as well), still spoke broken English, and still played the banjo. He also continued to insist that he was "intitled to his Freedom," and he remained very good at evading capture. Five months after his escape, his new owner advertised in the *Pennsylvania Gazette* on the theory that he might have returned to Philadelphia. The posting took care to remind readers that Scipio had been "the Property of Mr. Marcus Kuhl" and was *not* a free man.[8]

Scipio could have been a "typical" runaway slave; he fit the remarkably consistent demographic profile for advertised runaways that lends an artificially timeless quality to such notices.[9] Yet Scipio insisted he was free, and he might not have been a slave at all. Marcus Kuhl's advertisements acknowledged this claim even as they sought to deny it. Authorities in some jurisdictions, moreover, apparently gave Scipio the benefit of the doubt. The ambiguities surrounding Scipio's status are the most important features of his story for the purpose of understanding the differences between his and Jane's predicaments. Though ads for Jane and Scipio appeared parallel in many respects, Jane's status as a wife made her, by definition, "free" and left her multiple avenues for redress not available to unfree household dependents such as Scipio. Colonial law took extraordinary measures to define household hierarchy in ways that limited slaves' and servants' options for legal and extralegal recourse, preserved the economic value of their labor for masters, and upheld the system of slavery as a whole.

REDEFINING HOUSEHOLD HIERARCHIES IN THE COLONIES

By the mid-eighteenth century, colonial labor statutes and runaway slave ads seemed to reinforce each other. Yet, on closer examination, the colonial statutes that redefined the meaning of bound labor also contain evidence of the equitable legal tools available to dependents under English law, as well as concern about implications that the rise of colonial slavery had for servitude and marriage. The regionally varied, gradual development of colonial labor regimes left legal loopholes through which people of color might challenge enslaved status. Runaways who fled from one jurisdiction to another created problems of comity that long predate those made famous in nineteenth-century American conflicts over fugitive slaves. If Scipio had pursued his claim to freedom in court, the grounds almost certainly would have been that he—like most free people of color and many colonial whites—was a temporary servant rather than a perpetual slave; he could also have appealed to legal rules that changed as he crossed colonial borders. Marcus Kuhl used his advertisements to override any power such loopholes might have provided Scipio, although Kuhl's decision to pursue Scipio was also shaped by statutory constraints.[10]

Our sampling of statutory ambiguity begins with the 1641 Massachusetts *Body of Liberties*. As noted in chapter 1, this document contained the first English law mentioning slavery, which managed to legitimize the institution even as it sought to limit it. The Massachusetts founding code outlined the "Liberties" of women, children, and servants in similarly paradoxical fashion, guaranteeing the right to community protection from "Tyrannical" husbands, parents and masters. The *Liberties* allowed householders more leeway regarding the physical "correction" of children and servants than for wives, but the code generally protected dependents who fled abuse and those who "harboured" them, insisting that magistrates rather than householders had the ultimate say in matters of household justice.[11]

The first English legal code for the middle colonies, the 1665 Duke of York's Laws, substantially based its provisions regarding "Masters, Servants & Laborers" on the Massachusetts "Liberties," but its sympathies lay foremost with husbands and masters. The code can be read as a post-Restoration critique of Puritan legal innovation. The mid-Atlantic region's first English governor, Richard Nichols, was a Royalist commander and newly minted lawyer who claimed he had compiled the Duke's Laws "out of the laws of the other colonies, only with such alterations as may revive the memory of old England in these parts, for democracy has taken so deep a root amongst us that the very name of a Justice of the Peace is an abomination."[12]

Nichols approved of some of Massachusetts's more coercive measures; he copied almost verbatim acts forbidding trade with servants and empowering local constables to pursue runaways at public expense. However, where Massachusetts empowered community members at large to intervene on behalf of abused dependents, Nichols's provision reserved that power for legal authorities alone. Servants were not entitled to find their own sanctuary by running away, but they were permitted to take complaints of masters' tyranny and cruelty to their community's "Constable & Overseers." It seems unlikely that this would have been a practical remedy. The penalty to masters for a first complaint was merely admonishment to "the Master or Dame not to Provoke their Servants." Upon the second complaint, the local authorities were empowered to "Protect and Susteyne" the servant in their own homes, provided they gave "Due Notice" to the master. The final arrangement for "Relief" was to be determined at the next court session. The statute freed servants whose masters "[smote] out the Tooth or Eye . . . or . . . otherwise Maym[ed] or Disfigur[ed]" them, although masters could release themselves from liability by demonstrating that this had been an accident of "moderate correction" rather than habitual "Tyranny." Seeking legal aid for lesser grievances was risky business, in part because masters might seek retribution after the first complaint. A servant judged to have "Causelessly Complained" was subject to three months of additional service. Like a servant, a "Woman Flying from The Barbarous Cruelty of her Husband" was also not entitled to choose her place of refuge. However, if she went to "the House of the Constable" or to the overseers of the parish, she could be "Protected . . . in the same manner as [was] Directed for Servants in such cases & not otherwise." Whereas in Massachusetts "any freeman of the same town" might provide aid, under the Royalist authorities' new laws, freemen were subject to punishment for taking in any such refugees.[13]

The development of Pennsylvania's statutes forbidding the "harbouring" of runaways is remarkable because here the analogy ran from wives to servants. The Duke's Laws prescribed a stiff fine—five shillings an hour—for any man who "Harboured, Concealed, or Deteyned" a married woman without the consent of her husband. The source for this provision is unclear. It might have preserved a rule established by the Dutch and Swedish settlers from whom Nichols had seized authority in 1664. Or it might have been Nichols's own innovation, reflecting the legal training he received in 1662 and 1663 when, as the previous chapter demonstrated, the issue of marital obligations much engaged Restoration England's high courts.[14] In any event, this provision was the *only* English-language statute with any bearing on newspaper notices for "eloped" wives, and it was fleeting. It disappeared from the legal codes drafted by William Penn and his supporters in the 1680s, long before colonial newspapers appeared on the scene. The language prohibiting "harbouring, concealing, and detaining" migrated from the marriage statutes to those concerning servants, and only this latter manifestation persisted in the statutes printed during the eighteenth century.

The penalty of five shillings for every hour was idiosyncratic. Time and labor were not generally measured in hours or even days in early America. The typical labor contract lasted at least a year, and more frequently four or seven years. Punishments extending service usually added months. And five shillings per hour was far out of proportion to the value colonists attributed to any woman's services. The measure seems to have been intended to intimidate and punish those who upset household order, rather than to compensate slighted patriarchs.

The legacy of this punishment reveals connections among efforts across the colonies to define household order by race. An hourly fine of five shillings reappeared in Pennsylvania's 1726 "ACT for the Better Regulating of Negroes in this Province," where it was directed against "any Free Negroe or Mulatto" who "shall Harbour or Entertain any Negroe, Indian, or Mulatto Slave, or Servant in his or her House" without the master's "Leave or Consent." The fine was softened somewhat in that it decreased from five shillings to one per hour after the first hour had passed, though it still amounted to several times what a servant's daily labor would have been worth. This provision otherwise emulated a passage in the 1707 Massachusetts "Act for the Regulating of Free Negroes, &c," which imposed a flat fine of five shillings for each offense. If the fine could not be paid, the offender was subject to "the discipline" of the "house of correction," where he or she "was to be kept at hard labor" valued at the rate of one shilling per day. In this context, provisions against harboring undermined the ability even of free people of color to establish their own households. Prohibitions against harboring wives upheld white husbands' claims to their wives' persons and labor. Restrictions on free blacks' right to "Harbour or Entertain" others of their race, in contrast, gave the claims of white masters precedence over ties of marriage, kinship, and community between African Americans, even in colonies not remembered for their investment in slavery.[15]

Even colonial Virginia took steps to "make certain" that servants and wives remained within the care of the legal system, again in ways that highlighted pervasive uncertainty about distinctions between forms of dependent status. Virginia's 1662 law defining slavery as a condition inherited through mothers invalidated paternal claims central to English law; it proved a pivotal step in turning people of color into a permanent underclass. As subsequent laws further deprived the enslaved of claims to legal protection, the colony added statues that explicitly required masters to "provide for their servants, wholesome and competent diet, clothing, and lodging," and warned them against using "immoderate correction."[16]

Virginia folded an explanation of the means by which wives might seek redress into its first comprehensive "Act concerning Servants and Slaves." The measure gave a detailed account of the procedures "all servants (but not slaves)" should follow to obtain legal arbitration in disputes with their masters. After these came an addendum declaring "that all servants . . . as well as feme coverts . . . shall upon complaints of misusage . . . have their petitions received in court, for their wages and freedom, without the formal process" normally required to undertake a lawsuit. This affirmed—for servants and wives—the customary equitable right of dependents to petition higher authority when the family patriarch acted unjustly. The inclusion of wives here seems an afterthought, given that their complaints could have nothing to do with "wages and freedom." The ill-fitting reference was symptomatic of the problems of analogy with slavery. Contemporaneous Virginia codes curtailed slaves' property rights and declared their masters liable for their unsupervised actions in ways that made them legally akin to wives. To avoid confusion on these points, the act's authors apparently deemed it necessary, though awkward, to codify prerogatives for wives as well as servants in order to make clear that both groups retained rights they were denying to slaves.[17] Such statutes marked the only places in which wayward wives entered written colonial laws.

LIMITED ACCESS TO THE LAW AND ITS REMEDIES

Pennsylvania's laws "concerning Negroes" were less stringent and comprehensive. They nevertheless extended regulations that had applied only to white "paupers" to *all* people of African descent. Local authorities had the power to "bind out to Service" the "Children of Free Negroes," "any Negro . . . set Free under the Age of Twenty one," or "any Free Negroe" they deemed underemployed.[18] Such measures made it very difficult for people of color to avoid bound labor in white households even when they were technically "free." However, these measures also meant that, in Pennsylvania and across the colonies, there were people of color who could exploit the spaces between the manifold forms of subordinate status, and claim the legal protection granted to life-cycle servants but not to slaves.

Under Pennsylvania's statute, if Scipio had been bound out as a child, his legally stipulated indenture would have ended when he turned twenty-four. This could explain why he started asserting his freedom so forcefully at "about 25 or 30 years of age." In his first advertisement, Marcus Kuhl implied that Scipio's "pass as a free Negroe" was fraudulent.[19] Some other authority might well have believed otherwise, and issued it in good faith. If Scipio convinced a local magistrate of his freedom or attempted to bring his case to court, the records do not survive in the archives of Philadelphia or its neighboring counties.

This absence of evidence made Scipio's case, once again, fairly typical. Even runaways who plausibly could have turned to the formal legal system seldom did so. Runaways' experiences with the law make this unsurprising. Neither Scipio nor most colonists had the opportunity to *read* colonial statute law, or to study the legal nuances and loopholes through which the well-informed might claim protection. Slaves and servants nevertheless encountered the law on a routine basis, and their experiences would generally have been even more intimidating than the codes themselves.[20]

In the treatment of runaways, the common early American—and early modern—fear of "people out of place" trumped concern about masters' abuses of power. Colonial runaway statutes derived substantially from English statutes that punished "vagrants" with whipping, forcible return to their community of origin, and bound labor.[21] As Pennsylvania's seventeenth-century laws suggest, even comparatively lenient codes were hardly encouraging. Laborers who sought legal protection could easily find themselves facing punishment instead.

In 1749 (when Scipio was once again on the run), two recently freed female indentured servants in Bucks County, Pennsylvania, explained why they had not sought legal remedies. Margaret Brown and Mary McWilliams had served more time than legally required, under conditions "as bad as the Egyptian bondage," because they knew "no better," and their master duplicitously denied them "opportunity to acquaint" themselves with any who might provide legal advice. They obtained "better advice," it appears, after McWilliams was not only freed but married. The "cover" of a husband helped McWilliams challenge their former master's claim that he held the right to retain, abuse, and possibly sell children both women had while in his service.[22]

Neither Brown nor McWilliams could write well enough to sign their own names, but they nevertheless found a sympathetic magistrate who helped them construct petitions. The judgment of other authorities was less certain. Their master's legal literacy saddled Brown with at least one extra term of service. After he brought to court an itemized list of his expenses for twice having advertised her as a runaway and four times having to pay for the men and horses who brought about her capture and return, Brown signed an indenture that added a year to her servitude. As an uneducated, unmarried Irish woman with a fondness for tobacco and "four or five" children of indeterminate paternity, Brown had little credibility.[23]

Scipio had little reason to hope he might fare better. In Maryland, he might have heard the colony's punitive measures regarding runaways read aloud by the county sheriff at a quarterly court session. The colony required that its acts "Concerning Servants and Slaves" be "published" orally, so "that no servants or slaves may have pretense of ignorance" of the law. In Virginia, the task also fell to the "reader of each parish" who was to "publish" them on specified "sermon Sundays . . . after divine service is ended, at the door of every church and chapel." Maryland, Virginia, and other colonies in which slavery anchored

the economy also inscribed the law on the bodies of the slaves themselves
with exemplary punishments for "incorrigible" slaves aimed at "terrifying
others from . . . like practices." Scipio might well have encountered slaves
whose ears had been cut off and faces branded with the letter *R* in punishment for running away.[24] Confronted with such evidence of the nature of the
law, Scipio would have been wise to distrust the legal system. And once there
was an advertised reward for his capture, he would have been a fool to show
his face in a printers' office to complain about the injustice of his masters'
advertisements.

REWARDS, HUMAN PROPERTY,

AND ADVERTISERS' LIABILITY

The offer of "THIRTY SHILLINGS Reward" that formed a banner headline
over the advertisement for Scipio and James created a visual contrast between
it and the neighboring notice for Jane Dorsius. Posted rewards reflected important underlying differences between ads for wives and ads for other runaways, both with regard to primary objectives and to the legal underpinnings
of such notices. The rewards also became a point of divergence between colonial and English handling of runaway ads. The expressed purpose of rewards
for colonial runaways was to assure "that their master may have them again,"
and in this respect, they offered a direct measure of masters' economic interest in their human property.[25] While rewards usually served masters' financial
interests, they were also products of a master's legal obligations to control
dependent laborers and liability for dependents' actions.

   Rewards for runaway slaves marked a direct connection between statute
law and the practice of advertising that did not exist in relation to ads for
wayward wives. By requiring that masters compensate those who "take up,"
"bring home," or "secure" runaways, colonial statutes sought to prevent negligent owners from letting disobedient servants and slaves escape.[26] More was
at stake in such measures than masters' individual property rights. Runaways
challenged the legal fictions that made people into property, undermining
the foundation of the colonial system of bound labor. Rewards were seen as a
necessary incentive to secure the participation of the entire free community
in policing those who ran away.

   The substantial fluctuations in the rewards Marcus Kuhl offered for Scipio
illustrate the advertisements' dual character as artifacts of masters' interests
and of their legal obligations. In his first ad, Kuhl promised thirty shillings
for Scipio's return. In his second—three weeks later—he offered only half as
much, less than the typical twenty-shilling bounty for horses, and much less

than the rate of forty shillings offered for most other runaways. Kuhl perhaps thought he had paid too much the first time, given the speed with which Scipio was captured. The following year, with Scipio roaming free in Maryland and western Pennsylvania, the reward went up to three pounds (sixty shillings). The dramatic increase certainly corresponded to the evident difficulty of capturing, holding, and especially returning Scipio to his master. It might also have been prompted by the hope of profit; the ad was cosigned by men in Lancaster, Pennsylvania, suggesting that Kuhl might have been trying to sell Scipio at a distance—if he could secure him.

Finally, fear of liability might also have explained the increase. Colonial laws gave local authorities (and in some cases free whites in general) broad powers to apprehend, advertise, and even sell suspicious persons. Required rewards meant that masters were likely to be charged for this process, regardless of whether they really wished to recover runaway dependents. Pennsylvania's minimum rewards were somewhat antiquated and not particularly onerous: ten shillings for servants taken up within "*Ten Miles* of the Servants abode," and twenty shillings for any greater distance. But if Scipio were captured in Maryland's "back Woods," the legally mandated reward and expenses could have made it more economical for Kuhl to simply let him be auctioned off by the authorities, thereby losing his "investment."[27]

The small, fifteen-shilling reward Kuhl posted in his final advertisement of Scipio might also be explained by the problem of liability, though in a different way. By this time, Kuhl might well have wanted to wash his hands of his troublesome and expensive human property. Were that the case, advertising Scipio could have served primarily to absolve Kuhl of responsibility for him. It might even have been cover for an illegal agreement by which he allowed Scipio to wander at will in exchange for a portion of his earnings. In the event that Scipio were captured, the cost to Kuhl would have been less than the fines imposed on masters who permitted "their Negroes to ramble about, under the pretence of getting Work" or gave "liberty to their Negroes to seek their own Employ, and so go to Work at their own Will."[28] Whether done deliberately or by default, such an arrangement would have given Kuhl time to decide how to dispose of Scipio more profitably.

Colonial runaway ads stood apart from their English counterparts in their emphasis on masters' right to profit by servants' labor. By the mid-eighteenth century, ads for runaway servants in England were usually *more* concerned with absolving masters of liability than with securing runaways' return. In this respect, English ads for runaway servants remained similar to those for eloping wives, and even used overlapping language. In the English press, servants might "elope" as well as run away, whereas in the colonies, "elopement" was used almost exclusively in reference to wives. And while English ads of runaway servants offered rewards, in the eighteenth century these were usually tiny, indicating that the master valued the service so little that he (or occasionally she) did not want the servant returned, but rather wished to make clear that he was no longer responsible for supporting the servant or paying any debts the runaway incurred. The exception lay with British newspaper ads targeting "servants" of color, which offered rewards and sometimes also used the language of "elopement" and "harbouring," often in ways that seemed to dodge questions about the legality of slavery in Britain.[29]

Colonial runaway ads in general, and rewards in particular, deserve the iconic status they have gained as evidence of the brutality and pervasive authoritarianism needed to sustain the system of slavery. Postings of wayward wives could be motivated by the same concerns, but (especially in the colonies) such ads sought literally to discredit wives, rather than to call for capture and return; in only a handful of exceptional cases did husbands offer rewards. However much they might want to, husbands like Peter Henry Dorsius could not legally dispose of their wives, profitably or otherwise. As a free woman of European descent, Jane Dorsius had more access to legal and public recourse than did Scipio. Marriage law assumed husbands' entitlement to the fruits of their wives' labor, but it preserved assumptions about wives' elevated status relative to other dependents. Rhetoric about protecting wives and children contributed to limited access to full divorce, and sustained policies protected communities from the burden of uncared-for dependents. Peter Henry Dorsius resorted to the press and public discrediting, as Scipio's master had, but in matters of marriage, the financial stakes for the community lay in Jane's favor.

Wayward Wives, Colonial Law, and a Shift in Practice

In ads about wayward wives, husbands' financial interests were inseparable from their legal obligations. Such legal dilemmas became a regular plot device for the novelist Daniel Defoe. His notorious heroine Moll Flanders, for instance, found herself advisor to a would-be suitor whose wife had "run away" with another man. He pleaded that she *tell me what must a poor abus'd Fellow do with* a Whore? *what can I do to do my self Justice upon her?*" Flanders responded that he might "Cry her down, *as they call it*," using a method "the Law" had supplied to clear himself of her debts. To be "cried down" meant most literally to be publicly denounced by the town crier, although it might also have encompassed other early modern forms of "publishing" official information. Notices like Peter Henry Dorsius's gave such practices new life in the eighteenth century. Flanders's description of them as a remedy "furnish'd" by "Law" gets things backwards. With such denunciations, the press, rather than established legal authorities, took the lead in defining, disseminating, and enforcing relevant "law."[30]

AN AMBIGUOUS CONTRACT

To understand why Dorsius turned to the press, we must first understand why he didn't turn to the law. Colonial marriage statutes tended to emphasize the contractual aspects of marriage, in contrast with the colonial innovations in labor law that reinforced the coercive powers of masters. The explicit links between runaway wives and servants found in Pennsylvania's early codes had disappeared by the early eighteenth century. (The manuscript containing Pennsylvania's earliest laws moldered in private English libraries until the twentieth century.) Marriage statutes that remained on the books stressed government interest in the "orderly" formation of households and in regulating the effects of their dissolution in the wake of death, or (before 1705) desertion or divorce. By carefully specifying the procedures necessary to contract a legitimate marriage, colonial legislatures sought to invalidate other customary practices and place all marriages under formal legal authority. This trend occurred not only in Puritan New England, but also in Virginia and South Carolina, where the Anglican Church was backed by the state. Anglican and dissenting colonies alike put in place provisions requiring marriage licenses or the publication of banns, along with some form of ministerial or judicial sanction for the match. In contrast, such "Puritan" measures were overturned by the Restoration in England and not reenacted there until the mid-eighteenth century.[31]

While colonial statutes framed marriage as a contract seemingly at odds with the violence and coercion evident in the law of slavery and servitude, they also made marriage central to maintaining the social hierarchy to which those other institutions belonged. Limiting what qualified as legal marriage reinforced legislative efforts to control household laborers—whether they were children, servants, or slaves. Laws requiring that household heads consent to their dependents' marriages helped cement its significance as a marker of independence. And measures denying legal marriage to slaves and interracial couples made marriage a privilege of freedom and whiteness.[32]

The few measures concerned with women's contractual rights *within* marriage also responded to the common disabilities of dependent status in ways that set wives apart from unfree laborers. Pennsylvania's "Act Concerning Feme-Sole Traders," for instance, bestowed economic powers on all wives left "at shopkeeping or to Work for their livelihood" by husbands who went to sea. The measure plugged a hole created by the absence of courts with explicit equitable jurisdiction, to which wives in England and other colonies sometimes turned when circumstances required that they be able to sue and be sued in pursuit of an occupation.[33]

The legal compromises made for wives contrasted sharply with the stark language and harsh punishments found in statutes concerning trade with servants and slaves. Acts "Against Trading with Servants" assumed that servants' efforts to "buy, sell, or receive . . . any coin or commodity whatsoever" were almost always illicit, and that those who traded with them did so at their own risk. Laws across the colonies promised to punish all who "imbezzell[ed] their masters goods," as well as the "divers lewd and evil minded persons" who, "for the sake of filthy lucre," encouraged them to steal. Massachusetts law on the subject proscribed trade with "Indians, mulattoes, negroes, and other suspected persons" in general. The extension of restrictions on trade to free blacks and Indians was simultaneously a reflection of the increasingly racial nature of American servitude and a means to ensure it. It placed yet another hurdle in the path of nonwhites who wished to establish independent households.[34]

All the laws regulating trade with dependents recognized the inability to make binding financial agreements as a defining "disability" of dependent status; yet such laws simultaneously acknowledged that married women, servants, and slaves were indispensable participants in the day-to-day transactions of the colonial economy. Where acts concerning servants and slaves aimed to protect masters, provisions for wives aimed to prevent female-headed households from becoming public responsibilities when "Husbands . . . lost sight of their Duty."[35]

PUBLIC NOTICE

Neither statute law nor case law, however, resolved the question of how an aggrieved husband might absolve himself of liability for a wife who had lost sight of *her* duty. In the face of this ambiguity, public notices became a self-perpetuating solution. Defoe's Moll Flanders accurately represented English practice of the 1720s when she described "crying down" as an intermediate step between desertion—a method she herself had effectively employed—and a "tedious and expensive" divorce through England's ecclesiastical courts.[36] Ads about wives became relatively common in the English papers in the 1710s and 1720s, appearing in numbers comparable to those of ads of other runaways. "Elopement" became a topic for less specialized legal handbooks (and Defoe's fiction) in reaction to this phenomenon. Defoe's characters recognized, but were not particularly scrupulous about, the uncertain legality of their remedies. Moll Flanders knew that ecclesiastical divorce did not guarantee the legitimacy of a subsequent marriage, but she did not much care. Legal treatise writers aimed to be more authoritative, but they were often less clear.

A husband "Abus'd" by his wife's adultery, most legal handbooks concurred, might indeed denounce and discredit his wife. Adultery was implied by the mere use of the term *elope*. Giles Jacob's *New Law-Dictionary* and his popular *Every Man his Own Lawyer* defined elopement as "where a woman that is married, of her own accord goes away and departs from her husband, and lives with an adulterer." The 1732 *Treatise of Feme Coverts: or, The Lady's Law* reproduced an oblique pronouncement from the 1632 *Lawes Resolutions of Womens Rights*: "Elopement, says a Writer of Antiquity, by the Sound of the Word and Nature of the Offence seems to be derived *a Lopex* a Fox; for it is when a Woman goes away from her Husband, and seeks her Prey far from Home, which is the Fox's Quality."[37] The legal presumption was that the chastity of a woman who left her husband was necessarily suspect.

The handbooks remained vague and internally contradictory about what a man could do if his wife left him but did not commit adultery. *Baron and Feme, The Lady's Law*, Giles Jacob's textbooks, and many other "modern" reference works invoked *Manby v. Scott*'s authority in ways that gave the force of law not only to the prevailing verdict, but also to the many caveats of Catherine Scott's defenders. The prevailing Royalist authorities in *Manby* had been prepared to let a wife starve if she would not submit, declaring a husband's ability to discredit his wife essential to his ability to compel her obedience, fidelity, and service. The compilers of handbooks (and also colonial authorities) tended to share the dissenting view that "women will be more tempted by want of maintenance than by abundance." This sentiment was echoed by Defoe's "abus'd husband," who complained to Moll Flanders that his wife was "a Whore not by Necessity, which is the common Bait of your Sex, but by Inclination, and for the sake of Vice."[38]

Like most of the "abus'd Fellows" who resorted to the press, Peter Henry Dorsius was more concerned with what he believed to be his prerogatives as a husband than with legal technicalities. Had he wanted to, Dorsius could have found many of these contradictory legal opinions on the shelves in David Hall's and Benjamin Franklin's printing office when he went to place his advertisement. An edited set of case reports that interpreted *Manby v. Scott* and a subsequent case as establishing the rule that a "wife's contracts bind the husband from his presumed assent only; not where he expressly dissents beforehand" was listed for sale on the same page of the *Pennsylvania Gazette* as the ads for Jane and Scipio.[39] But so were Jacob's *Law-Dictionary* and

Pufendorf's *Nature and Nations*, a seventeenth-century republican tract that a recent English case had used to uphold a husband's obligation to support a wife who had left him simply because he denied "her the respect due to her sex."[40] Moreover, Franklin and Hall had advertised *Every Man His Own Lawyer*, the legal reference most accessible in the colonies, some seventeen times in the decade prior to Dorsius's ad. In the two paragraphs it devoted to elopement, *Every Man* asserted that "the putting of the wife in the *Gazette*, or other news-papers, is no legal notice to persons in general not to trust her."[41] That did not stop Henry Dorsius or others from trying, however.

Newspapers, not statutes or legal handbooks, supply our only record of the formula employed to denounce one's wife. Henry Dorsius's advertisement illustrates the conventions of the genre. The full text of his notice reads:

> Philadelphia, June 9. 1748.
>
> Whereas Jane, the wife of Peter Henry Dorsius, of Philadelphia county, the daughter of Derrick Hogeland of Bucks county, hath eloped from her said husband; this is to desire all persons not to trust her on his account, for he will pay no debts of her contracting, from the date hereof.[42]

Almost without exception, elopement notices adopted formal legal language, marked first by the opening "Whereas," a term generally reserved for legal petitions and pronouncements. They proceeded to identify the people involved, the husband's place of residence, and frequently the husband's occupation as well. A description of the wife's transgressions generally followed the identifying information; elopement was the standard charge. In seventeenth- and early eighteenth-century usage, the term referred more frequently to wives who ran away from their marriages than to children who ran away to get married. Advertisements concluded with a literal discrediting: that is, "this is to desire all persons not to trust her on his account." The denial of credit—both in the economic and the social senses of the term—was always the expressed purpose.

The formulaic language in husbands' postings masked considerable variety in actual circumstances underlying them. Notices were prompted not only by "eloping" wives or household economic instability, but also by deserting husbands, domestic violence, mental illness, quarrels over property or household authority, or sometimes simply spite. (Or, as we saw in the cases in the first two chapters, all of the above.) The advertisements could also have very different and even contradictory objectives. Some husbands sought to force a "runaway" wife to return home, occasionally citing the damage to their estates caused by loss of their property in their wives' labor—the same grievance that motivated most ads for runaway servants and slaves. Others, in direct contrast, sought to be rid of their wives. Their ads aimed at community recognition of marital separation in an era when full divorce was not an option for most warring couples, even in Puritan New England.

Manby v. Scott's declaration that denouncing a wife in a "News-Book" was *not* good legal notice provides the earliest evidence of the practice. Printed newspapers first appeared in England during the seventeenth-century Civil Wars, and Edward Scott had presumably used them to discredit Catherine sometime prior to 1663. However, his notice does not survive, nor do any similar newspaper postings of wives before the late 1690s. Ads of runaway slaves and servants, in contrast, first surfaced in the late 1660s, as families who had obtained wealth in the "plantations" began to bring colonial customs and colonized people home to old England. People of African descent made up only a tiny part of the population in the metropole, but they were the targets for roughly one-fifth of seventeenth-century English runaway ads. For English servants, moreover, simply absconding was not usually sufficient crime to warrant publication. Especially early on, ads targeting white runaways also included accusations of theft or other crimes that would have warranted a general "hue and cry" under established criminal law.[43]

Royalist distrust of the press made innovations like runaway advertisements especially remarkable. Restoration authorities conveniently blamed the "miserable confusions and Calamities" of the Civil Wars on the "monstrous and exorbitant disorder" of unregulated printers. William Berkeley, who served as governor of Virginia for much of England's Civil War period and for nearly two decades into the Restoration, expressed a common Royalist sentiment when he attributed sectarian chaos in England to the twin evils of print and education. He hoped Virginia would have neither "free schools nor printing" for a hundred years, "for learning has brought disobedience, and heresy, and sects into the world, and printing has divulged them, and libels against the best government. God keep us from both!" Whether God had a hand in it or not, it would take nearly a century for Virginia to acquire a newspaper. The Restoration sharply curtailed England's press. *Manby*'s 1663 judgment against "News-Book[s]" came as the Crown prosecuted printers and established a monopoly that left only the staid *London Gazette* in publication from 1665 to 1679.[44] The attenuated state of the papers, rather than *Manby*'s specific authority, likely explains the absence of wife ads.

The press was not to blame for marital conflicts, but its ability to "divulge" them became a crucial element of debates about marriage law from the 1680s forward. English state interest in controlling the press waned with the collapse of the Stuart monarchy in the "Glorious Revolution" of 1688, and newspapers began to proliferate in number and form. In 1692, John Dunton, an ambitious and idiosyncratic dissenting printer with ties to New England, began dishing out marital advice of all sorts in his weekly *Athenian Mercury*. Correspondents wrote to the paper with queries about everything from cosmology to public health; courtship, sex, and marriage were of consistent interest to male and female readers from a range of backgrounds. Those whose poverty kept them from seeking "Council for Advice" on marriage law, as well as those who did not like what their lawyers had to say, found the paper useful. Dunton supplied detailed instructions on how an aggrieved husband should handle "an Elopement," mixing dubious legal advice with the assurance that "to print the Case, describe the Persons, and disperse the Papers" was "the best way" to discover an absconding wife. Dunton did not print such notices himself, but by 1698 they had begun to appear in several other London papers.[45]

Printers like Dunton also kept the public informed about the "Many Divorces Lately Granted by Parliament." During the 1680s, John Locke and other republican theorists revived John Milton's analogies between the marital and social contracts, divorce and revolution. Their writings provided the Whig-dominated Parliament of the 1690s with a rationale for revisiting the issue, and politically well-connected candidates for divorce were waiting in the wings. Although only a handful of cases gained a hearing, published accounts of these trials fed public appetite for stories of sex, violence, and aristocratic extravagance. The press thus kept full legal divorce alive as an imaginative possibility for the growing metropolitan reading public through the eighteenth century. The imaginative element played a crucial role, because even as publicity fueled demand, it also generated a legal backlash.[46]

Husbands' newspaper notices inspired immediate and conflicting responses from the judiciary. In the first case for which a printed advertisement survives, the Court of Common Pleas, like the judges in *Manby*, rejected the form of the newspaper notice and deemed the husband liable for his wife's debts. William Holt, chief justice of King's Bench, on the other hand, reached the opposite conclusion in a different trial related to the same marital dispute. In a second case in 1698, Holt went out of his way to extend and correct *Manby*, specifying circumstances under which a notorious separation freed a husband from his obligations, and in which newspaper desertion notices might be legally valid.[47]

In 1700, the anonymous compiler of *Baron and Feme: A Treatise of the Common Law concerning Husbands and Wives* undermined Holt's conclusion. In his prefatory note "to the reader," the editor boasted that he had "abridged and reduced" *Manby*'s "long Arguments" in an effort to quell legal inconsistency "as to what Acts or Contracts made by the Wife shall bind the Husband." Yet his contribution only further confused *Manby*'s legacy. His six relatively concise propositions highlighted the caveat regarding husbands' newspaper notices. A husband's general prohibition against extending credit to his wife, he explained, was "void in itself . . . because if such a prohibition should be good, the law gives her a fruitless power in enabling her" to contract for necessaries "when there is no person may contract with her."[48] This particular limitation on husbands' powers was a *dissenting* argument in the original case. This anonymous version of *Manby* had much longer legs as a precedent than did Holt's competing "clarification," because *Baron and Feme* became the main reference work on marriage law for the duration of the eighteenth century.

Baron and Feme remained noncommittal on the question of divorce. Like its seventeenth-century predecessor, *The Lawes Resolution of Women's Rights*, it gave conflicting advice that could be read multiple ways. Paradoxically, Parliament's momentary willingness to grant full divorces made it more difficult for those in the colonies to cross this legal line. Around 1702, the House of Lords sharply restricted the cases in which it would consider acting, reserving divorce for men of extraordinary wealth and rank whose notoriously adulterous wives left them in danger of dying without heirs. Simultaneously, the Privy Council (acting for the queen and Parliament) disallowed dissenting Pennsylvania's late seventeenth-century statutes granting full divorce in cases of adultery.[49]

Rather than opening the "road to divorce," Parliament's interventions narrowed it. For the next fifty years, legislative interventions in marriage law became more muted on both sides of the Atlantic. Parliament passed a few private bills of divorce each decade, but general measures condemning adultery and attempting to regulate marriage formation went down to defeat.[50] Colonial legislatures continued to innovate in other areas of marriage law, however, because they faced a common set of jurisdictional problems. None of the colonies fully replicated the complex set of interconnected legal and religious institutions that regulated marriage in England. Colonies founded by religious dissenters, as we have seen, deliberately chose to eliminate separate systems of ecclesiastical and equitable courts. During the seventeenth century, even colonies that wanted to emulate the Anglican-English model lacked the resources or population needed to sustain its multiple layers. All folded the separate bodies of precedent established in canon law and in equity—both of which tended to give dependents more power than did the common law—into their developing legal practice in a piecemeal manner.

Whether by design or by default, colonial marriage became the concern of secular civil authorities. Everywhere in the colonies, therefore, *Manby*'s attempt to place marriage outside the common law and reserve jurisdiction to the ecclesiastical courts was indeed—as Catherine Scott's supporters had claimed—"more specious then satisfactory."[51]

ABUSE OF AUTHORITY

Dorsius's disregard for legal technicalities became a problem for him—and in turn for the printers of the *Gazette*—because Jane was not a "Whore." His notice provoked the reply shown in figure 3.2.

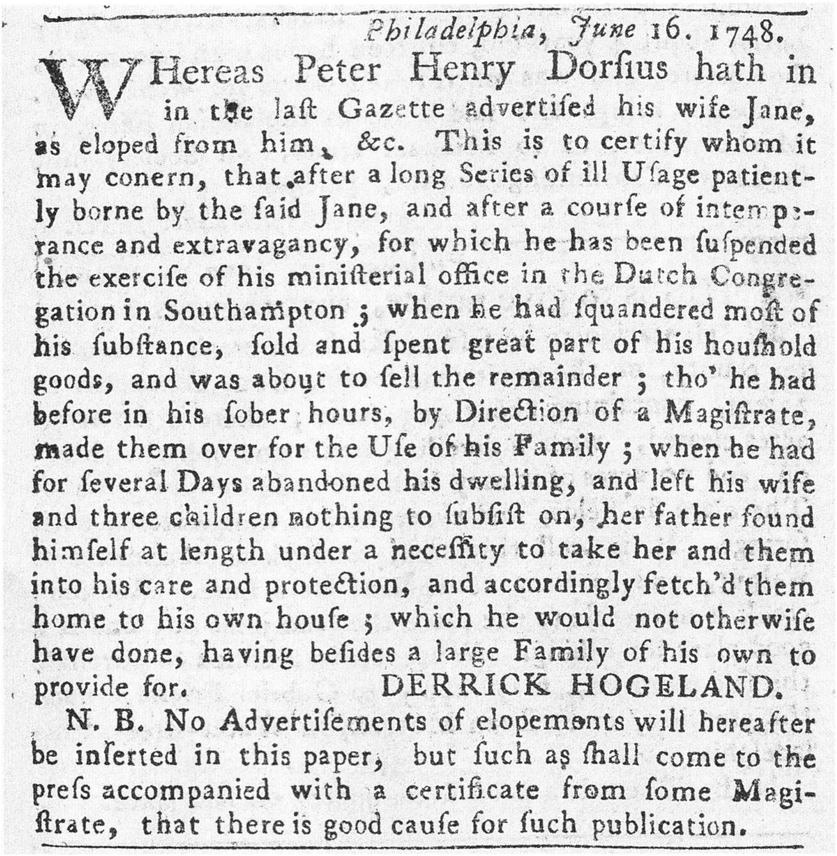

Philadelphia, June 16. 1748.

WHereas Peter Henry Dorſius hath in in the laſt Gazette advertiſed his wife Jane, as eloped from him, &c. This is to certify whom it may conern, that after a long Series of ill Uſage patiently borne by the ſaid Jane, and after a courſe of intemperance and extravagancy, for which he has been ſuſpended the exerciſe of his miniſterial office in the Dutch Congregation in Southampton ; when he had ſquandered moſt of his ſubſtance, ſold and ſpent great part of his houſhold goods, and was about to ſell the remainder ; tho' he had before in his ſober hours, by Direction of a Magiſtrate, made them over for the Uſe of his Family ; when he had for ſeveral Days abandoned his dwelling, and left his wife and three children nothing to ſubſiſt on, her father found himſelf at length under a neceſſity to take her and them into his care and protection, and accordingly fetch'd them home to his own houſe ; which he would not otherwiſe have done, having beſides a large Family of his own to provide for.   DERRICK HOGELAND.

N. B. No Advertiſements of elopements will hereafter be inſerted in this paper, but ſuch as ſhall come to the preſs accompanied with a certificate from ſome Magiſtrate, that there is good cauſe for ſuch publication.

FIGURE 3.2 Derrick Hogeland and Jane Dorsius advertisement, *Pennsylvania Gazette*, June 16, 1748
Courtesy of the American Antiquarian Society

In this rebuttal, Jane Dorsius's father, Derrick Hogeland, cast Henry Dorsius as an abusive drunk who had failed to manage his professional or household affairs, and whose negligence demanded the intervention of legal authorities and of her family. Hogeland's notice is most remarkable, however, for the note appended to his advertisement, in which the printer announced that in the future ads like Henry Dorsius's would require certification from a magistrate before they could be published. This expression of uncertainty about the printer's right to publish "Advertisements of elopements" without approval from legal authorities was at once a response to the particular, local circumstances of this controversy, a product of legal ambiguity surrounding ads for wives, and an attempt to address long-standing concerns about the appropriate relationship between the press and the law.

The Dorsius case offers a superb example of the gradual and repetitive process by which the press reshaped local practices of communal regulation. The significance of the periodical press as "new media" in the eighteenth century is especially striking in the colonies. The colonial press lagged behind that in England, and its small scale and uneven development make it comparatively easy to track the new media's impact on ordinary people and its power as an agent of change. In the colonies, advertising was an innovation, and when printers took up the business of publishing legal notices, it had unforeseen consequences for legal practice.

Outraged community reactions to ads for wives were particularly common whenever the practice was first introduced. In a pattern that recurred as new newspapers established themselves in new communities over the course of the eighteenth century, when wife ads threatened to become an established practice, they elicited challenges on multiple fronts. In Boston in 1725, a husband's repeated attempts to discredit his wife in the papers, and the appearance of a copycat ad, seem to have prompted legal authorities to give the wife a sympathetic hearing in court. While the record of the relationship between the court case and the ads is not explicit, it was several years before another husband discredited his wife in the Massachusetts press. In 1731 in Philadelphia, a string of three desertion notices was broken by an angry published challenge by an aggrieved wife. And similarly, the advent of husbands' advertisements in the young *New-Hampshire Gazette* provoked a flurry of vehement objections from advertised wives and their supporters between 1759 and 1762.[52]

Local politics were always a factor in such disputes. The fact that Hogeland was a powerful man provides a concrete explanation for why the *Pennsylvania Gazette's* printers expressed insecurity about their role. Direct

rebuttals by wives were far more common than defenses through an intermediary, but none prompted printer commentary. Hogeland was one of the
largest landholders in Southampton Township and a prominent member of
the community's Dutch Reformed Church. He represented Bucks County's
Dutch population in the legislature eight times between 1746 and 1758. When
Henry Dorsius named Hogeland as Jane's father in his initial advertisement,
he escalated the dispute, which appears to have been as much a quarrel with
the community that Derrick Hogeland represented as it was a falling out with
Jane. Derrick Hogeland's personal authority allowed Jane to mount a more effective defense than could the women who took out ads on their own behalf. [53]

The printers might also have faced official pressure prompted by the open
question of who would support Jane. Despite Derrick Hogeland's wealth,
this seems to have been as much a real concern as a rhetorical strategy. At
twenty-seven, Jane was the eldest of his and Marytje Slodt's eleven children.
The other ten were still at home, and the youngest was actually born during
the newspaper controversy. Jane's own children were all under six years old,
and might well have been a burden on even such a prosperous household.[54]
Derrick Hogeland stressed this difficulty in his advertisement, carefully noting that although he had taken Jane and his grandchildren "into his care and
protection," Peter Henry Dorsius was still obligated to provide for them. The
implication was that Henry, rather than Jane, was the runaway.

Runaway husbands were a matter of public consequence because, as we
saw in the previous chapters, unsupported wives had economic and moral
claims on their communities that were not easily dismissed. Wives could appeal to court officials to force their husbands to support them and their young
children; Jane had probably used such a petition to order Henry "by Direction of a Magistrate" to make over his household goods "for the Use of his
Family." Independent record of her suit does not survive, but in 60 percent
of the cases leaving records of similar legal judgments, husbands used their
newspaper notices to openly defy local authorities.[55]

Husbands' notices called attention to the power that the press gave individual husbands to circumvent local efforts to mediate marital conflict. Although comparatively few elopement ads were as clearly illegal as Henry's,
the vast majority of them were extralegal. Most advertisements left no direct
paper trail because husbands used them to avoid the formal legal system altogether, in some instances motivated by ignorance and distrust of the courts,
and in others by a canny sense that the legal ambiguity tolerated by the press
was to their advantage. Henry's newspaper notice must have been especially
galling to the leaders of his residential community because there could be
little doubt that he knew what he was doing.

Had his tenure in Pennsylvania ended differently, Henry might have claimed a different place for himself in history as the founder of the German Reformed Church in America. He had arrived in Pennsylvania in 1737, the first minister sent with the official sanction of the church. Hogeland was an elder in the congregation Henry was to serve. Henry's newspaper spat with the Hogeland family was probably rooted in tensions over the congregation's obligation to support him—a conflict that began even before his marriage to Jane. Henry had taken his post expecting a church, a rectory, and a respectable salary. None of these were ready for him on arrival, and even after the church and homestead were provided, the salary remained inadequate. In his defense, his "extravagency" might simply have been his refusal to support himself by farming. The itinerant preaching required by the shortage of Dutch and German Reformed ministers could conceivably have been the reason that "he had for several Days abandoned his dwelling." These excuses aside, by 1748 Henry had managed to alienate not only his congregation, but also his fellow ministers. He wanted to return to Europe, and his attempt to "sell the remainder" of his worldly belongings was likely meant to fund this move. He left Pennsylvania for good two months after he discredited Jane.[56]

Henry's intransigence threw responsibility for supporting Jane back to her father and her community, who did not want it. The ensuing debate over responsibility for Jane played itself out in local policy in two ways. First, it affirmed the community's right to enforce husbands' obligations. The actions of local officials stood against the strand of legal argument that most strongly asserted husbands' abstract patriarchal rights. High courts might argue that wayward wives should "submit or starve," but this principle made for awkward local policy. In cases of "Ill Usage patiently borne" and abandonment, it was a burden to communities as well as to wives.

Second, although Jane's neighborhood sought to preserve its power to mediate the affairs of its constituent households, local inability to control Henry spurred a far more expansive understanding of community when it came time to settle the matter of support. Jane ultimately obtained relief from across the Atlantic, through a petition to the Dutch Reformed authorities who had sent Henry to Pennsylvania. They paid her an annuity for thirty years, ceasing when Hogeland died and left her a substantial bequest. Jane's case prompted the Reformed Church on both sides of the Atlantic to set up a fund to provide for the widows and impoverished families of ministers in the colonies.[57] This seemingly modest change in institutional policy reflected significant problems of jurisdiction, to which the next chapter will return at greater length. European and English legal systems theoretically placed both the clergy and marriage under the jurisdiction of ecclesiastical authorities.

In this case, the Reformed Church claimed the responsibilities expected under that system. Imperial authorities were happy to hold dissenting religious groups liable, but—as with husbands—they were less sanguine about granting them autonomous legal power.

The Rise of the Press

The disintegration of Jane and Henry Dorsius's marriage would have made a splash in their local community and religious network even had it not appeared in the press. The newspapers, however, allowed it to ripple outward along entirely new channels, reaching people with whom Jane and Henry had no connection of kinship, proximity, or faith. In appending the note to Derrick Hogeland's ad that required future postings to come to them "with a certificate from some Magistrate, that there is good cause for such publication," the *Gazette*'s printers marked momentary uncertainty about the power of the press to disrupt established patterns of authority.

The printers' nota bene highlights the difference between newspaper advertisements and more traditional forms of "publishing," all of which were mediated by local authorities. The original senses of the term *publish* was "to make publicly known" and "to announce in an official or formal manner." To literally have had Jane "cried down," Henry would have needed to take his complaint to the town crier, who was often a constable and who was inescapably party to local legal proceedings. Alternatively, he might have used one of several other procedures suggested in colonial statutes. Couples wishing to marry, for example, were expected to obtain a certificate of their eligibility signed by "a credible person where they have lived" and by a justice of the peace. They then published this formal notice by "affixing [it] on the Court-house or Meeting-house Door in each respective County where the parties" resided, for a month in advance of the ceremony. Notices concerning strays and runaways who had been "taken up" were also to be posted on church and courthouse doors. The statutory mandate for public readings of Virginia's and Maryland's acts "Concerning Slaves and Servants," as well as of other law, also evidenced the connections between oral and written forms of publishing. As late as the 1770s, newspaper desertion notices occasionally refer to publication by these more traditional means. Thomas Baker of Boston, for instance, thought better of his decision to "publish" his wife "in the public prints and by the Cryer of this town." He then took out a second newspaper advertisement revoking "all and every Sentence that has been printed or said by the Cryer . . . in my Behalf."[58]

A newspaper ad might use the same words "said by the Cryer," but it did not reach the same audience, nor did it have the same relationship to local authorities. The community the papers served was simultaneously wider *and* narrower than that reached by local forms of publication and established oral networks. Printed papers first appeared in colonial port cities—Boston, Philadelphia, and New York—between 1705 and 1730. Their initial purpose, as the historian Charles E. Clark aptly puts it, was to link "provincial Americans with the metropolitan center of their pan-Atlantic English world" by printing correspondence and items from the English press for American consumption. They catered to literate and prosperous paid subscribers throughout their respective regions; the *Pennsylvania Gazette*, for example, was based in Philadelphia, but it served readers in New Jersey, the Pennsylvania backcountry, Delaware, Maryland, and Virginia. Although print runs were small, the early papers reached many more elite readers, over a wider geographic area, than the manuscript newsletters they replaced.[59]

However, until the last part of the eighteenth century, newspapers did not reach as broad a swath of the local community as did more traditional forms of publishing. Even in New England, where literacy among ordinary people was more common than elsewhere in the colonies, local news was still transmitted primarily through word of mouth. Reading the papers, one could find that the news from Paris in 1723 was that an ass had died in the street after drinking from a pan an apothecary had left to cool in the window; if something of that sort happened locally, however, one would hear about it from a neighbor, not the press.[60]

The earliest colonial printers expected that subscriptions and state support would make their papers sustainable ventures. They competed for state sanction and the right to claim that they were "printed by authority"; status as the government's official press brought lucrative contracts, and seemed the obvious route to financial success. Printers introduced ads in a bid to demonstrate the papers' local and regional usefulness, not because they expected them to bring in much revenue or take up much space. The first printers took pains to educate their readers in the potential of the press by actively soliciting ads for "Houses, Lands, Tenements, Farmes, Ships, Vessels, Goods, Wares or Merchandizes, & c. to be Sold, or Lett" and of "Servants Run-away, or Goods Stoll or Lost."[61]

Such functions for newspaper advertising might seem obvious in retrospect, but it took decades for the papers to become a widely used and accepted means of broadcasting most types of local official information. A few advertisers appear to have readily adopted the medium as a prompt way to find missing people or goods, immediately submitting notice of a servant "this day runaway" or a cow "stray'd on Monday last."[62] In the first years of a paper's existence, however, many notices were clearly experiments, attempted only after other methods had failed. The earliest ads for runaway slaves and servants were typically for those who had been missing for months or years. A reader of Franklin's infant *Pennsylvania Gazette* in 1730 sought to recover a mare that had "stray'd away about 3 years since."[63] Only a handful of stray wives appeared in the papers prior to 1730, when the practice began to gather momentum. In this instance too, newspaper notices supplemented but did not supplant other forms of publication. John Taylor's 1732 denunciation of his wife Rachel, for example, simply reprinted the two-year-old notice he had "posted . . . already" in his home county, presumably on the courthouse door.[64]

Notices for runaway slaves and servants were among the first ads of any sort to appear in the colonial newspapers, where they became part of a calculated effort to show that the press could act on behalf of public authority. The printer of the *Boston News-Letter*, the first (and until 1719 the only) colonial paper, was an active intermediary in the recovery of runaways and strays during the paper's early years. On several occasions, he invited readers to return missing servants and livestock directly to him, thereby putting himself in the business of paying rewards and of confining and returning captives. After a few years of this, his delight was evident when he had opportunity to demonstrate the value of the paper's communicative power alone. In April 1706, he proudly informed his readers that "a Negro man Slave, and an Indian" servant advertised the previous December had been "apprehended . . . by vertue of said Advertisements coming (in the News Letter) to South-Carolina, whither [they] had travelled." Perhaps because of this demonstration of the efficacy of newspaper advertising, after this date he offered himself as a conduit for "Intelligence" regarding runaways, but rarely as a direct agent in their capture and return. Such indirect engagement with the traffic in runaways (and in the sale of slaves and servants) was the typical pattern observed by printers throughout the century.[65]

The *News-Letter*'s success in recovering men who had run from New England to South Carolina demonstrates the power of ads to extend the reach of the authoritarian infrastructure created by colonial laws governing slaves and servants. Such notices quickly became a staple of colonial advertising, and, in 1720s Jamaica, they appear to have been a primary reason for the newspapers' existence.[66] The ready acceptance of runaway ads did not mean, however, that authorities readily trusted the press in general. Paradoxically, one of the only statutes to explicitly sanction advertisements as legal notice also expressed reservations about the potential of the newspapers to encroach on traditional channels of communication and authority. In 1750, the Virginia legislature mandated advertisements in the *Virginia Gazette* as the last resort for locating owners of valuable found goods and of unidentified slaves imprisoned in the Williamsburg jail. The state here assigned the *Gazette* the same official function that the printer of the *Boston News-Letter* had attempted to claim, without success, in 1704. Even as it turned the press into an arm of the law, the Virginia legislature noted concern about its reach and anonymity. Newspaper advertisements were to be used only after notice had been given for several months at the courthouse and in the churches of the county where the runaway had been taken up. Moreover, because the press might allow "dishonest persons to pretend themselves as owners," the statute made special provisions to prevent fraud. A master wishing to reclaim a runaway "published . . . in the *Gazette*" first had to prove before his local court that he had "lost a slave, answering the description" found in the papers. Certification from a local magistrate, and the face-to-face communication and verification of credibility the process required, were still deemed necessary to the integrity of the legal process.[67]

As a genre, ads about wives were slower to appear in the colonial press than ads for other runaways, and colonial papers and authorities remained ambivalent about the practice of advertising wives long after it became common in Britain. Ads of eloping wives first appeared in colonial papers because individual husbands saw them as a potential remedy, not because printers solicited them, and not because local authorities found them useful. The practice developed in response to advertisers' demands and through imitation. In the colonies, published ads of wives obtained legitimacy in part through their similarity to other runaway ads. If ads of runaway servants and slaves or notices calling in debts were acceptable, advertisers and printers appear to have reasoned, why should desertion notices be any different?

Yet desertion notices provoked controversy in a way that other ads did not, and they did so repeatedly. Legal hazards kept Scipio out of the printing office, but Jane Dorsius was not so constrained. The Dorsius conflict is particularly remarkable because the newspapers turned the local conflict into a border-crossing debate.

For a dozen years after the initial 1731 furor over the desertion notices in Benjamin Franklin's *Gazette*, ads of wives had appeared only sporadically in Pennsylvania's two weekly papers. Since the ads appeared once or twice a year, the form was not unknown, but neither was it routine. During the 1740s, Franklin dramatically expanded the *Gazette*'s circulation and its physical size, making it the largest colonial paper in both respects. Increase in the number and variety of ads the paper contained accounted for a significant part of its physical and financial transformation—the number of ads in each weekly issue doubled from thirty to sixty in the three years prior to Henry Dorsius's notice, and they now took up half of the paper's column space. Ads concerning laborers made up the single largest category of notices before and after this transformation, and runaway notices and ads offering slaves and servants for sale accounted for roughly a quarter of all advertisements.[68] In contrast, before 1745 wife ads had been rare, but by 1748 they too appeared regularly, with one or two in any given issue of the *Gazette*. In the June 9 paper, Jane Dorsius found herself in company with a New Jersey woman named Deborah Shippey.

In the Dorsius–Hogeland dispute, the *Gazette's* printers found that they had become victims of their own success. When they printed legal notices, they inadvertently assumed the responsibilities of the local magistrates who vetted the notices that appeared on church or courthouse doors. The printers were ill suited to the task of mediation. Their community of readers had never corresponded to any single neighborhood, and during the 1740s it grew into a much larger group of people than could be known by face or reputation. The paper's region-wide readership undermined the ability of advertisers' residential communities to intervene in the process of publication, increasing the power of individual heads of household to assert their authority over runaways of all sorts. The *only* eighteenth-century challenge to a runaway slave ad raised precisely this issue. The objectionable runaway ad mislabeled a servant as a slave, and, its challenger complained, it might therefore have allowed the runaway to be taken up "and sold as a Slave at 100 Miles from any one who knew his Freedom."[69] Henry Dorsius similarly demonstrated the ease with which advertisers could use their anonymity to circumvent local judgment. Had he been as "notorious" in Philadelphia as Derrick Hogeland claimed he was in Southampton, Dorsius would have found it difficult to "publish" Jane.

The printer's self-correction inspired a significant, if temporary, reconsideration of the practice of using the papers to discredit wives. The *Boston Gazette* announced a similar change in editorial policy in the issue that picked up news from the issue of the *Pennsylvania Gazette* containing Derrick Hogeland's ad. Coincidentally, the *Boston Gazette* had itself recently published an especially provocative notice discrediting a wife from a wealthy and politically prominent family who intervened behind the scenes. The printers, having heard "the Matters of Charge ... fairly ... related," took it upon themselves to repudiate the controversial ad. Following the *Pennsylvania Gazette's* example, they declared that they too would publish "no more Advertisements of Elopements . . . without" the signature of a justice of the peace "signifying the expediency thereof."[70]

The printers' admonitions had some impact on the practice of publishing elopement ads in both locations. One Philadelphia husband was motivated to attend to legal niceties he had previously neglected, retracting an ad he had "inadvertently" placed "about a year ago." He explained that he had "made use of the word Eloped, which [he] intended only for Absenting," a subtle distinction that suggests he had encountered legal opinion equating elopement and adultery. His wife, like Jane Dorsius, was not a "whore." It was several months before the *Boston Gazette* printed another elopement ad, and the next one to appear dutifully assured the public that it came to press "properly certify'd by one of his Majesty's Justices of the Peace." The *Pennsylvania Gazette* also observed this formality in the two elopement notices that followed immediately on the heels of Derrick Hogeland's ad.[71]

This shift in editorial policy demonstrated concern about the ways in which the press expanded the authority of individual husbands over and against that of their communities and their wives. But printers' efforts to provide elopement ads with official legal sanction proved short lived and had only a fleeting impact on the growth of the practice. The printers of both *Gazettes* dispensed with noting certification by magistrates after one or two ads, and idiosyncrasies in the immediately subsequent notices suggest that their silence was not simply a matter of editorial convenience. The second ad published by the *Boston Gazette* following the controversy occupied tenuous legal ground. The husband tacitly admitted that he was the one who had left his wife, citing her "misbehavior" as the reason "he cant [*sic*] live with her."[72]

The third elopement ad to appear in the *Pennsylvania Gazette* after Derrick Hogeland's notice—some three months later—showed that readers had been paying attention to the debate, although not in the way the printers intended. The husband's initial ad, like Henry Dorsius's, seemed routine and unremarkable, but it too provoked a challenge from the advertised wife. Lydia Rue took her grievances, and apparently Derrick Hogeland's notice, to the *Gazette*'s rival paper, the *American Weekly Mercury*, and there published a rebuttal that was substantially copied from Hogeland's. She too claimed that "after a long series of Ill-usage" which she had "patiently borne," her husband "had abandoned his Dwelling for several Days and left her nothing to subsist on." Her "Father, finding himself under a Necessity to take" her and her newborn "Child into his care, accordingly fetched [them] home to his own House, which otherwise he would not have done, having a large Family of his own to provide for." Lydia sandwiched her own story in between these borrowed phrases. She had not been "a Month brought to Bed" with a new baby when her husband left her, and he soon made things worse by returning "in a frightful Manner" and locking "her out of Doors, refusing to let her and his Child have any Maintainance, (for he had little enough to pay his Debts)." She was therefore "obliged to go to some of the Neighbours for that Night, and the next Day she came and broke into the House, and found he had taken away many of the Goods." When her husband found that she had returned, he "told her *If she would not go she might stay there and starve to Death*; he likewise kept a Man in the House to keep her out whilst he went and published an Elopement."[73]

If Lydia is to be believed, her husband went to extraordinary lengths to make it seem that she had eloped, forcing her to stay out of the house so the complaint he brought to the printers would have at least the semblance of truth. Her notice performed its own complicated dance to prove that she was in no way responsible for their separation. The baby her husband would not support, she carefully noted, was "his Child," and by implication she was not an adulteress. She left her husband's dwelling only when he forcibly "obliged" her to seek refuge with a neighbor, and then only for one night. Her husband, moreover, threatened to let his dependents starve. We will never know who technically had legal right in this dispute, and that fact is in itself telling. The Rues' notices were shaped by some knowledge of marriage law, but the couple seems to have been using the press to keep their battle out of the courts.

It is ironic that a notice aimed at reconnecting elopement ads with the formal legal system should inspire such a striking example of the way in which newspaper notices became a self-perpetuating, extralegal phenomenon. Lydia Rue's imitation of Derrick Hogeland's ad was an unusually clear instance of the sort of mimicry that turned such notices into a common, if not fully accepted, practice. The pattern is harder to spot in husbands' notices because they were so brief and formulaic; but it can be found in the repeated use of irregular phrasing and even in printer's typographical errors. One imagines an angry husband, or in Lydia Rue's case, a desperate wife, carrying a past issue of the paper to a printer's office and requesting "an ad like this one." By midcentury, husbands' notices had become common enough that printers could comply without even substantially resetting their type. Such time-saving measures sometimes led to the intermingling of the names of past and current advertisers, when copy setters changed the name of the subscriber to a notice but neglected to alter its text.[74] Readers' imitation of one another added momentum to the forces that were turning advertising into an indispensable part of life in urban communities. At the same time, it reinforced long-standing reasons to be suspicious of the trend. Imitation allowed newspapers to establish a body of quasi-legal precedents virtually independent of the opinions of local legal authorities and of distinctive traditions in colonial marriage law, creating contested uniformity out of the diversity of colonial law.[75]

Jane Hogeland Dorsius and Scipio appeared side by side in the press, but nowhere else. Scipio's story is lost to us after his last advertised escape in 1757. Marcus Kuhl's ads may have been a tool to defraud Scipio of a legitimate claim to freedom, but we will never know because in 1748—and when he ran away again in 1749 and 1757—Scipio did not risk bringing his case to a printer or magistrate. Colonial laws sought at every turn to undermine alternative means by which slaves and servants might renegotiate the terms of their dependence, ignoring and undermining their kin networks, devaluing their religious commitments, and otherwise defining them out of the community served by the law and the press. In contrast, though the trail of records left by Jane's efforts to obtain financial support is fragmentary (and the responses reluctant), it nonetheless documents the multiple channels by which she might do herself justice. Kin, church, law, and the press all enabled Jane, and other women in similar circumstances, to use husbands' obligations to temper husbands' authority. These resources provided wives with the means to defend the privileges of their status, and to remain free people despite (or perhaps because of) their dependence.

The colonies' economic dependence on bound labor and institutionally weak legal systems led to innovations in the regulation of households, ranging from brutal slave codes to the informal regulation made possible by runaway advertisements in the press. Where this chapter has focused on these developments from the "bottom up," the next reorients us to the "top down" perspective of English authorities during the same period from the Restoration of the 1660s to the emerging colonial crisis of the 1760s. The rapidly expanding press and increasingly chaotic Anglo-imperial legal system inspired a new quest for order, in which eighteenth-century legal systematizers revived *Manby* and once again foregrounded the parallels, more than the distinctions, between wives and slaves.

Marriage, Slavery, and Anglo-Imperial Jurisdictional Politics

"So great a favourite is the female sex of the laws of England," William Blackstone infamously noted in his 1765 *Commentaries on the Laws of England*, that "even the disabilities, which the wife lies under, are for the most part intended for her protection and benefit."[1] Blackstone's apology for women's legal disabilities echoed that found a century earlier in *Manby v. Scott*. In both instances, such apologetics accompanied attempts to disguise legal innovation as ancient principle. This chapter examines the context underlying the innovations—and apologies—in Blackstone's enormously influential synopsis of the law of domestic relations. It traces a loosely defined "conversation" among powerful figures in English government, colonial cases that demonstrate the practice of "local law" as well as cognizance of larger debates, and English treatise writers and colonial and Scottish intellectuals who engaged with imperial directives between the 1720s and the 1760s. Attention to this complicated conversation alters a number of historical stories usually told separately: the story of marriage law and the rise of divorce, the emergence of antislavery, and the significance of seemingly technical debates about religious authority and jurisdiction to the imperial conflicts that produced the American Revolution.

Notwithstanding the Restoration-era efforts to buttress household hierarchies and jurisdictional boundaries attempted in *Manby*, the late seventeenth and early eighteenth centuries saw gradually intensifying legal drift and growing moral anxiety on the part of imperial authorities. By the mid-eighteenth century, anxiety had turned into legal and moral panic, intensifying jurisdictional conflict and spurring Enlightenment efforts to impose order. The "conversation" that gave rise to this panic had roots in the 1690s, when Parliament overrode Anglican resistance to full divorce by granting the right to remarry to a few wealthy lords whose adulterous wives had deprived them of heirs. The periodical press, recently freed from tight government control, widely circulated sensational accounts of these parliamentary trials. Such stories of sexual scandal prompted new conversations about marriage and morals. In the same decade, the Anglican Church began new missionary efforts in the colonies, driven by the fear that dissenting groups (especially Quakers) were winning the contest for the evangelization of enslaved Africans and Indians. Denominational competition and the development of intergenerational slavery also renewed a conversation about whether conversion to Christianity should confer freedom upon slaves. Pennsylvania's Quakers and New England Congregationalists were among those most troubled by the emergence of perpetual racial slavery, as it undermined the rationalization that slaves were captives taken in just war. Could Christian converts and their children still be kept as slaves?

Conflict over this question and an unusual curiosity about the behavior of his parishioners contributed to the moral admonitions and political jockeying of Edmund Gibson, a powerful cleric and scholar of canon law who served as bishop of London from 1723 to 1737. Gibson's extensive reform agenda included multipronged efforts to restore the ecclesiastical legal authority that *Manby* had theoretically, but not practically, affirmed in wake of the English Civil Wars.[2] His assertion of ecclesiastical jurisdiction in Britain and the colonies in turn drove further debate over both marriage law and slavery; Gibson's agenda gave rise to both the infamous 1729 Yorke–Talbot opinion declaring that baptism did not free slaves and the 1753 Marriage Act (the Hardwicke Act). These landmarks reinforced legal trends emphasizing the "possessory rights" of husbands. In the English common-law courts, cuckolded husbands sought damages from their wives' lovers in suits charging "criminal conversation" (shortened to *Crim. con.* and meaning adultery) and "alienation of affection." Extralegal practices that made wives appear similar to slaves were also on the rise, including newspaper advertisements for wayward wives and, less commonly, "wife sale" as an informal attempt at divorce. The Hardwicke Act also manifested renewed imperial interest in imposing uniform, Anglican norms of marital practices throughout the empire; it played an underrecognized role in Scottish Enlightenment theorists' interests in domestic law as a measure of civilization, American Quakers' parallel repudiation both of lax marital discipline and of slavery, and shifts in colonial practices with regard to divorce. Newspaper reporting of these phenomena, as well as of parliamentary petitions for full divorce, helped escalate demand for legal and quasi-legal remedies to marital conflict on both sides of the Atlantic.[3] Blackstone's synopsis of domestic law, with its emphasis on the parallel powers of husbands and masters, attempted to impose order on this shifting and contested legal terrain.

Disorder in the Legal System: Common Law, Equity, and Ecclesiastical Jurisdiction

Manby had affirmed the jurisdiction of England's newly reinstated ecclesiastical court system in marital disputes, while simultaneously upholding the superior powers of secular courts of equity and especially of common law over the financial fallout of those disputes. In the century between the 1663 decision in *Manby* and Blackstone's 1765 *Commentaries*, competition between the many parallel branches of England's court system intensified, and colonial expansion increased opportunities for jurisdictional conflict. The growth of the press amplified perceived disorder in the legal system and inspired a generation of politicians and jurists who sought to impose a rational, centralized imperial legal order.

In the eighteenth century as in the seventeenth, this generation invoked patriarchal authority as a stable, timeless foundation for a neatly nested hierarchical legal order as a political argument. Such claims manifested anxiety about pervasive jurisdictional disorder, and flag historical moments of instability and uncertainty. Between the 1670s and the 1730s, Anglo-imperial marriage law and practice were neither settled nor uniform. Variety *was* the norm. Local communities privileged expediency over ideological consistency, drawing as needed from a grab bag of post-Reformation arguments about marriage law. In this regard, marriage law aligned with more general imperial policy. Colonial and imperial legal authorities alike understood a certain amount of legal divergence and ambiguity as inevitable. They handled jurisdictional conflicts largely by avoiding them, and gravitated to legal solutions that, in the historian Mary Bilder's words, privileged "nuance and context" over rigid consistency or insistence on the primacy of metropolitan rules.[4]

The connections between these developments defy orderly schematic descriptions. They emanated from the bottom up *and* from the top down, from the empire's center *and* from its periphery. Conversation is as apt a metaphor as any, though this was no orderly dialogue. It mirrored, on a transatlantic scale, the chaotic and noisy character of court sessions themselves. In Westminster Hall, England's high courts of common law (King's Bench and Common Pleas) met simultaneously with the equitable Courts of the Exchequer and Chancery in an open space, divided from one another only by the stalls of booksellers and other traders that lined the walls. The Old Bailey, London's main criminal court, met partially in the open, and observers paid admission as in the theater. Not far away, at Doctors' Commons, lawyers trained in continental civil law carried out the business of the central ecclesiastical Court of Arches and London Consistory Court before an audience that included printers eager for salacious tales of marital scandal. In these crowded spaces, the elevated seats of the justices could not guarantee that their voices would be heard over the competing arguments of the lawyers, law students, litigants, and sometimes rowdy observers who passed in and out of the scene below the bar.[5]

The mid-eighteenth century saw the erection of wooden screens in Westminster Hall that demarcated a twenty-five-foot-square space for each of its courts. Some sources say that these were ordered by Philip Yorke, Lord Hardwicke, who served as attorney general from 1725 until 1733, as chief justice of King's Bench from 1733 until 1737, and then as one of the most powerful lord chancellors in England's history until 1756. Others date the screens to the 1760s, shortly after Hardwicke's protégé, William Murray, Lord Mansfield, began his nearly three-decade reign over King's Bench. William Blackstone's own efforts to delineate boundaries between the common-law and equitable and ecclesiastical jurisdictions grew out of Hardwicke's and Mansfield's programs for reform. The partitions in Westminster gave physical form to the intellectual barriers these leading figures in the development of eighteenth-century English law sought to reinforce; the screens symbolized the somewhat ironic motives and consequences of their efforts.[6]

The year 1750 marked the nadir in the prestige and use of England's central—and particularly of its common law—courts. "The intricate, delatory, chargeable, oppressive, endless practice of the Law" had been a major complaint in the era of the English Civil War, and it remained a source of grievance across the eighteenth century. Despite persistent demands for reform, court costs rose steeply during the late seventeenth and early eighteenth centuries. Insistence on formal adherence to "intricate" legal procedures expanded outward from the central courts to local courts of record, and the common-law courts' business declined accordingly. Competing jurisdictions—ranging from Parliament to local magistrates, courts of conscience and newspapers— picked up some of the slack.[7]

Such jurisdictional rivalry was not new, but two interrelated developments made it seem newly threatening. The first was the ever-spreading reach of the press. The sheer volume of legal commentary found in Westminster booksellers' stalls and in the newspapers that Lord Mansfield read as he heard cases distinguished this eighteenth-century courtroom scene from those of earlier centuries. The press allowed local events to assume legal significance throughout the empire. In this echo chamber, wayward colonial husbands like Peter Henry Dorsius, the titillating matrimonial trials of Britain's aristocracy, and freedom suits by people of color generated a new kind of noise. Second, a new, multinational wave of Protestant religious reform amplified the effect. Reformers attacked vice, injustice, and one another, and in the process reinvigorated debate about the relationship between church and state. Competition for jurisdiction and the perception of pervasive disregard for the law helped turn inevitable legal variety into intolerable inconsistency in the law of domestic relations.

TRANSATLANTIC LEGAL LOCALISM

In England and her colonies, the legal treatment of marital discord was marked by continuity in variety. There was variety in the types of low-level officials who handled such complaints: they might be local constables or justices of the peace, parish officers, town selectmen or—in England—commissioners in a local court of conscience. They were usually legally literate, but for the most part they were not trained lawyers. There was also variety in the arguments that aggrieved spouses used to claim redress, although these typically drew on the reasoning and scripts outlined in chapters 1 and 2.

Continuity stemmed from the fact that marital disputes—like most labor disputes—remained in the hands of local officials and were seldom pursued to the limits of the law. Jurisdictional differences in prescribed formal legal remedies (and in particular access to full, as opposed to bed and board, divorce) defined exceptions, not norms. Legal action was more often threatened than pursued, and ambiguous outcomes were the norm. Local authorities gravitated to solutions that secured local stability, even if those solutions loosely interpreted formal legal rules and blurred the jurisdictional boundaries that the English legal system erected between common law, canon law, and equity. Legal principles that affirmed wifely submission were all well and good, so long as they did not make local taxpayers responsible for the support of starving dependents.[8]

This localized approach to justice was essentially equitable even when the jurisdiction in which it took place was not specifically labeled as a court of equity. As a branch of law, equity offered flexible and specific remedies in cases where common-law rules denied them. Equity was particularly important in conflicts over unpaid debts, and to wives, servants, and children, all of whom were technically "disabled" at law. Equitable jurisprudence did not fundamentally challenge social hierarchy, but rather sustained it by making it bearable. Its forms and arguments consequently held considerable appeal for the local officials who mediated most marital disputes. For wives, equity offered remedies that were seldom equal; the goal of equity was not to give women the same economic resources and redress available to men. Yet, as the seventeenth-century treatise *The Lawes Resolutions of Women's Rights* had put it, equity nonetheless allowed some women to "shift" their common legal disabilities "well enough."[9]

England was peculiar among European nations and even its own empire in placing "equity" and "law" (meaning common law) under the auspices of different courts. Scotland followed the continental model, in which equity and law coexisted as different forms of reasoning within a single institutional context. The colonies, as we have seen, adapted English institutions in varying ways, but none correlated perfectly with England's complex and divided jurisdictional system. This gave colonial litigants, lawyers, and jurists leeway to determine the appropriate argumentative frame for each case. Studies of local legal practice have found that precepts of coverture were frequently acknowledged and frequently ignored. Even courts that attempted to differentiate between various jurisdictional hats might forget which one they were wearing at a particular moment, often to the irritation of legally savvy observers. Instances in which courts disregarded common-law precedent look surprising when viewed through the lens of arguments about jurisdictional boundaries that proliferated in later decades; they are less so when one considers English jurisdictional politics from the 1720s through the 1740s.[10]

EMPIRE, EVANGELISM, AND SLAVERY: THE YORKE–TALBOT OPINION

The 1720s don't generally make it onto timelines of the history of antislavery or of changes to marriage law. Yet fragmentary evidence from colonial disputes about marriage and slavery suggests connections between such local conflicts and better-known transatlantic debates about religious jurisdiction. During this decade, New England saw renewed conflict among Massachusetts's established Congregationalists, Rhode Island's proudly disestablished Quakers, and disgruntled Anglican clergy, who were appalled at dissenters' legal power in the colonies. This conflict was compounded by moral concern and colonial outreach on the part of the charismatic English Anglican bishop Edmund Gibson, who aspired to impose uniform Anglican authority over both marriage and slavery in a larger bid to expand the power of the Anglican Church.

Edmund Gibson, who became bishop of London as well as de facto minister to the Crown and patriarch for the colonies in 1723, was a key actor in English politics. Gibson had become convinced that England and the empire were threatened by rampant moral decline. The new publicity garnered by people who moved in and out of marriages as they moved across jurisdictions helped fuel his sense of urgency. Defoe's 1722 novel *Moll Flanders*, for instance, had turned vice into popular entertainment, with a heroine who, among other things, "Was Twelve Year a Whore, Five Times a Wife [Whereof Once To Her Own Brother], Twelve Year a Thief, and Eight Year a Transported Felon In Virginia." Critics feared that such works not only amused but mis-educated "honest Dick and Doll"—servants who spent their time "down in the kitchen . . . studying Colonel Jack and Flanders Moll." The factual accounts of impiety and vice that Gibson solicited from his pastoral underlings only confirmed his fears, and his political ascendancy in the late 1720s gave him the opportunity to act.[11]

Gibson was an early member and staunch supporter of the Society for Promoting Christian Knowledge, an organization formed in 1698 by Anglicans alarmed at Quakers' superior missionary networks in the colonies. Gibson was also a legal scholar with long-standing interest in reviving the ecclesiastical courts, which he saw as a crucial tool for combating vice and spreading the Gospel and Anglican authority at home and in the colonies. When he discovered that the bishop of London's responsibility for the spiritual welfare of the colonies was not grounded in formal law, he began pressing for reforms that would achieve these multiple ends, thereby shaping a conversation about jurisdiction that affected marriage and slavery.[12]

Gibson's influence was evident in several important opinions on the relationship between colonial and imperial laws that Attorney General Philip Yorke (the future Lord Chancellor Hardwicke) issued between 1725 and the mid-1730s. Yorke was also a moralist and a strong believer in the need for a more orderly and centralized legal system. On questions of revenue, he inclined toward extending English statute law and English sovereignty to the colonies. However, he was not disposed to make concessions to the Anglican church at the expense of secular authorities, despite his sympathy for Gibson's moral aims. When Gibson demanded that Yorke challenge the statutory establishment of dissenting Congregational churches in Massachusetts, Yorke acknowledged the legal irregularity but made pragmatic arguments against the bishop's effort to extend Anglican ecclesiastical authority. Prior Crown approval of the objectionable colonial statutes meant that they could not lightly be revoked, and while the Anglican Church certainly had a right to jurisdiction over its clergy, the colonial laity would not tolerate such claims. In this instance, colonial legal variety merited toleration.[13]

On the question of slavery, Yorke and Gibson agreed to indulge colonial innovations in the service of imperial ends. In 1729, together with Solicitor General Talbot, Yorke infamously declared that neither baptism nor time spent on English soil untied the legal bonds of colonial slavery. Their signed opinion accepted slavery as both a Christian and an English institution, rather than a colonial aberration. Eighteenth-century antislavery activists would later disparage the Yorke–Talbot opinion, portraying it as the non-binding product of a wine-sodden dinner hosted by nervous colonial planters, who were eager to close loopholes through which slaves challenged their authority. Historians long accepted this account, despite the obvious political stakes it held for opponents of slavery. More recent scholarship suggests instead that the opinion was a product of Anglican missionary zeal. It appears to have been solicited by a protégé of Gibson's, who had just embarked on an evangelizing mission in the colonies and aimed to secure slaveholders' cooperation in the conversion of their slaves. It first circulated in Rhode Island and in the *Boston Gazette* and became a matter of English record through London papers that reprinted the *Gazette*'s news from the colonies.[14]

The Yorke–Talbot opinion turned (or at least tried to turn) the policies of slaveholding Virginia, the Carolinas, and the Caribbean into imperial law. In New England and the mid-Atlantic, it would have registered less as a concession to colonial divergence than as an effort to rein in religious and legal dissent. Anglican leaders' eagerness to show that their own evangelical efforts were compatible with slavery distinguished them from reformed religious groups who challenged slavery as un-Christian and inhumane.

The latter point was hotly contested in imperial circles during the 1720s and 1730s. London creditors were lobbying for uniform policies that allowed slaves to be treated as a liquid form of capital so that they might more easily be able to recover colonial debts. As things stood, colonial rules regarding the transmission of enslaved property were varied and changeable; Virginia, for instance, attempted to class slaves as real estate, and thereby limit the circumstances by which they could be seized by creditors or separated from inherited lands. Slaveholders and religious moralists alike objected that imperial policies threatened masters' control of community and familial networks within slavery. Masters knew this power was essential to securing slaves' cooperation without the relentless use of violence. Moralists—including both the Congregationalist Samuel Sewall (whom we shall meet momentarily) and the Anglican Edmund Gibson—dreamed of using masters' paternalist pretenses to spread Christianity among populations of infidels.[15]

Colonial Household Conflicts, Local Law, and the Shadow of Imperial Norms in the 1720s

Three case studies from Massachusetts and Pennsylvania help illuminate the ways in which these imperial concerns touched colonial households, as well as the practice of "equity" and local law in the colonies. Dorothy Jackson of Massachusetts and Anne Ashton of Pennsylvania were the first women in their respective colonies to challenge husbands who attempted to discredit them in the newspapers. Anna Margareta Boehm's divorce petition to Pennsylvania's legislature was the first test of whether colonial legislatures outside New England could follow Parliament's example and grant full divorce. These are not stories that suggest a happily-ever-after. But they are stories in which wives and their communities expected women to have access to legal remedies, and to be included rather than excluded by law. That inclusion—in the Jackson case, at least—was paid for by household interest in slave property. These stories exemplify the case-specific approach to household justice that provided continuity amid the legal variety of the eighteenth-century Anglo-imperial world. They also document the careful dance that colonial lawyers, judges, printers, and future political "founders" performed around rules emanating from the imperial center.

THE JACKSONS' CASE: EQUITY FOR A WIFE, PAID FOR BY A SLAVE

The fragmentary records left by Dorothy and John Jackson in Massachusetts begin with marital complaints and end with an estate dispute about widow's rights and the status of a slave. This instance of local law resembles the Lawsons' case in chapter 1, but it displays a greater concern for Massachusetts's compliance with English precedent, as well as discomfort with what this meant for the enslaved man whose fate hung in the balance. The case followed a common pattern in colonial equitable remedies for abused wives, in that relief for a white woman came at the expense of an enslaved black man.

In 1725, after her husband had denounced her for desertion in the *Boston News-Letter* twice in the space of a few months, Dorothy Jackson petitioned the Suffolk County Court for a separate maintenance, charging that "he utterly refuses to provide her support and has forbid any person to Credit her, or have anything on his Account." Her current "Deplorable Circumstances" followed many years of "grievious" treatment. Her husband had repeatedly beaten her "and abused her by calling her whore, Bitch," and other harsh names. He had also "turned her out of Doors" on multiple occasions, most recently by thrusting her "headlong" out of the house, catching "up a Hatchet in his hand," and threatening "to spill her Brains out." John Jackson's efforts to discredit his wife in the newspapers confirmed community skepticism about his already poor marital track record. Witness testimony for Jackson's lawsuit does not survive, but in the crowded living quarters of eighteenth-century

Boston, domestic violence was not a private matter. John Jackson's advertisement warned Dorothy's allies "against harboring or entertaining her at their Peril," providing a concrete record of the kind of threats that might persuade a couple's "Friends" that official intervention was warranted. Such intervention, in turn, usually only carried as far as needed to secure promises of "Good behaviour" and protect the "public Peace."[16]

After giving both Jackson and her husband a hearing, the Massachusetts court ordered him to take her "home again to his house and support her as his Wife" and to give bond for his "Good behavior towards her." Should he refuse to comply with these conditions, she was to receive the alimony she had requested; such "separate maintenance" amounted to a bed and board divorce, though the records did not call it that. No records tell us whether this verdict in fact relieved Dorothy's "Deplorable Circumstances." Three years later, John had left the province and died without a will, and Dorothy hired a lawyer to assert her claims to the estate. Her place of residence cannot be determined, but her plea made no explicit mention of their separation. She never turned to the press.[17]

The property Dorothy sought to control after her husband's death was a man named Adam, whom her lawyer argued had been fraudulently transferred out of the estate by the court-appointed administrators in a deliberate effort "to protect him from Jackson's wife." Dorothy Jackson's lawyer (the London-trained Scotch Irish Anglican Robert Auchmuty) was simultaneously giving advice in the dispute over church property and taxation that inspired Edmund Gibson's complaints about New England's Congregationalist religious establishment. In the dispute over religious jurisdiction and privileges, the lawyer supported the distinctiveness of colonial practices. In Jackson's case, on the other hand, the lawyer invoked English examples, citing recent decisions in the London Mayor's Court and King's Bench to show "the preference all Courts give to the wife's Right of Admin to the Husbands Estate."[18]

In 1728, Dorothy seems to have won her legal point. Precedents from the London Mayor's Court, which itself merged equitable and common-law jurisdictions, persuaded Massachusetts Judge Samuel Sewall that Dorothy Jackson, and not the trustees who had provided security for John's "Good behavior" and Dorothy's separate maintenance, had the right to administer John's estate. The implication was that, even in technical legal matters, London knew better, and also that slaves needed to be treated like any other property in the settlement of estates and debts. The case remains a typical instance of local law in that it tells us nothing about how such legal concessions in fact played out in practice.

Though the Jacksons were minor figures, Judge Sewall was prominent in his time and has earned lasting fame for his early opposition to slavery; cryptic elements of the case hint at conflict over the extent of masters'—and especially mistresses'—power over slaves. Sewall had authored one of the earliest antislavery tracts. He had also actively (if largely unsuccessfully) worked behind the scenes to ensure that Massachusetts laws did not place black or Indian slaves in a wholly different category from English servants, particularly with regard to expectations about sexual behavior and religiously sanctioned marriage.[19] The same court-appointed trustees who had promised to enforce John Jackson's "good behavior" to his wife had "leased" Adam for a term of service, most likely to provide Dorothy's maintenance. Selling the labor of enslaved people was a common means by which wealthy families guaranteed an income for widows throughout the eighteenth-century colonies. Less common, however, was Sewall and the trustees' apparent desire to "protect" Adam from being sold outright by Dorothy Jackson. They appear to have been trying to allow Adam to remain in Boston, where he may have had kin and some claim to legal protection, if not a finite term of service. They might even have been successful, as he last appears in the records in the household of Nathaniel Wheeler, whose family later became famous for its evangelical aspirations and ambivalence about slavery (his daughter Susannah Wheeler Wheatley at once cultivated and exploited her enslaved protégé, the brilliant African poet Phillis Wheatley).[20]

While Adam's case offers only oblique evidence of the aging Sewall's ongoing engagement with debate about slavery in the 1720s, Sewall's writing was simultaneously finding a new public outlet in Pennsylvania. In 1729, even as more conservative Anglican activists procured and disseminated the Yorke–Talbot opinion, the Quaker merchant Ralph Sandiford borrowed liberally from Samuel Sewall's critique of slavery in an essay that Pennsylvania Quaker leaders thought too controversial to publish. Sandiford brought his essay to press anyway, only to be disowned for his stance. The young Benjamin Franklin anonymously arranged the printing. In 1720s Pennsylvania, as in Massachusetts, simmering debates about marriage, slavery, and religious authority also threatened to boil over into larger imperial jurisdictional conflicts. As we shall see, for Franklin these were issues of private as well as public concern.[21]

THE ASHTONS' CASE: BIGAMY, ADULTERY,
AND RECONCILIATION

Anne Ashton was the first Pennsylvania woman to challenge her husband's effort to discredit her as an eloping wife. Where Dorothy Jackson had turned

to the Massachusetts courts, Anne Ashton turned to the press. Dorothy and
Anne's specific grievances differed, but their stories both illustrated patterns
common in the "local law" regulating marital discord across colonial and English jurisdictions. Both women's responses manifested, first of all, community
(as well as individual) indignation at the power that newspaper discreditings
gave to husbands. Each marked the first instance in their respective colonies
at which multiple postings by husbands occurred within a few months of each
other, and at which the reading public might begin to wonder whether such
ads were going to become regular practice rather than rare events.

On January 26, 1731, Anne Ashton placed an ad in the *Pennsylvania Gazette*, arguing that she was much "abus'd" by the notice Benjamin Ashton
had published two weeks before. He had acted—and advertised—contrary
to community-mediated efforts to secure their reconciliation. On January 8,
Anne had obtained his promise, "before several Gentlemen," that he would
"put away the red hair'd Girl." She had taken this to mean that "every thing
was made up between" them, but Benjamin was not content. "Instead of putting" the girl "away, he locked himself up with her in the Room, and shut his
Wife big with Child into the Kitchen to lie by the Fire." A few days later, he
advertised that Anne had eloped from him—a charge she refuted. Although
she had apparently sought shelter elsewhere after being turned out of bed, she
had since "offered herself several Times," had returned "home and stay'd with
him" for at least a few days, "and would gladly have continu'd, being by reason
of her Condition unable to shift for herself at present."[22]

Benjamin Ashton had demonstrated that he was not overly scrupulous
about the obligations of the marriage contract even before his marriage to
Anne, who was probably his third wife. In 1724, he had entered a marriage
that ended in an informal separation soon after. Benjamin moved a few miles
away, and the woman he had left behind formed a new alliance. The couple's
self-initiated divorce turned into a criminal matter after Benjamin's abandoned wife bore a child in 1727. She was prosecuted first for fornication and
bastardy, a charge that treated her as a single woman. She defended herself by
claiming that she was married to the child's father, but this maneuver backfired by calling attention to her complex marital history. She and her new
husband were then indicted for bigamy—a far more serious matter.[23]

Benjamin's estranged second wife bore the legal consequences of their
separation, but it is unlikely he emerged from the ensuing controversy with an
untainted reputation. On one hand, the prosecutions probably served his interests and may have been at his behest. His wife's conviction for bigamy would
have protected his estate against the claims of her children, and entitled him to
request from the governor a divorce from bed and board (but not permission

to marry again). On the other hand, the trial called attention to the fact that he had knowingly allowed her to live apart from him and to remarry. He might even have been the one who deserted.

English and colonial courts routinely deemed husbands' tolerance of an informal separation as grounds for denying them claim to legal redress; by abdicating their authority as husbands, they shared some measure of their wives' guilt.[24] Benjamin Ashton never sought a formal divorce. His second wife disappeared from the records after her indictment for bigamy. Whether she (conveniently) died or simply sought to rebuild her life elsewhere cannot be determined, but one way or another Benjamin was permitted to enter a legally binding marriage to Anne. The education in marriage law that Benjamin received during his second wife's trials might have been what prompted him to dissociate himself publicly from Anne in the newspapers at the first hint that she might leave him. His community had already given him a new chance to play the role of husband, however, and they were reluctant to let him again define the part.

Dorothy Jackson's and Anne Ashton's cases also had similar outcomes. The right to return "home" and the right to respect for her status as a wife were Anne Ashton's stated objectives from the beginning. In theory, she might have obtained a divorce from bed and board (essentially the settlement Dorothy Jackson sought) under the same set of statutes that had entangled Benjamin's previous wife. The relevant Pennsylvania statutes explicitly granted this option to aggrieved husbands and wives in cases of adultery, bigamy, sodomy, and bestiality. If convicted, Benjamin would also have faced twenty-one lashes and either a year of imprisonment at hard labor or a fine of fifty pounds. Neither of these remedies would have helped Anne solve the problem of how she was to "shift for herself." But the case never came before Pennsylvania's courts. Benjamin took Anne home again, and she bore him several more children in the years that followed. A will he made in 1737 honored her status as his "tender and loving wife" and named her his sole executor; she assumed this responsibility without incident upon his death five years later.[25]

THE BOEHM MILLER CASE: RELIGIOUS CONFLICT AND COLONIAL LEGISLATIVE DIVORCE

While Benjamin Ashton's marital history made him a poor candidate for legal redress, his wife Anne might also have been deterred by another wife's very public failure to obtain a legislative divorce. In 1729, Anna Maria Boehm

Miller gave Pennsylvania's divorce laws and England's newly revived example of parliamentary divorce the most direct test of the early eighteenth century. The case exemplifies the swirling currents of religious radicalism that fueled jurisdictional conflict and broader debates about marriage and slavery in the 1720s; it highlights the ways in which conflict between different religious groups could ultimately strengthen secular state authority.

Anna Maria Boehm Miller's marital trouble attracted attention both because of who she was and because of the content of her petition. Her father, John Philip Boehm, was a German reformed preacher and schoolmaster who migrated to Pennsylvania with his family in 1720, after his theology and his temperament left him out of work at home. In 1728 and 1729 he was embroiled in a bitter fight about jurisdiction over Pennsylvania's German-speaking religious communities. Anna Maria's appeal to English colonial authorities for a decision on marriage law is particularly intriguing in this context because it appeared to test English authorities' openness to German Protestants' legal expectations. (As noted in chapter 1, continental Protestants were more open to full divorce than the English.) Upheaval and conflict among Pennsylvania's German religious factions made the imperial state the neutral arbiter for a matter that would otherwise have remained under religious jurisdiction; religious conflicts ended up reinforcing secular authority. John Philip Boehm's eventual victory over a succession of religious competitors, including the Moravians and Peter Henry Dorsius, earned him the status of founder of the German Reformed Church in America. The hagiographical histories through which we know of his life have relatively little interest in his female relations in general, and they do not tell us what happened to this daughter.

Anna Maria Boehm Miller created a stir by petitioning the governor and council for a divorce from her husband George, using the legal grounds that his malformed testicles had prevented him from consummating their marriage after two years of daily effort. Dutiful and unsatisfying sex of the sort was clearly not conducive to domestic harmony, but Anna Maria's overarching concerns were her husband's violence and threats to take her away from the colony and her parents and friends. Anna Maria's petition was legally well constructed; it probably would have passed muster with Bishop Gibson, who argued that canon law allowed annulments on the grounds of impotence. She did not, however, win her divorce. She and her supporters likely expected that her husband would leave town of his own accord rather than submit to a trial. He surprised them by enduring a humiliating medical inspection, in which he demonstrated before physicians that he could manually obtain "sufficient erection & length of Penis to convey and emit" semen "into the feminine Matrix." This was enough for the prominent colonial officials trying to maintain their dignity as they sat as a court of chancery, and they eagerly washed their hands of the case.[26]

Two years later, a few months after he published the Ashtons' advertisements, Benjamin Franklin reported sardonically that Anna Maria had returned to her husband and now declared that "GEORGE IS AS GOOD AS DE BEST." Whether she in fact returned is debatable; the only independent records have her married to someone else in the 1740s.[27]

Franklin's humorous dismissal encapsulates the strategy that limited the political impact of sectarian tension and debates about slavery and marriage within the empire for the next two decades. Marriage and its discontents made for lively fiction and created a ready market for advice literature. It was a topic fit for manly jokes. But neither unhappily married couples nor the authorities benefited from testing the limits of marriage law. Indeed, Franklin's aptitude for ridicule might have helped restrain the legislature from revisiting the question of divorce, which did not surface again in Pennsylvania until the 1760s, when he was out of the colony. Controversies about faith and the morality of keeping slaves could similarly generate good business, but prudent printers and politicians indulged them without becoming invested—as Franklin well knew from personal experience.

BENJAMIN FRANKLIN: RUNAWAY APPRENTICE AND HUSBAND

Benjamin Franklin's own complicated marital history developed in parallel with the Ashton and Boehm Miller controversies. His career during this period demonstrates his long-standing and intimate familiarity with debates about marriage law, slavery, and the rights of dependents. Franklin came to Philadelphia as a runaway apprentice in 1723 and went to work for a printer who had himself run from a failed marriage, debt, and religious and political controversy in London, and who held radical ideas about both marriage and slavery.[28] Franklin promptly performed the same maneuver in reverse, leaving a woman to whom he had promised marriage to go to London, accompanied by a friend who had deserted his own wife and child.

Five years later, in 1728, Franklin returned to Philadelphia and proceeded to drive his old master out of business. Unlike his rival printer, Franklin had a feel for politics and knew that some deeds are better left unpublished. Franklin's political caution landed his overtly ideological predecessor with the responsibility for some of Franklin's controversial actions, including printing Ralph Sandiford's contested antislavery work. Franklin avowed his role fifty years later, after antislavery became a politically viable stand. Franklin approached marriage with similar circumspection. Deborah Read, his onetime fiancée, had married and been deserted during his absence in London. Rather than renew his relationship with Deborah, Franklin sought a more secure and profitable match. This courtship brought him an illegitimate child rather than the marriage settlement he had in mind. In this awkward situation, after some quiet conversations with lawyers, he "made amends" to Deborah by marrying her despite her own uncertain legal status; she in turn raised his son William as her own. We know these details (and not others, such as the identity of William Franklin's mother or whether Deborah Read's first husband had really died or simply agreed never to return) because Franklin used them to make political points decades later. Franklin's account of Deborah's possible bigamy and William's illegitimacy remained unpublished until after Deborah was dead and William had become disloyal.[29]

Compromises and obfuscations of this sort—whether about legitimacy in birth and marriage or responsibility for controversial publications—render the political details of the ferment in the 1720s murky. In the short term, conflict was avoided rather than settled. Leaders of the groups that would become Methodists and Moravians and "new light" Protestants of various other stripes sought common ground with Anglicans like Gibson in a universal Christian mission aimed at converting Indians, slaves, and uncouth colonial masters. In the decades that followed, religious awakening turned into religious schism, and stances on marriage and slavery became integral to the ways competing sects defined their own identities and their relationship to state power.

Bishop Gibson did not obtain most of his short-term objectives. A 1732 act of Parliament, intended to ensure the "more easy Recovery of Debts and his Majesty's Plantations and Colonies in America," made a starker statement of uniform imperial policy on slavery than the Yorke–Talbot opinion. When it came to settling debts, slaves were now chattel, and neither the benevolence nor the self-interest of colonial masters and legislatures could protect them from the reach of metropolitan creditors. The furor over the establishment of Congregational churches in Massachusetts not only failed to produce a colonial episcopacy, it almost undermined the Anglican establishment in England: Quakers, whose interests aligned with the Anglican challenge to Massachusetts policies giving state support to Congregationalist churches, used similar antiestablishment arguments to lobby for a parliamentary act exempting the group from tithes that supported the Church of England. Gibson stepped away from formal political power in 1737, after the Ministry failed to support his efforts to defeat this measure. The Quaker lobby remained ever

vigilant, however, with important consequences for the next round of controversy over both marriage and slavery.[30]

Gibson's legacy carried over in the career of Philip Yorke, who by 1737 had
become Lord Hardwicke and lord chancellor, reaching the pinnacle of his
power as Gibson stepped down. Over the long term, much as he had in the
1720s, Yorke would use Gibson's moral agenda to promote legal reforms that
consolidated secular imperial power. In the 1730s and early 1740s, however,
his respect for case-specific equitable justice and his personal stake in the
strength of England's courts of equity seemed compatible with varied local
legal traditions. He would have been unlikely to object to the equitable justice
meted out by Samuel Sewall in the Jackson marital and estate disputes or by
the local courts and neighbors in the Ashton conflict. Yet, as a politician, he
was probably glad that neither of these cases came to his attention. The more
prominent inaction of Pennsylvania's governor and council in their equitable
judgment of the Boehm Miller case also spared imperial authorities from
hard decisions. Such discretion allowed jurisdictional disorder to remain the
rule. In the business generated by marital conflict, local discretion gave equity
the upper hand over the common law.

Ancient Patriarchy and the Invention of "Possessory Rights"

Printers, lawyers, and the clergy all found new ways to profit from the ambiguities of marriage law in the 1730s and 1740s. First, legal restrictions on the
press lapsed during this period, as they had in the 1690s, leading to a new explosion in printed media, and in turn to anxieties about social and legal disorder. Competition between publishers of legal texts reinforced growing jurisdictional tension over marriage law, and new treatises generated confusion
rather than clarity. Second, common lawyers found in criminal conversation
litigation a lucrative way to intervene in marital disputes that might otherwise have been left to other jurisdictions; a few made this the foundation for
illustrious careers, including the powerful late eighteenth-century chief justice of King's Bench Lord Mansfield, as well as the future Lord Chancellor
Erskine. Mansfield attributed his rise to fortune to his acclaimed arguments
in a highly publicized 1738 criminal conversation trial. Between the 1760s and
1780s, Erskine established his own lucrative legal career on a similar trade.[31]
Publicity in high-profile cases fueled demand for similar remedies and for
more published stories of scandalous cases. Third, a similar dynamic was at
play on humbler terrain in the instance of wife sale—an extralegal form of divorce that exemplifies the process by which new practices acquire legitimacy
by inventing a history and claiming status as ancient custom. Finally, the

press also generated publicity for impoverished and sometimes unscrupulous clergy who made a business of performing marriages that bent, or outright broke, laws requiring communal oversight. Long-standing debate over such "clandestine marriages" would come to a head in the 1753 Hardwicke Act, the measure through which Philip Yorke would secure both his own and Bishop Gibson's legacy.

MANBY V. SCOTT IN THE 1730S:

EIGHTEENTH-CENTURY LEGAL TREATISES

FAIL TO REIMPOSE ORDER

All these developments contributed to a new wave of lawyerly efforts to disguise legal innovation with the rhetoric of ancient patriarchal rights, which has in turn confounded historians' efforts to assess continuity and change in mid-eighteenth-century marriage law and practice. The two English treatises on marriage law published during the first part of the eighteenth century, *Baron and Feme* and *The Lady's Law*, documented enduring legal ambiguities and escalating jurisdictional conflicts over the regulation of marriage. Competing accounts of *Manby v. Scott* anchored both works, perpetuating debate about whether coverture was meant primarily to protect wives or to empower husbands.

The first two editions of *Baron and Feme*, published in 1700 and 1719, had been specifically subtitled *A Treatise of the Common Law concerning Husbands and Wives*. In 1732, just after the expiration of the term of copyright established by statute in 1710, *Baron and Feme* acquired a whimsical competitor. *The Lady's Law* explicitly promoted itself as both more up to date and more faithful to *Manby*, notwithstanding the fact that it took much of its content from the early seventeenth-century *Lawes Resolutions of Women's Rights*. Like this predecessor, *The Lady's Law* promised to inform "the fair Sex" about the power the law gave them "to preserve their Lands, Goods, and most valuable Effects, from the Incroachments of any one; to defend themselves and their Reputations against all unlawful Attacks of Mankind, and to maintain Actions, and carry on Prosecutions and cases of Violation of their Persons, to the Death of a daring Offender." Unlike its seventeenth-century counterpart, however, the eighteenth-century treatise did not apologize for women's legal disabilities. Its intended audience of "all Practitioners of the Law, and other curious Persons" was decidedly masculine. It is hard to imagine a woman in need of legal aid finding much amusement in the items the treatise compiler included as "Things of entertainment, being writ long ago" and "mix'd with the Law." The compiler judged many of "our old Laws and Customs relating to Women . . .

very merry, though the Makers of them might possibly be grave Men." How
the reader was to determine the difference between law and farce was unclear.
The book's detailed discussion of "Rapes, Polygamy, and stealing of Women"
among other things "not so much as mentioned in the Treatise called *Baron
and Feme*" seems designed to titillate and perhaps repulse; neither the tone
nor the content was in keeping with literature addressed to female readers.[32]

In 1738, *Baron and Feme*'s publishers responded to this challenge with a
third edition that expanded its scope to include both "Law and Equity." The
shift in title reflected the jurisdictional balance of power in marital litigation
more accurately than the original. The "many additions" to the work included
a much fuller reprint of what purported to be Lord Hale's opinion in *Manby*
(to compete with "Judge *Hide's* remarkable opinion" in *The Lady's Law*). The
injunction against posting one's wife in the newspapers, discussed in the previous chapter, was now dropped, though it endured in other legal handbooks
into the nineteenth century. If this change was intended to increase the text's
fidelity to precedent, it was counterbalanced by sloppiness elsewhere. The expansion thoroughly undid the original compiler's claim that *Baron and Feme*
"methodized" English marriage law. Indeed, while *Baron and Feme* had more
(literal) heft and sobriety than *The Lady's Law*, both treatises were so disor-
ganized and full of conflicting edicts that they were unlikely to provide any
reader with much security.

CRIMINAL CONVERSATION, WIFE SALE, AND THE IMAGINARY "ANCIENT" ROOTS OF HUSBANDS' POSSESSORY RIGHTS

Common-law interventions in marital disputes followed from common-law
remedies in property disputes, and thus cast marriage as a property transaction. Suits for "criminal conversation"—the legal action that first made Lord
Mansfield famous—sought civil damages for husbands of adulterous wives by
imagining "seduction" as the equivalent of illegally trespassing on one's land.
As the historian Hendrik Hartog aptly notes, "Criminal conversation was neither a criminal action nor about conversation." An aggrieved husband could
sue his wife's lover for "trespass" upon his wife as upon other forms of property. Women disappeared as actors in such suits, making them the "paradigmatic example" of legal reasoning that treated wives as the property of their
husbands. Unlike ecclesiastical prosecution of adultery or the criminal adultery trials that continued in most colonies, criminal conversation thoroughly
erased the wife's agency or desire. As a *feme covert* under common-law jurisdiction, she was not a party to the suit, nor could she stand as a witness.[33]

Among people who could not afford expensive lawyers and lawsuits, mid-eighteenth century England saw the rise of (or at least an increase in newspaper reports regarding) "wife sale," an extralegal form of self-divorce that also construed marriage as a property relationship in which wives were akin to chattel. The phenomenon has been studied by social rather than legal historians, using anthropological frameworks that tend to render the practice peculiarly timeless. Those interested in affirming folk customs have found themselves caught, in the historian Deborah Valenze's words, "between an interpretation that seems painfully obvious—the demonstration of the subjection of women to chattel status—and an equally superficial assumption that marital relations among the poor were barbaric." The phenomenon is better understood as an innovation "coterminous with the financial revolution, a contemporary upheaval in marriage arrangements (at least until mid-century), and a colonial trade in persons and slaves." Criminal conversation and husbands' published threats to those who "harbored" eloping wives were similarly tied to these three trends.[34]

The idea that criminal conversation suits and wife sale were ancient remedies owe more to the popular press than to legal authorities. The earliest reference I have found to either phenomenon comes from the peripatetic printer John Dunton, who invented a variety of legal and extralegal remedies for elopement in the 1692 *Athenian Mercury*.[35] Rather than seek revenge "by Man-slaughter upon the provocation" (i.e., a duel), an abandoned husband "might have some remedy perhaps by Law." Dunton claimed that "if there should be occasion to sell her to him with whom she has Eloped," the husband might find "a Form, or an Instrument in Writing ready drawn up for that Case, . . . in Cook's [*sic*] Second Institutes." However, the best way to determine how to proceed on this sale of his wife to her seducer, the printer assured his reader, was first to place an advertisement in the newspapers that would expose those who harbored her.[36]

Notwithstanding the allusion to the renowned early seventeenth-century legal authority Sir Edward Coke's *Institutes of the Laws of England*, the relationship of these remedies to the law in the 1690s was uncertain. It remained so in the 1730s and 1740s, when the wife-selling practices Dunton described first became common enough to register on the social historian's radar with any frequency. Neither *Baron and Feme* nor *The Lady's Law* had much to say about them, nor did Coke's *Institutes*. The "ready drawn Instrument" for wife sale that Dunton described *might* have existed in another handbook that invoked Coke's authority, but if so, it was neither widely disseminated nor accepted by formal authorities. Instead, newspaper anecdotes by printers like Dunton and Franklin and published complaints by disgruntled officials helped spread the practice of wife sale during the eighteenth century. The earliest *legal* evidence I have found of such a practice comes from the papers of a late eighteenth-century colonial lawyer.[37] Dunton's remedies acquired their reputation as "ancient" patriarchal rights through eighteenth-century debates about their legitimacy.

When Dunton suggested that an aggrieved husband would find better remedies at law than through a duel, he was probably referring to suits for criminal conversation, which had begun to gain a foothold in the courts in the late seventeenth century. Dunton's argument seems to affirm the prevailing historical narrative that portrays criminal conversation as moderating older patriarchal norms by providing an alternative to the violence traditionally assumed to be warranted in defense of aristocratic notions of masculine honor. As Hartog, following Lawrence Stone, puts it, the action was in keeping "with the era's general commercialization and commodification of property relations, the reduction of all things, even honor, to a monetary equivalent." Criminal conversation certainly commodified the prerogatives of husbands. But it was a practice invented by opportunistic lawyers, publicity-driven demand, and parliamentary policy that developed to its fullest extent in the mid- and late eighteenth century, not simply a moderate form of an older patriarchal tradition.[38]

In general, historians would do well to avoid echoing the embarrassed pleading of eighteenth- and nineteenth-century jurists, who insisted that, legal forms aside, by the 1790s criminal conversation suits were about husbands' injured affections and the "loss of the comfort and society" of a wife rather than a man's claim to property in his wife's body. The companionate reframing of criminal conversation suits and enlightened contempt for "barbaric" customs like wife sale deflected attention away from the novelty of the possessory claims underlying both actions. In criminal conversation and attacks on those who "enticed" away or "harbored" wayward wives, women *became* possessions to which husbands had rights. If such actions represented an "enduring form of male hegemony," they gave it new form and new power during the eighteenth century.[39]

THE 1753 HARDWICKE ACT: MARRIAGE LAW EXTENDS
PATERNAL AND IMPERIAL AUTHORITY

Possessory rights came to center stage with the 1753 Marriage Act, also known as the Hardwicke Act or Lord Hardwicke's Act, which gave fathers possessory rights to counterbalance the expanding claims of undesirable sons-in-law. The measure resembled seventeenth-century Puritan marriage statutes that were still on the books in many colonies. Like those laws, the Hardwicke Act required that minors obtain consent from their parents or guardians before marrying, and that couples broadcast their intention to marry weeks in advance. The publication of the banns was supposed to assure a hearing for those who questioned the legitimacy of the match. Supporters of such measures declared them necessary protection against unscrupulous seducers who stole gullible children—particularly, innocent heiresses—away from their families. The 1753 Marriage Act went beyond similar colonial laws in the extent to which it construed children (and not just children's inheritance claims) as property, over whom fathers had possessory rights until well past the age of puberty. Advocates and opponents alike imagined such patriarchal powers as ancient phenomenon. Yet by making improperly formed marriages voidable, it gave paternal authority a novel place in English law.[40]

The debates about clandestine marriage used stories of family tragedy to disguise broader jurisdictional concerns. Seventeenth-century Puritan reformers used their marriage statutes to make the theological point that marriage was a civil contract, not a sacrament. Their attempts to place marriage firmly under the control of the state targeted not only would-be seducers, but Anglicans, Catholics, and more radical Protestant groups with competing views on the proper formation and regulation of marriage. From the Restoration until the 1740s, repeated efforts to outlaw "clandestine marriages" in England ran aground on such jurisdictional and sectarian rivalries. With one hand, the Marriage Act affirmed ecclesiastical power by placing the Anglican Church firmly in control of the new apparatus for licensing and registering marriages. With the other, Parliament sharply restricted the lucrative and often ethically dubious business of private licensing and ceremonies and affirmed that marriage was foremost a civil contract over which secular legal bodies defined the terms. Supporters and opponents of the measure alike invoked divine as well as natural and national law. Nevertheless, those who linked the doctrine of marital indissolubility with ecclesiastical authority had reason to be worried. Only "superstition," Attorney General Dudley Ryder argued in the Commons, had interfered with previous efforts to allow the annulment of secretive marriages by minors; the current age made "Christianity consistent with common sense."[41]

The 1753 law did not originate with Phillip Yorke (now Lord Chancellor Hardwicke), but it bears his name because it would not have passed without his substantial intervention. Hardwicke was by all accounts a grave man who was distressed by the propensity for marriage law to make the legal system into a source of merriment. (Neither he nor Bishop Gibson would have been amused by *The Lady's Law*.) An anonymous defense of the Marriage Act encapsulated both men's concerns. It declared Lord Hardwicke's Act simply a new means to enforce ancient rules, the breach of which was "daily and openly, and impudently avowed, and Invitations to transgress the Law hung out upon Signs, and published regularly in common News Papers." Unenforced earlier laws were a serious problem, as "Laws unexecuted are not only an Incumbrance and a Reproach, but a real Evil of pernicious Tendency to a State." The Marriage Act gave Hardwicke direct means to combat "the degeneracy of the present times, fruitful in the inventions of wickedness," which he thought required new statutes. As we shall see, the act's connection to Hardwicke's vision for a more orderly system of imperial law had repercussions in Scotland and the colonies that have been unnoticed even by historians who position the statute as a source of significant social change.[42]

Repercussions of Imperial Intervention in Marriage Law

The Hardwicke Act explicitly exempted Scotland, Quakers, and Jews from its provisions for contracting legitimate marriages. The Welsh, Catholics, and England's myriad other dissenting religious groups, on the other hand, were expected to conform to its Anglican rules. (Ireland already had similar measures that targeted secret marriages between Protestants and Catholics.)[43] The act's exceptions were a testament to the vigilance of Quaker, Jewish, and Scottish groups' political lobbies rather than to parliamentary solicitude. Quaker and Scottish efforts to defend their autonomy provide a concrete political context for these groups' mid-eighteenth-century interest in marriage reform and antislavery. Both groups played an outsize role in developing and disseminating social theories that turned "domestic relations" into measures of the progress of civilization, and on the colonial debates about marriage examined in later chapters.

ENLIGHTENED SCOTS: JURISDICTIONAL BATTLES AND STADIAL THEORY

Lord Hardwicke exempted Scotland from the 1753 Marriage Act only out of political necessity; his private papers contain a draft bill for submission to the Scottish Court of Sessions that demonstrates his intent to extend the measure there. The measure aligned well with his concern about the "arbitrariness" of Scottish legal proceedings and his general desire to bring Scotland more effectively under English jurisdiction, by force when necessary.[44] This fraught political context made things difficult for elite Scots who (like Mansfield) had cast their lot with England. Even those who concurred with Hardwicke about the need for Scottish law reform parted company with him on the means.

The Scottish Enlightenment's distinctive interest in marriage and slavery as indices of civilization emerged in tandem with the debates about jurisdiction over marriage associated with the Hardwicke Act. Although David Hume was not a defender of Scottish autonomy, the musings on polygamy and divorce that he added to the 1748 edition of his *Essays, Moral and Political* anticipated other, more nationalistic responses to English jurists' complaints about the differences between Scottish and English marriage law. Hume opened with the observation that it was "mere superstition to imagine, that marriage can be entirely uniform, and will admit only of one mode or form." The piece formally supported the English policy of marital indissolubility, but it supplied arguments that ran more effectively in the opposite (Scottish) direction. And in the end it summarized itself as a defense of common "European" practice, which Hume defined through diversity. The famous conversation about the "increase of mankind" in which Hume, Robert Wallace, and Benjamin Franklin engaged via between 1751 and 1754 similarly reflected on the significance of imperial policies regarding marriage, inheritance, servitude, and slavery for subordinate jurisdictions.[45]

The Hardwicke Act gave these general jurisdictional anxieties a specific focus. In the sensational case that precipitated the 1753 law, a respectable English marriage had been undone by a prior clandestine Scottish one. Upon her husband's death, the innocent English wife found herself disinherited and her children bastardized when his first wife and children placed a claim on his estate. For those in the know, questions about the morality of Scottish law framed the issue from the outset. There were immediate signs of a nationalistic reaction, and the parallel measure Hardwicke intended for the Scottish lawmakers did not go through.[46] Erskine's classic *Principles of the Law of Scotland*, published just months after the Hardwicke Act went into effect, carefully noted that Scottish tradition recognized the legality of clandestine marriages; later Scottish Enlightenment notables reiterated concern about jurisdictional conflict and the need to defend superior Scottish marital practices from English rules that promoted domestic and civil tyranny and corruption. Tensions escalated in subsequent decades as Scotland became a refuge for eloping couples. Weddings in the border town of Gretna Green became a staple of English fiction, and the question of whether England ought to recognize such marriages emerged as a key forum for the development of the legal principle of comity.[47]

QUAKERS: MARITAL DISCIPLINE AS THE PRICE
OF RELIGIOUS AUTONOMY

After George II closed the parliamentary session that finalized the Marriage Act in June 1753, an anonymous Quaker woman who had been observing from the gallery stood up and held forth for half an hour on the decadence and corruption evident in the chamber. The speaker might well have been Mary Peisley or Catherine Payton. These traveling Quaker ministers departed soon after for North America, where they launched the internal reform movement famous for turning antislavery into an article of Quaker faith, as well as a push for marital discipline with repercussions that lasted generations. Antislavery has overshadowed Quaker reformers' parallel concern with marriage discipline in most historical accounts. Yet marriage practices and domestic ideals were fundamental not only to Quaker opposition to slavery but also to the many other aspects of Quaker culture that anticipated "modern" norms and institutions, including intimate, egalitarian familial relationships, advocacy of women's rights, capitalist industrialism, separation of church and state, and principled pacifism.[48]

Seventeenth-century Quakers obtained political tolerance through internal discipline. As we saw in the first two chapters, seventeenth-century Puritans and Royalists alike regarded the sect as a threat to "all laws and order." The group survived by making themselves into a model of orderly familial and communal self-government. (Their mass exodus to Pennsylvania in the late seventeenth and early eighteenth centuries also did not hurt.) They adhered to the belief that marriage should be spiritually motivated, beginning with divine inspiration that shaped the couple's desires. They trusted neither the established church nor lay magistrates with the task of solemnizing those intentions, and instead instituted a communal vetting process that was far more rigorous than either its Anglican or Puritan counterparts. Couples had to declare their intentions months in advance to their families and before their local men's and women's meetings. Women's meetings, aided by officially recognized itinerant male and female ministers, ran background checks, consulted the couple's families, and offered spiritual counseling. In theory, they would only approve a match deemed likely to create a household governed by "holy conversation." Tight policing of the formation of godly and harmonious households secured familial networks and group boundaries. Such networks and boundaries were essential to Quakers' economic success and also to the legal exemptions they demanded from the imperial state on everything from the maintenance of their own poor to military service and wartime taxes, to the swearing of oaths.[49]

The power to exercise jurisdiction over their community's marriages—and thus to define the community—underpinned all other Quaker claims of autonomous jurisdiction. English Quakers had therefore vigorously opposed the many attempts to crack down on "clandestine marriage" prior to the 1753 Marriage Act, and they had won exemptions to earlier licensing measures that they had not defeated outright. This vigilance (and the Quaker lobbying machine that had given Bishop Gibson such trouble in the 1720s and 1730s) made it unsurprising that they alone among dissenting groups obtained an exemption from 1753 law.[50] The jurisdictional threat posed by the success of the Hardwicke Act, however, deserves a place alongside the Seven Years' War as an explanation for the timing and nature of the Quaker reform movement of the 1750s. Peisley and Payton certainly knew of the controversy when they sailed for the colonies, and it may explain their subsequent denunciations of lax marriage discipline as a source of communal malaise. The 1754 outbreak of war served to confirm their warnings about divine displeasure, spurring a change in Quaker leadership and policy with dramatic consequences. It pushed Quakers who wished to remain within the religious fold out of political power in Pennsylvania, leaving behind men like the future revolutionary leader John Dickinson, who had already fallen out with the community over marriage discipline.[51]

The political impetus behind efforts to purge the Society of Friends of slaveholding and of those who had married out of the faith is easy to miss because Quaker reformers explained their movement in theological terms. Lax marital discipline and slavery both tempted Quaker children away from godly ideals. Slavery had long been a controversial matter within the Quaker community because, as Ralph Sandiford had argued in the 1720s, it originated in and was sustained through violence. Reformer John Woolman condemned slavery not simply as a sin, but as a social threat to godly families. White children in slaveholding households learned to tolerate physical violence against slaves and to overlook the violence slavery did to the families of people of color. Perhaps worst of all, they became inured to the ways in which their confidence in their own righteousness rested on prosperity acquired through slavery. Quakers needed not only to free their slaves, Woolman argued, they also owed people of color restitution for the sacrifices forced on them over generations in the service of Quaker families. The French-born, English-educated Quaker saint Anthony Benezet turned such reasoning outward, using Quaker communication networks to implement what became a multilingual, international propaganda campaign for the abolition of slavery. Yet through the 1760s, Benezet remained as busy with the enforcement of marital discipline as with the censure of slaveholding Friends. Both measures helped preserve the Friends' precarious privilege of self-government at the cost of shrinking the tribe. Many raised within Quaker families left for new faith and political allegiances, carrying Quaker domestic ideals with them.[52]

The post-1753 spread of jurisdictional concerns about marriage and domestic relations into the colonies was also evident in Massachusetts. As we saw in the first chapter, Massachusetts and other Puritan New England colonies enacted radical provisions for full divorce during the English Civil Wars and did not withdraw them with the Restoration. Massachusetts did make some compromises after its near loss of its charter in the 1690s. Early condemnation of "bed and board" separations for fueling sexual temptation gave way to divorce provisions that more closely resembled the canon law proceedings of England's ecclesiastical courts, allowing separations like that in the Jacksons' case. Neighboring Connecticut, with a more secure charter, refused to make this concession, and continued the Puritan practice of granting full divorce. Despite these compromises, Massachusetts nevertheless granted full divorce on grounds that would have led only to separation in England. The years immediately following the 1753 Marriage Act mark what the historian Nancy Cott labels a "curious exception" to this pattern. From 1754 through 1757, the Massachusetts Governor's Council suddenly became scrupulous about English procedures and granted only bed and board separations; six couples with adulterous spouses turned instead to the colonial legislature for divorces that resembled those granted by Parliament. (The English Privy Council took note and exception, but apparently allowed them to stand.) Massachusetts reverted to its long-standing procedures again in 1758, after Thomas Hutchinson became lieutenant governor, and then in 1760 chief justice of the Massachusetts Superior Court. Like Samuel Sewall, Hutchinson was the proud descendent of prominent Puritan forebears, with a stake in preserving Massachusetts's distinctive legal traditions. On his watch, the number of divorce petitions heard and granted increased, and the newly conquered territory of Nova Scotia implemented a marriage law allowing full divorce on the Massachusetts model.[53]

As was typical of colonial legal proceedings, official records made no note of the reasoning behind these apparent shifts in policy. But as Hutchinson carried out his legal responsibilities, he drafted his *History of the Colony of Massachusets-Bay, from the First Settlement Thereof in 1628*, the main point of which was to defend Massachusetts's claim to independent and distinctive jurisdiction. Hutchinson's discussion of marriage law triangulated between

English rules and Scottish objections. Massachusetts's long-standing policies, he implied, could teach the English a thing or two about civilization and legal progress. He affirmed that from its beginning, Massachusetts had placed marriage under civil authority. The colony had rejected the canon law rules regarding marital separations as inhumane to the injured party and allowed full divorce without dire social consequences. He invoked the colony's 1641 prohibition against domestic violence as evidence of the "tender sentiments" of its Puritan founders. English common lawyers who defended a husband's power to "moderately correct" his wife had some catching up to do. Massachusetts's long experience led Hutchinson to concur with unnamed "Scotch writers" who argued that magistrates were no less fit to conduct marriage ceremonies than were clergy. English and Scottish anxieties about the Hardwicke Act's requirement that marriage be contracted publicly, on the other hand, seemed overblown to Hutchinson. Massachusetts's century of experience with such requirements suggested that the English could also adapt and be better for it: "Perhaps, in a few years, the people of England will be equally well satisfied with the provision made by the late Marriage Act, and no body will be at the pains of a journey to Scotland to avoid conformity with it."[54]

Hutchinson addressed slavery and marriage in adjacent paragraphs. The juxtaposition demonstrated his engagement not only with Scottish Enlightenment debates, but possibly also with Quaker critiques. The Quaker antislavery activist John Woolman had personally carried an antislavery message and printed propaganda to New England while Hutchinson was drafting his book. Hutchinson's brief discussion of slavery in Massachusetts framed it as a foreign institution. He insisted in a few sentences that the Puritan founders had thought it illegal and improvident; a footnote acknowledged John Josselyn's account of "Mr. Maverick's Negroes," citing the same page describing the rape of a slave woman discussed in chapter 1. Hutchinson did not acknowledge the local tradition of opposition to slavery established by Sewall and preserved by Sewall's grandnephew Jonathan, who had a hand in litigation by individual slaves that would take on new political significance in the 1760s. Had Hutchinson called attention to the colony's internal debates about the legality of slavery, he would have compromised his effort to portray the institution as an external imposition and undermined the colony's ability to challenge policies that turned the rules of plantation colonies into imperial norms.[55]

The Rise of Blackstone

Generations of reformers and historians have scoffed at Sir William Blackstone's attempts to portray women's legal incapacity as a privilege. However, they do not question his foundational status in American law or his formulation of the law of domestic relations, which drew tidy parallels between the law of parent and child, master and servant, and husband and wife. Blackstone's apologies for women's legal incapacities were necessary because his interpretation of them was novel and contested. His 1765 *Commentaries on the Laws of England* would become the standard work on English law and the vehicle through which Americans of the next two generations were most likely to encounter Enlightenment political ideas. But they began as an intervention in the jurisdictional conflicts and debates about religion, marriage, and slavery described in this chapter, and their application in the colonial context created problems he did not anticipate.[56]

Blackstone's personal and intellectual engagement with marital politics, as well as his ambition to "restore" coherence and harmony to the common law, emerged early in his career. Like Lord Mansfield (the head of the common-law Court of King's Bench), as a young lawyer Blackstone did some of his most lucrative business in marriage law. Unlike Mansfield, Blackstone was not a gifted speaker; he made money by drafting clever written agreements designed to circumvent equitable trusts protecting the property of married women, not through sensational criminal conversation trials. Blackstone found it difficult to be heard in the chaotic atmosphere in Westminster Hall. In 1753, he left the "bustling practical Part" of the law for the "thinking theoretical Part," and took up a lectureship at Oxford. The letter that announced his career change also discussed the 1753 Marriage Act. Hardwicke's law, Blackstone gossiped, had reportedly been printed but not "published, & that for two Reasons; first, because it is so incorrect that it will reflect dishonor somewhere," and secondly because in the antisemitic uproar that followed a law for the naturalization of Jews that passed near the same time, "the Clause exempting the Jews from the Restrictions & Penalties imposed upon the Christians, might increase the present Ferment."[57]

Blackstone's Oxford lectures became his *Commentaries on the Laws of England*. This is pertinent to our discussion of marriage and authority for two reasons. First, it reminds us that Blackstone's approach to the law began circulating via his students for years before the first volume went to press in 1765. A printed abstract was available by 1756, and his work was known in the colonies by the early 1760s, where, as the next chapters will argue, it contributed to a shift in legal culture with significant consequences for the handling of marital disputes. Second, both Blackstone's lectures and his *Commentaries* served concrete political ends. They broke with curricular requirements legally prescribed at Oxford during the seventeenth century, and Blackstone intended them to help the university gain legal autonomy. His broader ambition was to elevate the common law above rival equitable and ecclesiastical jurisdictions within England's complex legal apparatus.

Blackstone pursued this agenda from a position of jurisdictional weakness rather than strength. The business of the common-law courts at midcentury was in decline. Parliament, moreover, was addressing persistent complaints about the expense and complexity of common-law rules with new statutes that created new courts with special, equitable jurisdiction (i.e., power to challenge common-law proceedings and decisions). From Blackstone's perspective, these changes, along with others, "altered and mangled" the system.[58]

Lord Chancellor Hardwicke might have agreed with Blackstone's negative assessment of many of Parliament's interventions. Hardwicke's efforts to render the law more orderly, however, had enhanced the status and prestige of Chancery and subsidiary equitable courts by making their operations more systematic and dependent on precedent. This move was paradoxical because, as Blackstone (following Hugo Grotius) observed, equity depended so fully on "the particular circumstances of each individual case," that "no established rules and fixed precepts of equity" could be "laid down, without destroying its very essence, and reducing it to a positive law."[59] Hardwicke was well aware of this tension, but pursued his agenda nonetheless because it offered a means to rein in the "arbitrary" case-dependent exercise of legal power not only in subsidiary jurisdictions in England but also in Scotland, where there was no institutional separation between common law and equity.

Henry Home, Lord Kames, chief patron of the Scottish Enlightenment and, like many of its key players, a lawyer and judge, turned Hardwicke's program to his own ends. His 1760 treatise *The Principles of Equity* aimed to reform both Scottish and English law by effectively placing supreme lawmaking power in the hands of judges with equitable jurisdiction. His arguments conveniently elevated the Scottish Court of Sessions, Scotland's highest legal body, over both Parliament and the claims of English common law.

Blackstone's account of English law borrowed the historical frame Kames had used to develop his critique of Parliament. However, Blackstone inverted the position of common law and equity. Kames described the common law as a system developed by "our rude ancestors" to provide "regulations to restrain individuals from doing mischief and enforce the performance of covenants." It was a primitive set of rules that utterly neglected the "more refined duties of morality." Only the robust application of equitable correction could bring it in line with the economic structures and elevated sensibilities of modern society. Blackstone and critics of equity, on the other hand, argued that "law without equity, tho' hard and disagreeable, is much more desirable for the public good, than equity without law; which would make every judge a legislator, and introduce most infinite confusion; as there would then be almost as many different rules of action laid down in our courts, as there are differences of capacity and sentiment in the human mind."[60]

Kames embraced innovation and thought the common law so twisted and inconsistent as to be beyond saving; Blackstone, in contrast, portrayed his own efforts as restorative rather than innovative. Reforming the study of law in England, he suggested, simply returned it "to its ancient course."[61] Both strands of historical argument distorted subsequent understanding of domestic law. The debate placed Blackstone in an awkward position, for he faced the challenge of depicting the common law as simultaneously more ancient *and* more progressive than its competitors. To accomplish this, he invented a historical narrative that cast legal support for absolute patriarchal authority as "old," and legal protection of dependents as a "new" paternalism. As we saw in chapters 1 and 2, these aspects of householders' authority had long been two sides of the same coin, and Blackstone's account was if anything an inversion of actual trends. In the English context, the increasingly absolute authority granted to slaveholders was the novelty in the eighteenth century, and it tilted the scales to erode "ancient" protections for servants and wives.

This ironic twisting of history is particularly evident in the literal recapitulation of *Manby* found in Blackstone's influential chapter on marriage law. Unlike the author of *The Lady's Law*, Blackstone did not invite his readers to laugh at the law, nor did he follow previous treatise writers in explicitly invoking *Manby*'s authority. *Manby* was nevertheless his second-most-cited source; even his apologetic claim about women's favored status in law took its wording directly from a manuscript opinion in *Manby*.[62] By obscuring his debt to *Manby* and the treatises from which he had probably learned of the case, he gave his synopsis the weight of what appeared to be multiple "ancient" sources and distanced his own work from the ambiguities, equitable counterarguments, and general sloppiness of earlier syntheses. In his *Commentaries*, the common law provided definitive answers, and he buttressed his claims about its supremacy by omitting or dismissing the alternatives available in competing equitable and ecclesiastical jurisdictions.[63]

Blackstone was less overtly misogynistic than earlier treatise writers or the justices in *Manby*. Yet he established his enlightened "sensibility" *not* by substantively altering *Manby*'s most restrictive legal claims, but rather by insisting they represented a departure from an even starker set of ancient patriarchal norms. Progressive moderation of the "antient privilege" of husbands under the "old common law" had begun in the "more civilized reign of Charles the second." The prevailing jurists in *Manby*, in contrast, had positioned their *immoderate* claims about husbands' authority as continuous with the ancient "laws, and the genius, custom, and constitution of the people."[64] The equitable remedies that Blackstone cited as moderating innovations, moreover, were at least as ancient as the common-law precepts on which he bestowed the authority of antiquity.

Blackstone made similar historical arguments with the categories he used to organize personal law. His chapters on the law of master and servant, husband and wife, and parent and child did not follow earlier legal treatises, but rather adopted the structure found in advice manuals describing godly household government, a genre pioneered by seventeenth-century Puritan ministers and updated by both Bishop Gibson and Daniel Defoe. This ordering of domestic relationships mirrored—but also pointedly differed from— the Aristotelian parallels between master and slave, husband and wife, and parent and child found in Roman law, which in turn was the basis for canon and continental civil law. English liberties, Blackstone contended, did not countenance slavery.[65] Dependents who could not hold property were not the same as dependents who were property.

When we look closer at the fine print and at later editions, Blackstone's position on slavery shifts in response to political pressure. The outline of Blackstone's lectures published in 1756 unequivocally declared that "slavery is unknown to our laws." The first edition of the first volume of his *Commentaries* retained this claim in a general discussion of the "rights of persons" and the liberties "deeply implanted" in the English Constitution. By asserting the deep historical roots of English commitment to liberty, Blackstone placed England at the forefront of the progress of civilization within the historical schema developed by Montesquieu in his 1748 *Spirit of Laws* and by various Scots.[66] But he also made some of the more coercive aspects of the law of master and servant difficult to explain.

The logic of possessory rights solved the puzzle of how to position the law as progressive without ceding rights to subordinates—whether slave, servant, or wife. The "reason and foundation" of a master's power to litigate for a servant, to sue for damages for beating or maiming a servant, and to prosecute others who hire a servant away from him, Blackstone mused, "seems to be the property that every man has in the service of his domestics; acquired by the contract of hiring, and purchased by giving them wages."[67] This list of legal disabilities, as we have seen, was one that servants and wives shared. Blackstone did not invent the connection, but his possessory logic and tidy categories gave the parallels new legal vitality. Subsequent editions of the *Commentaries* accommodated slavery by emphasizing the possessory rights of masters. As servants became legally more like slaves, so too did wives.

   Paradoxically, antislavery activists (many of whom belonged to the marriage-
reforming Quaker lobby we saw responding to the Hardwicke Act) had a hand
in Blackstone's shift from decrying to rationalizing slavery. Anthony Benezet
made sure that statements against slavery from a wide range of sources ended
up in the hands of those in positions of power and influence on both sides of
the Atlantic. Blackstone's initial defensive assertions about English liberty might
have been reacting to Benezet's work, and his subsequent revisions of his statement certainly were. In the 1765 first edition of the *Commentaries*, Blackstone
invoked a late seventeenth-century decision in which Chief Justice William Holt
momentarily balked at efforts to enforce Virginia's slave laws on English soil and
declared (as Blackstone interpreted it) that "a slave or a negro, the moment he
lands in England, becomes a freeman; that is, the law will protect him in the
enjoyment of his person, his liberty and his property." Benezet and English abolitionist Granville Sharp saw to it that this passage from Blackstone—without
the distracting caveats about the limits servitude could impose on a freeman—
quickly received wide circulation and created problems for jurists and politicians engaged in the "bustling practical Part" of the law.[68]

   Lord Mansfield was quick to remind Blackstone that the 1729 Yorke–Talbot
opinion and subsequent rulings by Lord Hardwicke deliberately contradicted
Holt's arguments, but the admonition could not avert controversy. Blackstone's revival of Holt spurred the activities of people of color who insisted
that if they were "christened or married" in England they would become free.
It also undermined the political compromises of the 1730s at a particularly
inopportune moment. As Blackstone went to press with his second edition,
government officials promoting the deeply unpopular 1765 Stamp Act were
citing as precedent the 1732 parliamentary statute that insisted that slaves
be treated as chattel for the purpose of "the more easy recovery of debts."
The 1732 legislation, the argument went, had opened the door to safer trade
and the colonies' present prosperity—and proved the superiority of imperial authorities' long-term vision for the colonies by achieving imperial ends.
With colonial slaves and land guaranteed as collateral, English creditors lent
more freely, spurring what historians have labeled a mid-eighteenth-century
"consumer revolution" in all the colonies, as well as the growth of the slave
trade and the expansion of plantation economies. From the perspective of
rebellious colonials, English moralists seemed hypocritical. They reproved
the colonies for practices of enslavement that England had encouraged, and
they demanded increased colonial revenue while condemning the basis of
much colonial wealth.

   Neither Blackstone nor Mansfield wanted to aggravate the growing imperial crisis. Blackstone removed the antislavery passages from his *Commentaries*.

Lord Mansfield tried to limit the implications of any ruling he made from the bench. Benezet's antislavery propaganda machine, however, ultimately thwarted their efforts by keeping their strongest antislavery statements in circulation; the press once again shaped perception of the law.[69]

The Echo Chamber of the 1760s

The complaints of late eighteenth-century observers suggest that the wooden barriers mid-eighteenth-century authorities erected in Westminster Hall did little to resolve—and may even have exacerbated—the noise and the crowds. Similarly, Hardwicke's, Mansfield's, and Blackstone's efforts to impose order on the jurisdictional disorder endemic to English imperial law increased jurisdictional conflict and confusion. Blackstone's insistence on system in English law and on neatly nested hierarchies of authority within that system was symptomatic of the broader shifts in policy fueling the imperial crisis of the 1760s. Blackstone, the historian Mary Bilder has argued, exemplified the rhetorical intolerance of "dual authorities" characteristic of late eighteenth-century political thought: "There is and must be" in all governments, he wrote, "a supreme, irresistible, absolute, uncontrolled authority, in which the jura summi imperii, or the rights of sovereignty, reside." Earlier generations, in contrast, had understood colonial and imperial legal systems to be "in tension," but not incoherent.[70]

The inclination to think of the jurisdictional tensions of the 1760s in terms of conflict between "dual authorities," with the colonies on one side and the imperial state on the other, was itself a revolutionary oversimplification. It positions the competition between Parliament and colonial legislatures as the primary conflict and differentiates these "public" politics from intractable "private" debates about religion, slavery, and marriage. Histories that accept this restricted understanding of the political realm have frequently misconstrued or outright overlooked the household and religious terrain cordoned off by eighteenth-century theorists. Yet no less a political authority than John Adams contended that "the apprehension of Episcopacy . . . contributed as much as any other cause" to the American Revolution. During the 1760s, rumors that the late Bishop Gibson's long-forestalled plans to install an Anglican bishop for the colonies were about to come to fruition "roused the attention not only of the inquiring mind, but of the common people." Adams framed the issue as one of parliamentary power, not only to appoint bishops but also to "introduce the whole hierarchy, establish tithes, forbid marriages." Pennsylvania Presbyterian leader Francis Alison, writing in 1766, concurred that the issue was not simply the imposition of bishops or even parliamentary authority (as Adams's postrevolutionary story had it). Rather, Alison feared Anglicans' "political power, and their courts."[71]

Blackstone's *Commentaries* were controversial in England and popular in America precisely because of his interventions in this complex jurisdictional landscape. Like the justices in *Manby v. Scott*, Blackstone sought to make the common law, and especially common-law judges, the ultimate arbiter of political power. Blackstone turned the common law into a tool through which "English liberties" might triumph over the claims of the church, Chancery, and even Parliament (his affirmation of the sovereignty of Parliament and the Crown notwithstanding).[72] In England, robust institutions sustained equitable and ecclesiastical power, and his critique had limited effect. In the late eighteenth century, quite contrary to Blackstone's prescriptions, Parliament actually stepped up the creation of new special courts of equitable jurisdiction.[73]

However, in the colonies—particularly those where equity fell under the loose purview of local law—Blackstone's attacks on equity had striking consequences. Whereas *Manby* had championed the near-absolute authority of the household head over his dependents in order to shore up the monarchy, in Blackstone such claims helped ensure that ordinary men could not escape liability for their household debts. Blackstonean pressure to practice law without equity was an important factor in the explosion of colonial newspaper marital disputes and demand for legal divorce in the 1760s, which the next chapters will explore in greater detail.

This chapter began with courtroom metaphor applied to a transatlantic conversation about the politics of marriage. A marital metaphor applied back to transatlantic jurisdictional politics provides an apt way to wrap up this intellectual history. In the mid-1760s, Benjamin Franklin was again in London, seeking a new kind of fortune as a political agent for the colonies. Since retiring from active control of his press in 1748, he had become internationally known for his scientific investigations and had grown rather tired of his marriage. Deborah again stayed behind in Philadelphia, running their affairs on her own for the last eleven years of her life.[74] Franklin did not want for female companionship, but in 1766 he was engaged in a different sort of courtship. He had well-established personal and intellectual ties to the leading figures of the Scottish Enlightenment, and he considered the colonies' position within the empire analogous to Scotland's before the political union of 1707.[75] He could not understand, therefore, why most Enlightened Scots seemed to be taking England's part in the brewing dispute. After a patriotic English reader attacked both the Scots and the Americans in a London newspaper, Franklin, writing as "Homespun," sought to enlist the reader's sympathy. Why was it that the English despised the Scots, who (denied access to power at the center of the empire) had dispersed to "fight and die for you all over the world?" The relationship was, he suggested, like a marriage gone awry. "Remember," he admonished his English readers, "you courted Scotland for 100 years, and would fain have had your *wicked will* of her. She virtuously resisted all your importunities, but at length kindly consented to become your lawful wife. You then solemnly promised to love, cherish, and honor her, as long as you both should live; and yet you have ever since treated her with the utmost contumely, which you now begin to extend to your common children" in the colonies. The remedy, Franklin implied, might be divorce.[76]

A Matter of Credit:
Husbands' Claims

Ads of eloping wives became commonplace in the colonial newspapers by 1750, as did reports of England's emerging practice of parliamentary divorce. Both trends reflected masculine economic vulnerability. By the mid-eighteenth century, expanding imperial credit networks touched even humble households, and seemingly never-ending cycles of war and economic crisis created real peril for householders throughout the colonies. Husbands' advertisements were about preserving credibility, in every sense of the word. The efforts to systematize and expand the reach of the common law seen in the previous chapter had been significantly motivated by desire to facilitate the recovery of debt. The top-down affirmation of husbands' authority in treatises like Blackstone's *Commentaries* was also an affirmation of husbands' liability. Husbands invoked that authority in the newspapers in an attempt to evade the legal system, which then—as now—favored the wealthy and entrapped the poor. Even as they pushed back against husband's legal obligations, elopement advertisements publicly reinforced ideas about men's possessory rights to their wives.

Chapters 5 and 6 use aggregate data to examine common tropes and coded language in husbands' and wives' advertisements, and to reveal connections between household unrest and larger economic and political change. On a case-by-case basis, advertisements placed by quarreling husbands and wives appear to be personal conflicts about private grievances. Understanding the genre gives new and often surprising meaning to such stories. The more personal and remorseful a husband's ad sounded, for instance, the more likely it was to reflect his genuine legal peril for egregious misbehavior and domestic abuse.

Philip Wood's advertisement (figure 5.1) compiles the grievances most frequently cited in newspaper notices concerning wayward wives, and it is typi-

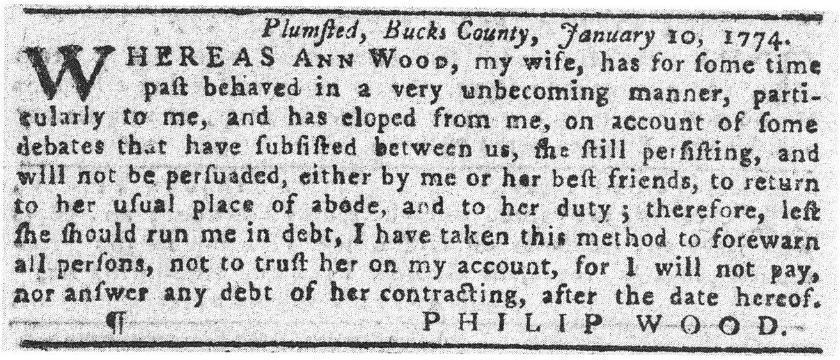

> *Plumfted, Bucks County, January* 10, 1774.
> WHEREAS ANN WOOD, my wife, has for some time paft behaved in a very unbecoming manner, particularly to me, and has eloped from me, on account of some debates that have fubfifted between us, fhe ftill perfifting, and will not be perfuaded, either by me or her beft friends, to return to her ufual place of abode, and to her duty ; therefore, left fhe fhould run me in debt, I have taken this method to forewarn all perfons, not to truft her on my account, for I will not pay, nor anfwer any debt of her contracting, after the date hereof.
> ¶   PHILIP WOOD.

FIGURE 5.1 Philip Wood advertisement, *Pennsylvania Gazette*, January 19, 1774
Courtesy of the American Antiquarian Society

cal of its genre in that it is at once evocative and enigmatic. In the winter of 1774, this prosperous yeoman farmer gave a short narrative of his marital woes in the *Pennsylvania Gazette*. "My wife," he explained, "has for some time past behaved in a very unbecoming manner, particularly to me, and has eloped from me, on account of some debates that have subsisted between us." She persisted in this misbehavior "and will not be persuaded, either by me or her best friends, to return to her usual place of abode, and to her duty. . . . Therefore," he concluded, "lest she should run me in debt, I have taken this method to forewarn all persons, not to trust her on my account, for I will not pay, nor answer any debt of her contracting, after the date hereof."[1]

Wood's advertisement serves as a cipher with which we can look past the formulaic nature of such notices to the varied circumstances that prompted husbands to post them. Wood touched on wifely misconduct, family quarrels, community concern and intervention, and the fear of financial distress. He outlined a complex plot, but disguised its details in a string of conventional phrases that provide an index to the form's common tropes, which included: (1) the attempt to deny wives' access to credit and to absolve husbands' of liability for their debts; (2) invocation of women's "elopement" and "misbehavior" to imply the kind of sexual scandal that would justify lack of spousal support; (3) expressions of remorse for household conflicts or (4) invitations to return and reconcile intended to preempt legal challenges based on domestic violence; and (5) veiled threats to anyone inclined to assist wives, which were usually a sign that a husband lacked community support.

Every ad tells stories, but not only the ones intended by its author. The genre was fraught with paradoxes. Advertisers asserted patriarchal rights to control household resources and determine where their wives and other dependents lived and worked—their "place of abode and duty," as Philip Wood put it. They cast themselves as the judges of their wives' behavior. Many went even further than Wood in their claims to private jurisdiction, threatening those who "harboured or entertained" their wives with the "Peril of the Law." Yet such stark assertions of private authority generally manifested weakness rather than strength. The very public nature of husbands' advertisements belied their claims to private jurisdiction over their households. Many, if not most, advertisements were desperate measures taken by men whose crumbling household and economic affairs threatened their solvency and their personal autonomy. When husbands' advertisements attempted to deny wives' economic agency, they testified instead to married women's claims to property and active participation in trade. Husbands addressed their invocations of domestic privacy to "friends" and neighbors who understood domestic affairs to be a communal concern.

Philip Wood shared a code with men in seventeenth-century England and the nineteenth-century United States, and this chapter's explanation of those conventions can be used to interpret ads across this historical span. Notwithstanding this continuity in form, the larger, aggregate patterns in the advertisements by colonial husbands that anchor this analysis also document significant shifts in married couples' experiences of legal peril. Husbands' advertisements were always controversial, and they were a poor means to their purported ends of preserving the man's authority, reputation, and financial credit. As the ever-apropos Daniel Defoe put it, "A Tradesman's credit, and a maid's virtue, ought to be equally sacred from the tongues of men." Husbands' advertisements turned the economic competence and the sexual virtue of both the advertiser and his wife into profane topics for tea table and tavern gossip.[2]

By the 1760s, prescriptive literature and popular fiction carried expectations about domestic virtue and discretion to new heights. Tradesmen and their families enjoyed the bawdy advice of Defoe and Franklin, but after midcentury, the educated and ambitious turned to the more refined fare offered by the emerging culture of "sensibility."[3] Massachusetts politician Thomas Hutchinson and English jurist William Blackstone both invoked this culture when they portrayed seventeenth-century legal protections for abused wives as innovations that anticipated their own refined sentiments and enlightened paternalism. But the legal remedies for women that Blackstone described as signs of progress were not new. Rather, what was new in the 1760s was the number of men, of all backgrounds, who asserted possessory rights to their wives. In England, lawsuits for criminal conversation and requests for parliamentary divorce jumped dramatically during the 1760s. Advertisements

TABLE 5.1: Husband-initiated desertion notices compared to English actions for possessory rights, 1730–1789

Year	Reported English wife sales[†]	English parliamentary divorce petitions[†]	Criminal conversations[†]	Colonial husbands' ads[*]
1739	3	5	0	49
1749	4	4	4	171
1759	2	18	7	214
1769	10	13	5	438
1779	13	35	25	411
1789	18	20	11	217

[†]Possessory rights data from Lawrence Stone, *The Road to Divorce: England 1530–1987* (Oxford: Oxford University Press, 1990), tables 6.1 (429), 9.1 (430), and 10.1 (432).

[*]Ads from Pennsylvania, Massachusetts, New Hampshire, and Virginia compiled for Sword Research Database; Ireland (1738–1770) from Ruth Watterson, "Disagreeable Necessities: The Role of Newspaper Advertisements in Regulating the Household in Eighteenth-Century America and Ireland," unpublished manuscript, with permission. Undercounting likely, especially after 1780, due to missing papers and sampling.

about wayward wives increased at a similarly striking rate, and in quantitative terms the practice was far more significant and widespread (table 5.1). In the colonies, not even the dramatic population growth and expansion of the press that occurred during these years are sufficient to explain the rising number of advertisements.

Husbands' advertisements were at once a symptom and a source of changing legal consciousness. They were a symptom of men's sense of their own legal peril in a world of expanding commercial opportunities and risks. Advertising husbands invoked the law in order to avoid being brought to court, preferring to operate in what the historian Michael Grossberg has termed "the shadow of the law" rather than face the "black letter rules" and formidable expenses associated with the formal legal system.[4]

When advertisers set popular ideology and customary claims *against* official means of law enforcement, they contributed to larger changes that were sharpening the lines between the formal law and its popular "shadow." Advertising husbands' extralegal efforts to stave off lawsuits, ironically, helped secure the ascendance of Blackstone's version of coverture. Desertion notices taught the reading public to think of marriage in ways that privileged husbands' common-law legal rights. As commonplace reminders of the potential danger of giving credit to *any* woman whose marital circumstances were not well known, elopement ads enforced coverture more effectively than legal treatises or legal authorities.

The crucial point, developed across the remaining chapters of this book, is that a legal understanding of marriage that emphasized masculine economic

	Pennsylvania	Massachusetts	New Hampshire	Virginia	Ireland (1738–1770)	Total*
1734	15	4				19
1739	25	4		0	1	30
1744	38	25		0	2	65
1749	75	28		3	0	106
1754	71	17		7	10	105
1759	55	23	3	0	28	109
1764	73	42	24	3	45	187
1769	96	29	7	11	108	251
1774	116	59	14	29	47	265
1779	80	27	8	31		146
1784	50	62	7	9		128
1789	55	27	5	2		89
Total	**749**	**347**	**68**	**95**	**241**	**1500**

*Ads from Pennsylvania, Massachusetts, New Hampshire, and Virginia compiled for Sword Research Database; Ireland (1738–1770) from Ruth Watterson, "Disagreeable Necessities: The Role of Newspaper Advertisements in Regulating the Household in Eighteenth-Century America and Ireland," unpublished manuscript, with permission. Undercounting likely, especially after 1780, due to missing papers and sampling.

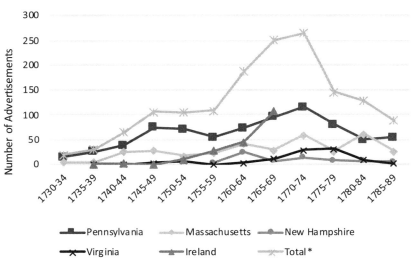

FIGURE 5.2 Colonial husband-initiated desertion notices, 1730–1789

rights and portrayed wives as a form of property did not assume full force until the mid- to late eighteenth century. Moreover, these coercive and hierarchical legal expectations emerged *simultaneously* with the eighteenth-century culture of sensibility that placed new emphasis on love and friendship as the primary basis for marriage. Advocates of sensibility imagined that by refashioning themselves and their most intimate relationships, they could bring about larger social transformation. The culture of sensibility accordingly condemned mercenary and exploitative relationships between men and women, though the alternatives it offered remained hierarchical. Husbands' complaints—and, even more strikingly, the wives' replies, discussed in chapter 6—reveal this ideology as complementing, rather than contradicting, changes in domestic law. Reverence for an intimate private world of familial refuge and feminine virtue provided an ameliorative counterpart to the legal changes underpinning the upsurge in husbands' advertisements.[5]

"Lest she should run me in debt": Credibility and Masculine Vulnerability

Advertisers' stories of desertion and wifely misbehavior can make it easy to forget that their ads were fundamentally an economic instrument, which husbands used to protect themselves as well as to punish their wives. The defining common element in all advertisements of wayward wives was the literal discrediting they prescribed. Whatever their various specific grievances, all advertisers warned the public "not to trust" or "give credit" to their wives on their accounts. Marital separation was not always the reason for this admonition. In many cases, husbands' ads reflected economic collapse *more* than marital discord. Ads' economic function, moreover, explains why the practice of advertising wayward wives flourished despite persistent questions about its legitimacy. Ads became commonplace during the eighteenth century as transatlantic commercial expansion drew increasing numbers of people into ever more vulnerable networks of credit and debt.

The legal arguments that shaped Woods' mid-eighteenth-century conflict echoed those we saw in case studies from the previous century. They were distinguished by the scale of their potential impact. The notices Christopher Lawson posted around Boston in 1656 caused a local stir. Philip Wood's advertisement reached thousands of newspaper subscribers and perhaps ten times as many newspaper readers across five colonies. In the seventeenth century, merchants like Lawson had credit networks with that kind of geographic reach, but few others did. By the mid-eighteenth-century, dramatic expansion in the colonial population and in the transatlantic commercial economy had drawn not only farmers like Philip Wood, but men from across the economic

spectrum into intricate webs of credit and debt, and into contact with local courts that had expanded to accommodate them. These developments
expanded opportunities for and expectations of masculine autonomy, and at
the same time, as the historian Bruce Mann has demonstrated, "multiplied
the risk of failure." It was now possible for "more people to fail owing greater
sums of money to larger numbers of creditors than" ever before.[6]

Credit sustained commerce and cemented social networks in the cash-
poor colonial economy. Credibility provided social as well as monetary currency to people in every walk of life, and communities depended on mutual indebtedness. For those in good community standing, accounts were
frequently left unsettled for years or even decades. Benjamin Franklin, for
example, made a conscious policy of floating debts to foster the goodwill and
loyalty of the many people who owed him money. When he died in 1790, he
made a final jest of bequeathing his unsettled accounts to the Pennsylvania
Hospital. This amounted to suggesting that his debtors make charitable do-
nations, because it quickly became clear to the hospital's overseers that not
much profit would be made by aggressively pursuing accounts that had been
outstanding, in many cases, for forty or fifty years.[7]

Damaged credit could have devastating financial and personal consequences regardless of where a husband fell along the social spectrum, and the
risks were amplified further by the growing commercial use of transferable
written credit instruments. Debts recorded in store or tradesmen's account
books tended to be anchored to a particular set of social relationships. As-
signable promises to pay originated in such contexts, but when they circulated in the wider marketplace, it became "difficult for debtors to know when
they would return for repayment or from what quarter they would come. All
that was certain was that reports of a debtor's distress would bring all of his
promises back at once."[8] Most free men had reason to fear the demands from
creditors that would accompany compromised community standing.

The marked increase in the number of colonial husbands who were willing to risk their standing by advertising their wives in the 1760s reflected de-
rangement in the economic system and a new concern with order in the legal
system. By the 1750s, the explosion of litigation in the colonial courts had
turned lawyering into a profitable occupation. Although most litigants still
represented themselves, this midcentury expansion of the legal profession
helped increase the degree of legal literacy required to negotiate the courts.
Increased colonial concern with legal forms, as well as interest in the lessons about the law taught by Scottish and English lawyers like Kames and
Blackstone, made going to law more complex, just as a global economic crisis
made it more necessary. Imperial efforts to protect metropolitan creditors

compounded these problems in the 1760s by demanding greater accountabil-
ity and plunging the colonies into a deep depression.[9]

In this context, it is easy to understand how advertisements became a
widespread remedy that appealed to the prosperous and the poor alike. The
1,240 colonial wife denunciations analyzed in depth for this book were scattered among 460 towns and one hundred counties, documenting the success
of newspapers as a form of regional communication. Moreover, advertisers
closely reflected the free white male population at large in their range of occupations and distribution of wealth. English and colonial advertisers together
represented more than one hundred occupations. The list includes yeoman
and farm laborers, sea captains and sailors, merchants, ministers, bricklayers,
and butchers, though most American men seem to have worked the land or
the sea. And whether they lived in cities or the countryside, in Pennsylvania
or Massachusetts, there were no statistically significant differences between
the colonial advertisers who appeared on tax lists and their fellow "taxables"
in the range of their property holdings.[10]

While husbands of all backgrounds found these ads useful, their notices
reveal important distinctions in what credit and its loss meant to men of different statuses. Advertisers mirrored the economic divisions within their communities. The scale along which most of the population measured rank was
one of *competency*, a fluid ideal that encompassed financial independence,
material comfort, and status. As the historian Daniel Vickers has explained,
competency was grounded in the capacity for self-employment, in householders' possession of "sufficient skill and property to ensure that neither they
nor their spouses regularly had to look abroad" for work. It assumed the ability to accumulate enough wealth to launch one's children on their own path to
independence, and to cushion the household through hard times. Possession
of a competency enabled householders to "approach their neighbors for the
exchange of goods and services on an equal footing, because for the basic
opportunity to earn a living throughout the working hours that dominated
life they depended upon nobody." Competency meant independence, but not
self-sufficiency. It was achieved through collective family enterprise, though
most of its rewards fell to the male household heads who were assumed to
direct the labor of their dependents and redistribute its fruits. And it secured
a household's place in the interdependent community networks of exchange
that made material comfort possible; it conferred credibility, and with it respect and authority.[11]

The colonial advertisers who can be traced to surviving tax lists fell along a
spectrum that ranged from householders whose wealth allowed them to control not only their own labor but also that of others, to transient laborers with

no claims to property other than that in their own persons and (perhaps) in their wives and children. Those whose property holdings placed them among the top 30 percent of taxpayers were prosperous. Samuel Hindsdale, one of the wealthier advertisers in Massachusetts, had more than an ample competency. In the year he advertised his wife for the second time, he owned sixty-five acres of productive land, four horses, two cows, thirty-seven sheep, two pigs, and two ironworks and had two hundred pounds lent at interest. These resources probably enabled him to employ not only his large family—he had nine children from his first marriage and two from his troubled second one—but his neighbors as well. His property certainly produced surplus sufficient to buy some "luxuries" as well as "necessaries," and to provide insurance against hard times. His wealth also earned him a place in local leadership and eventually in colonial government. His duties in the Massachusetts House of Representatives might explain why his wife was "absent from him and at a distance" in the summer of 1771; he, not she, had left home.[12]

Advertisers between the fiftieth and seventieth percentiles of taxpayers generally held enough property to employ themselves and their families in good times, but their grasp on this competency was less secure. Hardship could send them tumbling into the lower ranks. The bottom half of the taxable population consisted of those who possessed little more than their freedom. Timothy Cavenaugh of Chester County, Pennsylvania, had a horse and a dozen acres of land, but identified himself as a "labourer."[13] When he advertised his wife in 1772, Benjamin Houghton might have had a horse and two cows, or he might have had nothing, depending on which name on the Lancaster, Massachusetts, list referred to him. In either case, he was deemed too poor to pay tax. The precise proportion varied from place to place, but like Houghton, between 10 and 35 percent of those who appeared on the tax lists had no taxable property at all.

Many advertisers were missing from the tax lists; of these, many were transient and, for the most part, poor. It was not in their interest to be found and taxed, nor was it worth the tax collector's time to track them down. Particularly in Philadelphia, several seem to have been recent immigrants from Germany or Ireland who lacked familiarity with the language.[14] Some 20 percent of the advertisers for whom occupational information can be obtained identified themselves as mariners, whose absences at sea rendered them nearly invisible to authorities.[15]

Uriah Snow was unusual in that he left a record of the itinerancy that led to his omission from the 1771 Massachusetts tax valuation. When he advertised his wife in that year, he described himself as "lately resident in Milton, but now of Boston." Two years before, Snow had been "warned out" of Boston by local officials, who gave him fourteen days to leave. Their records stated that he was "Last of Medford," suggesting that he moved frequently and that he had no fixed residence to which he could return. "Warning out" served as formal notice that the town government did not recognize a person as a resident and would not provide them with poor relief. So long as such illegal migrants could support themselves, the authorities might ignore their continued presence. Should they seem likely to require public assistance, however, they might find themselves loaded onto a cart and shipped to the last community to claim them.[16] Fearing such a consequence, Uriah Snow was probably not eager for further encounters with Boston town officers. And because he and his family were more likely to be a liability than a source of revenue, neither Boston nor any other town was eager to acknowledge him as a taxpaying resident.

For men in this uncounted underclass, and many of those in the lower ranks of the tax list, wife ads were evidence of a marital double bind. These were laborers of one type or another who needed to sell their labor—and that of their dependents—to survive. Their status as husbands was often the only thing marking them as householders and free men. Yet the obligation to support their dependents, particularly those who lived apart from them, was sufficient to threaten their freedom. Their ads were self-protective attempts to absolve themselves of these responsibilities, though at the cost of any pretensions to household authority and competency that they might have had.

John Taylor, a Delaware farmer, expressed the link between wives' subordination and husbands' freedom more concretely than most. "My wife," he complained, "has eloped any servitude in my house, [that] a housewife ought to do" and also "threatened to take on . . . debt to that degree to make a servant of me." His inability to control his dependents' labor and actions threatened him with dependency. Taylor referred here to formal debt servitude, in which local authorities were required by statute to indenture insolvent debtors to anyone willing to buy their labor by paying their debts. In Massachusetts and Pennsylvania, involuntary service of this sort had ceased to be formally sanctioned legal practice in the 1730s, but debtors still faced imprisonment. Throughout the colonies, confinement remained the standard means of coercing insolvent debtors to satisfy their creditors well into the nineteenth century. Most debtors obtained release from prison by relying on family and friends to scrape together the funds to rescue them or by turning over their assets. For those without such resources, informal private contracts promising labor for relief seem to have been a common strategy—though one that is difficult to document. The persistence of forms of debt peonage in the maritime industries in particular could account for the large numbers of mariners who discredited their wives. Such advertisers sought to avoid putting their labor at the disposal of their creditors, who might retain them from one voyage to the next to pay debts their wives accrued during their absences at sea.[17]

Numerous husbands blamed their wives for reducing them to "great Poverty and Distress," for the breakup of their households, and in some cases for actual imprisonment. The "misconduct" of his wife, claimed George Beck, forced him "to follow a circumstance in life" that left him "unable to pay any more debts." Abiall Smith, "by her great Mismanagement[,] obliged her . . . Husband to break up House keeping." George Simon Tampler declared that he had been forced to bind out his children to pay for his wife's extravagance. And Benjamin Crawfourd, a self-described "poor Man," had been "put in Prison" because his wife had "run [him] to unnecessary Expences." Crawfourd did "not chuse to mention" what those expenses were, but in other cases a wife's "imprudence" in "boarding herself and children out" was sufficient to get her husband "committed to Goal."[18]

In most of these instances, it is impossible to determine whether marital discord and wifely misbehavior were the causes of a household's poverty, or merely side effects of it. Uriah Snow claimed in his 1771 advertisement that his wife Lucy had "absented herself from the Family repeatedly for several Years past, and now broke it up." Yet Snow was himself transient and it is possible that Lucy Snow's "absences" were simply efforts to find support and lodging her husband could not provide. Martha Willington, the wife of another member of the transient working poor, explained the matter this way in a response to her husband's 1762 advertisement: "Altho' I am very sensible that neither he nor I are of much Importance to the Public, for he has not an Estate to entitle me to any Credit on his Account; yet I desire . . . to let the Publick know, That I never run him in Debt one Farthing in my Life, nor ever eloped unless it was to Day Labour, to support me and the Children, which I am of Necessity obliged to do." Willington assured the public that she would "be ever glad to do my Duty to [my husband], if only he would for the future behave to me in such a manner that I may do it with more Ease than heretofore."[19] When he renounced responsibility for his own wife, Uriah Snow may have been attempting to avert a forced move from Boston. Local authorities would have been unlikely to have much sympathy, however, for such an effort to distinguish his ability to support himself from his ability to support his dependents.

Regardless of the root cause, unresolved marital conflicts could destroy a poor man's aspirations to competence. The propertied laborer Timothy Cavenaugh, for example, slid down and ultimately off the scale of taxpaying householders. He and his wife spent eight years separating and reconciling, and by the time of their final breakup Timothy had lost his horse and twelve

acres of land. The last Chester County tax list on which he appeared registered him as an "inmate," or a dependent worker on another's property.[20]
After this he vanished from the records, suggesting that he had either moved
on or died without sufficient property to merit a will or an inventory. Collectively, the husbands shown by the 1772 Philadelphia tax list to have little or
no property were almost twice as likely as comparable taxpayers eventually to
turn up on the registers of the city's poor. Nearly two-thirds of these advertisers received some sort of poor relief, and several ended up in the workhouse
or almshouse.[21]

In prosperous households, ads could serve to shelter the husband from
creditors, as a means to control an overly independent and possibly "extravagant" wife, or simply as an affirmation of a husband's authority. Husbands
who had property sometimes expressed fear of "Ruin," and a few faced poverty or prison. In contrast with poorer men, however, only about 5 percent
of the prosperous advertisers on this list received institutional aid—a proportion that was not significantly different from that for other prosperous
taxpayers. Most of those who possessed a competency found the financial
consequences of their marital conflicts less dire, and their misfortunes were
not due solely to the loss of a wife's labor or the costs of separate maintenance.
Prosperous advertisers were more likely to be concerned with wives who controlled property or who were active participants in "trade," either as part of
a family enterprise or in their own right. These men sought to preserve their
own fortunes or means of livelihood, and perhaps also secure access to their
wives' estates.

According to her husband, Grace Lyon had "at sundry Times, without . . .
consent, presumed to Trade," giving "her Obligation," running him into debt,
and causing him "Damage." Vinkler Jones forbade the public from "trans-
acting any Business" with his wife Elizabeth, in the process indicating her
substantial involvement in his financial affairs. He deemed it necessary to
explain not only that he would not pay her debts, but also that he refused to
honor her receipts for payment of debts due to him, or accept responsibility
for "Orders . . . either for Money or Goods, or any Thing else of what Nature
so ever" that she made in his name. Similarly, Samuel Blaker warned "persons
indebted to him" that "they may depend on paying said debts again" if they
made payments to his wife Catherine. He claimed that she had "clandestinely
got into her possession bonds of her husband's, and received the money for
the same, and refused to give him any account of it."[22]

Grace Lyon, Elizabeth Jones, and Catherine Blaker all possessed economic agency one would not expect if one took Blackstone's account of the
law of coverture at face value. The timing of their husbands' advertisements

condemning their "dealings" as "presumptuous" and "unlawful," moreover, may well reflect heightened concern with common-law rules related to the arrival of Blackstone's *Commentaries* in the colonies. Their ads appeared between 1767 and 1773. Blackstone's first English edition appeared in four volumes between 1765 and 1769, and was available almost immediately through Scottish booksellers in all the colonial regions.[23]

These three cases are significant less as evidence of the formal limits on married women's commercial activities than of the fact that married women's economic participation remained fairly routine. Colonial wives still unabashedly performed not only essential, unpaid reproductive labor—"the servitude in my house that a housewife ought to do"—but also made measurable and necessary contributions to household accounts through other means. New England women's textile production, in particular, increased in its scope and ambition during the eighteenth century; dairying, brewing, and midwifery remained common female occupations. And if circumstances required, it was not only possible but *expected* that a wife would serve as her husband's "deputy," acting in his stead to transact the business that sustained their joint interests.[24] Eighteenth-century commercial growth in the colonial seaports of Philadelphia and Charleston made married women's independent economic activity so frequent that legislatures in both Pennsylvania and South Carolina enacted statutes clarifying the legal powers and obligations of "feme sole" traders. Elsewhere, prosperous and legally savvy men used written powers of attorney to delegate authority to their wives when their economic concerns drew them away from home, or, as we saw in the case of Elizabeth Lawson, when a wife had reason to travel. Grace Lyon seems to have been empowered by such a formal instrument; her husband's ad revoked "a former Power, I gave to [her] to transact for me in my absence." It is not clear, however, that such formalities were always observed or deemed necessary by communities in which couple's joint identities were well established.[25]

Grace Lyon and Elizabeth Jones, in fact, seem to have been posted *not* because of straightforward situations in which wives were overstepping legal bounds of their ability to transact, but because their husbands found themselves in trouble with creditors. Wives' financial mismanagement might have been partially responsible for their straightened financial circumstances, but it was unlikely to have been the sole cause. Complaints about female extravagance were a familiar and convenient cultural trope on both sides of the English Atlantic. Daniel Defoe's *Moll Flanders* once again offers us a fictional story that resembles an actual case. Elizabeth Jones's situation was reminiscent of an episode in which Moll colluded with her spendthrift second husband first in wasting their joint estate (most of which had been her inheritance from her first husband) and then in his desertion. With bankruptcy pending, Moll squirreled away what assets she could, some of them without her husband's knowledge and others at his behest. Yet when his creditors came to seize the property, Moll played the part of an innocent, abandoned, and helpless wife. Like her fictional counterpart, Elizabeth Jones had apparently known of her husband's financial difficulties and agreed to arrangements she thought were meant to protect her from them. She claimed that he had deliberately sent her away after having her make payments "by his Order." These had proved "to be bad" and "he was afraid of being taken up [arrested], and that there would be farther Trouble about it." What she had thought was a strategy to shelter her from his financial and legal problems turned out to be an attempt to use her as a scapegoat for them.[26]

Cases in which a wife stood accused of stealing or concealing assets often marked instances in which she was shielding property from her husband's creditors, whether the husband desired it or not. Virginian John Berrow, for example, complained that after he fell "under Misfortunes," his wife had "made away with several of my Goods." And a New Jersey advertiser noted that his wife had carried away "with her sundry . . . effects, some of which were under execution." There is no way to know whether these women were colluding with their husbands in their flight from "Misfortune," but they do illustrate the self-protective function of husbands' ads. Berrow promised to "prosecute . . . to the utmost Rigour of the Law" those discovered to be retaining his property, a move that tacitly assured his creditors of his efforts to find the means to repay them.[27]

At the same time, Berrow's ad acknowledged that many people were willing to "harbor" his wife and the "Goods" she had taken. Such cases mark conflicts within families, within communities, and between legal traditions over women's entitlement to separate marital property. In most such disputes, the "Goods" and "Effects" wives took with them were things they regarded as their own. Husbands' lists of embezzled items typically included "Household Furniture," "a bed and bedding," or "a part of her best clothes." This was personal, "moveable" property of the sort women brought with them into marriage (one husband acknowledged as much in his ad), and wives retained customary claim to it.[28] In eighteenth-century England, wealthy families increasingly protected their married daughter's separate property with complex equitable agreements like those in Catherine Scott's seventeenth-century case. American wife ads, with very few exceptions, did not refer to such formal arrangements. They did, however, set the interests of wives and their supporters against those of husbands and their creditors in ways that echoed conflicts between the wifely prerogatives upheld under equity and the common law as defined in *Manby v. Scott* and redefined by Blackstone.

Samuel Blaker seems to have been more concerned with asserting masculine competence and control than with direct threats from his creditors, but he too faced a community that believed his wife had a claim to separate property. Five years after his initial posting, Samuel published a second advertisement conceding as much. The bonds he accused Catherine of "clandestinely" concealing from him, he now admitted, belonged to her in "her own proper right, being a part of her dowry by a former husband." (And her debts, he had found, "were only such as were necessary towards housekeeping.") He had "been misled by evil disposed counsellors" when he published his first advertisement, but now "upon more prudent examination of my wife's conduct, found her to be innocent and faultless."[29]

Some months later, Samuel drafted a will that again affirmed Catherine's claim to separate property and suggested that the "evil disposed counsellors" on whom he blamed their disagreement might have been his own children from a prior marriage. Samuel made a generous settlement of cash and land on Catherine and bequeathed to her "his Household Goods and Furniture of every Sort . . . , and also *her* Beds and Furniture, &c." This distinction between his furniture and hers formally recognized her right to the property she had brought to the marriage. Moreover, Samuel carefully stated that money he had given to Catherine prior to drafting the will was also part of her inheritance, quite possibly to dispel any doubts about who had claim to the bonds and money that had been the source of their dispute.[30]

Samuel left only token amounts to all but one of his adult children, reserving what remained for his grandchildren. This uneven distribution of goods probably reflected property already settled on his children, their relative need for support, and perhaps also a desire to keep property away from his daughters' husbands. One son-in-law was singled out for particular ire, accused (like Catherine before) of "unjustly detaining" bonds from Samuel and of refusing to repay a sizeable debt. According to Samuel, this relative took advantage of "my Weakness and Infirmities," knowing "that I cannot stir about to look for and recover" the missing documents. After Samuel's death, Catherine and her coexecutor advertised the offender in the *Pennsylvania Gazette*, implying that he had stolen the bonds and warning the public not to use them as a basis for crediting him.[31] If this son-in-law was one of the "counsellors" that Samuel had blamed for his effort to discredit Catherine, the tables had now fully turned.

While the personal details of the situation are lost to us, Samuel's ad and will together make clear that his age—he was well into his seventies—and "Infirmities" were probably salient issues in both controversies. His wife and son-in-law might have been trying to cheat him (and each other), or simply working around the failing judgment of an elderly man. When seen from this perspective, his advertisements testify as much to his anxiety about age-related loss of competence and authority as to his actual power as a patriarch.

In either event, Blaker's anxieties illustrated the fears about debt that made the concerns expressed in advertisements at once universal and particular. Masculine identity and economic status were closely intertwined regardless of where a husband fell along the economic spectrum, and all men feared sliding down, or off, the scale of competency. Yet the specific financial grievances of advertisers varied, and in many instances—especially for the prosperous—worries about debt and credit were peripheral to other reasons for advertising. Forty percent of those whose ads mentioned the fear of a wife's debts used the future tense; they did not claim that their wives had done them economic harm, just that they "perhaps may want to" do so, "as was usual in such cases" of marital conflict and separation.[32] When an advertiser tacked the prospect of financial injury onto a laundry list of other complaints, as Philip Wood did with the phrase "lest she should run me in debt," it was a strong indication that he was more interested in punishing his wife than in self-protection.

"Behaved in a very unbecoming manner . . . and has eloped from me": Implied Sexual Scandal

Sarah Wiggin did not know whether or not her husband "had any particular meaning by the word Eloped," but having been informed that "it means a married Woman's leaving her Husband, and living with an Adulterer," she assured the readers of the *New-Hampshire Gazette* that her "Character is too well established to be blasted by his Suspicions." Virginian Thomas Elliot discredited his wife Mary for her misconduct but carefully noted that he did not "accuse her of incontinency." John Stickney of Newbury, Massachusetts, explained that he had "advertised the publick, that Joanna my wife had eloped from me" because the word was "commonly used on such occasions." He subsequently deemed it necessary to "publickly declare, that I think she is a chaste woman." He "did not design any thing to the contrary" with his advertisement, but merely "intended to signify that she went without my knowledge." Like Samuel Blaker, Stickney blamed his children from a previous marriage for the conflict. Philadelphia storekeeper Edward Jones also found it necessary to clarify a general warning forbidding the public "from trusting any one on his Account, without . . . [a written] Order from him." To his dismay, "Some disaffected Persons . . . reported that" the advertisement was "put in . . . wholly upon [his] Wife's Account," when he had meant it only to signify a change in his business practices.[33]

Whether a husband wished it or not, ads were about more than just financial matters. Market values and family values were not divisible. Postings of wives and—as Edward Jones's ad suggests—newspaper discreditings in general operated within a legal framework that assumed they were rooted in sexual scandal. A wife's infidelity was the surest (and by some lights the only), legal reason for refusing to support her. As we saw in chapter 3, it was certainly implied by the term *elope*, which was by far the most common charge advertisers brought against their wives. Fifty-five percent of colonial English-language advertisers used this word. Another 20 percent accused their wives of leaving them but employed different language. Such women "absconded," "departed," "left," "absented," or "refused to live with" their husbands; more rarely they had "run away," "abandoned," "deserted," or "forsaken" them. Sometimes these alternative words reflected a strategic decision to avoid the charge of "elopement"; in other instances the terms were used interchangeably. Most of the remaining 15 percent justified discrediting with references to wifely misbehavior. Their ads were also colored by the implication of adultery, making it necessary for men who did not accuse their wives of "incontinency" to take exception to the form.[34]

Despite these underlying assumptions, relatively few notices appear to have been prompted by actual infidelity. Only 7 percent of colonial advertisers explicitly accused their wives of adultery in the papers. In cases traced to other records, evidence of adultery surfaced no more than 12 percent of the time.[35] While the fragmentary nature of the sources probably accounts for part of this discrepancy between the actual and implied justification for advertising, the grievances underlying most postings clearly bore only a loose relationship to such formal legal requirements.[36]

Advertisers' tendency to broadly construe their prerogatives as husbands at the expense of legal niceties does not mean that they were unaware of the "particular meanings" of the words and phrases they employed. Thomas Jacob "revoked" an ad he had placed a year earlier, noting that his wife had merely "absented" herself and not "eloped." Presumably, his wife had *not* committed adultery, and he wished to clear her reputation (as well as his own). In the wake of the controversy over Peter Henry Dorsius's advertisement (see chapter 3), Jacob had learned that his own ad might not have been approved by a magistrate. Jacob blamed ignorance for his error, and it is quite probable that he—and many like him—made technically inaccurate claims in careless imitation of other ads.

Nevertheless, Jacob's case also shows that advertisers became legally educated when they needed to be. Newspaper discreditings appealed to most advertisers as a way to keep their marital problems out of the courts; if a wife was prevented from running up debts in his name, a husband was that much less likely to be sued for her support. When circumstances threatened to transform an ad from a convenient form of extralegal action into a cause for legal action against the husband, he might retract his notice. Thomas Jacob apparently feared that the heightened legal scrutiny given to ads in the wake of the Dorsius–Hogeland dispute made him vulnerable to suits from his wife's supporters and perhaps also to charges of slander. He found reclaiming liability for his wife himself preferable to having it forced upon him at law.[37]

Most advertisers performed a precarious balancing act, claiming just enough legal authority to make their notices appear legitimate, while trying to avoid giving a wife or her allies a basis on which to challenge them. The delicacy of this balance helps explain, on the one hand, the willingness of some advertisers to admit to having been cuckolded and, on the other, the imprecise nature of the charges found in most ads. Like Thomas Jacob, John McGlaughlin posted a second advertisement a year after his first attempt to discredit his wife. In contrast with Jacob, he seemed almost delighted to be able to announce that he now had "sufficient" evidence "of her Infidelity to my Bed" to remain "fully determined not to pay any Debts" she may contract. McGlaughlin's need to take out a second advertisement indicates that his first posting—based on his wife's threats to "run me in Debt in order to send me to Goal [sic]"—was not entirely effective. The second, with its explicit charge of adultery, left no trail in surviving court records, suggesting that at minimum the ad helped keep him out of jail for debt.[38]

"Unbecoming," Philip Wood's adjective, was the single most common descriptor used in accusations of wifely misbehavior, and like most explanations it was purposefully vague. It left room for readers to imagine that husbands had legal grounds for their actions, without explicitly stating what those grounds were. Adultery was certainly "unbecoming" conduct, but only two of the forty-five American advertisers who used this expression explicitly stated that that was the issue. Others used more suggestive vocabulary: twenty-two advertised wives in my American sample were "disorderly," nine "indecent," seven "indiscreet," six "shameful," and four "scandalous." Seven went "strolling about from house to house" and five kept "bad" or "lewd company."[39] In some cases, several epithets appeared together. William Pyle, for example, accused his wife Hannah of "strolling about the country, and sometimes the city of Philadelphia, drinking to excess, and keeping bad company, in an odious and scandalous manner." Hannah's behavior tested the limits of what her community would tolerate, but it is noteworthy that William did not accuse her directly of "keeping company with other men," a statement (used by five other advertisers) that would have solidified his case. Even "keeping company" was a far cry from the allegations of a New York man who reported that his wife had been found "Naked in Bed" with another man, who "was immediately confined to Gaol."[40]

Investigation into records outside the newspapers indicates that William was being deliberately ambiguous. This was his second attempt to discredit Hannah, twenty-two years into a tumultuous marriage that endured (at least in name) from 1749 until his death in 1789. The couple's difficulties began shortly after they were wed. In 1753 they were censured by their Quaker meeting for having "fallen into divers errors," Hannah "by taking strong liquor" and William "by giving way to an unguarded passion & c." William first posted Hannah in the newspapers in 1757, and she responded with a lawsuit. As she explained it, he had allowed an "idle strumpet" to assume her rightful place in his household, and they had driven her out with beatings and abuse. Proving that *he* was the adulterer helped her win a separate maintenance.[41]

The couple cycled through separations and reconciliations for the rest of their married life, and the early 1770s marked a period of particular conflict. With the 1771 advertisement quoted earlier, William tested his community's memory and resolve with regard to his obligation to support Hannah. She seems to have returned to him in the wake of the advertisement, perhaps because she could no longer find people to "trust her on his account." A year later she again left him—or was turned out, depending on whom one believes. William then took out a third newspaper notice, this time stating that she had "eloped." A few months later, Hannah took him to court on the grounds that he "refuseth me any support & will not alow me to live with him & my Age and bodily weakness Renders me unfit to support my Self." She was awarded alimony yet again, and she succeeded in having the amount raised two years later.[42]

William's notices were crafted with apparent thought to their legal implications. His first two remained technically accurate in their description of his grievances against Hannah, although those complaints did not give him certain grounds for refusing to support her. His third advertisement used legally acceptable language, but because Hannah had not committed adultery, her behavior did not match the formal charge. This last legal battle followed shortly after the release of the Philadelphia edition of Blackstone's *Commentaries*, and the timing suggests that the consciousness about legal forms that it inspired might have played a role in William Pyle's renewed assertion of his powers as a husband.[43] All of William's ads had mixed results. They complicated Hannah's attempts to support herself and were evidently honored to an extent sufficient to prompt her to resort to the courts. Within the legal system, however, the extralegal evidence that William was serious about *not* supporting Hannah turned against him. Blackstone's admonitions notwith-standing, the authorities in Chester County, Pennsylvania, still deemed fe-male poverty a greater problem than wifely behavior that, while "unbecom-ing," was not unmistakably illegal.

"Some debates that have subsisted between us": Domestic Violence

William and Hannah Pyle, like most of the couples whose marital difficulties found their way into the press, were clearly no strangers to argument. Never-theless, husbands' advertisements very seldom referred to the "debates" un-derlying the disintegration of their households. Philip Wood's use of the term was unique, and he was one of just twelve colonial advertisers (1 percent) who referred in some way to "disputes," "disagreements," or a wife's refusal to "live peaceably at home." (In contrast, 155 advertisers [13 percent] bluntly asserted that their wives had acted "without cause.") As was true of William Pyle's careful avoidance of reference to adultery, husbands whose ads openly acknowledged household quarrels seem to have been trying to deflect atten-tion from their own questionable behavior. More than half of these notices provoked responses from wives—a rate of challenge that was several times that for the overall pool of newspaper denunciations. The women's answers verified that these were cases where the community recognized a two-sided "debate," and might not accept a husband's unilateral condemnation of his wife's behavior.

Mention of "disputes," in fact, seems to have been an oblique reference to domestic violence. All the cases where wives responded involved violent households. In five—including that of Philip and Ann Wood—wives cen-sured their husbands for far exceeding the "moderate correction" heads of household were allowed to exercise on their dependents. In the other two, documents point to physically aggressive wives, one of whom was aided by members of her natal family in attacking her husband. In comparison, vio-lence beyond the bounds of community norms also surfaced in 12 percent of the Pennsylvania cases that were cross-checked against court records and in just over half of the cases in which wives used the press to respond to their husbands' charges.

Most advertisers structured their notices so as to preserve the illusion of complete authority, although all ads marked instances where their power was in question. Labeling a wife as disorderly or disobedient carried a subtly dif-ferent message than the statement that husband and wife "could not agree."[44] When husbands acknowledged "debates" with their wives, they were admit-ting to a greater degree of household disruption and tacitly accommodating a public who may well have been aware of and involved in their disputes. In Philip Wood's case, mention of "debates" was just one of several clues that marked his advertisement as exceptional.

"Will not be persuaded, either by me or her best friends, to return": Preempting the Law

More than any other aspect of his ad, Philip Wood's reference to his own and to friends' efforts to persuade his wife to return draws attention to the form's awkward position between informal and legal means of mediating household disputes. With this phrase, Wood evoked a long-standing practice in which separation and community-mediated reconciliation were routine ways of negotiating power with households. At the same time, the Woods' story demonstrates how husbands' use of ads to assert their independent jurisdiction over their households could propel such disputes into formal legal channels. Ads' propensity to escalate marital conflicts helps explain how—eventually—the courts became where, and divorce became how, separating couples settled their grievances. In the vast majority of eighteenth- and early nineteenth-century newspaper marital disputes, however, mediation remained in the hands of "friends" rather than the courts.[45] A teleological emphasis on the rise of divorce risks misunderstanding ads' importance in a world where divorce was seldom a goal, even where it was an imaginative and legal possibility.

Wives—much like slaves and servants—used temporary separations as a means of coping with household discord and violence. Historians have observed that dissatisfied slaves and servants frequently ran away for brief periods, using such "strikes" as leverage in attempts to win better treatment. Slaveholders' journals indicated that advertised runaways counted for only a small fraction of those who absented themselves.[46] In cases of marital conflict, the best evidence of "absenting" as a negotiating strategy comes from the newspapers themselves.

Elopement notices document the use of temporary separations as a strategy for negotiating points of conflict and for inviting outside intervention. Ninety-five (8 percent) of the couples whose marital problems appeared in the press left evidence of multiple separations and reconciliations. Hannah Pyle, whom we met earlier, provides an unusually well-documented example of a wife who "absented herself" from her husband "sundry times," and of community expectations that made even the most miserable marriages indissoluble. Hannah and William's family and Quaker meeting mediated their disputes for years, and Hannah appears to have gone to live with her mother on at least one occasion before the press and the law became involved. This early estrangement would have gone unrecorded were it not for Hannah's 1758 suit for alimony, in which husband and wife both submitted lists of accumulated grievances. Hannah's lawsuit was an extraordinary measure, but it was seen by none of the parties as an attempt to end the marriage. The language of her award framed it as a provisional remedy that would last "during the Present Separation." William's obligation to make payments would end "Upon a Reconciliation," an incentive that appears to have helped reunite the couple in the following decade. Hannah and William's renewed conflict in the press and the courts during the 1770s might have marked a permanent breach between them, but it still did not end the marriage in the eyes of the law. In 1782, when William drafted his will, he made careful provision for her, apparently taking into account her court-awarded maintenance and her litigiousness. The conventional reference to her as the "beloved" wife was conspicuously absent from the document, which acknowledged that their marriage endured but attempted to bar Hannah's dower.[47]

William and Hannah Pyle exemplified the early American—and early modern—predominance of a structure of marriage that was, in the historian Hendrik Hartog's phrase, "unambiguously permanent." Studying nineteenth-century separation agreements, Hartog cautions against interpreting this extralegal form of "marital exit" as strictly parallel to divorce. "Many husbands and wives," he argues, "contracted not because they wished to end a marriage, but because they wished to continue it, separated."[48] Wives who "absented" themselves, and husbands who advertised their "elopements," employed a similar logic. They more often sought to renegotiate the terms of their relationship than to terminate it. They might advertise their marital difficulties, but they rarely pursued divorce.

The weak correlation between newspaper elopement notices and the pursuit of legal divorce offers evidence of the prevailing commitment to marital permanence at the institutional, if not necessarily the individual, level. In colonial Pennsylvania and Virginia, newspaper denunciations of wives corresponded to petitions for divorce in less than 1 percent of cases. The difficulty of obtaining a divorce in these colonies before 1770 perhaps makes this result unsurprising, but even in divorce-friendly Massachusetts the correspondence was under 7 percent. Furthermore, divorce meant permanent dissolution of the marriage in only a slim majority of these Massachusetts cases. In almost half, the wife was the petitioner, and husbands' advertisements were either a defensive measure in a suit already underway, or the trigger that spurred the wife to take legal action. Three-quarters of these women sought—and won—separate maintenance rather than a full divorce. One couple later reunited, after a second legal proceeding that assured the wife of "better treatment from her husband in the future." Evidence ranging from husbands' published retractions to wills that bequeath property to an again "beloved" wife suggests that couples who advertised their troubles in the papers were more likely to reconcile than to divorce.[49]

This remained true for generations. A study of such separations in early nineteenth-century Connecticut and Vermont—states with divorce policies that were among the most liberal in the early United States—found that no more than a third of the couples who appeared in the papers sought legal divorce. Instead, more than a third reconciled, and roughly another third stayed legally married but lived apart.[50] Husbands' notices thus remind us that extralegal modes of separation remained the primary solution to marital conflicts long after divorce became a relatively accessible legal option.

Few elopement notices corresponded to divorce, but the connection is stronger when inverted. While less than 7 percent of Massachusetts elopement notices pertained to divorce cases, 16 percent of Massachusetts couples who divorced had already appeared in the papers. In such cases, ads could help secure legal remedies. Female petitioners cited them as evidence of their husbands' stubborn refusal to support them. Men used them to demonstrate their prompt and outraged response to their wives' misbehavior. In both situations, petitioners were granted divorces with much greater frequency than those who had not used the press.

One of the ironies in the conventions governing elopement notices was that husbands who, like Philip Wood, explicitly mentioned their attempts to persuade their wives to return were the least likely to desire reconciliation. Such references were made by almost 5 percent of advertisers, and they varied in tone. John Ross sternly sought "to require" his wife "Elizabeth to . . . return to her Husband, who hath provided her with a convenient House to live in, and shall provide her with warm Cloathing, wholesome Food, and Work suitable for one in her Station." Edward Day patronizingly offered to "overlook" his wife's "Misfortune" in choosing to leave him "and to provide for her and Children, in the best Manner he is [able], provided she and they will return Home, and be contented as far as a Wife ought to be." Obadiah Cookson appeared more generous. He promised to "receive and entertain" his wife "with all that Pity, Love and Courtesy that a Husband ought, and also to proclaim with great Chearfulness her good Deeds, as publickly" as his notice had proclaimed "her Evil." John Holbrook sounded plaintive as he "earnestly lovingly kindly" invited his wife Joanna "to return home to" him; like Cookson, he also declared that he would "receive her and conduct towards her in all Regards as a kind & tender Husband ought to do towards his Wife."[51]

However sincere such entreaties might sound, they were a strong indicator that the advertiser had not behaved as "a Husband ought." In over half of the cases where ads have been cross-checked against court records, explicit invitations to return were related to wives' attempts to obtain redress for failure to provide, cruelty, or both. Husbands' promises of better treatment were made with an eye to impending legal consequences, and their concessions usually came too late to be convincing. As one Connecticut wife explained in the press, her husband "always was excellent at promising, but very forgetful to perform."[52] At least a quarter of these advertised wives won divorces or separate maintenance agreements, giving this subset of ads a much stronger correlation to genuinely broken marriages than was true of the genre as a whole.

"To her usual place of abode, and to her duty": Husbands versus Communities

Husbands' promises that returning wives would be "kindly received" take on a different tenor when one notes that 60 percent of the time these were paired with injunctions forewarning "all Persons . . . from harboring or entertaining" them at the peril of being prosecuted to "the Extremity of the Law." Threats of legal action against those who gave shelter and food to fugitives were the starkest form of overlap between ads of wayward wives and those of other runaways. Roughly 15 percent of colonial ads targeting wives *and* ads targeting slaves and servants made such provisions. English advertisements for runaway servants resembled wife ads in that they usually coupled such warnings with a discrediting rather than a reward for return, making the provision more clearly a matter of advertisers' liability than of claims to property in the person and labor of their dependents.[53] In the case of colonial slaves and servants, admonitions against harboring register differently. Statutory provisions (discussed in chapter 3) made threats of prosecution significant, if also unsurprising and redundant. In wife ads that ran parallel to such notices, the overlapping language provided a sharp reminder of coercive aspects of marriage law that were ordinarily disguised behind the rhetoric of mutual obligation. An injunction against "harboring" a wayward wife was as close as most husbands came to ordering her captured and returned. It was stronger than a simple denial of credit, because with it a husband declared not only that he would not pay his wife's debts, but that he might sue those who helped her.

Philip Wood's admonition to his wife to return to "her usual place of abode and to her duty" was a more tempered expression of husbands' power, but one that nonetheless asserted his right to determine the place and conditions in which she lived and worked. Advertisers who explicitly invoked this authority—and particularly those who used it to forbid others to "entertain," "receive," or "harbor" a wife "in their Houses"—registered their dissatisfaction with community mediation of their marital conflicts, though not necessarily in ways that worked to their advantage. By insisting on their formal legal rights, husbands set "return" against "reconciliation." If their marital debates had not already found their way into the courts, this sort of advertisement was often enough to put them there.[54]

To appreciate the significance of advertisers' injunctions against "harboring" their wives, it helps to review the ways in which such notices were otherwise careful to distinguish themselves from ads for slaves and servants. Wives "eloped," "absconded," "left," or "absented," but especially in the colonial English-language press they almost never "ran away." Colonial German-language papers, in contrast, were somewhat less stringent about the distinctions. With few exceptions, rewards and descriptions did not appear in advertisements concerning wives because the blatant coercion required to capture a runaway was out of step with the notion that marriage was a voluntary relationship and a prerogative of free status. Offering a reward for the capture of one's wife was not explicitly illegal, but it simply was not done. In all but the most exceptional circumstances, it would have raised questions about a husband's motives that might well have given a wife grounds for legal action against him.[55]

The handful of notices that did contain a bounty generally offered it for the return of stolen goods or children. In only nine cases did a husband order that his wife be apprehended. In all but one of these instances the woman had run off with another man, who was the one being held legally accountable.[56] John Brown, for example, promised that anyone who secured his wife's lover "so that he may be prosecuted according to law, shall be handsomely rewarded." "THREE POUNDS reward" went to "whoever secure[d]" Brown's wife, "so that her husband may see her."[57]

Nicholas Sournas's notice appeared at first glance to be a straightforward runaway ad for a servant man. The careful reader discovered, however, that the man "went off with the Wife of the Subscriber." Nicholas proceeded to describe his wife as one would a servant: Mary Sournas "is a short, thick Woman of a dark Complexion, with black hair, black Eyes, aged about 30 Years, and has lost one of her front Teeth: She is a neat Woman in Sewing, Spinning, and knitting Stockings, and can do almost any Manner of Taylors Work, but is oblig'd to use Spectacles when at Work." Mary had taken elegant clothing and a fine horse with her, and the pair were "supposed to pass for Man and Wife." However, the consequences Nicholas prescribed for this subterfuge differed for each. Mary was to be discredited as an "eloped" wife. For securing the "Run-away"—meaning only the servant—"and Horses and Saddles," he offered "two Pistoles Reward" above "what the Law allows."[58]

Adultery and theft made husbands' extraordinary measures and language in these cases acceptable. Their ads documented breaches of duty through which a wife might forfeit the prerogatives of her status, yet the legal consequences of these cases were primarily borne by the man who enticed her away. Assuming their claims were true, John Brown and Nicholas Sournas could have won divorces, though neither appears to have sought one. Samuel Huggins, an advertiser with a similar complaint, forgave his wife and her lover "on their . . . repentance and promise of reformation," only to have them run away together again nine years later.[59] Prosecution "according to the law" might have involved criminal charges; adultery remained punishable by lashes and fines in most colonies.[60]

There is remarkably little evidence, however, of cases in which husbands actually used the law to enforce the claims their advertisements made about their legal rights. Brown and Sournas might, theoretically, have sued their wives' lovers for criminal conversation, but they did not. Two related New Hampshire cases offer the best examples of what happened when colonial husbands pursued their advertisements' legal threats in the courts. Both cases tested the rights of husbands against the affection of fathers, and both bear witness to the enduring primacy of localized law. Early in May 1760, William Holt took out a newspaper advertisement in which his emphasis on his wife Bulah's duties attempted to mask his own apparent negligence. She had "eloped" from him, refused "to live with [him] as an obedient wife ought to," and had "run [him] in Debt." "Notwithstanding" these grievances, Holt promised to provide for her and treat her "with all the Love and Tenderness she can reasonably expect" should she and her child return to him. He regretted that her behavior "obliged [him] to take this Method with her to inspire her to that Obedience which the Marriage Covenant obliges her to." To the end of his notice, Holt attached "an evidence" of Bulah's debts and of the primary source of his ire. He had been "sued by her Father, and taken with a single Writ" for an odd assortment of debts. The list began with a bill for a cow that his father-in-law had sold him a year before. Some months later came charges for "2 Days and a half Work at Mowing and Raking of Hay." In November, Bulah's father billed him for "cutting Wood, taking care of his Cattle," and miscellaneous other tasks related to "taking Care of his Family . . . for three Weeks, when . . . Holt was gone from home." Finally came the costs of Bulah's "elopement," when she returned to her father's house to give birth and generated charges for her mother's "Nursing" and her father's "Time in taking care" of her, rent for her room, and assorted costs "in excess of what . . . Holt provided."[61]

Under ordinary circumstances, most of these debts might never have been recorded. Exchanges of labor and assistance in times of need were everyday occurrences between kin and neighbors in rural communities. And as we saw in previous chapters, paternal care was indeed a well-established tradition.[62] By publishing the charges and assuring his readers that the whole account had been paid to his "good Father in Law," Holt accused Bulah's father of petty litigiousness. His objection to having been "taken with a single Writ" implied, moreover, that the whole affair was legally improper. Book debts like this one had long been a common way of keeping and settling accounts in small communities. The form suited people who dealt with each other over extended periods of time and in multiple capacities, not simply as debtors and creditors but, in the historian Bruce Mann's words, as "neighbors, relatives, fellow church members, companions in the local militia company, suppliers of goods and services that each needed, . . . parents whose children had quarreled or whose livestock had eaten each other's grain." "The procedural and evidentiary flexibility of book debt," Mann argues, "invited the parties to explain their dispute in ways that would place the legal issue of indebtedness in the larger context of their social relations." In the mid-eighteenth century, litigation of this sort was being displaced by disputes over formal written promissory notes that used increasingly technical modes of pleading, where an improperly constructed writ could doom a case regardless of its merits.[63]

Suits over book debt, in contrast, allowed parties to air (if not to settle) grievances other than those legally at issue in a particular case. In this instance, Bulah Holt's father presumably brought his suit to "inspire" William to meet his obligations as a husband. The seemingly unrelated charges fit together as an itemization of things William was *not* doing to support Bulah. The cow, one suspects, might have been intended to supply a want of milk and meat. One can imagine William insisting it was not needed, leaving Bulah and her father to provide it with feed for the winter and thus explaining her father's "Work Mowing and Raking" Holt's hay. Then Holt left his pregnant wife alone without firewood as the New Hampshire winter set in, and perhaps also failed to make provision for her lying-in, forcing her to retreat to her parents' house. The court records for this case would probably not clarify its substance, even if they had survived. Holt's own admission that his father-in-law won the case suggests that judge and jury in his home community deemed him negligent, and that they supported a father's right to provide refuge to a needy child even against her husband's wishes. However, the case does not tell us whether Holt's advertisement would have made a difference in these legal proceedings. We know that Bulah returned to him, because local records show the births of more children to the couple during the next decade. But we cannot know whether this was because his notice inspired "her to . . . Obedience," because her father's lawsuit chastened him into responsibility, or because all the parties compromised with regard to what they could "reasonably expect" of the marriage.[64]

A similar lawsuit filed by the father of another estranged New Hampshire wife has more bearing on the question of the enforceability of elopement notices, although it was similarly inconclusive. A few weeks after William Holt placed his advertisement, mariner Patrick Markham and his wife Elizabeth engaged in an extraordinarily contentious newspaper exchange. The crux of the couple's dispute seems to have been where and in what style Elizabeth would live during Patrick's voyages—his ability to determine her "usual place of abode." Elizabeth claimed that "when he went to Sea, he provided no Place for my Residence . . . nor any Thing for my subsistence;—so far from it, that he deposited his Effects in the Hands of another, with Orders not to supply me with any Thing." Had she not had "a Father's House for an Asylum," she "should have been left to the Alms of the Parish." Since his return, she further claimed, Patrick had "never expressed any desire, neither to my Father (that I ever heard of) nor to myself, that I should return and live with him." Elizabeth professed herself "little concerned at" Patrick's "Caveat against giving me Credit," pronouncing it nothing but "a Piece of Cunning" by "a Churlish Husband" who sought to "exonerate himself from the Charge of affording a Wife sufficient Alimony." And she hinted that soon "perhaps a Time may come when the Effects of such a Caution may be bro't to the Test."[65]

Patrick Markham, for his part, replied with a detailed description of his arrangements. "Just before I went on my last Voyage," he claimed, "I gave her Sixteen Dollars in Gold and Silver, a Note of Hand of one Gage for £85, (which sum she received soon after my Departure) and I directed her Father to pay her £108 O.T. which he owed me for Goods: I gave her a Piece of Holland, Ditto of Cambrick, Plenty of Cotton Wool, Corn of all Sorts, 20lb. of Coffee, 7 Cord of Wood ready Sawed, Store of Roots, an Order to receive Molasses." This was certainly enough to "content any reasonable Woman for the Space of four Months." He argued, moreover, that Elizabeth had no need of an "Asylum," for he "had hired Part of the House of the Widow Davis in Portsmouth for her," and was not to blame if "that Place did not suit her Intrigues." In response to her veiled threat to take him to court for alimony, he asserted that "I myself am Judge of my own Behaviour, and that of my Wife." Legal interference with his right to pass judgment in his own family, would lead to a time, "prophesied by" Elizabeth, "wherein Cuckoldom is to be unrestrained,

Indolence and Extravagance encouraged by Law, and the gray Mare . . . the better Horse by Authority."[66]

These dire predictions about challenges to masculine jurisdiction did not deter Elizabeth's father from bringing a lawsuit a few months later. He charged Patrick for the costs of supporting Elizabeth during the contested voyage and after the advertisement, concluding—like Bulah Holt's father—with expenses incurred when she gave birth to the couple's only child. The suit may well have been inspired by the advertised success of the Holt case. After a year of legal wrangling that seems to have focused more on legal technicalities than on issues, Patrick Markham won an appeal that exempted him from paying any damages and awarded him court costs. His discrediting of Elizabeth was sustained, but in a backhanded way. In the absence of legal arguments, it is impossible to say whether the court meant to affirm his newspaper notice, or rested its decision on other aspects of this complex case. Rather than making a defining statement on the rights of "Churlish Husbands" or "gray Mares," the New Hampshire court maintained its authority to deal with such matters on a case-by-case basis.[67]

Markham's legal victory, however ambiguous, was exceptional. Husbands whose advertisements coincided with legal challenges from their wives generally did not fare well before the law. I have identified thirty cases in which an advertised wife was engaged in legal proceedings against her husband. Most of these women sought a separate maintenance; a few prosecuted their husbands for assault and battery and wanted security for their "good behavior."[68] A husband's ad was a response to legal action that was already underway in one-third of these cases. Some of these advertisers apparently intended to deter the wife from going forward with her suit; others sought directly to contravene a verdict that had gone against them. In most of the remaining cases, the husband's ad appears to have pushed the wife into the courts by undermining her position in informal negotiations over the terms of their relationship. In none of these cases did the courts make a decision that validated a husband's advertisement. Two-thirds of the time, wives won their suits outright. Three wives met with outcomes other than those they desired, but which were not clear victories for their husbands. And in seven cases the verdicts are not known, either because the records are missing or because the couple resumed their negotiations outside the legal realm. They worked, in short, as localized law generally did.[69]

Advertisers, for the most part, do not seem to have engaged in legal action that would have tested the enforceability of their attempts to discredit their wives. Only fifteen of the nearly four hundred advertisers traced to local records buttressed their notices with court proceedings. Twelve of these were those who sought—and for the most part won—divorce, enjoying an extraordinarily high rate of success because they had compelling evidence of their wives' adultery. The wives of two others were convicted of adultery, though their husbands did not attempt divorce. The only one to venture a defense of a possessory right to his wife was laughed out of court. The legal records do not survive, but the *New-Hampshire Gazette* reported that John Parry had sought four thousand pounds in damages in a suit for criminal conversation, only to have the "Jury give the Defendant his Cost without going off the Stand."[70] Although many men threatened to sue those who harbored their wives, none seem to have done so in the eighteenth-century colonies.

One can interpret this limited evidence of the enforcement of husbands' notices in contradictory ways. On one hand, it highlights the resilience of local equitable practices. On the other, it suggests that advertisements worked well enough for most advertisers. Ads' sustained popularity would be difficult to explain if they were wholly ineffective. Between 1760 and 1775 in the colonies, husbands' advertisements acquired practical legitimacy by becoming commonplace, though they were still not so ordinary as to make the scandal they implied unremarkable. Ads may not have deterred family and neighbors who were convinced that a husband was in the wrong, but they did interfere with a wife's ability to solicit aid from outsiders. Samuel Blaker presumably would not have needed to retract his notice five years after the fact had this not been the case. The fears about the power of the press expressed in *Manby v. Scott* seem to have been realized: husbands' advertisements, more effectively than *Manby*'s general pronouncements, created a climate that made tradesmen wary of granting credit to any woman whose marital status and reputation they did not know well.

Nevertheless, even if desertion notices enabled men to escape liability for their wives' debts, such advertisements remained a poor way to salvage one's credibility. The corporate identity of husband and wife meant that a man could never fully rescue his own credibility by tarnishing that of his wife. In defending their formal rights as husbands, advertisers admitted to personal failures as men. Their wives, we shall see in the next chapter, were only too willing to drive this point home.

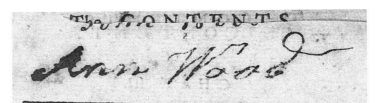

THE
CONTENTS.

CHAP. I.

THE Confideration of Marriage in the Eye of the Law. Of Affiances, and where the Breach thereof is punifhable. When the Solemnization of Marriage in the Church began; and how the ancient Manner of Efpoufals was. If Marriage be once done by one in Orders, not to be diffolved for a Defect of Ceremony, as to Time, Place, or Licence.

CHAP. II.

The Nature of a Feme Covert. Wherein a Feme Covert and an Infant differ as to Privilege. What Acts the Husband may do to the Wife, and what the Wife to the Husband; and the Explication of the Rule that they are one Perfon in Law. And in what Refpects fhe is faid to be fub poteftate viri. Of the Change of her Name and Dignity.

A 3   CHAP.

FIGURE 6.1 Signed contents page, *Baron and Feme: A Treatise of Law and Equity, Concerning Husbands and Wives* . . . (London: in the Savoy: E. and R. Nutt, and R. Gosling [assigns of E. Sayer, Esq.] for T. Waller, 1738)
Harvard Law School Library, Historical & Special Collections

6

"In Justice to my Character":
Wives' Replies

The special collections of the Harvard Law School Library hold an intriguing copy of the English legal treatise *Baron and Feme*. The book offers, at first glance, a testament to the enduring power of the common law over American households and to the enduring power of legal texts as sources of legal authority. It is a compilation of legal precedents dating, for the most part, from the 1600s, in an edition published in 1738, with marginal notes documenting its continued use in the United States well into the 1800s. T. Rosseter wrote on the front sheet that the book had been "Bot at Philadelphia May 11th 1823," and whimsically Americanized the text with the alternate title, "Trouble in the Wigwam." In small regular cursive, another nineteenth-century reader carefully marked instances where Coke's *Commentaries on Littleton*, the classic early seventeenth-century synthesis of the common law, seemed more authoritative. These annotations emphasized legal continuity rather than change. They evidence the tendency of nineteenth-century Americans to take the ostensibly ancient common-law rules propounded by authorities like Coke and Blackstone as the received law of marriage, and to disregard the debates and contradictions that had shaped earlier legal practice in England and her colonies.[1] The writer also indicated the very few places where Pennsylvania's statutory legal tradition diverged from English precedent, unconsciously making the point that the only noteworthy alteration in formal marriage law during the past century—despite the political changes wrought by the American Revolution—had been the new state's 1785 Act Concerning Divorce.[2]

The marks left by an earlier owner, however, hint at a different story, in which changes in written law were only partial and imperfect manifestations of mid-eighteenth-century contests over the terms of female dependence. On the contents page, written in a dark, deliberate eighteenth-century female hand, is the name Ann Wood. The signature is remarkable as evidence of a woman's quest for legal literacy, and also because of the effort Ann put into asserting her ownership of this book. She signed so forcefully that the quill punctured the paper at the top of the *A*, and the ink left a dark shadow on the preceding page. And she obliterated the names of previous owners, taking a knife to two signatures near the top of the title and contents pages, underlining them with a single cut and ripping away the sides that remained. A third name was rubbed and inked away; slicing it out would have damaged the printed text. Ann then claimed the only remaining empty space on the book's first two printed pages for her own name.

If the signer was the same Ann Wood who passionately rebutted Philip Wood's charges of elopement and misbehavior in the *Pennsylvania Gazette* in 1774, it is easy to imagine this mark of ownership as an act of defiance.[3] She might have hoped that asserting control of this object and the arguments it put at her disposal would also empower her to assert control in her disordered household. Philip Wood's wife Ann displayed a familiarity and facility with marriage law that makes the connection seem plausible, though she left no documents that tell us whether this book in fact belonged to her. She left even fewer traces in the historical record than was ordinarily the case for women of her time and place; were it not for her public attempts to seek justice from her husband, we might not know that she had lived.[4] Ann's rebuttal of Philip's advertisement acknowledged the expectations of public invisibility that account for her absence from documentary sources. What "occasions me to make this reply," she claimed, was the fact that Philip had *already* "acquainted the public of the shameful division of his family, and laid all the odium upon me"; advertising was a "disagreeable task" undertaken only because Philip had failed to give "the public a genuine account of the debates which he says subsisted between us."[5]

Ann Wood's story provides a window on the individual and institutional circumstances that "occasioned" wives to publish challenges to their husbands' authority and on the arguments that gained women a public hearing. Wives' advertisements were not simply a reaction to the proliferation of husband's elopement notices, but rather reflected the impact of a changing legal culture on women's opportunities for redress. Wives' publications were most common and most creative in colonies that lacked institutional support for equitable remedies or divorce. Women's presence in the press thus marked the triumph of Blackstone's culture of legal answers over the ambiguity and flexibility of earlier colonial practices.

Husbands' ads anticipated legal danger and were motivated by fear of being drawn into the courts. Wives, in contrast, advertised after they had tried to find legal remedies and found them wanting. Wives' advertisements consequently made more complicated arguments, interweaving legal claims with biblical allusions and appeals cast in the eighteenth-century language of sensibility. Wives sentimental appeals to lost "love and affection" and revolutionary sounding references to "intolerable grievances" became necessary because of the ways in which enlightenment legal systemization closed down other avenues by which women could obtain legal redress. The conventions that enabled wives to claim moral high ground made it still more difficult for them to make specific legal demands. They substituted the right to be left alone for the right to economic support.

Wives published their own versions of their marital debates in nearly all of the papers surveyed for this project. In comparison with husbands' postings, wives' advertisements were sporadic and relatively rare occurrences. In several American colonies, however, wives' publications became both more frequent and rhetorically innovative around 1760. In Pennsylvania and New Hampshire, in particular, publications by wives accounted for between 10 and 20 percent of the newspaper notices pertaining to marital discord during America's revolutionary decades. In contrast, in England and Ireland during the eighteenth century and in America after 1810, rates of response to husbands' advertisements seldom exceeded three percent (table 6.1). What accounts for these differing cultures of reply?

Wives' advertisements bore a different relationship to the formal legal system than did husbands' complaints, although both sorts of notice operated in the shadow of the law.[6] Husbands used that shadow to extend their own authority and *preempt* the claims of those who might bring them before the courts; their advertisements typically reflected loose assumptions about marital unity and masculine power rather than close attention to legal niceties. A man might employ legal formulas in inappropriate ways and later excuse his ad as the result of ignorance or "the Heat of Passion and Inconsideration."[7] Wives' notices, in contrast, were carefully considered. To advertise, wives had to make more sophisticated arguments and meet a higher standard of evidence than did husbands. Women usually turned to the press *after* they had tried and been frustrated by available legal remedies. Their publications marked perceived inadequacies in the law in a way that husbands' advertisements did not.

Women like Ann Wood consequently employed legal scripts and also drew on alternative sources of authority to defend their own visions of household justice. The rhetorical strategies they used to establish legitimacy—in all senses of the word—provide striking evidence of ordinary women's creative adaptation of eighteenth-century intellectual resources. During the revolutionary era, the balance between legal rhetoric about marital rights and duties and other strands of argument in wives' notices underwent an ironic shift.

TABLE 6.1: Wives' rebuttals / wife-initiated desertion notices, as percentage of husbands' ads, 1730–1789

	Pennsylvania		Massachusetts		New Hampshire		Virginia		Ireland (1738–1770)*	
1734	1	7%	0							
1739	0		0						0	
1744	2	5%	0				0		0	
1749	3	4%	2	7%			0		0	
1754	2 / 1	4%	1	6%			0		0	
1759	1	2%	0		0		0		0	
1764	6 / 1	10%	1	2%	4	17%	0		3	7%
1769	8 / 2	10%	1	3%	1	14%	1	9%	1	1%
1774	6 / 2	7%	4 / 1	8%	0		3 / 1	17%	1	2%
1779	4 / 6	13%	0		2	25%	0			
1784	2 / 4	12%	0		0 / 1	14%	0			
1789	6 / 5	20%	1 / 2	11%	1 / 1	40%	0			
Total	**41 / 21**	**8%**	**10 / 3**	**4%**	**8 /2**	**15%**	**4 / 1**	**5%**	**5**	**2%**

*Ads from Pennsylvania, Massachusetts, New Hampshire, and Virginia compiled for Sword Research Database; Ireland (1738–1770) from Ruth Watterson, "Disagreeable Necessities: The Role of Newspaper Advertisements in Regulating the Household in Eighteenth-Century America and Ireland," unpublished manuscript, with permission. Undercounting likely, especially after 1780, due to missing papers and sampling.

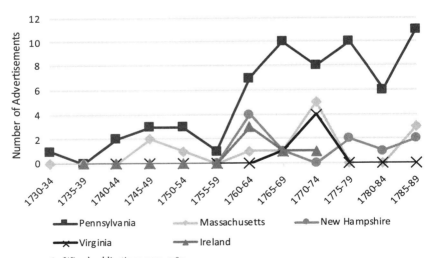

FIGURE 6.2 Wives' publications, 1730–1789

Before 1760, most American wives' publications sought to reign in husbands who had used the press to avoid local legal judgment, and they explicitly invoked wives' legal claims and community support. After 1760, it became imperative that wives' publications appear to be first-person "genuine accounts" of their marital woes, told in an increasingly sentimental style. Wives' notices continued to observe legal formalities, but they sought to avoid appearing formulaic or litigious. They appealed instead to readers' emotions and empathy—their "sensibility," in eighteenth-century parlance—and crafted their stories to feed the growing public appetite for sentimental literary forms.

Eighteenth-century legal theorists and even some aggrieved wives depicted such appeals to sensibility as signs of social progress. The sense of injustice they reflected, the argument went, was founded in an unwillingness to tolerate forms of tyranny acceptable to earlier, less civilized and enlightened generations. The distinctive patterns in American wives' replies were indeed products of the Enlightenment, particularly the Scottish variety. They corresponded almost perfectly to the arrival of the Scottish booksellers and printers who became the primary purveyors of Enlightenment texts in America.[8] The association of wives' sentimental arguments with progress, however, is less straightforward. That narrative obscures the ways in which Enlightenment culture contributed to the problems it purported to solve.

American wives experimented with arguments drawn from sentimental novels because Enlightenment legal culture imposed new constraints. The absence of a comparable culture of reply in England is best explained not by Americans' love of liberty and English tolerance for tyranny in households or in government, but by the sustained ability of England's complex and multilayered legal system to give aggrieved wives a hearing. In the colonies, on the other hand, locally varied practices and ideas about the legal privileges and protection due to wives proved more vulnerable to enlightened legal theorists' efforts to subordinate equitable jurisprudence to the common law. Even more clearly than husbands' complaints, wives' replies offer evidence both of the jurisdictional disorder that inspired Sir William Blackstone's account of coverture and of the real and immediate practical impact of his and other legal theorists' efforts to impose order. Women's publications also testify to the opportunities and the costs of rhetorical alternatives. The conventions of sensibility changed expectations regarding masculine behavior and gave women reasons to undertake the "shameful" task of publicizing their marital grievances, allowing—even requiring—them to publish on their own authority. But sentimental appeals tended to cast marital disputes as moral dilemmas outside the realm of legal (or political) redress. The arguments that legitimated a woman's efforts to "do Justice" to her "Character" in the press mixed uneasily with those needed to obtain justice through the law.

A Change in Values or a Change in Venue?
Patterns over Time and Place

To a modern eye, the passion and assertiveness of wives' replies may suggest a nascent feminism. The historian Clare Lyons, for instance, reads Pennsylvania elopement advertisements as evidence that revolutionary-era women were challenging "patriarchal marriage" and asserting that "personal satisfaction and individual choice in intimate relationships were indeed legitimate goals of a new configuration of gender, sexuality, and the ordering of society." However, looking at the ads in a broader geographical and historical context shifts our understanding. Joanne Bailey's work on English marital disputes stresses continuities across the seventeenth and eighteenth centuries and portrays newspaper conflicts simply as augmenting an array of legal and communal practices for negotiating marital difficulties that remained notably unaffected by sentimental rhetoric celebrating romantic marriage and loving domesticity.[9]

Differences in the ways that wives used the newspapers, rather than substantial contrasts in English and colonial attitudes toward marriage, likely account for these disparate approaches to the evidence. Wives' newspaper replies barely figure in Bailey's study because they were rare. Nevertheless, she has ample evidence of women who sought justice through parish officials, who in turn placed advertisements and otherwise attempted to punish deserting husbands, particularly in the 1770s and 1780s. Her sources include several wives who left their husbands to find more satisfying intimate relationships. Yet such cases recurred frequently enough from the seventeenth century onward to cast doubt on historical interpretations that emphasize late eighteenth-century changes in behavior.[10]

Some first-person narratives of marital grievance that appeared in Pennsylvania's and other colonies' papers with increasing regularity in the 1760s do seem, at first glance, to support claims about a new and distinctive assertiveness on the part of wives. Prior to 1760, colonial women advertised only to rebut notices by husbands. As in England, such challenges were rare, and when they did appear, they occurred in clusters that registered community discomfiture with the novel powers newspaper ads gave to husbands, making general measures of their average incidence misleading. Forty percent of these early notices were posted by wives' supporters—by fathers like Derrick Hogeland, by other family members and friends, or occasionally by local authorities—rather than by the women themselves. After 1760, indirect rebuttals all but disappeared, accounting for less than 3 percent of colonial wives' advertisements. Wives took public responsibility for responding to their husbands, and they did so with rapidly increasing frequency. In Pennsylvania's English newspapers, the average incidence of wives' publications between 1760 and 1774 was more than three times what it had been from 1745 to 1759. Wives' advertisements were still unusual enough to be startling, but readers of any given Pennsylvania paper could expect to see at least one new challenge almost every year during the decade prior to the American Revolution, and in 1773 the genre inspired a revolutionary parody. In New Hampshire and Virginia during the same period, nearly one of every ten husbands who advertised received a response, though the overall incidence of ads by husbands and wives was lower than in Pennsylvania. Even Massachusetts, where the culture of reply was generally more muted, saw a dramatic increase in wives' ads during the 1760s. Between 1705 and 1790, the Massachusetts papers contained only nine advertisements placed by wives on their own behalf; six of these appeared between 1762 and 1773.[11]

The basic legal framework of wives' rebuttals remained consistent, but their tone shifted, and they were joined in the papers by new types of ads. Sporadic protests against husbands' abuse of power became carefully crafted—and by some accounts obligatory—defenses of character. Elizabeth Markham, for example, feared that silence in the face of her husband's public libel would "be imputed to a Consciousness of Guilt, and having nothing to say."[12] Consciousness of having something to say in their marital disputes and of a right to a public hearing perhaps explains a new form of wifely publication that also began to appear in the 1760s. A few wives began to take the initiative in denouncing their husbands, inverting the masculine genre and defying the precepts of coverture. Yet these examples speak even more clearly to the tension between varied local legal cultures and the Blackstonean effort to impose English common-law norms. The women who discredited their husbands were almost all German American, although a few mid-Atlantic women of English descent followed their example and turned the form on its head in creative ways. Such ads for the most part registered German communities' adherence to practices with regard to married women's property and credit that differed from those of their British counterparts.[13]

Ann Wood and her fellow advertisers denied that they were challenging patriarchal norms; they asserted themselves in the press chiefly because the communal and institutional alternatives they expected to come to their aid had failed. Philadelphia from the 1760s through the 1790s was certainly a laboratory for experiments with new ideas about gender and the ordering of society. Its booksellers' inventories contained the restrictive legal answers that pushed debtors and unhappy couples to look for extralegal alternatives, as well as an attractive array of Enlightened and sensible texts that pulled them toward particular solutions. Elopement notices need to be understood using both halves of this equation. They might—or might not—have reflected a new sexual culture. They certainly reflected changing economic circumstances and legal consciousness on the part of husbands, who had discovered that accusations of adultery shored up their efforts to absolve themselves of liability for their wives' debts.

The presence of a legal culture that accepted responsibility for marital disputes dampened innovations by wives in the press. This helps explain the generally low response rates in England and in Massachusetts, as well as American patterns after the revolution. In the 1770s, the petitions of women (and men) who sought divorce from colonial legislatures and courts began to appear in the papers, functioning as public notice to deserting spouses or other people who might "shew cause (if any they have) why" the divorce should not be granted.[14] A few of these were submitted to the papers directly by the petitioners, but by the 1780s state legal authorities had assumed responsibility for placing such ads. Published divorce petitions stood apart from discreditings and rebuttals because they were tools of the legal process rather than attempts to work around it. Such proceedings remained far less common than desertion notices well into the nineteenth century. Wives' ads became less frequent and more formulaic as the law, once again, became the place to which they were expected to take such complaints.

Ann Wood's Advertisement

Ann Wood's notice exemplified the multiple strands of argument characteristic of wives' notices in the 1760s and beyond. She skillfully interwove the legal arguments common to most rebuttals with other scripts, subtly calling for divine as well as earthly justice and also invoking new, sentimental tropes. Her ad was at once a legal plea, a biblical prayer, and a literary appeal to her readers' sensibility. It exemplifies three strategies common to wives' replies, which this chapter will examine in turn: first, legal claims akin to those made by wives whose husbands had attempted to divorce them, including failure to provide "necessaries" for one's family and excessive violence; second, invocation of a higher, religious standard of justice than the law; and third, sentimental tropes designed to elicit community sympathy for a wife's powerlessness and dependence, albeit at the expense of direct claims to power.

Before we begin to disassemble its strands, it is worth reading Ann Wood's notice in its entirety; the whole is greater than the sum of its parts. After summarizing her husband Philip's charges that she had "behaved in an unbecoming manner," "eloped" from him, and refused to "return to . . . her duty," Ann Wood put forth the following as the "genuine account" of their "debates":

> I do now declare to the world, with a sorrowful heart, that, were it in my power to live with him in peace, I would continue with him, even in the greatest poverty or distress, as he is my husband, as well for the fulfilling of my marriage vows, as for the credit of four children which are all his by me; but he has, for many years past, treated me with unkind scurrilous language, harsh ill names, and struck me with iron pots, chairs, and even any thing that lay ready to his hand; he once beat me so unmercifully with a bridle, that I bore the marks of the bitts for several weeks after;—-he has abused his obedient dejected children, with such harsh language and immoderate correction, and kept from them a sufficient allowance of the necessaries of life, that not one of them is living with him at present, yea, it is well known that some of them chose rather to seek their bread among strangers, when almost in infancy, than put up with the base and uncharitable usage of their father, when at the same time his estate is worth about 15 or 16 hundred pounds.—- These intolerable grievances are the cause of the unhappy debates that subsisted between us, and which cause me to decline living with him any longer, or returning to my place of abode, and to my duty, as he deceitfully expresses it;—-that I eloped from him is a shameful falsehood, since it is well known he turned me and some of the children out of doors, burned a part of our clothes, and turned us off partly naked; and, when some of our neighbours, through pity to us, entreated him to let us return home, he absolutely refused, and immediately bolted the door.—-Thus have I given the public a short account of the cause of our separation, which I solemnly declare was not of my choice; for I am now an old woman, much enfeebled with hardship and grief, and not capable of procuring the necessaries of life; yet, rather than endanger my life by dwelling with him any longer, I am resolved, with the advice of almost all my friends and neighbours, not to solicit him to let me return any more, but [to] depend on the Providence of God and my poor weak industry for my sustenance, during the few remaining days of my disconsolate life.

Taken as a whole, Ann Wood's advertisement appears to be an almost spontaneous outpouring of "hardship and grief"—a powerful, sympathetic appeal. Yet its details were carefully framed and might well have been designed with the legal precepts outlined in *Baron and Feme* in mind. Read through this lens, her notice highlights the fundamental similarities, as well as important differences, between legal pleas and public appeals.

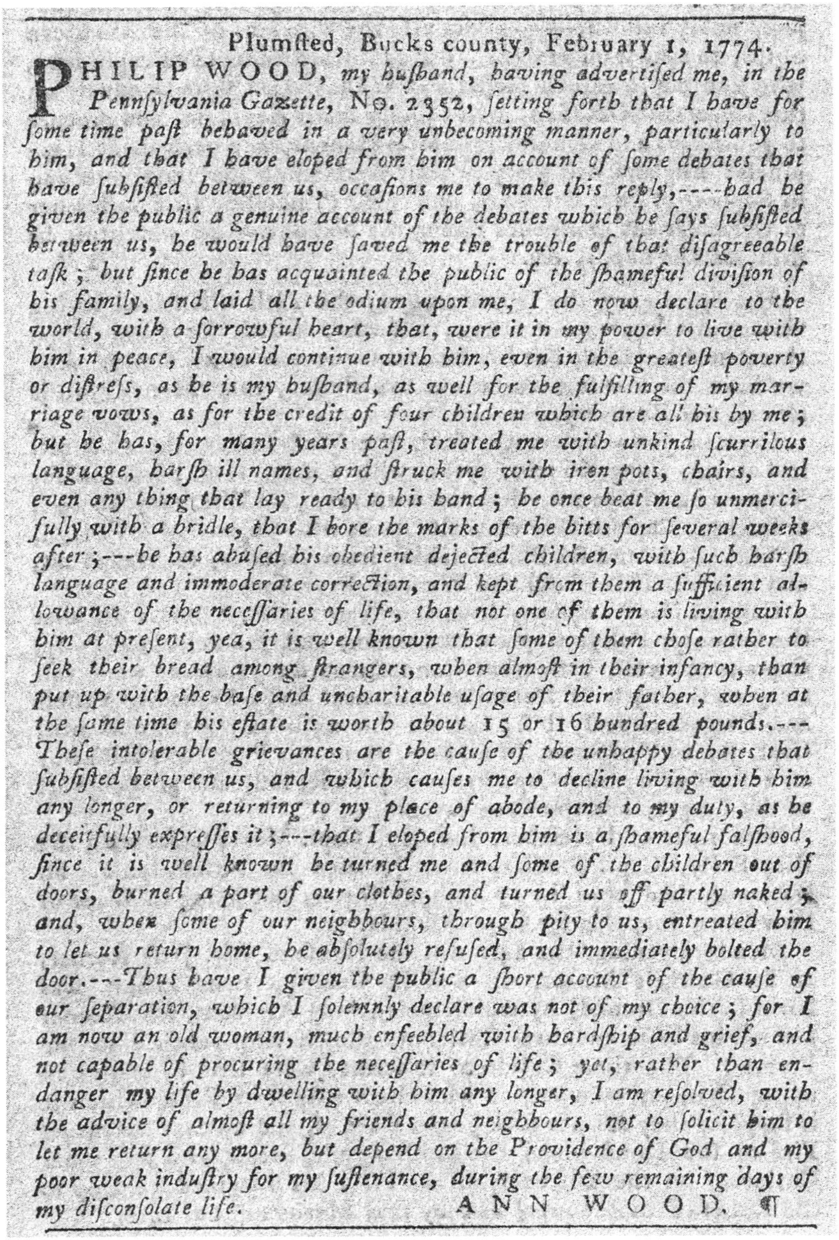

Plumfted, Bucks county, February 1, 1774.

PHILIP WOOD, my hufband, having advertifed me, in the Pennfylvania Gazette, No. 2352, fetting forth that I have for fome time paft behaved in a very unbecoming manner, particularly to him, and that I have eloped from him on account of fome debates that have fubfifted between us, occafions me to make this reply,----had he given the public a genuine account of the debates which he fays fubfifted between us, he would have faved me the trouble of that difagreeable tafk; but fince he has acquainted the public of the fhameful divifion of his family, and laid all the odium upon me, I do now declare to the world, with a forrowful heart, that, were it in my power to live with him in peace, I would continue with him, even in the greateft poverty or diftrefs, as he is my hufband, as well for the fulfilling of my marriage vows, as for the credit of four children which are all his by me; but he has, for many years paft, treated me with unkind fcurrilous language, harfh ill names, and ftruck me with iron pots, chairs, and even any thing that lay ready to his hand; he once beat me fo unmercifully with a bridle, that I bore the marks of the bitts for feveral weeks after;---he has abufed his obedient dejected children, with fuch harfh language and immoderate correction, and kept from them a fufficient allowance of the neceffaries of life, that not one of them is living with him at prefent, yea, it is well known that fome of them chofe rather to feek their bread among ftrangers, when almoft in their infancy, than put up with the bafe and uncharitable ufage of their father, when at the fame time his eftate is worth about 15 or 16 hundred pounds.---- Thefe intolerable grievances are the caufe of the unhappy debates that fubfifted between us, and which caufes me to decline living with him any longer, or returning to my place of abode, and to my duty, as he deceitfully expreffes it;---that I eloped from him is a fhameful falfhood, fince it is well known he turned me and fome of the children out of doors, burned a part of our clothes, and turned us off partly naked; and, when fome of our neighbours, through pity to us, entreated him to let us return home, he abfolutely refufed, and immediately bolted the door.----Thus have I given the public a fhort account of the caufe of our feparation, which I folemnly declare was not of my choice; for I am now an old woman, much enfeebled with hardfhip and grief, and not capable of procuring the neceffaries of life; yet, rather than endanger my life by dwelling with him any longer, I am refolved, with the advice of almoft all my friends and neighbours, not to folicit him to let me return any more, but depend on the Providence of God, and my poor weak induftry for my fuftenance, during the few remaining days of my difconfolate life.   ANN WOOD. ¶

FIGURE 6.3 Ann Wood advertisement, *Pennsylvania Gazette*, February 9, 1774
Courtesy of the American Antiquarian Society

"Endanger my life by dwelling with him":
Ann Wood's Plea

Baron and Feme was unlikely to have been a comforting text for Ann Wood. Its author, unlike Blackstone, made no apologies for legal misogyny. Yet the book's unsystematic treatment of marriage law explained equitable remedies that received at best a cursory nod in Blackstone. With careful study, Wood might have collected a handful of passages on which to build her case.

Baron and Feme's introduction simultaneously limited and affirmed a husband's right to use physical force: "Though our Law makes the Woman subject to the Husband, yet he may not kill her but it is Murder; he may not beat her, but she may pray the Peace, . . . but he may give her moderate Correction." An abused wife could "pray the peace"—that is, she could petition local authorities for protection, upon which they were expected to secure her husband's promise (on penalty of a sizeable fine) to "keep the peace towards his Majesty's subjects and especially his Wife." This action was the early modern equivalent of a temporary restraining order. Historians debate its effectiveness. A husband's "good behavior" until the next court session was usually enough to end the matter in the eyes of the law. A wife who wished to pursue her case had to prove, as Ann Wood claimed, that her husband routinely exercised *immoderate* correction that amounted to life-threatening cruelty. For many women and their communities, a return to relative peace, rather than legal vindication, was the objective. "Praying the Peace" might not end a husband's violence, but it could moderate it. It was a remedy that could be invoked repeatedly, and one that enlisted the wider community in monitoring a husband's behavior. Historians of English practice have argued persuasively that at least until the mid-eighteenth century, the procedures worked well enough for women to be satisfied that the law offered them justice, albeit in a context in which forcible "correction" of household dependents was thought to be occasionally necessary, if not desirable.[15]

Two other paragraphs, buried deep in *Baron and Feme*, provided key details about such equitable remedies for abused wives. On page 259, the reader would learn that if "A Husband turns away his Wife, or uses her with Cruelty; by which means she is obliged to leave him, Chancery will upon her own, or Prochein Amy's [sic] Application, decree her a separate Maintenance, suitable to her Degree and Quality, the Fortune she brought and her Husband's Circumstances." Near the end of the book, a brief discussion of divorce explained that "If a husband take from his Wife Apparel; and other Necessaries" it might constitute sufficient cruelty to merit legal redress. The same chapter categorized life-threatening cruelty as cause for a full divorce, though the few examples that the text provided implied that bed and board separations were all that could be expected.[16]

Each phrase here mattered for Ann Wood. She sought to establish that Philip had "turned her away," bolting the door against her and her children. He had burned her clothes, depriving her of "Apparel and other Necessaries." His repeated beatings "endangered her life," and were not within the bounds of ordinary household "correction." And finally, his "Circumstances" were certainly sufficient to afford her separate maintenance. She might not have brought a "Fortune" to her marriage; nor was she of the elite "Degree and Quality" with which *Baron and Feme* and the English chancery courts were chiefly concerned. But as the wife in a competent household, with a claim on an estate of "15 or 16 hundred pounds," she also had an equitable claim on her community's attention when her husband's mistreatment brought her and her children into poverty and distress.

Ann Wood's legal arguments echoed those of women who petitioned the courts for separate maintenance. Elizabeth Lawson and Dorothy Jackson, whom we met in previous chapters, had made similar claims before justices in seventeenth- and early eighteenth-century Massachusetts. Virtually every published rebuttal of a husband's newspaper notice used some combination of the same arguments. Seventy percent charged advertising husbands with cruelty. Seventy percent cited their failure to provide. And 95 percent raised at least one of these two grievances.[17] At their core, then, wives' published rebuttals were modeled after the legal challenges mounted by wives whose husbands sought to divorce *them*.

The historian Cornelia Dayton has examined this latter phenomenon in colonial Connecticut, where the "most liberal divorce policy in the eighteenth-century English-speaking world" had actually decreased the options available to abused wives during the eighteenth century. Connecticut granted only full divorce with permission to remarry, deeming separations from bed and board "popish inventions" that encouraged the sin of adultery. But for most of the eighteenth century, it would not grant divorces where cruelty was the exclusive grounds. It granted hundreds in cases of desertion or adultery. In these circumstances, Dayton explains, husbands had abdicated "their prime marital responsibilities of economic support and fidelity. By walking out, these men unilaterally transferred their patriarchal authority over their household dependents to the state." Petitions based on cruelty, however, asked "the state to inspect the way in which a man governed his family." Over the course of the eighteenth century, lawyers and judges in Connecticut became increasingly reluctant to interfere with a husband's exercise of his household authority.[18] In consequence, charges of marital cruelty came into the Connecticut courts almost exclusively as a means of defense, used by wives whose husbands charged them with desertion.

Comparison of these Connecticut cases with those of wives who rebutted their husbands' newspaper advertisements in other colonies reveals striking similarities in the profiles of the women involved and in their arguments. The Connecticut women who mounted legal challenges to their husbands' governance had resources that typically included "separate wealth, a secure place to go to, sympathetic family or friends," as well as intangible qualities like confidence in their ability to manage alone in the "fierce resolve" required to do so.[19] Women who challenged their husbands in the press also had more than the usual array of resources. A third of wives' rebuttals explicitly referred to their own claims to separate property. The proportion of cases in which this was an aspect of the dispute was probably even higher; almost 60 percent of wives' responses condemned their husbands' (mis)management of property. Women's separate holdings were often substantial. Louise Leddel's husband had spent "Four Hundred and Fifty Pounds Sterling, of her money," and Lydia Anderson's had gone through "near Three Hundred Pounds" of her estate in the space of three years. Mary Dicks claimed to have brought her husband a marriage portion of three hundred pounds, but to have fled his violence with only the clothes on her back. Jane Tennent, Margaret Bannerman, and Mary Meyer were all prosperous widows fighting to protect the estates they had inherited. Though a few women who advertised were clearly poor, those for whom information is available were overwhelmingly from the upper half of the economic spectrum, in marked contrast with the full spectrum represented by advertising husbands.[20]

Women who advertised routinely invoked the support they received from their local communities in order to buttress their positions, but they differed from the women in Dayton's study in that they did not necessarily have secure places to go. In many cases, a woman would advertise either because sympathetic family and friends were unable to provide long-term charity or because the husband's threats made the wife's supporters reluctant to take further risks. In response to her husband's charge that she was a "strolling worthless Woman," for example, Sophia Connor replied that "his wretched Behavior . . . drove me to it." She accused him of running through the estate left to her and her children by her first husband and then abandoning her to "shift for" herself, returning only when "Christian People bestowed their Charity upon" her so that he might spend what she had. "If he had not taken a Suit of Clothes that was sent to my Son from London for a Present," she contended, her husband "would not have a Stitch" on his back. She concluded her notice by warning the public that she would no longer pay *his* debts.[21] Sophia had a transatlantic network of people willing to assist her, but her husband's periodic assertion of his marital rights forced her to "stroll" about from one refuge to another. By discrediting him, she sought to protect her claim to the support of her friends.

A woman who disputed her husband's charges of willful desertion, whether in the papers or in the courts, *had* to make the legal arguments found in Ann Wood's petition, lest she make herself even more vulnerable to her husband's and the law's authority over wayward wives. She had to establish that her husband had forced her "out of doors" and abdicated his responsibility for supporting his dependents. She also had to make her charges in a way that protected her own character as a dutiful and submissive wife. A woman whose anger was too overt could be portrayed as a scold whose ill temper excused her husband's violence.[22] "Were it in my power . . . ," Ann Wood asserted, "I would continue with him, even in the greatest poverty or distress," not only to fulfill "my marriage vows," but also for "the credit of four children which are all his by me." In one sentence, she simultaneously affirmed her commitment to marriage as an institution, warded off implications of adultery on her part, and emphasized the communal stakes in this dispute. Philip's failure as a household head threatened to make his entire family a burden on the community.

This underlying legal framework remained a consistent aspect of wives' ads throughout the eighteenth century on both sides of the Atlantic. In the 1760s, however, the tenor of colonial women's notices began to change in ways that set them apart from women's legal suits. Early colonial rebuttals were much more likely than later ones to set a wife's legal rights against those of her husband and to contain demands as well as defenses of character. In 1742, Elizabeth Dunlap responded to her husband's attempt to discredit her not only by denouncing his violence, but by interfering with what she claimed was the imminent sale of his estate. She warned the public against purchasing any of his lands, because she would "not join in the sale of any part of" them and she intended "to claim her thirds (or right of dower)." Several other women—or their supporters—made specific objections to a husband's handling of their joint property, implying that they might challenge these transactions in court.[23]

After 1760, wives could still call into question their husbands' economic circumstances and credibility—Sophia Connor was a case in point—but the manner in which they did so was usually more circumspect. Priscilla Butler, for example, charged her husband with "turn[ing] me out of his House, with a Child three Years old, to shift for myself and Child" and with keeping "all the Houshold Furniture, and my Cloaths, which I carried to him." The mention of these items suggests that she wished to have them returned, but she refrained from making any overt material demands. "Though I could expose him in many Instances," she continued, "I forbear, in hopes he will be sorry for what he has done, and restore my Character, (which he has unjustly injured) in as public a Manner as he has endeavored to take it away." The proportion of ads that specifically challenged a husband's management of his property declined. Ads by wives' supporters virtually disappeared, marking another move away from explicit links between wives' publications and the legal process. Such indirect rebuttals were the equivalent of filing a plea in court through her "next friend"—in *Baron and Feme*'s awkward law French, "her Prochein Amy"—a legal maneuver by which dependents "disabled in the law" could select trustees to defend their interests. The shift to first person appeals to the "impartial public" reflected a new strategy that protected a wife's allies and allowed her to invoke a range of powerful, but not necessarily legal, arguments about justice.[24]

This shift in strategy appears to correspond with changes in the ways the laws of coverture were being enforced, and if Blackstone was not specifically to blame, the emphasis on common-law rules over equitable alternatives certainly was. Studies of debt litigation note that this trend was especially marked in Massachusetts. It factored into the tale of woe that Precillia Howard published there in 1773. Precillia grudgingly conceded that her husband's "proper creditors" had legal claim to "her paternal estate," even though she found it "hard" to have been "turned out of doors" for her husband's debts. Because her husband had deserted her to escape confinement for debt, she thought "he might safely have omitted to forbid any person trusting her on his account" in his own advertisement. He also threatened legal action against those who harbored or entertained her—an assertion of possessory rights that, as chapter 5 noted, does not seem to have been enforced during the colonial era, but which in the uncertain legal climate of the 1760s and 1770s might well have made Precillia's allies unwilling to be too vocal on her behalf. Precillia condemned it as "a species of cruelty all the circumstances considered, upon which he is left deliberately to reflect."[25]

Wives increasingly emphasized abstract moral principles rather than concrete material goods because the press had become an outlet for women who found themselves disappointed by the law. Ann Wood, for one, had not hesitated to make explicit economic demands when she went to court. In November 1773, Ann had filed a criminal complaint against her husband Philip before a Bucks County magistrate. Her actual petition does not survive, but related documents make clear that she sought to freeze his assets and secure a separate maintenance. She claimed that Philip intended "speedily to Dispose of all his Considerable Estate and leave his Wife and Children unprovided for," an accusation quite similar to the one Elizabeth Dunlap had placed in the papers thirty years earlier. Philip was ordered to answer her charges at the next court of quarter sessions and to give bond for his good behavior toward her. He apparently chose to go to jail rather than comply.[26]

Although Philip and Ann clearly constructed their newspaper notices with an eye to their legal ramifications, neither one made explicit reference to their encounter with the courts. Legal records (once again) did not report an outcome for Ann's suit, but its retrial in the press suggests that neither party was satisfied with the results. It appears likely that Philip staved off formal legal action. He might have made a private separation agreement with Ann, only to renege on it in the papers. Or it is plausible that the offers of reconciliation described in his advertisement persuaded the authorities not to consider Ann's plea. The pathetic aspirations outlined in her ad suggest as much. She made no mention of her hopes for alimony or of her attempts to interfere with his ability to sell their property, asking only to be allowed to live separately and unmolested, depending "on the Providence of God and my poor weak industry for my sustenance, during the few remaining days of my disconsolate life."

"On the Providence of God": Prayers and Curses

The multiple scripts that shaped Ann's notice intersected in her allusion to her dependence on God. It could be read as an acknowledgment, first, of the divine laws dictating wifely submission found in *Baron and Feme* and in other accounts of marriage law. Legal imperatives provided the basic framework for Ann's account, but as in Elizabeth Lawson's seventeenth-century petitions, they were not the source of its most powerful arguments. Perhaps because she had lost faith in legal justice, Ann wrote a prayer for divine justice into her petition, and with it turned the rhetoric of submission into a form of power.

Ann's advertisement glossed the structure and the content of Psalm 109, a biblical prayer for "vindication and deliverance." The connection was subtle, leaving in doubt whether it was the result of conscious design or an unconscious parallel made by one whose religion shaped her understanding of daily life. Psalm 109 simultaneously invoked God's mercy and God's judgment. The psalmist was a male head of household who stood unjustly charged with oppressing the poor and the weak, and whose accusers had cursed his household with debt and dispersal. The prayer elaborated and inverted this curse, turning it against the psalmist's enemies. Ann Wood's advertisement cast her as the psalmist, though her sex complicated her relationship to the prayer, much as it confounded her options within the legal process. Neither the psalm nor the legal doctrine of marital unity comprehended enmity between husband and wife. Because her enemy was her husband, turning the curse (or the law) against his household did not free her from the malediction.

The psalm began: "Hold not thy peace, O God of my praise; For the mouth of the wicked and the mouth of the deceitful are opened against me: they have spoken against me with a lying tongue. . . . And they have rewarded me evil for good, and hatred for my love."[27] Ann's denunciation of Philip's "deceitful" claim that she refused to return to her "duty," and her affirmation of her commitment to her husband and her "marriage vows," echoed these passages. The evils that afflicted the Wood household matched well with the psalmist's description of the evils that had befallen him, and which he prayed would be turned instead upon his enemies.

Set thou a wicked man over him: and let Satan stand at his right hand.
When he shall be judged, let him be condemned: and let his prayer become sin. . . .
Let his children be fatherless, and his wife a widow.
Let his children be continually vagabonds, and beg: let them seek their bread also out of their desolate places.
Let the extortioner ["his creditors" in more modern translations] catch all that he hath; and let the strangers spoil his labour.
Let there be none to extend mercy unto him: neither let there be any to favour his fatherless children.
Let his posterity be cut off; and in the generation following let their name be blotted out. . . .
Because that he remembered not to shew mercy, but persecuted the poor and needy man, that he might even slay the broken in heart.
As he loved cursing, so let it come unto him: as he delighted not in blessing, so let it be far from him.[28]

Perhaps Ann saw Satan at Philip's right hand when he stood over her and struck her "with iron pots, chairs, and even any thing that lay ready at his hand," or when he beat her "so unmercifully with a bridle, that [she] bore the marks of the bitts." Through his refusal to "shew mercy," Philip had cursed his own house. He had, in effect, rendered his children "fatherless, and his wife a widow." He had turned his children into "vagabonds," even when his neighbors took "pity" on his family and "entreated him to let [them] return home." Philip's love of cursing, his abuse of his family with "unkind scurrilous language" and "harsh ill names" drove his children "to seek their bread" as servants in strangers' households. Ann's paraphrase here forcefully associated labor contracted outside one's own household with poverty, need, and the "shameful division" of the family. It meant seeking bread in "desolate places" and letting "strangers spoil [one's] labour." Independent labor increased one's dependency.

Ann's emphasis on the stigma associated with becoming a dependent outside one's own household added to the pathos and drama of her conclusion. It made all the more extraordinary her resolve, in the last days of her "disconsolate life," to rely on her "poor weak industry" rather than return to her place as Philip's wife.

Ann's self-portrayal as someone left abject and powerless by her circumstances is complicated by the next section of the psalm, however. It turns this litany of misfortunes back upon the perpetrators as a "reward of mine adversaries from the LORD." In the "Providence of God" there was the power to turn the maledictions of one's enemies against them. The "poor and needy" supplicant "became also a reproach" to those who had dismissed her, with the power to call down God's mercy and God's judgment. Seen through this lens, Ann's poverty became a sign of her righteousness. Her earthly resources—her neighbors' patience and support as well as her legal options—might have been exhausted, but her plea for divine justice held considerable power.

Understood within this biblical context, the undercurrent of anger that ran through Ann's notice explodes forth in a potent curse. The emotion and the mode of expression were at odds with the increasingly refined literary conventions governing newspaper correspondence, and they marked Ann as a transitional figure—an "old" woman in a new public world. In the 1740s, another woman of Ann's generation had been much more explicit in her invocation of biblical law, advising her husband that "he would do well to read and consider" Malachi 2:14, a verse that promised judgment against the man who "dealt treacherously" with the wife of his youth.[29] And a providential reading of her personal history would still have resonated with some in Ann Wood's audience. In 1769, for instance, Barbara Arndorff placed an ad that displayed her own belief in divine and diabolical wonders. Her husband, she claimed, had extracted a confession of adultery from her through physical violence mixed with supernatural threats. She had affirmed his accusations of infidelity in a fit of terror after he dragged her to a crossroads at midnight and summoned the devil to tear her to pieces.[30] Yet in the press of the 1770s and beyond, supernatural judgments and curses that slipped "like oil into . . . bones" were more likely to encounter skepticism, discomfort, and occasional ridicule. Most women of younger generations still made religious arguments, but they used the moral lessons embedded in popular fiction more often than the Bible as their guiding source.

Mixed idioms in both Wood's and Arndorff's advertisements acknowledged this trend. Barbara Arndorff advertised to "retrieve her character" and defend her credit, which was "full as good as his, he not being able to pay his just debts at present." Barbara's notice answered ads that her husband John had placed in the German-language papers, and her effort to deny him credit on *her* account reflected the distinctive practices regarding married women's credit and marital community property, as well as religious belief, observed in Pennsylvania's German communities. Barbara's ad prompted John, in turn, to address an English-language audience. John contended that an English-speaking magistrate and court had convicted Barbara of adultery, that she was mentally unstable, having attempted "to drown and hang herself," and that her claims should thus be dismissed as "a notorious falsehood." John's efforts to demonstrate his reason and character notwithstanding, the case would have confirmed readers' stereotypes about what one lawyer termed the "very superstitious" Germans.[31] Wood and the Arndorffs, like Elizabeth and Christopher Lawson a century earlier, lived in a world of wonders. The late eighteenth-century lawyers and judges from whom Ann Wood and Barbara Arndorff needed to turn for legal redress had not rejected that world, but they did their best to shut it out of the courtroom.

Historians tend to follow the lawyers and label explicitly biblical arguments and similar invocations of otherworldly peril "traditional" in contrast with new "modern" and seemingly secular arguments grounded in reason and sentiment. When we mark religious forms and regulatory practices as "traditional" and as distinct from the realm of the legal, however, it becomes easy to lose sight of the lively debates about ecclesiastical jurisdiction in which such characterizations intervened during the eighteenth century. The penumbra of tradition masked the ways in which varieties of religious practice and regulation of marriage continued to coexist and coevolve. The keyword that flags the interpretive dilemma here is *persistence*, which carries with it the presumption that "traditional" gender hierarchies and marital forms like polygamy must inevitably pass away. Their failure to do so points to the need for an alternative framework, and for closer attention to the ways in which "modern" forms of communication can give new life to marginal practices—a status that in the seventeenth and eighteenth centuries could be applied to divorce as easily as to phenomena like wife sale and polygamy.[32]

"The few remaining days of my disconsolate life": Sentimental Dependence

Ann Wood's assertion of her dependence "on the Providence of God" in the face of the hardships of this life can be read more comfortably as a sentimental appeal than as a curse. The pathetic conclusion to her advertisement could have been inspired by the extraordinarily popular, genre-defining novels of Samuel Richardson. The eponymous heroine of Richardson's novel *Pamela* similarly glossed one of the psalms during her time of trial, comparing her imprisonment by the rakish Mr. B—— to the Babylonian captivity. When Pamela's single-minded defense of her virtue was rewarded by the reform of (and marriage to) her persecutor, her poem served as witness to her piety and to the "moral and instructive sentiments" Richardson wished his works to convey. Pamela was commended for softening the original psalm into only "a little bit of a curse." "I think it one of my Pamela's excellencies," Mr. B—— remarked, "that though thus oppressed, she prays no harm upon the oppressor."[33] Ann Wood's prayer was at once more subtle and less benign.

The ending of Ann Wood's saga was closer to that of *Clarissa*, Richardson's most acclaimed work. The climatic event in *Pamela* was the heroine's marriage to her onetime oppressor. The story continued for some five hundred pages more, chronicling Pamela's ongoing reform of her converted rake and management of her household through her submissive, self-abnegating behavior. In *Clarissa*, Richardson set out to disprove the myth that *Pamela* had created—namely, "*that a reformed rake makes the best husband.*" In an attempt to escape a forced marriage to a man she despised, Clarissa fell into the power of the villainous Lovelace. He kidnapped her, imprisoned her, and finally drugged and raped her. Feeling remorse—and finding that possession of her body did not allow him to touch her soul—he then offered to make "amends" by marrying her. Clarissa steadfastly refused. Despairing of happiness in this world, she spent most of the final two volumes of this eight-volume work preparing for her death.

Those volumes included numerous departing speeches, all of which reiterated the theme of placing one's dependence first on God and of spiritual growth through trial. Like Pamela and perhaps Ann Wood, Clarissa adapted a psalm to her circumstances, asking for deliverance "on being hunted by the enemy of my soul," even as "my days are like a shadow that declineth." She interpreted her situation as the fulfillment of a curse laid upon her by her father for her perceived disobedience, and she sought release from his "Malediction . . . and a Last Blessing," after which "Death will be welcomer to me, than Rest to the most wearied traveller that ever reached his journey's end." Ann Wood's reference to the "few remaining days of my disconsolate life" concisely conveyed a similar sense of pathos.[34]

Ann Wood's notice was less overt than many others in its use of sentimental arguments, by which I mean language and story lines that echoed Richardsonian fiction, setting self-abnegating virtue against seductive villainy and soliciting readers' sympathy for the moral righteousness of the oppressed.

Sentimental tropes began to appear in wives' advertisements in the 1760s, and the arguments they made possible were at least in part responsible for the increasing frequency with which such notices appeared. By the 1780s, they were virtually a requirement of the genre.[35] This rhetorical strategy entailed a difficult set of trade-offs, hinted at in Lovelace's reaction to one of Clarissa's dying entreaties. When she offered him forgiveness on the "one condition" that he "molest her no more," he complained that, however generous her intent, "the whole Letter [was] so written, as to make *herself* more admired, *me* more detested."[36]

The sentimental mode created another point of entry for women who wished to advertise, making the defense of one's character sufficient grounds for a public hearing. It allowed wives to cast their husbands as villains of the worst sort for actions that might not have won consideration by the courts. The trade-off was an intensification of the requirement that women appear to be above reproach in their fulfillment of their marital duties. A wife who depicted her husband as "tyrannical," "barbarous," and "inhuman" needed to be like Clarissa—universally "admired," a "paragon of virtue," a "saint."[37] Her motives for advertising needed to appear disinterested and forbearing. She could defend "injured innocence," seek to prevent her errant husband from "deluding other simple women," and request to live unmolested.[38] Tit-for-tat accounting of marital prerogatives and concrete economic demands undermined her case. Even the palpable sense of "resentment," "injustice," and righteous anger expressed in wives' notices was at odds with the sentimental script.

On sentimental terrain, a wife had the advantage over her husband, whose public exercise of his patriarchal prerogatives necessarily raised doubts about his character. In eighteenth-century fiction, charges of elopement were a tool of duplicitous villains. In the wake of one of Clarissa's escape attempts, Lovelace contemplated advertising her "in the *Gazette*, as an eloped wife," and mused at some length about how he might best describe her for the papers. In the end, he was able to use the ruse of her elopement to recapture her without resorting to the press. Upon finding the boardinghouse where she had taken refuge, his servant spread the rumor that she was "but lately married to one of the finest gentlemen in the world," and had left him in a fit of jealousy provoked by his "gay and lively habits." By characterizing her as a "wilfull and sullen" wife, prone to run away "if she could not have her own way in every-thing," Lovelace explained her distress and deprived her of supporters. Richardson repeated the device in *Sir Charles Grandison*. Kidnapping and captivity were also central to the plot of *Pamela*, but Pamela's status as a servant made her fear being advertised as a runaway and a thief rather than as an eloped wife.[39]

When Richardson used elopement as a plot twist, he imitated novels by Eliza Haywood, another extraordinarily prolific and popular early eighteenth-century English literary figure.[40] In Haywood's rendering, however, the device demonstrated not only the evil nature of individual villains, but also the larger injustices permitted by the law of marriage. In *The Fortunate Foundlings* (as in *Clarissa*), the villain gained access to the bedchamber of the fleeing heroine by portraying himself as the overindulgent husband of an eloping wife. He won sympathy for his case by citing his desire "to reclaim her by fair means," rather than resorting to a magistrate and other legal officers to "force her to return to her duty." In this instance, he found himself thwarted by the arrival of the novel's hero; but both protagonists wound up in jail on the suspicion that they were indeed a runaway wife and her "gallant." Implicit in the telling was the argument that even the "fair means" by which a husband could coerce his wife were subject to abuse, both in and outside of marriage.[41]

Haywood made the point more clearly in her popular *Betsy Thoughtless*, detailing the degeneration of the heroine's marriage to a man who "considered a wife no more than an upper servant, bound to study and obey, in all things, the will of him to whom she had given her hand." He began to "throw off the lover, and exert the husband" only a few months after the ceremony. On the advice of friends, the heroine sought to "soften" his behavior through submission to his demands. Haywood and her protagonist balked, however, when the husband began to encroach on the financial provisions of the marriage contract; submission to this would have been "a meanness, which all wives must have condemned her for." The heroine continued as a dutiful but unhappy wife until she discovered her husband's adultery and returned to her family. To do otherwise, Haywood advised, "would have been an injustice not only to herself, but to all wives in general, by setting them an example of submitting to things required of them neither by law nor nature." Her husband was not persuaded by this view of "divine" and "human laws," reminding her instead that "a wife who elopes from her husband, forfeits all claim to every thing that is his, and can expect nothing from him till she returns to her obedience."[42]

Haywood depicted the husband's assertion of his legal prerogatives as the ultimate confirmation of his deceitful and brutal character. But she was a realist when it came to the actual workings of "human laws." The heroine's friends support her actions, but her family's lawyer informed her that she would have a difficult time making her case in court. Haywood did not bother to pursue justice for her even in a fictionalized legal system, and instead rescued her with the timely death of her husband. By dutifully nursing him in his last illness, the heroine put herself above reproach and was freed to marry

"Mr. Trueworth," the suitor she should have accepted in the first place and whom Haywood had also conveniently widowed.

Richardson and Haywood held differing views on the nature of female subordination, but the drama in both authors' works derived from struggles over appropriate relations of dependence. Their villains were villainous because of their tyrannical tendencies, expressed in their abuse of their power as masters, husbands, and men of independent fortune. Heroines' virtue was defined by their ability to differentiate between legitimate and illicit uses of masculine power, to balance submission in most things with resistance to excessive demands. Richardson in particular rewarded exaggerated female dependence with the power to challenge male prerogatives. "Well may I forget that I am your Servant, when you forget what belongs to a Master," the waiting-maid Pamela told the designing Mr. B——. Clarissa's primary dependence on God justified her disobedience to her parents and her refusal to consent to dependence on immoral men, though her actions were legitimized only by her Christlike sacrifice of worldly happiness. Dependence was the lot of a woman in "any State of life," but it should not make her "a slave . . . in spirit" or demand that she "desert" herself.[43]

In their newspaper rebuttals, ordinary women used the terms of sentimental fiction to tell their own stories, thereby shedding light on the real-world impact of the eighteenth-century "culture of sensibility."[44] Sentimental scripts gave female advertisers the opportunity to call public attention to grievances for which social institutions provided no remedy, but also demanded that their complaints be framed as personal suffering rather than as social critique. They could report their suffering with an eye to reforming their husbands. Criticizing the distribution of power within marriage, however, would have undermined their claim on the public's sympathy.

The story of Sarah Wiggin strikingly illustrates the connections between sentimental fiction and sentimental appeals. Wiggin cast herself as Pamela. Like Richardson's heroine, she had been "brought up" from an early age in her husband's "Family," and "had long refus'd his Addresses." In a gesture worthy of a novel, "she had even burnt a Licence he had bought twelve Months before" their eventual marriage. Her sense of obligation to him and his persistent and "Advantagious Offers" had at last won her consent, "though greatly against the Advice" of her "Friends" and probably also the wishes of his relations. At issue were the "Disparity of our Ages," and also of wealth. Tuften Wiggin was at least twenty years Sarah's senior and had children near her age.[45] He was a man of property, though not wealthy enough to have been a character in English fiction. She was a dependent in his household—whether his ward or his servant is unclear—who appears to have had no property of her own.

Sarah agreed to a complicated marriage settlement that limited her claims on his estate. After marriage, her husband pressured her to surrender the protections that agreement gave her. Sarah acquiesced to his financial demands, only to find, as Eliza Haywood warned her fictional heroine, that allowing oneself to be "menaced, or cajoled, out of even the smallest part of your rights" was the first step in allowing one's husband to "encroach upon the whole, and leave you nothing to call your own." Sarah finally protested after her husband confiscated all of her documents relating to their settlement, and her complaint prompted him to order her to leave. He promised to make some provision for her and send her personal belongings after her, but when she complied with his wishes, he reneged and "immediately Advertised me as an Eloper." She and the child at her breast were thus "exposed to the wide World" by the "Folly" of "one whose Duty it is to be my Virtue's Guard and preserve it from every stain."[46]

Sarah Wiggin went into considerable detail about the economic terms of her marriage; the problem of support for herself and her child was clearly her foremost concern. Yet she made no explicit financial demands. The ostensible reason for her advertisement was to do "justice" to her "injur'd Reputation" and to "vindicate" her "Character" as an obedient and faithful wife. Her advertisement resembled a missive from one of Richardson's heroines in that it unambiguously condemned her husband's "base" behavior and at the same time offered him forgiveness. Despite her suffering as a result of his "Persecutions," Sarah concluded her advertisement by wishing "him well," and begging "the Pardon of the Public, for the Trouble I have given them to read the Circumstances of my Misfortunes."[47]

Sarah Wiggin used sentimental tropes to turn her weakness into a source of strength. Like Anne Ashton and Ann Wood, she had investigated her legal options. Her ad was mentioned in chapter 5 for its specific challenge to her husband's use of the word *eloped*, which she had been "inform'd . . . means a married Woman's leaving her Husband, and living with an Adulterer." Her source for this information probably also apprised her of her tenuous legal circumstances. Her husband had treated her unfairly, but he had neither committed adultery nor threatened her life. Her financial claims against him were likely to be unenforceable, especially in the absence of the documents she accused him of stealing from her. In sum, she probably had no legal grounds for a permanent separation, and she needed to make the best of a bad situation. By advertising, she produced a public record of her claims that he could not destroy. In the press, moreover, she could make an argument that set moral right *against* legal power.

Sarah's ad, like most wives' rebuttals, implied that she was prepared to defend herself before the courts; it did not openly acknowledge that her case was weak. Legal constraints and the outcome of the case suggest, however, that the ad's purpose was to pressure her husband to come to terms before things went that far. As a tool in informal negotiations, sentimental arguments had power. Sarah's ad placed her husband on the defensive in their community. To preserve his reputation, he would need to show generosity and repentance for his affront to her "Virtue." In court, on the other hand, the details that gave her newspaper appeal its moral force could easily have been dismissed as irrelevant. Sentimental arguments began to appear in colonial divorce cases in the next decade, after they had become common in wives' advertisements. Even then they were a supplement to conventional charges, rather than a substitute for them.[48]

Sarah's claim that "her Character" was "too well established to be blasted" by her husband's affront appears to have been supported by her community. Hers was the only advertisement in this book's sample to secure a husband's public retraction of his charges. By portraying herself as the obedient Pamela rather than the resolute Clarissa, Sarah left open the possibility that she would be willing to return and work for the reform of her husband. Tuften Wiggin retracted his elopement notice, and the couple apparently reconciled. Sarah was recognized in her husband's will as a "well beloved" wife and made his sole executor. She appears to have enjoyed a long, independent widowhood, during which she did not remarry.[49]

Authorship, Agency, and Remedy

Ann Wood's invocation of divine judgment did not win her justice in this world. Ann's newspaper advertisement marked her last appearance in the surviving records, and it seems likely that she died not long after publishing it. The curse on Philip Wood's household remained, however. He kept his property from creditors, and without apparent difficulty, loaned a substantial sum out at interest a few months after Ann's notice; her lawsuit did not give the "extortioners all that he" had. But he nonetheless found himself dependent on the mercy of those he had abused. He was maintained by his son during the "infirmities" of his last years and reluctantly turned over much of his property to him in 1780. Philip's final legacy was one of family discord. On the day he drew up his will, one of his daughters "came suddenly into the apartment" and "by the dint of clamor [broke] up the Business," a disturbance that led to legal disputes between his children after his death.[50] Philip's attempt to insure his posterity was indeed "cut off," though not entirely "blotted out."

   Philip Wood's estate inventory noted "three books" among his possessions. It would provide the historian with a convenient conclusion if these
were *Baron and Feme*, the Bible, and *Clarissa*, but reality resists such tight
connections. We do not and cannot know whether our Ann Wood was the
signer of Harvard's copy of *Baron and Feme*, or even what her exact role was
in recording her story. The holes in the historical record are instructive in this
instance because they turn us from simple questions about Ann's knowledge
and actions to the bigger issues of what was—and is—at stake in authorship,
both with regard to its historical implications for wives' ability to obtain redress, and in modern historians' efforts to interpret their stories.

   Wives' ads encapsulated the paradoxes of their dependent status. While
wives (and servants, children, and even slaves) possessed the right to be supported and not to be "immoderately" abused, the assertion of that right required independent action at odds with their prescribed roles. The legally
established processes by which they might seek redress required that they put
themselves under the protection of legal authorities. Their actions had to be
framed as a desperate response to extraordinary duress and *not* as an expression of independent agency. An independent person other than a husband
had to be willing to assume the responsibility for the wife's cause. The outsider covered the wife's agency in seeking redress with his own. The process
placed the dependent and her champion at risk for charges of inappropriate
behavior—the dependent for being disobedient and undutiful, the champion
for meddling in another's household government.

   Given this context, the post-1760 shift away from ads authored by others
to wives' first-person narratives is remarkable. In such notices, wives became
unmistakable public actors, even as they masked this fact in exaggerated
rhetoric about their own dependence. The emergence of a culture interested
in authentic expressions of feeling allowed abused wives to describe marital
cruelty in terms of their human suffering, changing the debate in ways that
made it difficult for husbands to respond in turn. In practical terms, it did not
remove community intermediaries from the process. The friends and family
who had previously authored notices still played an essential role. But remov-
ing them from the public debate reduced their risks. It deprived an angry
husband of a convenient target for his complaints and of clear grounds on
which to attack his wife's allies, whether in the press, the courts, or on the
field of honor. If a woman's public appeal was well constructed, further challenge to her would only, as Lovelace complained, make him "more detested,"
reinforcing her charges of brutal and authoritarian behavior.

   The dilemma for husbands was real, but the effect was subtle and limited.
Patrick Markham, whom we met in the previous chapter, circumvented it by

challenging the appropriateness of his wife's authorship. He cited Elizabeth Markham's literacy as both a cause and example of her desire to usurp household authority. Elizabeth's erudition made her both unwomanly and deceitful, he argued. She had "a Knack at writing well, and tells her Story with great Plausibility, but," he charged, "(to my Sorrow), her Language to me in private, has not been quite so refined." He implied that Elizabeth used her (mis)education to attempt to make the "gray Mare the better horse by authority," and any rough treatment he might have given her grew out of the need of reminding her of her sex and her class.[51]

Patrick turned Elizabeth's literary allusions against her. A third of his long notice dissected her description of him as *Proteus.* He made his own ignorance of the reference into a virtue, using it to position himself with a respectable public whose class-appropriate education kept them ignorant of such classical affectations. He had first asked "several Masters of Vessels" if they knew of Proteus, but they had never "heard of him." Finally, "an Acquaintance of mine and Mrs. *Markham's* (who had been educated at Colledge, and had read her Advertisement) . . . informed me that this same *Proteus* was a Heathen God, who would turn himself into any shape." Patrick used the voice of this authority to condemn Elizabeth: "I don't know that the Comparison lies between you and him," the educated man replied, "but you may perhaps retort the Name of *Messalina,*" a legendary adulteress who had squandered her husband's fortune on behalf of her lover. Patrick's ally concluded that "It was a great Pity, that a Woman, who in her Writing discovered such a Knowledge of the Ethnic Mythology, and of Law, should behave so as to give me so much Trouble and Uneasiness." Patrick himself wished that "she had been addicted to reading some godly Book, rather than such Heathenish Authors, from which (I fear) she has learnt no Good," or better still, had given over reading entirely and "taken more Care of what was once our mutual interest." Her aspirations to intellectual and material refinement had, he claimed, made her "famous (or rather infamous) for keeping bad Hours, and leading a dissolute Life."[52]

The very literary skills that enabled Elizabeth Markham to bring her complaints before the public undermined her credibility as a dutiful wife. The irony of the case was compounded by the fact that her reference to Proteus might have been inspired by a reading of *Clarissa,* rather than a study of "Ethnic Mythology": Richardson used the comparison on multiple occasions to highlight Lovelace's ability to disguise his black nature with polished manners and deceitful writing.[53] The defiant tone of Elizabeth's 1760 advertisement was not that of a Richardsonian heroine, however. Patrick's rebuttal—and eventual legal victory—might have provided a legal lesson to Sarah Wiggin when she placed her own ad in the same paper a few years later, helping to explain her studied use of the sentimental model and her careful deference to her husband and to her audience.

Patrick Markham's reading of his wife's advertisement stood at odds with that of husbands who blamed "the wicked agency of others" for their wives' complaints.[54] Both interpretations remain perilous for the modern historian. On one hand is the risk of overstating the rhetorical skills and emancipatory aspirations of the women who took to the press. It is tempting to interpret these rebuttals as protofeminist declarations of independence. While this reading might apply in a very few cases, most wives' ads were in fact declarations of *dependence* motivated by personal belief as well as rhetorical necessity. Dismissing women's professed allegiance to household hierarchy as contrivance does an injustice to the authors and their context; it risks reaffirming, albeit to different ends, husbands' charges that they were neither good women nor good wives.

On the other hand, recognizing that even the most intimate accounts of marital suffering were carefully and collaboratively constructed raises questions about their "authenticity." With such questions comes the danger of inadvertently following the arguments of husbands who blamed wives' "friends" and family for their marital disputes, and who ascribed their wives' publications to the "wicked agency of others." (Present-day examples of this strategy can be found in claims that rape survivors like Chanel Miller did not write their own victim impact statements.[55]) Wives' authored their advertisements *and* they sought the help of "friends" in framing their stories. The familial and communal support structures on which they relied remained a consistent and essential source of strength. What had become difficult was honoring, or even acknowledging, that interdependence in a world that celebrated autonomy.

In a study of the late eighteenth-century invention of the concept of human rights, the French historian Lynn Hunt argues that the concept rested on an appreciation for autonomy rooted in "a new relationship to the world, not just new ideas." Particularly in the prerevolutionary Anglo-American context, Hunt observes that "the desire for greater autonomy can be traced more easily in autobiographies and novels than in the law." The "imaginative empathy" developed by the readers who engaged with heroines like Clarissa and Pamela, Hunt contends, laid the foundation for a political vision in which individual autonomy and equality were paramount. "Learning to empathize opened the path to human rights," even if "it did not ensure that everyone would be able to take that path right away."[56] Women who placed their personal testimony about the human effects of marital cruelty in the newspapers certainly played on sensible readers' sympathy in their quest for justice. Yet where Clarissa's fictional demise was poignant, Ann Wood's real and disconsolate life was dispiriting. It did not lend itself readily to worldly remedies. New legal emphasis on autonomy and rights, the next chapters will argue, were at least partially responsible for her predicament. Opening that path foreclosed and devalued others.

Lands unwa...

TO THE PUBLIC.

WHEREAS my wife AMERICAN LIBERTY, hath lately behaved in a very licentious manner, and run me confiderably in debt; this is to frwarn all perfons from trufting her, as I will pay no debts of her contracting from the date hereof.

Nov. 13 1773. LOYALTY.

TO THE PUBLIC.

WHEREAS my hufband Loyalty hath, in a late avertifement, forwarned all perfons from trufting me on his account : this is to inform the public, that he derived all his fortune from me ; and that by our marriage articles, he has no right to profcribe me from the ufe of it.—My reafon for leaving him was becaufe behaved in an arbitrary and cruel manner, and fuffered his domeftic fervants, grooms, foxhunters, &c. to direct and infult me. that purpofe, AMERICAN LIBERTY.

FIGURE 7.1 Liberty versus loyalty, *Boston News-Letter*, January 13, 1774
Courtesy of the American Antiquarian Society

Wives Not Slaves

In the 1774 advertisement that framed the previous chapter, Ann Wood aimed for pathos and sympathetic tears. Almost simultaneously, a different set of advertisements aimed for humor. In colonial newspapers filled with reports about the political crisis over the Tea Act, an imaginary husband named "Loyalty" discredited his wife, "American Liberty," claiming she had behaved "in a licentious manner" and run him "considerably in debt." American Liberty, in turn, defended her actions by citing Loyalty's violations of their marriage contract:

> WHEREAS my husband Loyalty hath, in a late advertisement, forwarned all persons from trusting me on his account; this is to inform the public, that he derived all his fortune from me; and that by our marriage articles, he has no right to proscribe me from the use of it.—My reason for leaving him was because he behaved in an arbitrary and cruel manner, and suffered his domestic servants, grooms, foxhunters, &c. to direct and insult me.[1]

Liberty's assertive tone, and the overt political stakes in this parody, contrasted sharply with real-life advertisements like those of Ann and Philip Wood, most of which avoided politics. As we have seen, it was not generally in a couple's interest to suggest that their domestic dispute had wider implications. Yet such implications were never far from the surface in a world where imagined connections between the household and the state justified both domestic and political order. During the 1760s and 1770s, this shared idiom created new problems and opportunities in both realms.

This chapter teases out the relationships between challenges to household authority, America's political revolution, and social change. It focuses on three distinct and contradictory eighteenth-century uses of the argument that wives were *not* slaves. The grievances of Eunice Davis, whose dispute with her husband opened this book, represented one strand. "If I am your *Wife*, I am not your *Slave*," Davis asserted in the pages of the 1762 *New-Hampshire Gazette*. Her consent to the marriage contract did not give her husband "unreasonable POWER to *tyrannize* and *insult* over" her. In the years immediately following the Davises' public conflict, such rhetoric became a staple of revolutionary politics, and in hindsight it is tempting to think of Eunice's ad as a real-life counterpart to the mock advertisement by American Liberty. Yet insofar as Davis's protest was "revolutionary," it hearkened back to the political debates of the *previous* century. Women on both sides of the Atlantic had long used analogies between marriage and slavery to secure protection from violence and degrading labor, and to challenge men who made excessive demands. Such protests fared best when they were not closely bound up with politics, and women in crisis usually went out of their way to frame their pleas as exceptions that proved the general rule that dependents ought to obey their household heads. This larger context gives new meaning to more explicitly political challenges to marital hierarchy in the eighteenth-century age of revolutions, including American Liberty's imaginary challenge to household authority, as well as Abigail Adams's proposal that the American nation's "new Code of Laws" should restrict the powers of tyrannical husbands.

American Liberty's arguments more closely resembled a second common use of the analogy between marriage and slavery. These arguments appeared in the complaints of wealthy white women from across the colonies who brought up slavery to defend their claims to property and to privileged status within the household. Such women, like Liberty, insisted on their authority to "direct" their domestic servants. More was at stake in disputes over what a real wife termed the "Privilege of my Negroe Wench," however, than social etiquette and household appearances. Women who claimed power as mistresses also set the equitable "privileges" of wives against the rights of husbands and creditors. The fortunes that secured those privileges and rights, all parties knew, depended on credit secured by the labor and bodies of the people they enslaved.

A third strand of argument inverted the others. In petitions against slavery and in freedom suits, people of color invoked the patriarchal authority of husbands in order to challenge the patriarchal authority of masters. Sir William Blackstone's unintended influence can be seen in litigation that insisted that the "service & conjugal comfort" a wife owed her husband took priority over all other obligations of dependence. Black men sought to free their enslaved wives by arguing that marriage gave a husband the right to "take away and hold" his wife "by law," regardless of her master's wishes. Because she was a wife, she could not be a slave.

Common threads connected these seemingly disparate arguments. Whether they emphasized the need for protection or asserted claims to property, all defined marriage against slavery. All participated in legal debates that defined women's marital power as an exceptional legal "privilege" rather than a basic right. And all demonstrated that household upheaval was fundamentally, and not simply metaphorically, connected to political unrest.

Liberty versus Loyalty: Marriage as Metaphor

One cannot understand the exchange between the husband Liberty and his wife Loyalty without recognizing households as political entities, but to reduce the joke to politics is to misunderstand the satirist's larger point and the larger, social stakes of revolution. The joke here was deliberately ambiguous. The satirist's foremost target was the press itself. The exchange between Liberty and Loyalty provided the climactic laugh in a series of sixteen comic "advertisements." Collectively, these fake advertisements indicted a culture that he believed allowed young people, and especially ladies and their chambermaids, too much leisure for the consumption of extravagant goods, romantic fantasies, and "Deistical" books by Hume and Voltaire. The dispute between Liberty and Loyalty was the only explicitly political reference, and the implication was that the domestic upheaval it represented was a side effect of the increased power of lawyers, of commerce and consumption, and of the press.[2]

To "get" the political joke here, one needs to recognize that Loyalty's and Liberty's advertisements were anomalous both as political rhetoric and in light of the conventions that shaped newspaper disputes between husbands and wives. It is tempting to imagine this exchange as supporting the right of the mistreated American colonies to depart from the tyrannical "husband" Great Britain, but such a reading overlooks the nuances both of this specific parody and the larger political situation. The legitimacy of such a separation, whether in politics or in marriage, was hotly contested. If Loyalty and Liberty were a married couple advertising in the press, it was by no means clear who had the right in the dispute. While a husband's public assertion of his marital authority could indeed suggest a tyrannical (or at least ungentlemanly) temperament, Liberty's response was hardly that of an appropriately deferential wife. In Massachusetts, moreover, the joke circulated in a *loyalist* paper shortly after the Boston Tea Party. In that context, it reads more easily as a critique of the extravagant and provocative disregard the Sons of Liberty displayed for Britain's authority and estate.[3]

If literal parallels in legal status were to be the criteria, marriage was a more accurate political metaphor than revolutionaries' more common claims that Britain treated them as slaves. Marriage, however, was *not* an ideal metaphor for those who challenged Britain's authority, precisely because it demonstrated the absurdity and the danger of such domestic analogies. The always politically savvy Benjamin Franklin had chosen his comparisons with care in the 1765 marital metaphor discussed at the close of chapter 4. He cast Scotland as England's aggrieved wife and the colonies as their abused children. Children (and especially sons) could reasonably remind their controlling father-king that, as they matured, they required some measure of independence. When colonists compared themselves to slaves oppressed by a tyrant, on the other hand, their only metaphorical option was revolt.

In 1773, violent rebellion remained an unappealing option to most colonists, and it was certainly not something white revolutionaries were eager to legitimate for their own slaves. English intellectuals accordingly dismissed colonial protests against enslavement as the hypocritical ranting of a spoiled child.[4] The Scottish Enlightenment figures to whom Benjamin Franklin had appealed as the colonists' mother sided with their English "husband" on this point. Even those who were politically sympathetic found colonial rhetoric insupportable. "It affords a curious spectacle," observed John Millar, a protégé of Adam Smith and influential professor of law, "that the same people who talk a high strain of political liberty, and who consider the privilege of imposing their own taxes as one of the unalienable rights of mankind, should make no scruple of reducing a great proportion of the inhabitants into circumstances by which they are not only deprived of property, but almost of every right whatsoever." Near the end of 1771, the decidedly republican Millar woefully noted that "fortune perhaps never produced a situation more calculated to ridicule a grave, and even a liberal hypothesis, or to show how little the conduct of men is at bottom directed by any philosophical principles."[5]

Revolutionaries did not represent *themselves* as wives. Marriage worked better as a symbol of social order than as a metaphor for injustice. The analogy, moreover, was a bit *too* apt. When he made American Liberty a wife, the Pennsylvania satirist highlighted the ways in which the relationship between colonies and Crown, while one of dependence, was *not* akin to slavery. Liberty's grievances—the misuse of her fortune, "cruel and arbitrary" treatment, direction and insult by "domestic servants"—captured the central sources of colonial discontent. Many of the specific charges in the Declaration of Independence could be reorganized under these headings. American Liberty's complaints about "domestic servants" in particular resonated not only with the Declaration's protest against the "swarms of officers" that the king had "sent hither . . . to harass our people," but also anticipated the charge that he "has excited domestic insurrections amongst us." As a wife, American Liberty asserted her privileged position in relation to other household dependents. As a political entity, she defended her place within the dependencies of empire, objecting to the Crown's enlistment of slaves and of "Indian savages" against her.[6] Read either way, she claimed power in domestic government, according to terms set in negotiated "Articles." As a wife, American Liberty could claim redress through avenues and on grounds not open to slaves. The parody's underlying message to those with political *and* those with matrimonial griev- ances was that everyone would be better off if they pursued those remedies quietly. In a less public forum, a settlement was possible. The complaints that appeared in the press, on the other hand, intensified the conflict, and left moral questions and political power in hands of greedy, amoral lawyers.

"If I am your *Wife*, I am not your *Slave*"

Eunice Davis's 1762 protest epitomizes the first strand of argument analyzed in this chapter. Her advertisement mixed political idiom with the language of sensibility. She was one of the first women to frame her ad as a defense of character and to label herself an "injur'd Wife"—two hallmarks of the sen- timental script. Unlike other women who employed these tropes, however, Eunice did not temper her assertion of individual personality with exagger- ated deference. In a strong first-person voice, she emphasized her consent to the marital contract, stressing that she had expected it to be based on "*Love and Affection.*" Instead, she (like American Liberty) had found that her hus- band governed his dependents as a tyrant. "When I acknowledg'd you as my Husband," Eunice informed John and her readers, "I . . . little thought . . . you would pretend to *assume* an unreasonable POWER to *tyrannize* and *in- sult* over me; and that *without any just Cause.*" Eunice demonstrated unusual confidence in her own ability to dictate new terms for the relationship. "Tho' for six Years past you have had the Power over me," she informed him, "you shall not any longer, if Justice can be obtain'd, unless something *Extraordinary* should happen in your conduct." He would be told of her "Proposals of Rec- onciliation . . . at a proper Season." "In the mean Time," she declared, "the first Step you have to take, is to make an *Acknowledgement*, in a public Manner, and retrieve *my Character*, which you have *unjustly aspersed.*"

The Davis household's predicament thus illuminates the economic pres- sures and intellectual culture that *generated* American revolutionary politics. The novelistic elements of Eunice Davis's protest were, in fact, novel. Her defiant political rhetoric, on the other hand, had long precedent. Her dec- laration "If I am your *Wife*, I am not your *Slave*" invoked language of revolt from the revolutions of the seventeenth century; the American Revolution was not yet at hand. When Eunice went to the press in 1762, England's North American colonists looked forward to a bright future within a mighty British Empire, which they had just helped to victory in the Seven Years' War. During that conflict, New Hampshire and Massachusetts had complained about jurisdictional and economic issues, but objections to political tyranny were *not* yet on the tip of every tongue. No one anticipated the conflict between the colonies and England that arose over the next decade.

John Davis was an early casualty of the rapid economic cycles of boom and bust that followed the end of the North American phase of the Seven Years' War. John was a tailor "from London," seeking Portsmouth clients who aspired to metropolitan gentility.[7] He was not so genteel as to be able to write his own name, but he appears to have been able to speak well enough to be a purveyor of fashion. As imports began to flow into the colonies after the wartime hiatus, John Davis overextended himself purchasing materials to entice customers who paid him with credit. Such borrowing and lending rested on the mistaken expectation that peace would bring prosperity. What occurred instead was a massive economic contraction. Britain stopped pouring resources into the colonies and focused on paying down England's wartime debts. Accordingly, imperial authorities stepped up enforcement of mercantilist restrictions on intercolonial trade and demanded colonial help with the empire's debt burden.

Davis's financial predicament in the early 1760s meant that he genuinely needed Eunice to do her "Duty," not only (as he specifically claimed) as a mother to their young children, but also by working at their trade and protecting him from his creditors. A man in danger of being sued for unpaid debts could "keep close" within his house to avoid litigation, relying on a legal custom that prevented authorities from forcing entry to serve him with a writ. This strategy required co-conspirators who conducted necessary business outside the home and made sure that only sympathetic persons gained entry. Eunice's departure made John doubly vulnerable, both by fueling creditors' fears of his insolvency and making it impossible for him to hide from them. A year after she left him, amid rumors that he was about to run away himself, his creditors tricked him into leaving the house, sued him en masse, and landed him in jail.[8]

Economic instability was not the sole source of John Davis's troubles. When she insisted she was not a slave, Eunice Davis employed language that had long served as a critique of domestic violence, and this was almost certainly the subtext for her advertisement. John had complained in 1760, before his economic woes became unbearable, that "evil minded People" were encouraging Eunice to leave him. A few months later, he placed an ad threatening those who "harboured" a servant Lad who had run away from him. Both complaints suggest that people in Portsmouth did not approve of the way he governed his dependents. The notice that provoked Eunice's response deviated from the standard formulas for husbands' ads in a number of respects, and in particular by soliciting her return. His promise to "kindly receive" her upon her "return to her Duty" was typical of men who feared that their wives would obtain legal remedy for their cruelty, failure to provide, or both. As was often the case in such notices, he alluded to family duty and affection, but also strongly asserted his possessory rights as a husband by prohibiting "any Person from entertaining or harbouring" Eunice. And he reserved for himself the right to determine whether Eunice's conduct was "agreeable to Reason," implicitly defending his power to "correct" her if necessary.[9]

Allegations that a husband treated his wife like a slave (and thus that wives, properly, were not slaves) appeared alongside charges of inappropriate demands for wifely service, violence, and sexual abuse in English and colonial court records from at least the early seventeenth century. In a 1619 English case, for example, a husband stood accused of deterring his wife from living with him by promising to make her "my Slave, and my sister Louther's Scullion." Rather than preside over his household, she was to do the dirty work reserved for the lowest (and usually male) kitchen servant.[10] A century later and an ocean away, Elizabeth Morgan also invoked slavery when she objected to her wealthy Connecticut husband's expectation that she would perform household drudge work unassisted. Notwithstanding his promise to "Hire what help he Could," she declared that "she would not Return, for She had ben his Slave long enough already."[11]

Morgan's complaints focused primarily on undue demands for her labor, but in most cases of this sort, violence and household work were intertwined. Testimony from a Massachusetts divorce case in the 1760s, for instance, recorded the husband's explanation that he treated his wife "as a Slave" because "Severity"—meaning violence—was required to make her serve his economic interests. Elizabeth Markham, whose heated exchange with her husband appeared in the *New-Hampshire Gazette* two years before Eunice Davis's, used the analogy to allude to sexual violence in marriage. Her husband, she claimed, "treated me much in the same Way that some Gentlemen I have heard of, do some of their young Negro Wenches,—lodge with them by Night, and give them the Strappado by Day; with this Difference, that they seldom beat them in Bed." The sexual abuse of enslaved women gave Markham a means to discuss openly a grievance that other women hinted at indirectly as a subject best "buried in silence." Even though her husband's violence was public knowledge in her neighborhood, Hannah Gardner explained, "the private abuses would be incredible" to them nonetheless. She had not told of them because, as a different Hannah had noted before the Connecticut courts several generations earlier, some abuses were not "fit to write nor" would "modesty allow mee to speak."[12]

AN INTELLECTUAL HISTORY
OF UNSPEAKABLE PROTEST

How was it that Elizabeth Markham had "heard of" unspeakable things? What prompted Eunice Davis to decry her husband's tyranny, if she was not parroting the politicians? And what did it mean for these women not simply to speak and write but to publish such rhetoric? Their appearance together in the press points to a conversation about power and jurisdiction *within* households as enduring and even more elusive than the conversation about legal jurisdiction *over* marriage and slavery outlined in chapter 4. Feminist thinkers (among them Elizabeth Cady Stanton and Virginia Woolf) have long argued that patriarchal systems maintain themselves by denying women their own history and intellectual traditions. Grievances left unspoken leave individuals, and successive generations, to invent their own, imperfect avenues for redress.[13] There is truth in this argument, but like lawyerly stories about ancient patriarchy, this story can perpetuate injustices it claims to resolve. Elizabeth Markham and Eunice Davis drew on a written and spoken tradition of protest, communicated by women across generations and across regions, that could simultaneously challenge and preserve patriarchal household forms.

As a defense of status within a hierarchical household order, the argument that wives were not slaves belonged to an abstract intellectual tradition backed by written authority. It was also a recurring vernacular trope. In both guises, it was reinforced and given new significance by the expansion of colonial slavery. The preponderance of New England cases among those in which the comparison served as a critique of domestic violence suggests that this usage had strong ties to radical Protestantism. In his early seventeenth-century guide to godly family life, the minister William Gouge argued that "God hath not ranked wives among those in the family who are to be corrected."[14] This premise acquired legal force through the seventeenth-century Massachusetts *Body of Liberties*, which denied husbands the authority to beat their wives and reserved the "correction" of female (and male) householders to the state. In 1764, the jurist and politician Thomas Hutchinson made it part of his effort to define (and defend) a legal tradition distinctive to Massachusetts. Hutchinson celebrated Puritans' refusal to countenance the "moderate correction" of wives *and* Puritan ambivalence about slavery in the same few paragraphs, turning both into evidence that Massachusetts laws were marked by "more tender sentiments" than their English counterparts.[15]

If Puritan restraint on householder authority counted as tenderness, it took a peculiar form, defined starkly against violence rather than by any positive attributes. It rested on an understanding of authority defined, ultimately, by the power to direct and "correct" others through physical force. Wives, as partners in household government, were not slaves not only because they "were not ranked among those in the family who are to be corrected," but also because they had the power to correct those who ranked below them: children, servants, and, lowest of all, slaves.[16] The language of sensibility thinly covered a legal order that assumed all men—and women—would be tyrants if they could. Hutchinson recognized the abuse of domestic power as a real and enduring issue, but like most of his politically minded contemporaries, he preferred not to speak about it more than minimally necessary.

Ironically, when Hutchinson attempted to categorize slavery as something outside the Massachusetts legal tradition, he obliquely referred his readers to John Josselyn's seventeenth-century story about an enslaved woman who had not only spoken, but "sang very loud and shrill . . . her grief" over sexual abuse that she disdained as "beyond her slavery."[17] Elizabeth Markham might have "heard" of such grievances from the ungodly books that her husband accused her of reading. She probably also knew of them more directly. She and her colonial contemporaries understood sexual exploitation as a nearly unavoidable element of slaves' experience, long before illicit and abusive interracial relationships became staple themes in antislavery literature. When she co-opted that abuse to portray her own unhappy marriage as beyond slavery, Markham testified to power relations that gave white and black women common grievances, but not common interests.[18]

WOMEN'S CRITICISM OF MARRIAGE, 1660–1776

Eunice Davis was participating in the same conversation as Elizabeth Markham; Portsmouth, New Hampshire, was a tiny town. Eunice might—or might not—have been reading the same books. The newspaper printers made it appear that she had signed her advertisement herself, a distinction they did not grant to her husband John, who signed with a mark. Yet legal records leave Eunice's own ability to write in doubt. The inability to write did not preclude the ability to read, to speak, or (as scornful memoirs by the printer Isaiah Thomas attest) even to compose poetry and other literature for printed media.[19] The Davises' imperfect literacy offers intriguing evidence of a transformation in literary culture through which ideas conceived by and for a leisured, genteel elite began to serve people of lower social status.

We can situate Eunice Davis and Elizabeth Markham in a tradition of literary critiques of marriage and women's legal disempowerment that extends back (at least) to Margaret Cavendish, Duchess of Newcastle, a member of the same seventeenth-century political circles as Catherine Scott (chapter 2), and forward through the English novelist Frances Brooke to the American revolutionary Abigail Adams. Common threads in their criticism include (1) skepticism about the marriage of very young girls; (2) an analysis of household hierarchy based on expectations about coercion and corporal punishment from which wives were exempt, but children, servants, and slaves were not; (3) questions about whether women's political disempowerment also exempted them from political loyalties and obligations; and (4) the use of cultural ventriloquism and the idea that men were "slaves to affection" to mute the political force of their arguments and render their criticism "safe."

The text that offers the closest analog to Eunice's protest "If I am your *Wife*, I am not your *Slave*" belonged to an elite literary tradition. One of the *Sociable Letters* that Margaret Cavendish published in 1664 provided a wry critique of aristocratic child marriages, framed as a fight between an aristocratic Lady and "her Pretty Young Daughter" and emphasizing the links between correction, dependence, and slavery. The daughter escaped physical punishment through skillful rhetoric, asserting that "she had rather be Racked as a Traitor, than be Whip'd as a Slave." Her insubordination to her mother was not treason, and she did not deserve "Thraldome or Slavery." At "Ten years of Age" she was "too Old to be Whip'd, [and] almost Old enough for an Husband." The child was "rescued" by marriage to a friend of her father's, who at first hesitated to take her because he wished neither to "be a Tutor, nor a Nurse" and thought it better to marry a more mature woman. The punchline of the story was that the father rewarded this wisdom with so large a dowry the that man accepted the girl, judging money a more faithful companion and source of happiness than a wife ever could be.[20]

Cavendish had spent the decades of the English Civil Wars in the inner circles of the Royalists exiled to Europe's French-speaking Catholic courts. Cavendish formally supported her family's alliance with the restored monarchy of Charles II while playfully using multiple voices in her fictionalized *Letters*—along with the analogy of enslavement—to criticize the limited options for women found in all forms of seventeenth-century political thought. A letter addressed to a dissenting republican female friend observed that women's exclusion from government could be interpreted as freeing them from it, or at least from the partisan loyalties that divided men. Women neither swore allegiance as subjects, nor were they made citizens of the Commonwealth. They were bound neither to the Crown nor to the state. "We are no Subjects," Cavendish observed, "unless it be to our Husbands, and not alwayes to them," for "we oftener inslave men, than men inslave us; they seem to govern the world, but we really govern the world, in that we govern men."[21]

Women secretly wielded power unacknowledged by men, but their own security lay with ties of female friendship and kinship not severed by marriage or by divisions among men: "Though there hath been a Civil War in the Kingdom, and a general War amongst the Men," Cavendish reminded her "Friend" and her readers, "yet there hath been none amongst the Women." And, all things considered, she advised her sister in a different letter, "where there is a Hazard in the Choice, and a Security in not Choosing, the Best" option for women was to remain "Mistress of your self." A "Single Life" was the "Safest Way." "All Wives if they be not Slaves, yet they are Servants, although to be a Servant to a Worthy Husband, is both Pleasure and Honour, for true Affection takes more Pleasure to Serve than to be Served, and it is an Honour to Obey the Meritorious."[22]

Wives "be not Slaves," but they were servants to an honorable cause—when the relationship was governed by affection. Cavendish's "Wishes and Prayers" for her sister were that "whether Married or not Married," she "may be as Happy as this World can make you."[23] When Eunice Davis, a century later and an ocean away, insisted that if she was a wife, she was not a slave, she too acknowledged the honor of serving in a well-ordered and affectionate household. "I always was, and still am willing to do my Duty," she told John, "provided you put it in my Power, and behave as you ought to do." John, as an unworthy husband, bore responsibility for any shortcomings in her own service as a wife and a mother; his own "Iniquities" had put this out of her "Power." Like most deserting wives, Eunice sought to make her husband the agent of their separation.[24] She was undeniably assertive about her own power to dictate the terms under which she would return to her duty. She directed her critique, however, specifically at her unworthy husband, rather than marriage itself. Cavendish had been more forthright. Marriage, as it was organized in this world, offered happiness chiefly by chance, or by the opportunity to escape the thralldom of childhood and become the mistress over other dependents.

It is unlikely that Eunice Davis was reading Margaret Cavendish. But Eunice stood on the fringes of a transatlantic circle of sociable readers who, in the 1750s and 1760s, revisited the same set of questions about marriage and women's relationship to the state. The journalist, playwright, and novelist Frances Brooke, for instance, was a noteworthy conduit for such ideas, though we don't know whether she drew on Cavendish directly or picked up similar rhetoric in the French novels she translated for English readers. Criticism of marriage as a form of slavery had been a central theme for the aristocratic seventeenth-century French women who invented the novel as a genre, in response to the same political crises that inspired Cavendish.[25] During the late 1750s and early 1760s, Brooke edited *The Old Maid*—a London periodical featuring humorous commentary on both marriage and politics—and wrote for a living, while her husband served as Anglican chaplain to the British troops in North America. At the war's end, husband and wife together became vocal proponents of the expansion of the Anglican Ecclesiastical hierarchy to the colonies. This issue, as chapter 4 noted, generated considerable controversy and patriotic ire, particularly in New England, and particularly because of its implications for legal jurisdiction over marriages and other aspects of domestic law. From 1763 to 1767, Brooke lived with her husband in Canada under the patronage of the newly conquered colony's Scottish governors, and there wrote *The History of Emily Montague*.[26]

This epistolary novel introduced readers to colonial politics and used colonial women as the foil for a radical critique of marriage. Brooke's characters opined that because "the civil government of America is on the same plan with that of the mother country, it were to be wished the religious establishment was also the same," for neither Catholic despotism nor Presbyterian republicanism meshed well with "a limited monarchy like ours." Brooke astutely argued that the rioting and upheaval produced by the 1765 Stamp Act grew out of the hardship produced by earlier measures restricting colonial trade; she thought colonial disquiet understandable, but concluded that "a good mother will consult the interest and happiness of her children, but will never suffer her authority to be disputed."[27]

A good husband, on the other hand, used different policy. Brooke's characters included a sprightly young woman who promised "to marry a savage and turn squaw (a pretty soft name for an Indian princess!)" after being told by Huron women of their freedom to "ramble 500 miles" without trouble from their husbands. This celebration Indian women's "freedom" inverted the cultural ventriloquism we saw in chapter 1, where colonists justified enslaving Indian women in English families on the grounds that it improved their circumstances. Brooke put her most radical recommendations in the mouth of the novel's hero, the dashing and sensible Col. Rivers. In letters to his sister, Rivers also admired the primitive simplicity and freedom in Indian marriages, though his reflections drew on Scottish Enlightenment assumptions as much as ethnographic observation. "The missionaries are said to have found no difficulty so great in gaining them to Christianity, as that of persuading them to marry for life," he reported. There was truth in such claims, but also convenient projection. Indians, as representatives of the state of nature, "regarded the Christian system of marriage as contrary to the law of nature and reason; and asserted that, as the Great Spirit formed us to be happy, it was opposing his will, to continue together when otherwise." Brooke ultimately rejected both "savage" marriages and the admirable but "unnatural" single life pursued by nuns in the convents in Quebec as artifacts of primitive, familial despotism. Her female coquette decided that she would "not be a squaw," for "in the most essential point," Indian children were "slaves: the mothers married their children without ever consulting their inclinations." Indian women chose their chiefs, "but what is that to the dear English privilege of choosing a husband?"[28]

"True freedom" lay only in England, but there was room for improvement. English men could learn from the gallant Rivers, who conceded that "in the true sense of the word, *we* are the savages, who so impolitely deprive you of the common rights of citizenship, and leave you no power but that of which we cannot deprive you, the resistless power of your charms." Brooke's hero, like Cavendish's wise suitor, aimed to marry a mature woman in her twenties rather than a girl who required a tutor or a nurse. Through him Brooke also expanded on Cavendish's argument that women's political exclusion could be a form of freedom. Rivers advised his sister that he did not think her "obliged in conscience to obey laws in which you have no share in making." Women's pleas for political rights "would certainly be at least as good as that of the Americans, about which we every day hear so much." Later in the novel, Brooke borrowed explicitly from the tradition of marital advice and critique founded by Cavendish and her French counterparts; she translated and reprinted several pages from the recently published memoirs of Madame de Maintenon, the politically savvy secret second wife of Louis XIV. Where de Maintenon depicted married women's lot as to "suffer and obey" the unjustified tyranny of husbands, Brooke's hero provided an alternative vision. He felt himself "obliged to own" that men "are generally tyrannical." Those who know "how to be happy," however, "willingly give up the harsh title of master, for the more tender one of friend." "The soul of friendship" is "equality." "Marriage, to give delight, must join two minds, not devote a slave to the will of an imperious Lord; whatever conveys the idea of subjection necessarily destroys that of love, of which I'm so convinced, that I have always wished the word OBEY expunged from the marriage ceremony."[29]

Abigail Adams, the rabidly patriotic wife of the rabidly patriotic Massachusetts lawyer John Adams, did not agree with Frances Brooke on matters of imperial or ecclesiastical politics. On the question of marriage, however, there was "no war amongst women." In 1776, shortly before John Adams was

appointed to the congressional committee that drafted the Declaration of Independence, Abigail wrote him a letter that has become famous for its entreaty "to Remember the Ladies" in "the new Code of Laws" she imagined
the new nation would require. "Be more generous and favourable to them
than your ancestors," she admonished, and "do not put such unlimited power
into the hands of the Husbands. Remember all Men would be tyrants if they
could." Scholars have only recently realized that most of what Abigail went
on to say on the subject was directly adapted from Frances Brooke's novel.[30]

The connection between Abigail Adams and Frances Brooke overturns
long-standing interpretations of Abigail's letter. Abigail's entreaty was *not* an
imitative byproduct of *American* revolutionary politics, though revolution certainly provided an opportunity to put her ideas in action. Neither was her plea
original, something imaginable by an exceptionally progressive woman but not
by the male revolutionaries with whom she interacted. Nor were the ideas she
expressed privately circulated only among her closest correspondents. Brooke's
transatlantically circulated novel was itself not entirely "new"; rather, it recapitulated a century-old (at least) tradition of female questions about marriage and
women's relationship to the state. Brooke might also have drawn some inspiration both from the alternatives presented by Huron squaws and Ursuline nuns,
and also from the plight of women like Eunice Davis and Elizabeth Markham,
who were publicly engaged in a revolutionary conversation about rights and
obligations within marriage a decade before Brooke's *History* went to press.

Davis's and Markham's arguments suggest that a real as well as metaphorical overlap between American challenges to political tyranny and challenges
to household tyranny was a matter of common sense as early as 1760. The
implications of such reasoning unsettled authorities, and as political tensions
rose it became increasingly unwise for wives to attempt to obtain justice by
comparing themselves directly to slaves. In the instances for which the outcome is known, the women whose cases have been discussed here did not
fare well in the courts.[31] Insofar as their complaints about their husbands'
"tyranny" and "insults" were taken to question masculine authority in general
and not simply the misbehavior of individual men, such rhetoric backfired.
Their defiance served as evidence of character flaws and an inclination to
disobedience, justifying their husband's attempts to "correct" them by means
that would otherwise have seemed "immoderate" or severe.

"The Privilege of my Negroe Wench"

In 1758, John Adams made note in his diary of a "conjugal Spat" between his
parents. His father, a member of their town's governing council, had brought

home Judah and Dolly, two impoverished girls whom the town had bound out as servants to secure their room and board. Race as well as poverty factored in the girls' inability to obtain support from their own families. Judah, at least, was a person of color, subject to the legal and economic constraints that made it difficult for nonwhites to maintain independent households. Elizabeth Adams, John's mother, was none too pleased about these new boarders. In front of the girls, she flew into a fury in which she accused her husband of wanting "to put your Girls over me, to make me a slave to your Wenches." John's father, in response, "resolutely asserted his Right to govern." Elizabeth Adams did not gain her point with her husband, but he was not the only audience for her tantrum. The two girls, who watched the scene through tears, were duly reminded of their precarious place in the household hierarchy, and of the effort that would be required to placate the mistress who would be directly responsible for governing them. Judah was still bound in the family's service five years later, when Elizabeth Adams loaned her for a season to Abigail, her new daughter-in-law. Abigail Adams accepted the favor grudgingly. She did not "fancy Judah," but she could not easily refuse an option that John *and* his mama judged the best way to contain their household expenses. Judah's thoughts on the matter went unrecorded.[32]

Elizabeth Adams's outburst illustrates a second sort of "wives not slaves" argument, in which women defined their status through their own power to wield authority over other dependents. When this strand of argument made its way into more public conjugal spats, it was less penitent, less explicitly political, and usually more powerful than protests like those of Eunice Davis. It did not threaten established hierarchies, but rather affirmed a social order in which rank was intimately tied to the power to govern and "correct." Such arguments could be intermingled with protests against a husband's unreasonable violence or expectations about labor. Elizabeth Morgan, the Connecticut wife who had been her husband's "slave long enough already," for instance, also demanded that her husband "buy her a Negro Wench" as a condition for reconciliation.[33] American Liberty's protest crossed categories as well; she not only criticized Loyalty's "arbitrary and cruel" behavior, but also specifically rebuked him for "suffering his . . . servants . . . to direct and insult" her.

Arguments that defended the right of wives to own and command slaves were delimited by class rather than region or historical period. Their recurrence during the late 1760s is significant because it illuminates the transformation of the marital "rights" the novelist Eliza Haywood had championed in the 1740s into "privileges" in the hands of enlightened lawyers like William Blackstone and John Adams. We can examine this change through the stories of two women whose protests anticipated "American Liberty's" claims that her husband had "derived all his fortune from me" and illegitimately sought to "proscribe me from the use of it."

Jane Tennent of Pennsylvania complained that her husband Charles had "not used me as a Wife," noting specifically that "he has refused me the Privilege of my Negro Wench to wait on me."[34] Virginian Margaret Bannerman's husband Benjamin had compelled her to "make over to him" her real estate and "five Negroes, of considerable value." This was an early step in a drawn-out process by which he took control of her fortune and "robbed" her of the prerogatives of her status. He denied her "the management of his house and servants" and used her money to clothe "a Mulatto bastard," who sat "next upon his right hand at table" and later took her place. He turned Margaret out into "a single room in a small house," where "deprived of servants" and unwilling to perform their work, she had become dependent on others' hospitality for the "benefit of a fire" and other "necessaries" of daily life.[35]

Jane Tennent's and Margaret Bannerman's complaints demonstrate the ways in which wives could define their status against that of other dependents, as well as the power of wealth to mediate the disabilities of gender. Jane and Margaret were rich widows, recently remarried, who found that their new husbands were more interested in their property than their persons. Charles Tennent and Benjamin Bannerman had behaved deceitfully, unjustly, perhaps even "brutally" in attempting to wrest control of Jane's and Margaret's estates. Most of their actions, nonetheless, fell within the legal rights of husbands found in Blackstone's account of coverture.

Jane and Margaret, however, were not about to accept such an intrusion on their own authority. They turned instead to some of the legal and extralegal equitable remedies available to wives outside of the purview of the common law. They also published powerful arguments contrasting their standing as persons—not women—of property with their husbands' mere pretensions to financial and personal credibility. Although they found themselves on tenuous and shifting legal ground and showed little regard for the conventional deference that informed the advertisements of most of the other wives, Jane and Margaret were both more successful than Eunice Davis at obtaining a measure of redress for their grievances.

The central charge in both Jane's and Margaret's advertisements was that their husbands were not the gentlemen they pretended to be. Jane Tennent used Charles's posting of her against him, wondering in her own notice how "such a man (as Mr. Tennent would endeavor to persuade the public he is) would be guilty of setting his hand to such a malicious piece of stuff." Charles Tennent wished the public to believe he was a minister and intellectual of equal standing with his father and brothers; he was the youngest (and only infamous) son in the family of the famous "Log College" revivalist William Tennent Sr. By marrying Jane, Charles seems to have been pursuing a strategy that had worked well for his better-known siblings. His brother William had been rescued from his creditors by a quickly arranged marriage to a wealthy widow, whose "skilful superintendence . . . of his temporal concerns" had made him "quite easy in his worldly circumstances."[36] Unfortunately, Charles was not content to leave his financial affairs to Jane's control; his advertisement discrediting her appeared within weeks of the marriage ceremony, and explicitly asserted his sole right to manage her first husband's estate.

Jane's counterattack accused him of ill treatment that, while ungentlemanly, was a far cry from life-threatening cruelty. In addition to refusing her "the Privilege of [her] Negroe Wench," he had also denied her the use of her "Horse and Carriage"—something explicitly granted her in her previous husband's will. She had consequently been obliged to leave the house on foot to get a tooth pulled, and (she claimed) returned the same day to find that he had "pasted up Advertisements around the Neighbourhood" declaring that she had absconded. While her complaints seem comparatively petty, her ad's effect on Charles's reputation probably was not. She demonstrated that Charles had not "used [her] as a Wife" because he could not afford to maintain the accoutrements appropriate to her status. Not only had she not run him into debt since she became his wife, she had paid money out of her "own Estate, to answer his Debts, and for Clothes both for himself and his Children."[37]

Margaret Bannerman charged Benjamin with even greater duplicity. Her first publication, in 1768, contended that Benjamin's behavior would "surprise all honest men, and raise their indignation against one who could act so brutally." Like Jane Tennent, she used his efforts to discredit her against him. As their conflict escalated, Margaret argued not only that his behavior was not that of a gentleman, but that he himself had no claim to the status. She portrayed him as a transatlantic con man. He had attained her speedy assent to marriage by passing himself off as a West Indies merchant who had recently inherited seven thousand pounds from a relative in Scotland. Too late, she discovered that he had in fact been sent to Antigua as a convict servant, and after serving his time, he had gotten "some Gentlemens effects into his hands, eloped" and come to Portsmouth. He then used her money to pay the debts accrued in this charade. She gave "honest men" warning that once Benjamin had disposed of her assets, he would no doubt leave Virginia without giving notice. It was only fitting that a former servant preferred the company of his "Mulatto bastard" to that of his wife.[38]

Jane's and Margaret's complaints differed from most others in that they emphasized their rights as wives with little or no mention of their duties.

Neither attempted to establish her reputation as a submissive or obedient wife; Jane in particular would have had a hard time sustaining such a claim. During her first marriage, Jane's husband had been forced to give bond for her good behavior after several neighbors charged her in court "with being a woman of vile and wicked Practices." They claimed that she habitually "raised wicked, false, invidious Reports . . . endeavoring to provoke" the entire neighborhood "to jealousies, animosities and acts of revenge to [their] utter Ruin." Jane was also twice convicted of assault, once in connection with this early suit and again in the course of her conflict with Charles.[39] Margaret did not leave external evidence of this sort, but Benjamin made (obviously self-interested) charges in a similar vein. He claimed that she "was a cruel, tyrannizing, drunken woman, in two of her former husbands time." He justified his treatment of her with the accusation that she'd tried to poison him and implied that her previous husbands, "both of whom she had buried in about thirteen months," might also have died at her hand.[40]

Jane and Margaret refuted their husbands' most serious allegations, but they did not themselves emerge as sympathetic figures. Remarkably, this did not matter much. As persons of property, they were able to make claims for justice unavailable to wives who traded only on their reputations for virtue. Margaret based her initial call for a public hearing on her status as a person who had "lived here many years in good credit, and laid out some thousands of pounds in trade." She answered Benjamin's accusations about her marital history in the same manner, noting that with one of her recently deceased "husbands I lived in good credit 16 years, and by our industry in trade gained upwards of £2500, which this deceiver robbed me of." Jane was less explicit, but her ad clearly established her control over her "own Estate."[41]

Jane and Margaret had independent claims to property because they were widows whose husbands bequeathed to them—and trusted them to manage—sizeable estates. It is worth noting, however, that widowhood itself was not the *source* of their confidence in their rights and abilities. Both had a direct hand in their deceased husbands' rise in status from local "shopkeepers" to prosperous "merchants." Their apparently childless marriages freed them to exert even more "industry in trade" than was usually the lot of good colonial wives. While their motives for marrying again are not clear, neither remained a widow for more than six months. Margaret had, as Benjamin charged, buried two husbands in the space of thirteen months. She waited only another six before marrying Benjamin.[42] Hasty remarriage might explain their inattention to legal provisions that would have secured their holdings from their second husbands. It is also possible that such protections did not seem quite necessary to colonial women in 1765 and early 1766 when these marriages were contracted; when they fell apart between 1767 and 1769, however, widely circulated copies of Blackstone's recently published *Commentaries* made such oversight seem a serious legal error. Their cases illustrate different ways in which legal and extralegal strategies could be employed to remedy this mistake.

Jane Tennent never sued Charles, but she seems to have accomplished more by indirect means than Margaret Bannerman was able to secure with a victory in court. Without clear legal documentation, Jane's efforts to retain control her estate must be inferred from a range of other evidence. In her advertisement, she chastised Charles for refusing to meet with her "before any Gentlemen in Town, to talk the Matter Face to Face." This type of arbitration probably played a significant part in their subsequent arrangements, and it placed Charles in an awkward position. Their marriage had almost certainly been facilitated by a prominent "gentleman of the town," the Reverend Doctor Francis Alison. Alison (who like both Jane Tennent and Benjamin Bannerman was a Scottish immigrant) remains famous as the founder of multiple institutions of higher learning in the mid-Atlantic. He was a coexecutor, with Jane and a Philadelphia merchant, of her first husband's will, and apparently also a patron for Charles. In both instances, he might have been stepping into the shoes of Charles's recently deceased brother Gilbert, the powerful pastor of the Second Presbyterian Church at Philadelphia where Jane was a member. Alison would have known Jane's precise financial circumstances and expectations, and he might have recommended the match as a way for Charles to stave off "embarrassment" and for Jane to secure social standing in accord with her affluence.[43]

Instead, the marriage was—in the words of the nineteenth-century church historian William Sprague—"fruitful of evils that continued to the day of his death." Alison seems to have stood by Jane in the dispute, lending moral if not legal support; she expressed her gratitude with bequests to his children in her own will. Shortly after the newspaper controversy, Charles was dismissed from his positions as a boarding school master and pastor to a large Presbyterian Congregation near Jane's home community in Chester County. The affair suggests that he had lost Alison's patronage as well as his own credibility. His nineteenth-century biographer described the last few years of Charles's life as marked by "painful relations with his Presbytery," brought on by "excessive indulgence in . . . the prevailing fashion of moderate and even immoderate drinking." Charles moved from Chester County to Delaware, where he was again dismissed from his ministerial position after a brief period of service.[44] He died in alcoholic ignominy in early 1771.

Jane does not appear to have accompanied Charles into exile, although it is not clear whether they made a formal separation agreement. Scattered court records from the years immediately following the newspaper conflict recognized both her independent agency and her continuing legal ties to her absent husband. In the summer of 1767, she was convicted of assaulting one James McCullough. (McCullough was almost certainly a relative—either her brother, her brother-in-law, or perhaps a young nephew—and he was also involved in the complicated settlement of her first husband's estate, but court records don't reveal the story behind the trial.) When Jane had been accused of "wicked practices" and assault a decade earlier, her first husband's intervention had protected her from the full force of the law; this time she gave bond in her own name and faced the consequences without her husband's "cover."[45]

In 1768, she was called to court again in a dispute "respecting the Farming . . . of her the said Jane's Farm or Plantation." The records of the case make clear that Jane managed land that she had purchased with and inherited from her first husband—that in the eyes of the community at least it was "her . . . Plantation." She *alone* had hired and evicted a tenant for the land, and she *alone* had agreed to the arbitrated settlement of the conflict that resulted. When she refused to comply with the arbitrators' decision, however, the tenant sued Charles.[46]

One can imagine a scenario in which this case served Jane's interests, allowing her to remind Charles that if he attempted to claim any of her property, he would also be liable for her debts. Alternatively, Jane might have been trying to avoid the specter of marital unity when she turned to equitable arbitration to resolve her dispute with her tenant. The lawsuit could then have been a savvy move by the plaintiff, compelling her to accept a settlement with which she was not pleased. Arbitration was ordinarily difficult to enforce at common law, and, with or without a formal separation agreement, Jane and Charles's marital strife made the matter exceptionally complicated.[47] The lawsuit had been dropped by the next court session, and so there is no way to know whether Charles or Jane satisfied the debt, or whether the disgruntled plaintiff simply gave up.

What these cases do demonstrate is that Jane's home community treated her in many respects as a *feme sole* and that she retained separate control of a substantial portion of her property. The means by which she accomplished this were not recorded in Pennsylvania's courts, and they have become invisible to us today. As with other cases of localized, equitable law, they involved intangibles such as the intervention of powerful allies and the force of her own potent personality, as well as more formal—though not strictly "legal"—arbitration. Whether or not Jane and Charles actually called on lawyers to document and defend their separation according to the principles of equity, they and their communities acted as if they had. Charles reportedly died in debt. When Jane died a few years later, she still possessed a considerable estate—less, to be sure, than what her first husband had left her, but more than the "widow's third" she might have expected if it had all passed to Charles.

Her will extended her control of these possessions beyond the grave, carrying over some animosities and mending others. She left her plantation to a nephew (and ward) with the provision that he bar two of his older brothers from ever setting foot on the land. A niece received a debt owed her by one of the disfavored brothers. Yet Jane chose one of the neighbors who had prosecuted her for "wicked carriages" as an executor; his daughter witnessed the will and received Jane's silver cream pot, her tea chest and canister, and her black paduasoy gown as expressions of favor. Her riding chair went to her current pastor's wife. The unnamed "Negro wench," however, was no longer hers to dispose of.[48]

WIVES' PRIVILEGES VERSUS CREDITORS' RIGHTS: DEBATING EQUITY

Margaret Bannerman turned, in succession, to neighbors, to the newspapers, and to the Court of Chancery. Benjamin's efforts to convert her property into cash were not discreet; he advertised the sale and his intention to travel out of the colony in the *Virginia Gazette*. Even as he did this, Margaret was able to turn to local merchants for clothing and household items to replace those he had denied her. These purchases were what prompted Benjamin to formally discredit her, setting the stage for her counterattacks in the press and the local courts. From this point, it took more than two years for Margaret to obtain a settlement. While the court records are relatively opaque regarding the process, periodic newspaper notices alluded to intense negotiations inside and outside of court. These public debates highlighted competing eighteenth-century visions of the "equitable" distribution of marital property: Margaret turned to contract logic that recognized married women's separate property, whereas Benjamin upheld a vision of limited female entitlements to a joint estate that, by virtue of marital unity, belonged indisputably to the husband.

Benjamin managed to delay a trial of the case with preemptive offers to pay different acquaintances for Margaret's room and board, though on restrictive terms. After about six months of stalling, Margaret took out another adver-tisement accusing him of making such promises in bad faith. He had used the time to load all of her "household and kitchen furniture, plate, wearing apparel, &c." onto a boat and carry them to another community where "he ex-posed [them] to publick sale." Three months later, following what must have been a sensational and contentious hearing, the Borough Court at Norfolk ordered Benjamin to pay her an annual stipend of sixty-five pounds per year, and to give bond for thirteen hundred pounds to ensure that it would be paid. These payments amounted to the interest off the cash assets that even Ben-jamin acknowledged Margaret had possessed at the time of their marriage.[49]

Although Benjamin retained control of all her real property, the award was relatively generous when judged against comparable English cases. The decision gave Margaret a portion in line with what she might have claimed had she been careful to draft "marriage Articles" before the ceremony. The court's award reflected legal thinking newly prominent in the mid-eighteenth century; namely, "the idea that the wife's support is to come from interest on property she brought to the marriage and be somehow proportionate to that property." For women who brought more property to marriage than did their husbands, this reasoning was a potential improvement from the common-law allotment of one-third interest in "his"—meaning their conjoined—estate. It recognized a wife's separate interest in property that lasted through and beyond the marriage. For women with less property than their husbands, on the other hand, it was not so advantageous—a fact that might explain Margaret's failure to draft marriage articles guaranteeing her separate interest in her estate. If she anticipated someday gaining title to Benjamin's purported seven-thousand-pound inheritance, she had little reason to arrange a pre-nuptial agreement that restricted her widow's share.[50]

Benjamin deemed the decree outrageous. After six months of unsuccess-ful attempts to appeal and otherwise avoid the decision, he attempted to dis-credit it in the press. His notice first attacked the justices of the local court, claiming that they were undignified, set against one another by local politics, and more concerned with their private interests than the workings of justice. He next attacked Margaret, pausing briefly to make a gentlemanly apology for "exposing my wife's character to the world, as it is the last thing I would be guilty of." (Margaret answered this by asking how it was that he did "not reckon imprisonment exposing, neither does he reckon turning me out of doors at 10 in the forenoon, before every person in *Portsmouth*, exposing; at the same time posted me in *Norfolk* and *Portsmouth*.") And finally, and at greatest length, Benjamin discussed finances.[51]

Benjamin rejected the court's reasoning as "unequitable." In its place, he suggested a model that preserved the unity of marital property and the primacy of the husband's interest and specifically cited the "equitable" interests of creditors as the reason for his possessory rights. Benjamin claimed that the court's award was roughly two-thirds of his annual income (all of which came from renting Margaret's properties), a proportion that unduly penalized him and threatened his creditors. He offered her instead sixteen pounds a year, or one-third of what he implied he was worth after making payments on his debts. "It must tend to bad consequences," he proclaimed, "for any court to think of compelling a man to maintain his wife at a higher expense than his estate will afford, either to distress himself, or deprive his creditors of their just due." He invited "the learned to make some enlargement on such proceedings," and asked "the publick to judge whether the court's decree, or my offer, was most equitable." He portrayed himself as virtuously fending off those authorities who sought to carry him "to jail on her account" while he sought to "secure" his creditors "from suffering by the said decree." After this business was done, he was "still agreeable to give [Margaret] a proportionate share of what is left." But "if she does not choose to comply with that, she may get her decreed £65 a year how she can."[52]

Benjamin ultimately prevailed, not only in practical terms, but also in anticipating legal trends in England and America regarding what constituted an "equitable" settlement on an estranged wife. Generalizations about awards for separate maintenance or alimony are difficult to make because these have not been much studied and because they varied substantially from case to case and jurisdiction to jurisdiction. Nonetheless, nineteenth-century English courts typically set maintenance at a third of a husband's net income, moving away from eighteenth-century views that emphasized a wife's claim to what she had brought to the marriage. The latter position, as already noted, favored only those women who had substantial property. Alimony became so problematic for nineteenth-century American courts that most divorcing wives did not seek it, lest it somehow bar the divorce. Courts would, however, recognize and provide for the return of property a woman had brought to the marriage. In most instances, this meant that the wife was worse off than she would have been with a proportionate share of the husband's property because it did not account for increases during the marriage.[53] Finally, enforcement was an enduring problem; unless a wife had managed to prevent her husband from liquidating his estate, she would be forced to "get her decreed" settlement "how she can."

Benjamin fervently insisted that all the property in question was "his." The Norfolk County Court, sitting in Chancery, was willing to acknowledge that some of it might be Margaret's, but neither came close to considering that she might somehow reestablish direct control over the entirety of the estate. The debate over what constituted an appropriate portion in this case validates the claim by the historian Susan Staves that "forced share rules"—whether based on contract logic or entitlements (i.e., "thirds")—sought primarily to balance the interests of male property holders and their creditors against the general community interest in preventing women and dependent children from becoming public charges. It was not, as later critics of coverture implied, that a wife could "own nothing." But when tested, property rights for women were construed differently than those for men. Courts protected them only insofar as they secured female subsistence; they did not intend wives to be able to contract, consolidate, and transmit wealth in the same manner as men. This was true in the seventeenth-century cases examined in chapters 1 and 2, and it remained so as mid-eighteenth-century jurists revisited the questions that *Manby v. Scott* had tried to settle a century before. The increased importance of contractual marital settlements affected the larger debate less by expanding women's legal claims than by turning these into negotiated privileges rather than basic rights.

In Margaret's case, the debate was about what constituted a class-appropriate "maintenance" and also about how to deal with an opportunistic outsider with less community credibility than his wife. Local politics factored into the matter, but not in a way that followed later "revolutionary" lines. Benjamin and many of Margaret's supporters remained loyal to the Crown in the years that followed. Though Margaret might have seen it otherwise, the legal question was never whether she should have meaningful independence or power.

The outcome of the Bannermans' dispute illustrates the difficulty of making simple statements about eighteenth-century white women's empowerment or powerlessness (legal or otherwise). A year after Benjamin challenged her to secure her decreed maintenance "how she can," Margaret received compensation through the forced sale of Aberdeen and Edinburgh, two men he enslaved and named to honor his history, not theirs. The total sum from the sale was perhaps one-tenth of the fortune she had had prior to the marriage, and it almost certainly would have translated to an annual interest income below the sixteen-pound annuity Benjamin offered. Margaret vanished from the records at this point, and she probably ended up comparably "poor." Benjamin, on the other hand, eventually parlayed her fortune into a forty-five-hundred-pound loyalist claim. Although Margaret's maintenance was unequal (and possibly also unequitable), the means by which she acquired it highlights the way in which the privileges of her status as a wife were defined against the disabilities of slaves.[54] When one compares Margaret's situation

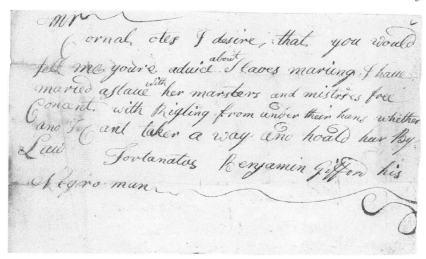

FIGURE 7.2 Letter from Fortunatus [Sharper] to Col. [James] Otis, undated
Otis Family Papers, Collection of the Massachusetts Historical Society

with that of the people who were confiscated and auctioned off for her benefit, analogies that make wives seem *like* slaves seem flawed indeed.

"Her service & conjugal comfort . . . which he had a right to have"

"Mr Cornal Otes, I desire that you would tell me your'e advice about slaves mariing [marrying]," began a brief query signed "Fortunatus, Benjamin Gifford his Negro Man."[55] This remarkable note introduces the third "wives not slaves" strategy, one found in revolutionary-era freedom suits. In legal pleas like Fortunatus's, we see the nascent transatlantic antislavery movement (introduced in chapters 3 and 4) seizing strategic opportunities from the confluence of "possessory rights" and reservations about slavery found in Blackstone, and also from American revolutionary rhetoric. As with Abigail Adams' protests against masculine tyranny, this movement has been casually attributed to the "contagion" of the American revolutionaries' demands for political liberty. The timing and transatlantic roots of these appeals complicate this narrative. Like challenges to marital tyranny, challenges to slavery were underway before revolutionary discontent gave them political traction. The stories of Fortunatus and his co-conspirators provide a window on these complex political dynamics and the larger, longer-term conversation about faith, family, and empire to which they belonged. Those who celebrated human equality in the abstract found it very difficult to bring these ideas "home."

In his note to Col. James Otis, Fortunatus Sharper identified himself by his relationship to his master. He thereby honored established household dependencies even as he mounted challenge to slavery with a political savvy evident in his choice of allies. Sharper had been born a slave, but when he penned his query he was in all likelihood *not* the property of Benjamin Gifford. In 1745, Gifford had promised his Quaker meeting that the "negro boy fortunatious sharper" would become free at age thirty-five. Assuming Gifford was true to his word, Sharper obtained his freedom in 1765, just as white colonists' anxiety about their own political "slavery" came to a boil.[56] The target of Sharper's inquiry was at the center of the controversy. "Mr Cornal Otes" was the elder James Otis, a prominent lawyer, merchant, and statesman in his own right, and father of even more famous children. His daughter Mercy Otis Warren was a close friend of Abigail Adams and an active participant in the transatlantic conversation about household and political tyranny; she had an illustrious career as a republican political writer and as the first historian of the American Revolution. Col. Otis's son, the lawyer James Otis Jr., carried arguments about natural human equality farther than any of his fellow American political agitators. In speeches and publications during 1764, he allowed for the possibility of political rights both for "negroes" and for women. Fortunatus likely took such sympathies into account when he sought a legal advisor.[57]

Fortunatus expressed seemingly more modest aspirations. "I have maried a slave with her marsters and mistreses free Concent with Rigting from under their hans," he explained. He wished to know "whither ano I Cant taker a way and hoald hur By Law." Could he, as the husband of an enslaved woman, exert the possessory rights associated with marriage? Implicit in this question were larger issues. By taking away and holding his wife, could Fortunatus (now free and well into middle age) establish his own independent household? Would that bring him the political rights accorded to white men on this basis? And, most important, would it end his wife's slavery?[58]

If Col. Otis or the local courts of Barnstable, Massachusetts, supplied answers to these questions, they do not survive. Records from elsewhere in both old and New England demonstrate that people of color used husbands' possessory rights to test slavery in precisely this way. In 1762, the London magistrate John Fielding complained that slaves brought from the West Indies were forming societies and persuading new arrivals to get "christened or married, which they inform them makes them free, (tho' it has been adjudged by our most able Lawyers, that neither of these Circumstances alter the Master's Property in a Slave.")[59] In the mid-1760s, this black community drew the white activist Granville Sharp into a concerted effort to challenge these lawyers' opinions. Husbands' possessory rights, as described in the newly published third volume of Blackstone's *Commentaries*, anchored the 1768 freedom suit of James and Mary Hylas, the second such case for which Sharp supplied legal advice. James Hylas, a freed slave who had married a slave woman with her master and mistress's consent, obtained a court order for Mary's return after her owners forcibly sent her back to the West Indies without his approval.[60]

Fielding not only disapproved of London blacks' legal activism in England, he also blamed unrest in the West Indies to "Blacks who have been sent back to the Plantations, after they have lived some time in a Country of Liberty, where they have learnt to read and write."[61] Fortunatus Sharper's note to James Otis shows traces of the transatlantic conversation Fielding feared, though it is not clear which direction the influence ran.

New England appears to have been the epicenter of efforts to undermine slavery through repeated, and often highly technical, litigation. The phenomenon remains poorly understood because these cases were very much the province of local law, and the evidence it has left behind is fragmentary and scattered across jurisdictions. Even more starkly than in marital disputes, judges resisted efforts to make (or record) general statements of antislavery principle in such cases, and efforts to force this point usually ran against the immediate interests of the person seeking freedom.[62]

Sharper's note demonstrates the bottom-up, grassroots nature of antislavery activism. Sharper was seeking legal advice on very specific grounds, and he appears to have learned of the strategy he proposed *independently* of the white lawyers who refined such challenges for the courts. If he already had a lawyer, he would not have needed to consult Otis. The geographic range of freedom suits based on women's marital status evidences wide-ranging channels of communication among blacks. In New England, such suits came from Cape Cod south of Boston, Salem to the north, and far to the west. The couples involved were isolated from one another; they consulted different lawyers; and yet they used remarkably similar arguments about marriage, slavery, and husbands' rights.[63]

These New England cases set wives' coverture against their servitude, turning women's subordinate position in marriage into a tool with which to secure their liberty. At the same time, they made female dependence critical to defining masculine independence. These lawsuits asserted husbands' proprietary claims to their wives more overtly than any other eighteenth-century colonial legal proceedings. Their legal language appears to have been adapted from Blackstone's *Commentaries*, and they document the rapid spread of his explanation of marital unity. They also helped reinforce and reify his account of patriarchal authority within marriage, even as they mounted a fundamental challenge to the patriarchal authority of masters.

The best documented of these New England cases, the 1783 suit of *Exeter, a negro v. Oliver Hanchett, Gentleman*, illustrates the paradoxes inherent in this strategy. The litigants were chiefly concerned with problems of masculine authority, but the story behind the dispute provides glimpses of female agency obscured by the nature of the records. Our tale begins sometime in the 1770s, when a slave woman named Flora protested the conditions of her servitude by running away. She may have been seeking freedom outright, making her one of many New England slaves who tested the resolve of their masters and of the legal authorities during the revolutionary period by simply leaving their posts. At the very least, her flight was a bargaining strategy designed to secure her master's recognition of the family arrangements she had chosen. She does not seem to have intended a permanent break with her community, because the two neighbors her master sent after her knew where to find her.[64] They went immediately to Exeter, a black laborer who lived in Southwick, Massachusetts, just across the border from her master's Suffield, Connecticut, home. They were surprised to discover that he had taken care to conceal her. After Exeter explained that this was because he and Flora "wanted to marry," the neighbors obtained her return by promising her master's consent for the match.[65]

These negotiations were facilitated by the fact that Massachusetts provided some legal protection for slave marriages, albeit in a less-than-generous context. The colony's 1705 "Act for the Better Preventing of A Spurious and Mixt Issue" had outlawed marriages between people of European and people of African origin, effectively turning interracial sexual relationships into criminal fornication. The early antislavery voice Samuel Sewall opposed the measure and secured, in his words, "some mitigation" for "the Negroes" in the form of a clause declaring that "no master shall unreasonably deny marriage to his negro with one of the same nation, any law, usage or custom to the contrary notwithstanding."[66]

Such mitigation was necessary because in the wider colonial world, "law, usage, [and] custom" did not recognize or respect slave marriages. Laws against interracial marriage were one facet of a colonial trend toward legislation that made legal marriage a privilege of free status and of whiteness. These measures used a variety of strategies to resolve the conflicting familial allegiances of slaves and servants in favor of masters rather than kin; they deliberately sought to prevent husbands like Fortunatus and Exeter from claiming patriarchal authority that might be used to challenge their wives' masters.[67]

Sewall's mitigating clause notwithstanding, masters retained ultimate control over slave families for most of the eighteenth century. Massachusetts legal authorities recognized slaves' marriages when it came to enforcing sexual norms and punishing adultery, but not as a means to allow enslaved couples the liberty to see each other regularly or raise children together. The marriage ceremony that took place when "Exeter brought Flora down to" her master's house illustrates how "usage and custom" could protect the power of masters even when statute law sought to limit it. According to later testimony by the slave-catching white neighbors, Flora's master granted his permission for the wedding on the condition that "his Title to . . . Flora should not be injured by such a Marriage but she should still continue in his Service and that Exeter could not take her away without [her master's] Liberty." The minister who performed the service also claimed that "he considered them as Servants and married them as Servants and informed them in the performance of the Marriage Ceremony that they were not discharged from Servitude or in any Manner freed from their obligations to their respective Masters."[68]

Flora and Exeter's marriage ceremony sounds as if it may have used the "Form of a Negro Marriage" found in the papers of another Massachusetts minister. The pair would have been admonished as follows: You, Exeter, "do now in the Presence of God, and these Witnesses, Take [Flora]: to be your Wife; Promising that so far as shall be consistent with ye Relation wch you now sustain, as a Servant, you will Perform ye Part of an Husband towards her; And in particular, you Promise, that you will *Love* her: And that as you shall have ye Opportty & Ability, you will take a proper *Care* of her in Sickness and in Health, in Prosperity & Adversity: And that you will be True & *Faithful* to her, and will Cleave to her *only, so long* as God, in his Provdce, shall continue your and her abode in such Place together." Flora would have taken similar vows; the surviving records of the ceremony do not indicate whether she would have been bound to obey Exeter as well as her master.[69]

The minister belabored the point that the couple was "not discharged from Servitude" by the marriage ceremony. He noted that at the pair's "Request, and wth ye consent of your Masters & Mistresses," he could give them "Licence . . . to be conversant and familiar together, as *Husband and Wife*," but only "so long as God shall continue your Places of abode as aforesaid; and so long as you shall behave your-selves as it becometh Servants to doe." The couple must "both . . . bear in mind, that you Remain Still as really and truly as ever, your Master's Property, and therefore it will be justly expected, both by God and Man, that you behave and conduct your-selves, as Obedient and faithfull Servants."[70]

Such compromised vows were a key grievance in the petitions against slavery that Boston's community of color placed before the Massachusetts legislature—and the British military governor—in the 1770s. The petitioners made savvy use of the language of sensibility and family feeling as they argued that slavery was morally incompatible with respect for marriage. Masters' power to decide whether and for how long their slaves were to be "marred or onmarred," they complained, made them strangers "to the endearing ties of husband and wife." When masters denied slaves the power to fulfill their obligations to their families, they "rendered [slaves] incapable of shewing [their] obedience to Almighty God." "how can a Slave perform the duties of a husband to a wife or parent to his child," the petitioners asked. "How can a husband leave master and work and Cleave to his wife How can the wife submit themselves to their Husbands in all things." Alienation from the prerogatives of masculine household authority headed the list of the deprivations of slavery in another petition. The writer exclaimed: "We have no Property! We have no Wives! No Children! We have no City! No Country!"[71] The petitioner here played with revolutionary emphasis on male household authority as the foundation for political rights. Men—and women—with "no City!" and "No Country!" could be flexible in their allegiances, as Massachusetts black's solicitation of *both* British and American authorities proved. With the 1776 departure of the British and of the loyalist lawyers who provided advice in most prerevolutionary freedom suits, black men's efforts to "take away and hold" their wives became a route to inclusion in the new state. For equal citizens even more than for colonial subjects, the limited marriage contract was anathema to independence and meaningful freedom.

Exeter and Flora seem to have abided with their limited set of marital rights until 1781, when Flora, with Exeter's help, tried to run away again. Their actions were motivated by the fact that Flora had recently been sold, and by the desire to protect their two children born since their marriage. In May, Oliver Hanchett, a Revolutionary War officer and prominent member of the local elite, had purchased Flora from her original master for thirty pounds. The transaction appears to have been carefully orchestrated to circumvent legal challenges. The bill of sale described Flora as "a Slave for Life and married to a Negro named Exeter," taking cognizance of her marriage but implying that it did not compromise perpetual servitude. It also certified her age as "upwards of twenty three years," thereby disqualifying her from the proposals for gradual manumission afloat in the Connecticut and Massachusetts legislatures and preventing her from claiming that she had been promised manumission at age twenty-four, a strategy used in other slave freedom suits.[72]

The document demonstrates that Flora's masters were clearly aware of the

legal assaults on slavery that were taking place around them. Flora and Exeter probably were as well. During the summer of 1781, the grapevine would
have supplied Flora and Exeter with additional reasons to challenge the authority of her new master. Not far from their home territory, Elizabeth and
Brom Freeman had brought a suit that not only aimed for their own freedom, but also challenged the constitutionality of slavery. Elizabeth later told
nineteenth-century abolitionists (some of whom she had helped to raise) that
she had known when to make a move because she had been "Been keepin'
still and mindin'" the conversation at her patriotic master's table. She had
heard not only the Declaration of Independence, but also of John Adams inclusion of the assertion that "all men are born free and equal" in the new
state Constitution passed in 1780.[73] A series of legal disputes involving a slave
named Quok Walker were also wending their way through the courts in another nearby county. In September 1781, the Massachusetts Supreme Judicial
Court sitting at Worcester allowed one of the Walker cases to become a forum for general arguments about the common humanity and natural rights
of African Americans and for objections to the specific disabilities of slavery,
including its threat to the sanctity of marriage. The details are murky, but the
verdict in this 1781 Walker case apparently declared slavery unconstitutional
in Massachusetts.[74]

That was enough for Flora. One month after this decision in the Walker
case, Flora packed up a bundle of clothing and other household items and left
Oliver Hanchett's house. Hanchett waited two days for her to return and then
took out a warrant for her arrest, charging her with theft. He supplied a detailed
list of the goods she had taken. These items included wearing apparel and other
things of small enough value that they could very well have been Flora's personal property, to which Hanchett as slave owner would have had legal claim.
The list suggests that Flora planned a journey. She took "womans shoes" that
were perhaps sturdy enough to have value to her master. A shift, petticoat, and
apron that might have provided a change of clothes. Two Holland shirts for
Exeter. A flask of liquor to keep them warm. The handkerchiefs, tea, remnants
of cloth, and sheep's wool could have been peddled to raise a little cash.[75]

Flora was apprehended and tried on the day the warrant was issued, and the
circumstances of her trial imply that—from the perspective of local authorities—
her primary offense may have been attempting to leave Hanchett's service. The
accusation of theft was a convenient way to bring her in line. A local justice of
the peace summarily sentenced her to be "publicly whipt on the naked body
eight stripes" and to pay triple damages and court costs. When she was unable
to pay the fine of five pounds, seventeen shillings, she was sentenced instead to
serve Hanchett for "the term of two years."[76]

If Flora was Hanchett's "Slave for Life," why did the court find it necessary or meaningful to bind her to him for a term of years? The prosecution
appears to have been a stopgap measure related to the growing uncertainty
about the legal legitimacy of slavery in Massachusetts and perhaps specifically
to the Freeman and Walker cases. The timing of Exeter's lawsuit against Oliver
Hanchett reinforces this impression. It coincided exactly with the expiration of
Flora's two-year term of service, and it followed by a few months the final 1783
Supreme Judicial Court decision declaring Quok Walker a free man.

In Exeter's suit, Hanchett was the one accused of stealing woman's shoes,
an apron, and a petticoat. The formal charge stated that he had taken by
"Force and Arms" not only Flora, but also a carefully itemized list of "Goods
and Chattels" that consisted of her apparel. The language in the case was ambiguous about whether Flora was also a "Good" or "Chattel," but it clearly asserted Exeter's property rights to the clothes on his wife's back. Exeter sought
six hundred pounds in damages for the loss of these possessions and of Flora's
"company and assistance." The dispute thus turned on conflicting claims to
Flora as a dependent; the question of her freedom was all but lost. The underlying issues were somewhat clearer in the case from which this section takes
its title. There a black couple sought damages from a wealthy Salem merchant
for holding the wife "in a state of slavery against her will & contrary to the
will of her husband." The merchant had threatened the wife's "life & liberty"
and deprived her husband of "her service & conjugal comfort . . . which he
had a right to have."[77] The complaint rested on the wife's autonomous—and
decidedly revolutionary—right to "life and liberty," and also on her husband's
possessory right to her person and services.

These cases reflected the same transatlantic conversation about marriage
that produced Frances Brooke's and Abigail Adams's overlapping protests
against marital tyranny. They were rooted in the importance of marriage as
an "endearing tie," but drew on legal opportunities created by Blackstone's
formulation of husbands' possessory rights. Reference to "conjugal comfort"
invoked the emotional, sentimental aspects of marriage that were celebrated
as the foundation of civic virtue in the period, yet this was paired with the
decidedly unsentimental reference to a husband's property in his wife's "service." These cases turned the legal aspects of marriage that made it analogous
to slavery into the key to enslaved women's freedom.

The tension between social ideals and legal language proved a stumbling
block in several of these cases. Lawyers for James Hylas (the man Granville
Sharp had assisted in 1768) had drafted a writ asking for damages as well as
for the return of his wife. This was probably because, according to Blackstone, the form was properly used *only* for damages, and not for possession

of a woman who had been seduced away. Counsel for Mary Hylas's owners snidely implied that Hylas, a poor black man, was only after the money. To Sharp's outrage, they persuaded the court to force Hylas to choose between the two options. Hylas obtained a court order for Mary's return; conventional accounts of the case do not say, however, whether authorities took steps to enforce it.[78]

In *Exeter v. Hanchett*, the lower, local court gave an affirmative answer to Fortunatus's questions about the rights of husbands to "take away and hold" their wives. Hanchett had based his defense on evidence of his title to Flora as a slave and a servant and on testimony documenting Exeter's assent to a limited marriage contract. The jury rejected this reasoning and ordered Hanchett to pay Exeter sixty-five pounds in damages and another ten in court costs.[79] Their verdict demonstrated sympathy for the argument that husbands, regardless of race, had preeminent claim to the persons, property, and services of their wives, as well as the claims even poor people with good credit could make on the neighbors who presided over local law.

Even as it reinforced and reified the patriarchal authority of husbands, the decision demonstrated the success of these suits' profound challenge to the authority of masters. The case and judgment together suggest that in the eyes of some Massachusetts residents—black and white—the Quok Walker cases provided the "solemn decision" against slavery that later historians have claimed. Although these suits were framed around individual grievances, they appear to have been coordinated in a way that the "wives not slaves" arguments that challenged the possessory rights of white colonial husbands were not. Through willful defiance and opportunistic litigation, Flora and Exeter took part in a collective movement that legally ended slavery in Massachusetts and, in the long term, radically altered early American relations of dependence.[80]

In the short term, however, the consequences were ambiguous. The year 1783 does seem to have marked the end of the Massachusetts courts' willingness to recognize slavery within the state. But it was only the beginning of drawn-out negotiations about what freedom meant for Massachusetts's African American residents. Exeter and Flora's fate makes this very clear.

The Supreme Judicial Court—the same court that a few months before had declared Quok Walker a free man and slavery "as effectively abolished as it could be"—overturned Exeter's victory on appeal. No documents survive to explain their reasoning, but national jurisdictional politics were probably a significant factor. Disputes about slave status thus joined the disputes about marriage law provoked by England's 1753 Marriage Act (see chapter 4) as the terrain on which an American understanding of the principle of comity would develop. Persuasive contextual evidence suggests that when Massachusetts authorities made the final decision in Flora and Exeter's case, they were newly concerned about the state's obligations under the Articles of Confederation to respect the rights (and particularly the property) of the free citizens of other states. Exeter and Flora lived in disputed border territory between Massachusetts and Connecticut, and Oliver Hanchett unequivocally identified himself as a Connecticut citizen. By vindicating him, the court demonstrated that it would allow citizens of other states to reclaim their "servants," even if it would not actively support state intervention on their behalf. The decision would thus have placated a South Carolina government disgruntled by its recent actions in another case.[81]

Regardless of its political context, the Supreme Judicial Court decision against Exeter and Flora also upheld distinctive "custom and usage" for "negro marriages," thereby preserving blacks' dependence in spite of their nominal freedom. The documents internal to the case suggest a line of legal reasoning in keeping with what Amy Dru Stanley has called the "legends of contract freedom" spawned by eighteenth-century liberalism.[82] The decision in *Exeter v. Hanchett* defined freedom in terms of the ability to make binding contracts and allowed these obligations to negate the privileges of status ordinarily accorded to male citizens. By agreeing, and perhaps even giving security, that he would not "take away" Flora without the "Liberty" of her master, Exeter had compromised what in other circumstances would have been seen as the fundamental right of a husband to determine where his wife lived and worked. The court affirmed Exeter's ability—as a free man—to make binding contracts with other men, and it held him responsible for abiding by them. Yet the decision simultaneously denied him the patriarchal authority that provided the practical basis for masculine autonomy. One hallmark of freedom thus served to invalidate another; the right to contract undid the privileges of marriage.

The unfavorable verdict may also have compromised Exeter's independence in a more concrete manner. It transformed him from a man possessing a modest estate into a debtor liable for court costs that now amounted to nearly twenty pounds. Flora had been unable to pay a debt of less than six pounds and had been forced to compensate with years of service. We do not know if Exeter was also forced back into service. It was punishment enough that he was left bereft of family and property. Hanchett carried Flora and their children to New York and sold them to a buyer from Virginia. Exeter, oral tradition had it, spent much of his remaining life as a poor man roaming New England in search of them, but never learned their fate. Their children and grandchildren remembered their claim to freedom, however, and in the 1840s would use it to mount another challenge to slavery.[83]

"We know better than to repeal our Masculine systems"

John Adams responded to Abigail's admonition that he "Remember the Ladies" by treating it as a joke. "As to your extraordinary Code of Laws, I cannot but laugh," he replied. "We have been told that our Struggle has loosened the bands of Government every where. That Children and Apprentices were disobedient—that schools and Colledges were grown turbulent—that Indians slighted their Guardians and Negroes grew insolent to their Masters." Abigail's letter, he contended, was the first hint he had seen that women, a "Tribe more numerous and powerfull than all the rest were grown discontented."[84] Abigail's demand for "new Priviledges" and her threats "to rebell," John speculated, must be the result of a "deep" plot by the English government designed to quash the colonies through internal dissent.

John proceeded to dismiss Abigail's request in language that echoed Margaret Cavendish's contention that men "seem to govern the world, but we really govern the world, in that we govern men." "Depend upon it," John assured Abigail, "We know better than to repeal our Masculine systems. Altho they are in full Force, you know they are little more than Theory. We dare not exert our Power in its full Latitude. We are obliged to go fair, and softly, and in Practice you know We are the subjects." "We oftener inslave men, than men inslave us" claimed Cavendish. "We have only the Name of Masters," insisted John. "Rather than give up this, which would compleatly subject Us to the Despotism of the Peticoat, I hope General Washington, and all our brave Heroes would fight."[85]

This was a joke, but like the exchange between the husband Loyalty and wife American Liberty that opened this chapter, it was a serious joke. In a subsequent letter to her friend Mercy Otis Warren, an outraged Abigail made it clear that her demands had been real, and that she found John's theory of sentimental deference poor protection from the marriage laws to which he gave "full Force." In a subsequent letter to his friend James Sullivan, John in turn demonstrated that he had been listening. In a debate over what the state should require of its voters, he defended property qualifications as a proxy for educated "understanding." "The Same Reasoning" that inspired democratically minded radicals like Sullivan "to admit all Men, who have no Property, to vote . . . will prove that you ought to admit Women and Children." "Men who are wholly destitute of Property," John warned, were "as much dependent upon others, who will please to feed, cloath, and employ them, as Women are upon their Husbands, or Children on their Parents." If poor men gained full political privileges, John warned, "Women and Children," who "have as good Judgment, and as independent Minds" as such men, would have equal reason to expect inclusion. "There will be no End of it," John predicted. "New Claims will arise. Women will demand a Vote. Lads from 12 to 21 will think their Rights not enough attended to, and every Man, who has not a Farthing, will demand an equal Voice with any other in all Acts of State, It tends to confound and destroy all Distinctions, and prostrate all Ranks, to one common Levell."[86]

The vote, in the early republic, was a "new Priviledge" rather than a right. In New Jersey, it was a prerogative enjoyed by women and by black men who met the statutory property requirement from 1776 until countervailing, masculinist, republican logic prevailed in 1807. This counterargument, as expressed in a 1785 Pennsylvania debate over the franchise, ran thus: "Every man in the state has what is supposed by the constitution to be property—his life, personal liberty, perhaps wife and children, in whom they have a right, the earnings of his own or their industry."[87] Husband's possessory rights became the means by which ordinary men might purchase political privileges and power.

Fortunatus and Exeter had hoped such logic would provide them—and their wives—with personal freedom. Where they saw opportunities, John and Abigail Adams saw dangers, although each interpreted the threat differently. Abigail's request was probably inspired less by the desire for "new" political powers than by the erosion of older rights that the new "masculine systems" of government redefined as privileges. When she invited John to be "be more generous and favourable to [the Ladies] than your ancestors," however, she promoted the Enlightenment logic (shared with and perhaps imbibed from Blackstone) that made such masculine systems into the essential, historical norm, to which female power was an exception.

John's laughter belied genuine fear that this new system would indeed "prostrate all Ranks to one common" level, distinguished chiefly by ignorance and vice. He, along with other revolutionary leaders, could imagine that hierarchies based on gender and race might be "repealed" by revolution. We turn next to the ways in which the revolutionary-era expansion of divorce law and of black husbands' patriarchal "rights" worked to contain those possibilities and create new distinctions.

Rethinking the Revolutionary Road to Divorce

American political revolutionaries did not heed Abigail Adams plea to "remember the Ladies" in their "new code of Laws." Historians looking for exceptions to this general reticence cite statutes regulating divorce, which passed in almost every state in the decades after the revolution. This chapter uses revolutionary-era divorce legislation, antislavery litigation, and divorce cases involving American "first families" to reevaluate an enduring historical narrative in which the legitimation of divorce and the gradual emancipation of slaves serve as parallel examples of the "radicalism of revolution." The politics of marriage and of slavery were intertwined for the United States' founding generation, but not in straightforwardly emancipatory ways. Changes in marriage policy, moreover, emerged from the transatlantic pressures and legal debates detailed in previous chapters. Demand for divorce was not specifically a "revolutionary" concern. As in the seventeenth century, highly contingent events shaped differences between divorce policy in England and her colonies. The prevailing principles on both sides of the Atlantic remained similar. Political leaders were most responsive to the desires of powerful men who wished to escape financial responsibility for adulterous wives. Leaders were less willing to accommodate poorer men with similar complaints. Authorities went out of their way to avoid confronting the tensions between revolutionary egalitarian ideals and entrenched household hierarchies, and the codification of formal procedures for divorce focused on preserving those hierarchies and limiting disorder. Authorities treated the disclosure of grievances by household dependents—whether wives or slaves—as a greater problem than the grievances themselves; whenever possible, they sought to settle them privately and to avoid public attention and precedent.

A pamphleteer in Philadelphia called out this tendency in a 1788 "Essay on Marriage; or, the Lawfulness of Divorce," concluding that legal change in marriage policy would only occur when people of "rank and character in the world, who shall have virtue and resolution enough . . . set some examples of separating and marrying again." Only through "remarkable exertions" like those radical antislavery activists could the "attention of mankind" be "roused or excited." Without people who were willing to risk their reputations and their public lives, and to share their stories of suffering and relief, "every thing goes on in its former course, and glides down the stream of time unnoticed."[1]

These observations capture the dynamics of patriarchal equilibrium that have been a theme throughout this book, and which were very much evident in the politics of revolutionary-era divorce. Late eighteenth-century celebration of sentiment-infused relationships and the pursuit of human happiness elevated expectations about marital happiness on both sides of the Atlantic. These potentially radical ideas were counterbalanced by a celebration of the "ancient common law" that gave primacy to—and grounded political authority in—the masculine rights of household heads. The distance between these compass points increased, but families seeking solutions to internal conflict in uncertain "revolutionary" times gravitated toward the midpoint and maintained the status quo. As in other eras, "revolutionary" divorce cases generally turned on circumstance, adhering less to fixed principles than to compromises that preserved familial "rank and character."

The anonymous (but self-consciously masculine) Philadelphia pamphleteer was steeped in Scottish Enlightenment arguments about the progress of civilization, adept with sentimental rhetoric, and also quite familiar with Pennsylvania's antislavery movement. This chapter uses his *Essay* to frame analysis of three tenacious but dubious arguments linking divorce, slave emancipation, and America's radical revolutionary character: first, that divorce was a product of revolution and of distinctively American "liberality"; second, that divorce and emancipation were analogous revolutionary challenges to household patriarchy; and third, that divorce was a "woman's remedy"—that is, an innovation intended to ameliorate wives' grievances and distress.

Historians of revolution still leave these premises unexamined, though historians of women and the family dispute them. In either case, the framing assumptions remain in place. They have generated a conversation that, in the historian Norma Basch's words, finds it "far easier to chart the connections between revolution and divorce at a high level of abstraction than it is to understand their influence on ordinary people."[2] This chapter argues that at least some of these revolutionary abstractions can be connected to the experiences of real, if not "ordinary," people. It analyzes three household conflicts whose cast of characters leaves no doubt about America's political founders' intimate familiarity with the complexity of marriage law and the ways in which it was entangled with practical and abstract concerns about slavery. As with the seventeenth-century *Manby* case that opened this book, obscure, inconclusive arguments citing legal jurisdiction or general principles in marriage law disguised the concrete but messy details of politically inconvenient real-world cases.

Our anonymous pamphleteer made ample use of revolutionary abstractions in his arguments for legal and social acceptance of divorce, portraying such reforms as the natural extension of American "liberality." He effused: "AMERICA has been famous for her love of liberty, and hatred of tyranny of every kind," and she has even "generously extended her liberality, in a great measure, . . . unto the African slaves." The next logical step would be to free unhappily married people "united in the worst of bondage to each other." His "Essay on Marriage" argued that provision for the "Lawfulness of Divorce" automatically followed from American revolutionary radicalism, a phenomenon he understood in expansively social terms. Communal happiness would be secure only when individuals were free to pursue their own happiness in marriages based on affection rather than obligation. That end required children to rebel against the patriarchal dictates of family and church, just as colonists had defied their authoritarian English parent. Greater "liberality" regarding divorce, the pamphleteer contended, would offer relief to women already in marital bondage; he had been moved to write, he claimed, by sensible concern for a female prisoner of an unhappy marriage, whose plight seemed to him every bit as tragic as the stories antislavery activists told to elicit sympathy for slaves. Emancipation and divorce were—or at least ought to be—parallel manifestations of revolutionary modernity.[3]

Subsequent generations of reformers and jurists reinforced these teleological arguments, and American historians have tended to look backward through this lens. But when we look forward, through the lens of events and laws regarding divorce starting in the seventeenth century, we begin to see the connections between individual and local concerns and the Atlantic dimensions of the eighteenth-century "road to divorce": a road that ran parallel to revolution rather than out of it. The revolutionary "abstractions" about divorce cited by Basch (and most other historians) include case notes by Thomas Jefferson, essays by Thomas Paine and our anonymous Philadelphia commentator, and statute law. In the two decades following the American Revolution, most state and territorial legislatures—with the notable exception of South Carolina—passed measures pertaining to divorce. Basch judges this "wholesale legitimation of divorce" to be "far more significant than the divergent terms that were being spelled out in state statutes." Such lumping is understandable for historians whose primary interests lie with later developments, and who see a world in which husbands and wives "looked to the law" for remedies to their marital conflicts because "courts were where one did such things."[4] In histories plotted around such mid-nineteenth century legal understandings of marriage, the gradual move toward the legislative recognition of divorce in the wake of the American Revolution necessarily becomes a pivotal "event."

When one looks forward from the eighteenth century, however, it becomes more difficult to see the postrevolutionary legitimization of divorce as a discrete event at all, much less as a radical one. In the context of the long-term, transatlantic conversation about jurisdiction over households described in previous chapters, the revolutionary politics of divorce seem less a rupture than a replay of previous conflicts. US historians' propensity to contrast postrevolutionary "American innovations" with "English legal traditions" overlooks the extent to which England's claims about those traditions were themselves shaped by revolutionary politics.[5] The demands of husbands whose grievances crossed class and partisan lines placed divorce reform on the political agenda throughout the British Empire during the 1750s and 1760s. Divorce became an *American* answer to these transatlantic pressures largely because English authorities defined it that way. England's reaffirmation of the Restoration-era compromises that entrenched marital indissolubility as English law was as "revolutionary" as the motley assortment of divorce laws instituted in the new American republic. In practice, moreover, English and American legal responses to the demand for divorce differed less than it might seem, and both were substantively shaped by the prodding of England's disgruntled Scottish "wife."

The 1788 Philadelphia "Essay on Marriage" appealed to "American liberality" and invoked local political traditions in Pennsylvania and New Jersey. It addressed itself first and foremost, however, to "the Feelings of Mankind." In these universal ambitions, as well as in its borrowed language and arguments, it was a work of the Scottish Enlightenment and of the transatlantic culture of sensibility. As with other such works, the author's professed sympathy for slaves and for women gave opportunistic cover to more complex (and less disinterested) masculine concerns.

Debates about slavery shaped the transatlantic politics of divorce, but not in the ways in which the anonymous essayist implied. Scottish Enlightenment logic and real political challenges by antislavery activists together provoked a prerevolutionary imperial overreaction; the anxieties of imperial authorities, in turn, made colonial demands for divorce into a revolutionary issue. Antislavery activists, on the other hand, spurned analogies between emancipation and divorce. The comparison ran counter to their own claims that slavery was immoral in large part because of its threats to the integrity of families. The families of people of color were put at risk not only by the breakup of white families who claimed them as property, but also by arguments for divorce that could justify breaking up the families of the poor—a power claimed not only by masters, but also by the government in newly "free" states. The experiences of freed people of color after the revolution offer painful evidence of how the "revolutionary" marital regime could use the obligations that went with masculine independence to revive old dependencies. Most antislavery activists consequently opposed divorce.

Enlightenment parallels between emancipation and divorce had long-lasting, conservative consequences in American states that clung to slavery. Defenders of slavery inverted the analogy. Like seventeenth-century defenders of absolute monarchy, slaveholders saw indissoluble, hierarchical marriage as an important foundation for arguments that portrayed slavery as an indissoluble, "natural" hierarchy. Slave states were therefore slower to grant full divorce in any form, and more likely to carry stringent canon law procedures into civilly regulated marriage. Slave states also jealously guarded control of all aspects of "domestic law" from federal infringement, fearing that national rules for marriage might open the door to national limits on slavery. Regional conservatism in marriage law was thus rooted in slavery, and has outlasted it.

Finally, revolutionary state legislatures did not portray divorce as a "woman's remedy," and when it came to the details, even our essayist was ambivalent. Rather, changes in divorce statutes responded to the same economic and legal pressures that drove demand for extralegal remedies and the expansion of masculine possessory rights. In jurisdictions that made desertion grounds for full divorce, women later seized on this option in disproportionate numbers. In divorce cases as in newspaper marital disputes, educated women became adept at using sentimental scripts to support their cases. This helped secure community sympathy but only occasionally translated into legal redress. In instances where elite white women did obtain a measure of "justice," it frequently came at the expense of enslaved families. The shadow of the claims of husbands' creditors to familial property loomed over both male and female divorce petitions. Mid-eighteenth-century demands for new means to dissolve marriages emerged from pressures on the family that were *fundamental* to revolutionary politics, not products of them. Masculine fears of debt and dependence, not feminine grievances, drove the rise of legal full divorce. The trend was a mark of "American liberality" insofar as liberalism gave men individual rights purchased at the expense of their dependents.[6]

Abstract analogies between divorce and emancipation demonstrate, however, that political leaders could imagine possibilities that they did not choose to pursue. The trope was common in discussions of household order on both sides of the Atlantic. The 1788 pamphleteer was one of many writers who professed sympathy for women and slaves to establish his credentials as a sensible, enlightened gentleman, even as he turned his sentimental arguments to other ends. Comparisons of marriage and slavery helped political figures of all stripes contain potential challenges to household hierarchy by literally domesticating them. Top-down analogies between forms of household dependency obscured conflicts between them. The interests of aggrieved white wives often directly *opposed* those of freedom-seeking slaves. Top-down accounts of domestic order also worked to depoliticize the grievances of household dependents. On the occasions when they could not be silenced outright, "domestic" complaints could be dismissed with satire or trivialized as scandal.

Divorce and the Jurisdictional and Personal Politics of Revolution

Pennsylvania's 1785 Divorce Act is the most commonly cited example of a provision for divorce "adopted as part of the republican renovation" of American society, but like the 1788 "Essay on Marriage" it had hybrid origins that combined local custom with transatlantic ideals. The 1785 Pennsylvania law was indeed more "liberal" than the colonial measure it replaced. It allowed for full divorce with permission to remarry in a number of circumstances, and it was unusually expansive in its definition of marital cruelty, though this remained grounds only for separation.[7] It was not, however, an *American* innovation, as it derived its language almost entirely from a 1779 *Scottish* legal treatise. Even more striking than the anonymous 1788 "Essay on Marriage," Pennsylvania's divorce law demonstrates how even supposedly revolutionary departures from English precedents extended earlier imperial practices and long-standing debates about jurisdiction.

Simmering conflict between English and Scottish law defined the revolutionary politics of divorce in England and America. With the 1753 Hardwicke Act, Parliament had attempted to set uniform requirements for legitimate marriages and, in the process, to override traditional powers claimed by ecclesiastical and local jurisdictions. The measure created new conflicts between England's marriage laws and those of its dependent states and colonies. The threat of English imperial encroachment on Scottish marital practices prompted many of the reflections on the relationship between household

arrangements and the progress of civilization for which the Scottish Enlightenment is particularly known. As debates about jurisdiction over marriage played themselves out in Britain, legislatures in Pennsylvania and other
American colonies whose laws were subject to review by the imperial government avoided the issue of divorce. English authorities' increasing emphasis
on the primacy of English law made the question politically risky. In the first
half of the eighteenth century, moreover, demand for divorce in the colonies
generally came from the desperate rather than the powerful, and thus gave
colonial legislatures little incentive to pursue the matter.

In the late 1750s and most markedly in the 1760s, demand for full legal
divorce resurfaced and intensified throughout the empire. England's Parliament had heard only twenty petitions for divorce during the first half of the
eighteenth century, and had refused almost half of those requests; between
1750 and 1760, it heard eighteen petitions and granted almost all of them.
During the 1760s, Scotland's consistorial courts saw a gradual increase in divorce cases that proved to be the beginning of a "spectacular rise." So too
did Massachusetts and Connecticut.[8] In 1758 and 1761, Nova Scotia passed
general legislation providing for divorce along the model found in Massachusetts. Legislatures in colonies without such general provisions, including New
Hampshire, New Jersey, Virginia, and Pennsylvania, also began to consider
individual petitions for private bills of divorce.[9]

Divorce petitions were a byproduct of the same forces that drove the increase in extralegal separations advertised in newspapers: masculine troubles with liability created by expanding credit networks and an increasingly
rule-bound legal culture, and a growing press that disseminated both legal
rules and examples of novel remedies. Requests for full legal divorce were nu-
merically insignificant relative to extralegal alternatives, but the heightened
jurisdictional tensions of the 1760s gave colonial petitions disproportionate
legal import. Parliament had started granting full divorces not simply to titled
lords in need of legitimate heirs, but to a broader class of wealthy men with
adulterous wives. If colonial assemblies held analogous powers, unhappily
married men wondered, could they do the same?

These questions were explicit in the petition of John Goggin, whose 1766
plea for divorce was the first to gain a formal hearing from Pennsylvania's
legislature since Anna Maria Boehm Miller's ill-fated 1729 attempt. Goggin
had been "advised, that the Legislature of Great Britain have, at several times,
passed Acts of Parliament, in cases of adultery, to divorce the parties from
the bonds of matrimony, and to allow the innocent party to marry again."
Goggin contended that his estranged wife, Catherine O'Brien, was not simply
unfaithful, but "a Prostitute to Negroes" who had given birth to a "Bastard

Mulattoe Child." He begged the legislature to have mercy on his "distressed Condition" and grant him a full divorce.[10]

Catherine's infidelity was probably distressing, and it was undoubtedly necessary to Goggin's legal case. However, financial distress, rather than Catherine's adultery, was named as the primary motive behind John's quest for a legislative remedy. Goggin and O'Brien began living together "as man and Wife" in 1756. By 1764 they had separated. Goggin had gone to sea in the interim, as a result of marital difficulties, he claimed; when he returned, John found himself facing prosecution and imprisonment for failing to maintain Catherine and her children. So he announced in the newspapers that he had renounced Catherine for her "Misdemeanors" and secured her written promise "never to claim Right to Title to the said John, or any thing belonging to him." He begged "the Favour of the Public not to credit" her on his account, for he was "determined not to pay one Farthing for her."[11] Philadelphia's overseers of the poor—local authorities who determined the fate of people who could not support themselves—rejected his position. While they accepted and enforced Catherine and John's informally contracted marriage, they refused to honor an informal separation that would result in starving dependents. Like many other local authorities across time and place, they found it more expedient to uphold a wife's "Right to Title" to her husband—and his credit—than to address her husband's complaints about her misbehavior.

The language of possessory rights in John's ad is striking. He framed marriage as mutual ownership ("Right to Title") of the person of one's spouse. In his divorce petition to the legislature, he suggested that Catherine had broken their agreement by granting other men possession of her body, and thereby forfeited any claim on him. When he married Catherine, he testified, he thought her "an honest industrious Woman." He found, however, that she had an "extravagant Fondness for strong Liquors," which he had been unable to control despite the use of "all Moderate Means . . . to reform her evil Habits." Philadelphia city authorities had already determined that Catherine's "wickedness" remained John's fiscal responsibility. His legal advisors informed him that neither her conviction for interracial "fornication," nor a bed and board divorce obtained from the colonial governor, would change that.[12] Consequently, his petition to the legislature took pains to demonstrate his own powerlessness and innocence, and drew explicit parallels between his case and the divorces recently granted by Parliament.

The legislature considered—and rejected—Goggin's plea. There were probably some lawmakers who were moved by the racial animus in John's petition, and who agreed that Catherine's transgression of racial boundaries aggravated the crime of adultery and made the case worth hearing. Others

were likely swayed by the petition's comparison of their own legislative powers to those of Parliament. Goggin's plea came as tensions over the Stamp
Act reached their peak, and a few in the legislature might have welcomed the
opportunity to assert their own sovereignty. The majority, however, did not.
In 1766 (and even in 1776), most of Pennsylvania's elected officials favored
reconciliation with England. The legislators were also, for the most part, the
kind of men who served as overseers of the poor and understood the costs to
local communities of abandoned dependents. Whatever masculine sympathy
Goggin's plea might have elicited, the cause of a poor Irishman with a dissolute wife was hardly worth the political risk.[13]

Three years later, in 1769, a husband of somewhat higher status met with
more success, probably because his petition revealed less. Masculine liability
and the claims of a "bastard child" were an underlying concern in the case;
unlike Goggin's, though, the complaint avoided explicit reference to such issues. The petitioner's estranged wife had married bigamously elsewhere, and
neither she nor her child were a burden to the public treasury. The Pennsylvania legislature granted him a private bill of divorce that carefully followed
English example. The Privy Council—the imperial body responsible for the
review of colonial laws and affairs—greeted the measure with skepticism because political tensions made them alert for challenges to the sovereignty of
Parliament and English law. Nevertheless, after Richard Jackson—a lawyer
and MP who served as colonial agent for the divorce-granting Massachusetts
and Connecticut, as well as Pennsylvania—declared the Pennsylvania bill
consistent with English practice, the council let it stand. Word of its success
appears to have spread, and in 1772 and 1773, Pennsylvania's legislature found
itself facing four new petitions for divorce.[14]

The Pennsylvania legislature handled these petitions cautiously. Only one
passed its scrutiny, and it forwarded this to England in a private bill of divorce
virtually identical to the one the Privy Council had approved in 1769. This
time the council interpreted the case as a political test and invalidated it on
jurisdictional grounds. Legal advisor Jackson, who had approved the earlier
Pennsylvania divorce, now tied himself in knots explaining the April 1773
reversal. Such divorce acts themselves might not be "repugnant" to English
law, but they were measures of "a new and extraordinary Nature." As such,
the council deemed it of "very great importance . . . that the assemblies in
your Majesty's colonies do not assume the exercise of powers beyond what
the nature and principles of the Constitution admit." They objected that the
Pennsylvania cases established dangerous precedent for other colonies, and
perhaps for England itself, because these colonial measures did not depend
on prior decisions by ecclesiastical courts or "a court of common law." A few

months later, the council drew an even harder line. It voided similar bills from New Jersey and New Hampshire, and issued a blanket edict forbidding colonial governors from giving royal assent to such measures.[15]

These imperial instructions renewed jurisdictional conflict. Couples who had thought themselves legally divorced now stood in legal limbo. The legislative bodies and governors who had supported them were called to heel. More insidiously, the council's edict called into question the divergent terms under which England's imperial dependencies governed marriage, and by extension the legitimacy of the diverse judicial structures operating in the colonies. The disputed acts of divorce had not involved suits in the ecclesiastical courts because Pennsylvania and New Hampshire neither had nor wanted such courts. If adultery convictions in colonial courts did not count as actions under the "common law," what were they? English legal practice with regard to marriage and sexual misconduct changed more than colonial practice during the eighteenth century. England belatedly incorporated "Puritan" reforms that it had rejected after its seventeenth-century civil wars, but which many colonies had sustained without interruption. England's internal conflict over such changes brought colonial practices under closer scrutiny, especially during the imperial crisis.[16]

It is unlikely that John Goggin or the Philadelphia butcher and New Hampshire carpenter whose suits provoked this imperial reaction intended such political consequences. The desire to shed the obligations of a defunct marriage was not a partisan issue. The political analogies in Goggin's petition might have gained him a hearing, but they ultimately undermined his cause. The parties to a "conjugal spat" seldom fared well when their cases became a testing ground for political principles. In addition, the relatively low status of these petitioners meant that their divorces were unlikely to have wide-reaching political consequences. The Virginia case of *Blair v. Blair*, on the other hand, had set the transatlantic rumor mill turning in the months prior to the Privy Council's resolution against colonial divorces, and deserves in-depth consideration.

BLAIR V. BLAIR, SOMERSET V. STEUART, AND IMPERIAL ANXIETY ABOUT HOUSEHOLD POLITICS

The Privy Council framed its 1773 change in policy on colonial acts of divorce as a matter of abstract jurisdictional principle, and this reasoning was consistent with its increasingly rigid insistence on colonial deference to parliamentary authority in the context of conflict over taxation and trade. However, this formal reasoning distracts from the more concrete desire to avoid political scandals grounded in household conflicts. Throughout 1772, Charles Steuart, a Scottish merchant and prominent imperial official who was advising the Crown on colonial affairs, received a steady stream of rumors regarding a politically fraught Virginia marital dispute. The case of *Blair v. Blair* thoroughly entangled the colony's "first families" and the interconnected, elite network of colonial and imperial agents. In the winter of 1773, Virginia's assembly was expected to consider a bill of divorce in which the colony's Scottish governor, Lord Dunmore, stood accused of adultery with the wife of a patriotic colonial subject and, by extension, of being the sort of corrupt imperial servant whose presence was an "insult" to "American Liberty." The Blair case merits attention not only for its likely impact on imperial divorce policy, but also because it was debated and decided by lawyers and legislators who became American political founders, leaving no doubt about their familiarity with controversies in marriage law.

Charles Steuart was probably not the only conduit through which news of the Blair case reached London, but he had especially strong reason to raise alarms about litigation targeting unpopular Scottish agents of empire. Steuart spent much of 1772 as the defendant in *Somerset v. Steuart*, a freedom suit that became the most famous legal challenge to slavery in England's history. Steuart had begun his imperial career in Virginia and ended it as the chief colonial customs officer charged with enforcing the Stamp Act and other deeply unpopular duties. Between 1765 and 1770, Steuart became personally known and politicly compromised in every colonial seaport from Virginia to Quebec, while James Somerset, his enslaved personal attendant, quietly established connections to opponents of slavery in many of these locales. After Steuart retired to London in frustration in 1770, Somerset secured baptism and a set of evangelical allies who helped him sue for his freedom before Lord Mansfield in the Court of King's Bench during the spring and summer of 1772. Steuart's unpopularity in the colonies and political expendability as a Scot in England made him a superb target for antislavery activists. Despite Mansfield's efforts to limit its actual legal implications, propogandists turned *Somerset v. Steuart* into the "Great Case of the Negroes" that declared English air "too pure for slaves to breathe," and thereby freed all slaves on English soil.[17]

The *Somerset* case primed Charles Steuart and other imperial policy makers to be wary of letting household litigation become a public concern. He and many other London agents were familiar with the transatlantic cast of characters involved in the *Blair* divorce case, and would have recognized it as potentially explosive news. (Steuart had even played a part in introducing Kitty Eustace Blair, Dunmore's purported mistress, into Virginia society.) The market for salacious tales of elite marital discord was such that no "pro-divorce lobby" was required to ensure unwanted publicity. Open debate in Virginia's assembly would have been hard to suppress, and Kitty Blair's mother threatened to publish her daughter's side of the story in a pamphlet if the case went against them. However it came to light, *Blair v. Blair* threatened to tarnish the image and authority of multiple factions in the debates over colonial governance. It remained a local "Williamsburg scandal" by chance. Before the bill of divorce came before the Virginia legislative session, Kitty's aggrieved husband died; or, as her sympathizers more euphemistically reported to London: "very opportunely took his departure for the other world."[18] The Council on Colonial Affairs had likely heard the dangerous rumors connected with this domestic insurrection—but not of Dr. James Blair's death and the consequent end of his divorce petition—when they rejected the Pennsylvania butcher's divorce bill as bad precedent on April 7, 1773.[19]

The cast of characters in the Blair case documents America's political founder's familiarity with debates about marriage and divorce, and also the difficulty of aligning a position on these matters with coherent political principles. As the Scottish lawyer and social theorist John Millar observed of American colonists' protests against their "enslavement" through taxation, colonial household politics showed "how little the conduct of men is at bottom directed by any philosophical principles."[20] When it came to marriage—as with slavery—the personal circumstances and family interests of revolutionaries were not always well served by legal or philosophical consistency.

Kitty Eustace was the daughter of Margaret Campbell Eustace and Dr. John Eustace, educated and accomplished Scots who appear to have settled in the colonies with the hope of securing wealth commensurate with their sense of status. Kitty's father, an Edinburgh trained physician, had left Margaret, Kitty, and a younger son in New York in 1764 and established himself in North Carolina, where he became known as much for his literary and social endeavors as his medical practice. In what appears to have been clever social marketing by his surviving family, after his death in 1769 he was remembered in colonial newspapers as a man of "wit and understanding" whose correspondence with the famed novelist Lawrence Sterne merited a wide readership. All the members of the Eustace family appear to have been well versed in Sterne's raunchy humor and sentimental literary tropes, as well as law and medicine. Kitty's few surviving letters suggest that she was exceptionally well educated for an eighteenth-century American woman; in contrast with Abigail Adams (and with most of their male contemporaries), Kitty's spelling and grammar were excellent. Kitty and her mother traveled from New York to North Carolina to retrieve Kitty's father's valuable library in the winter of 1769–70, and soon after settled in Norfolk, Virginia, from where Charles Steuart's correspondent pronounced both Margaret Eustace and her "pretty daughter" exceptionally "agreeable ladies."[21]

The pair's performance of sentimental gentility and their family connections to an international circle of medical professionals helped Kitty win the hand of the very eligible Dr. James Blair. Charles Steuart's correspondents noted that Kitty's "clever managing" mother had "played her cards exceedingly well" in arranging the match.[22] The Blair family were of Scottish descent, but were also thoroughly Virginian. James Blair's father had been a multiterm president of the Virginia Governor's Council and had served as acting governor of the colony on more than one occasion. His brother was a member of the General Court, clerk of the Governor's Council, and a friend of Thomas Jefferson; after the revolution, he went on to help draft the US Constitution and serve on the Supreme Court. James, the youngest son, had been sent back to Scotland to study medicine alongside Arthur Lee, who became a colonial agent and the United States' "first diplomat." (We will meet Lee again later in this chapter.) In 1769, James Blair had joined Lee in London to study law and pursue politics, but his tenure was interrupted by a "violent nervous disorder" that forced his return to Virginia about six months before his marriage to Kitty.[23]

The families who facilitated the Eustace-Blair marriage appear to have intended the match to tighten the bonds between Virginia's Scottish American and Scottish expatriate communities. Instead, it helped sever them. The couple parted on their wedding night, for reasons that survive only in gossipy letters alluding to physical incompatibility and to James Blair's mental and physical incapacity. Over the next year, the couple went through the usual rounds of local community mediation, as well as some less usual medical consultations. Kitty filed a suit for separate maintenance based on the couple's prenuptial agreement, but was initially turned down in the hope that reconciliation could be forced. The Blairs' difficulties were "talked of all over the country" and beyond.[24] The dispute took on ominous tones after James accused the governor, Lord Dunmore, of having adulterous designs on Kitty. With the mediation of his brother, James backed down from this politically dangerous charge. It nevertheless cast a pall over attempts at a settlement, not least because Dunmore was the Crown officer who would have been responsible for making an equitable decision about marital separation.

By late 1772 both sides had employed the best lawyers in Virginia, and James Blair had requested a bill of divorce from Virginia's burgesses. Historians know of the case because Blair's friend Thomas Jefferson prepared the pro-divorce arguments, which ranged widely in order to legitimate divorce on grounds other than adultery (or James's reputedly unusual masculine "instruments").²⁵ Jefferson's detailed case notes highlighted the conceptual importance of household government to republican political thought, and built a radical case for divorce from the bonds of matrimony from more ambivalent arguments by Pufendorf, Milton, Locke, Hume, and Montesquieu. In many respects, his brief anticipated the case for divorce from the bonds of empire he made three years later in the Declaration of Independence. While Jefferson performed the research for Blair's case, Virginia's premier orators stood charged with presenting them before the bar; these included Edmund Pendleton, James Mercer, and Jefferson's teacher, the College of William and Mary law professor George Wythe.²⁶

It is not clear what would have become of James Blair's divorce bill had he lived. His erratic behavior and attacks on the governor had undermined his community support, in spite of his excellent legal team. Kitty Blair adeptly appealed to the refined sentiments of Virginia's elite men and women, including her sister-in-law Ann Blair. On James's death, Kitty sued for her widow's share of the Blair family estates using arguments that made sympathy for female distress the measure of American "liberality." A conservative interpretation of received marriage law—not divorce reform—provided the remedy. Without James's evidence and with the new imperial injunction against colonial bills of divorce, it became much harder to posthumously declare her marriage invalid. Jefferson's radical arguments for divorce surfaced in the legal pleading by James Blair's family, but they failed to persuade even those who agreed with Jefferson's politics. John Randolph—Virginia's attorney general, Dunmore's confidant, and an eventual loyalist—and the rabidly revolutionary lawyer Patrick Henry together carried Kitty's case. (St. George Tucker, another George Wythe student and future American revolutionary and judge, provided her with unofficial advice.) All but one of the members of a General Court headed by Lord Dunmore determined in Kitty Blair's favor, awarding her a plantation and sixteen enslaved people. Kitty's elated mother attributed their success "in a land of Strangers" to arguments by Patrick Henry that shone "in the cause of Justice, backed by Law." Jefferson dismissed Henry as having "avoided, as was his custom, entering the lists of the law" and instead "running wild in the field of fact." Historians suspect that Dunmore and Randolph moved behind the scenes to arrange the trial to lay to rest the rumors of Dunmore's adultery and to prevent Dunmore's overt intervention in the case. We are left with these conflicting interpretations because the Eustace women were content, the Blair family was outmaneuvered, and no cadre of activists cared to pursue the matter.²⁷

Charles Steuart and other London authorities would have been relieved at this ambiguous legal outcome, which avoided jurisdictional conflict and the attention of colonial propagandists. Time-honored damage-control strategies had proved more effective than in the *Somerset* case. Although authorities would have preferred informal, private settlements as a means to defuse political tension, murky and technical legal judgments were almost as effective, especially when they left few records that could serve as precedent.

While the Blairs' case did not become the sort of overt legal and political challenge that London feared, it remains significant as an example of the ways that threats to the integrity of familial—and especially patriarchal—claims to property, power, and happiness inspired revolutionary political passions. Animosities stirred by the case helped divide Virginia's Scottish gentry into differing revolutionary camps. The future US Supreme Court Justice John Blair, brother of the unfortunate James, split with Lord Dunmore as the legal dispute played itself out. And while the General Court ruled in accord with Dunmore's interests, his and Attorney General Randolph's behind-the-scenes machinations gave ammunition to those who saw Dunmore as an unscrupulous tyrant, bent on using his position to further his own interests and denying Virginians impartial justice.

Links between grievances about domestic law and revolutionary politics were not consistently tied to a specific emancipatory agenda, however. They cut both ways, creating loyalists as well as revolutionaries. Benjamin Bannerman, an adventuring Scot whom we met in the previous chapter, became a loyalist in response to colonial officials' support for the legal claims of his household dependents. Bannerman had been outraged by a local Virginia court's 1769 decision to award alimony to his estranged wife. In 1774, he ran into trouble in Pennsylvania when antislavery activists targeted him in a failed attempt to produce an American counterpart to *Somerset v. Steuart*. Bannerman appears to have chosen sides due to his outrage at what he saw as colonial affronts to his honor and credibility, rather than from enthusiasm for the Crown. Affronted honor, beginning with the rumors in the Blair case, also shaped Lord Dunmore's marked hostility to Virginia's revolutionaries, including his famous 1775 promise of freedom to the slaves of rebellious colonists.[28] The Declaration of Independence's complaints about the "domestic insurrections" fostered by representatives of the Crown had multiple layers.

The Blair case is also another reminder of the frequency with which liberality to a wife entailed an illiberal and uncertain future for enslaved families. Within two months of the decision granting her dower, Kitty Eustace Blair auctioned the estate's livestock and farm equipment and rented out half her interest in the land and its enslaved workers. Her advertisement noted "5 workers" and a "handy cook" available for hire. She and her mother remained in Williamsburg, and in high society's good graces, until Kitty remarried a revolutionary officer and future governor of Georgia in 1777. She died young, but her mother (and eventually her brother, who became an international revolutionary adventurer) ultimately returned to the family estates in New York, where they socialized in the circles of still more American "first families" who shaped ambiguous postrevolutionary divorce policy.[29]

THE CREATION OF AMERICAN LIBERALITY

In the wake of the Privy Council's prohibition on colonial divorces, purveyors of the culture of Enlightenment and sensibility gradually established explicit connections between marital reform and "American Liberality." These advocates for divorce—like the ideas they propounded—were primarily migrants. Thomas Paine, whose 1776 *Common Sense* was the first of many revolutionary pamphlets to earn him international renown, arrived in Philadelphia late in 1774, fleeing debts and a failed marriage. His first publication was an essay on "Unhappy Marriages," which placed a critique of Christian marital indissolubility into the mouth of a wise "American savage." Like Paine, the Philadelphia bookseller Robert Bell had left a wife and debts behind in Britain. He published the 1771 American edition of Blackstone's *Commentaries* and was among the most important distributors of Scottish Enlightenment texts and sentimental novels in the colonies.[30] We have no overt statements of his interest in marital reform, but the arguments of our anonymous 1788 pro-divorce pamphleteer were aimed at people who had been spending time in his bookshop. Bell was probably the conduit for the obscure Scottish legal handbook that provided the template for Pennsylvania's "revolutionary" 1785 divorce law.

Written by Robert Boyd, a student of the Scottish Enlightenment stadial theorist John Millar, this 1779 treatise emerged from the imperial debates about jurisdiction over marriage prompted by the 1753 Marriage Act. Boyd claimed the authority of ancient "custom" for Scotland's practices regarding marriage and divorce, and asserted that England's policies had diverged from their common cultural roots. Incursions by English legal treatises (like Blackstone's) and the specter of imperial insistence on uniformity made it necessary to enshrine Scottish custom in print. In a subsequent work, Boyd carried the conversation from law to culture, explicitly connecting concrete questions of legal policy with his more famous mentor's (Millar's) abstract meditations on marriage, slavery, and civilization. It behooved the student of law, he argued, to blend "political and moral inquiries with the nomenclature of statutes, the arrangement of cases, and the collecting of legal opinions." A narrow focus on legal texts left the law "cramped and manacled," when it ought instead to be an area of "liberal study which bestows additional energy upon every faculty of the soul, . . . quickens its perceptions, discovers the principles of legislation, teaches how to provide against, or how to remedy disorders in the state." Such a capacious understanding of law, he further argued, explained Americans' ability "to auger misgovernment at a distance, and snuff the approach of tyranny at every tainted breeze." Thus justified, he dove into a long conjectural history designed to show that Scottish marriage practices were agreeable to the "the dictates of religion and nature," whereas England's promoted tyranny and corruption.[31]

When Pennsylvania legislators borrowed his language for the state's 1785 Divorce Act, however, they sought to contain revolutionary enthusiasm, aiming to "remedy . . . disorders in the state" rather than challenge tyranny. The most direct reasons for reform were merely pragmatic. Legislators found the task of handling private bills of divorce frustrating and burdensome. Between 1777 and the passage of the 1785 act turning authority over to the Supreme Court, the Pennsylvania Assembly heard thirty-five appeals and granted eleven divorces. Relative to population or even to the number of couples advertising their disputes in the press, this caseload was small. But it was equivalent to that handled by England's Parliament during the same period, when the time-consuming and tedious procedural requirements associated with such bills prompted new efforts to restrict access to them.[32]

In 1785 Massachusetts similarly responded to growing *demand* for divorce—manifested in legislative petitions as well as in the courts—with an act clarifying the process by which it should be obtained. The measure essentially affirmed the proceedings of the past century, but narrowed the available grounds by excluding desertion. This restriction cut against any revolutionary implications the law might have had in two ways: it left husbands of wayward but not adulterous wives in as awkward a position as ever; and it deprived women of the grounds that—in other jurisdictions, at least—most commonly gave legal divorce the semblance of being a "woman's remedy." (In eighteenth-century Connecticut, desertion was the primary ground in 67 percent of divorces awarded to women.) New York's 1787 divorce act was even more limited, recognizing only adultery as sufficient cause. In these instances, the move to make divorce legal was motivated substantially by the desire to make increasingly visible forms of extralegal marital dissolution illegal. As Basch succinctly puts it, "To make divorce legitimate was to make all other dissolutions illegitimate."[33]

The move to regulate divorce was also intimately connected to new efforts to regulate matters of credit and debt. Pennsylvania passed a "radical" bankruptcy act and its Act Concerning Divorce and Alimony in the same 1785 legislative session. The measures had much in common. Pennsylvania's revolutionary legislatures found pleas for relief from insolvent debtors even more tedious than divorce petitions. The legislature was inundated with both sorts of petition not only because of the social and economic turmoil produced by the revolution, but because shifting conceptions of law made such equitable relief at once more necessary and harder to obtain at the local level. Finally, while Pennsylvania's divorce and bankruptcy statutes departed from previous *colonial* practice, they aligned the new state's practices with those established elsewhere in the British Empire. The Scottish divorce law after which Pennsylvania's Divorce Act was modeled had been accepted practice since the 1680s. Pennsylvania's 1785 Bankruptcy Act followed English practices, particularly in limiting its provisions for relief to wealthy, commercial debtors.[34] Both "revolutionary" measures, in short, served relatively conservative ends. They clarified and relocated equitable jurisdiction that the assembly found burdensome, and limited relief to a deserving few whose grievances could be addressed in ways that affirmed old hierarchies.

Divorce and Emancipation: A Useful False Equivalence

Revolutionary-era antislavery activists successfully created an organized transatlantic movement for slave emancipation and quietly undermined legal support for the institution in most northern states. There was no equivalent "movement" in support of divorce and the reform of marriage law, but parallels between revolutionary divorce and emancipation have nevertheless acquired enduring historical currency. In broad terms, responsibility for this lies with Scottish Enlightenment stadial theorists who portrayed indissoluble marriage and slavery as equivalent forms of bondage, fated to subside with the progress of civilization. More concretely, our anonymous Philadelphia pro-divorce essayist appears to have co-opted the analogy for his own political purposes, in spite of the knowledge that antislavery activists would have rejected it outright. Eighteenth-century opponents of slavery found that the cause was better served by religious arguments for marital indissolubility that challenged the destruction of enslaved families. When freed people of color did leave records of marital separation in the wake of the revolution, it frequently reflected efforts by former masters to reimpose old hierarchies. White authorities readily held black men responsible for the financial obligations of marriage, though they declined to grant black families the right to preserve family integrity. In the American South, supporters of slavery inverted Scottish Enlightenment arguments, using the supposedly "natural" dependence of women in indissoluble marriages to help justify the "natural" dependence of black men and women in a state of slavery. Opposition to divorce became a proslavery principle, contributing to regional conservatism in domestic law that outlasted the institution of slavery.

ANTISLAVERY ACTIVISTS' OPPOSITION TO DIVORCE

Between 1785 and 1788, a transatlantic group of Anthony Benezet's followers strategically reshaped antislavery into distinctive national movements in America, England, and France. This was the same network of people who, before the war, had created political headaches both for imperial officials and for colonial advocates of rebellion through their efforts to make antislavery a universal rather than partisan cause. In *Somerset v. Steuart*, in the Pennsylvania freedom suit that spurred the founding of the world's first antislavery organization, and in the *only* challenge to a runaway slave ad to appear in the colonial press, they carefully targeted unpopular slaveholding agents of empire such as Charles Steuart and Benjamin Bannerman. In the satirical conjugal spat discussed in the previous chapter, such men were the "servants, grooms and foxhunters" that the tyrannical husband Loyalty allowed to "direct and insult" his wayward wife American Liberty. Antislavery activists hoped that if they redirected the ire of both Liberty and Loyalty to such scapegoats, they might also inspire the warring couple to put aside petty disputes over taxes and instead find a higher, shared calling in "common duty in defence of the rights of mankind." Conflict and the threat of war, activists believed, reflected divine judgment for the sin of slavery; the eradication of this root evil would bring about redemption and peace. During the revolution, this activist cohort aimed for pacifist neutrality but inclined toward loyalism. After the war, it became politically necessary for them to reinvent antislavery with a nationalist spin.[35]

When the author of the 1788 "Essay on Marriage" reframed local concerns and transatlantic arguments to make marriage reform an "American" cause, he followed the example antislavery activists had already set in lobbying efforts in Congress and at the 1787 Constitutional Convention. From its opening paragraphs, the pamphlet demonstrated considerable knowledge of the strategies of Philadelphia-based activists. When he claimed, for example, that his production had been inspired by "a paragraph in a newspaper, relative to a woman in the city who had destroyed herself on account of some infelicity in marriage," he directly echoed a story told by antislavery activists about their motives for resuming and expanding their activities in the wake of Revolution. The Quaker Benezet featured an account of two Philadelphia men who had thought themselves freed by the revolution, and had committed suicide rather than return to slavery, in his final inspirational missive. Neither Benezet nor the people of color with whom he worked would have agreed with the use to which the pro-divorce advocate put their emancipatory efforts.[36]

Even as he invoked antislavery as a model for reform, the 1788 pamphleteer acknowledged the limits of his analogies between emancipation and divorce. He encouraged readers to disregard public opinion and emulate the provocative and controversial antislavery activist Benjamin Lay. The writer praised, among other things, Lay's famous disruptions of religious services; he was known for entering meetinghouses and sprinkling the congregation with blood, informing them that "the blood of the slaves was in like manner upon their heads, if they did not repent and free" them. Lay, like his inspiration Ralph Sandiford, had been disowned by the Quakers. By celebrating this example, the writer disparaged those who remained within the Quaker fold. This backhanded dismissal of the Quakers suggests that the writer knew that his views on marriage were at odds with those of Benezet and other reformers whose primary commitment was to the abolition of slavery, and that he did not care.[37]

Benezet and other spiritual and intellectual leaders of the early antislavery movement rejected analogies between divorce and emancipation. Antislavery commitments became Quaker policy during the 1750s as part of a communal purification movement anchored by marriage reform. In what appears to have been the price for their exemption from the terms of England's 1753 Marriage Act, Quaker communities on both sides of the Atlantic rigorously enforced oversight of the formation of marriages, disciplining those who married without the blessing of their meetings and disowning those who married out of the faith. The pro-divorce pamphleteer saw this paternalist religious meddling as profoundly unjust, and seems to have disliked Benezet for his role in it. Benezet (as well as the Anglican Granville Sharp and the nominally Presbyterian Benjamin Rush) regarded the inviolability of godly households as a crucial theological plank in arguments against slavery. Divorce, *like* slavery, was a practice permitted under "Old Testament" Mosaic law but forbidden to Christians. New Testament prohibitions *against* divorce stood as evidence that Christ had ordained a new household order.[38] To argue for divorce, then, was to undermine activists' claims that the eradication of slavery was part of a Christian project of global redemption.

Our pamphleteer, in contrast, treated the emancipation of slaves and the legal right of divorce as directly parallel, characterizing both slavery and marriage foremost as civil relationships subject to legal authority rather than "natural" or divinely ordained bonds. He argued that having "granted relief to a less respectable class of mankind, without request, in a less painful situation" (i.e., to slaves), state legislatures should certainly also be willing to provide legal remedy to those unhappy "free citizens of America . . . unto whom the bands of wedlock has entailed wretchedness instead of joy!"[39]

This critique of marriage drew on the racist ventriloquism common in Scottish Enlightenment speculation about marriage. A defender of slavery could have been proud of the pamphlet's discussion of the ways the primitive simplicity of "Negroes" and the paternalistic benevolence of masters rendered enslaved people's situation "less painful" than an unhappy marriage. Although the enslaved were "always at call to come and go," the pamphleteer argued, "their common portion of labour" was "seldom equal to that of a free person," and they were "relieved from the care and concern of providing for themselves and families." Regarding "bodily correction," they could "mostly avoid [it] by submission and fair promises, and this they often regard no longer than it smarts, which is soon over." Unlike unhappy husbands and wives, slaves were "not confined to their master's apartment, to be always tormented and abused." The author asserted, moreover, that "slaves,* almost always, by complaint or remonstrance to their master or others, may change their master, until they have found out the most moderate." (The asterisk flagged a qualifying footnote "alluding to the slaves of Pennsylvania and New-Jersey," suggesting that the author was aware of the fantastic nature of many of his claims.) Presumably because their exclusion from participation in civilized society kept them closer to the state of nature, the enslaved were also "under no restraint from religion, morality or fear of losing their reputation, or of excommunication; their love is all delight; they feel no dread from future consequences; they marry with whom, and for as long as they please, and no longer." Slaveholding might be a "detestable practice," but this strain of Scottish Enlightenment argument attempted to make exclusion from the constraints of civilization into an enviable form of freedom.[40]

MARITAL OBLIGATIONS AND THE PRESERVATION OF RACIAL HIERARCHY

What the pamphleteer depicted as virtues of slaves' experiences, African Americans portrayed as profound grievances. Revolutionary-era freedom petitions and court cases expressed both worldly and religious "dread" of the "future consequences" of masters' control over marriages. Enslaved men's inability to "provide for themselves and families" was a key marker of their subordinate status and their exclusion from the polity. When the enslaved "changed their masters," it was more generally in transactions in which their wishes were at best a peripheral concern. In an economic system built on slaves' value as mobile capital, the paternalism of individual masters provided scant protection. When a master's own household fell under threat, the law required that he sacrifice African American families and communities to preserve his own.[41]

The specter of debt and liability hung over emancipation, as over divorce, in ways not acknowledged by our pamphleteer. Squabbles over financial responsibility for former slaves and their families, for instance, followed immediately on the heels of the final legal decision in the Quok Walker cases credited with ending slavery in Massachusetts. In the face of courtroom defeat, Walker's master petitioned the state legislature for relief from the statute that made masters liable for their manumitted slaves. He requested "that if the servant is set free, the master may be free too." The obligation to "maintain and support . . . a Negro Servant" when one could "have no control over him," he protested, inverted God-given relations of dependence and made white Christians into slaves.[42]

Newspaper ads of African American runaways shifted to reflect similar concerns about liability by former masters. Notices demanding the capture and return of runaways all but disappeared from the Massachusetts papers in the wake of the decision against masters in the 1783 Walker case. Masters instead placed ads that forbade "All Persons" from "harboring, trading with, or trusting" their former slaves, discrediting them in nearly the same terms used for eloping wives.[43]

This shift in runaway ads from offering rewards to discrediting indicated that contemporaries recognized the Walker cases as a meaningful legal landmark. Other advertisements that emerged at the same moment, however, demonstrated immediate efforts to reinstitute racialized dependence, using the very right to legal marriage that African Americans demanded as they sought their freedom. In the New England press during the early 1780s, identifiably African American men took out a spate of newspaper notices discrediting their runaway wives. Following the practice long used by white husbands, they charged that the women had "eloped" from them and declared that they would not pay their debts. The overall numbers were relatively small—some twenty-seven across New England between 1780s and 1800. Yet in Boston papers during the 1780s, black men's notices accounted for 14 percent of the total at a time when blacks made up less than 3 percent of the population. Hundreds of elopement notices appeared in earlier decades, but none were by African American men.[44] The phenomenon suggests that masters' who had balked at conferring the privileges of marriage were quite happy to transfer its economic burdens. They made sure that freed men were "bound to maintain and support" their wives, regardless of whether they had control over them.

Black men's advertisements differed in subtle ways from ads taken out by whites, and further document how the obligations of marriage could be used to compromise aspirations to independence by people of color. Black men's notices were far more explicit about wives' obligation to labor than were those of white men. A white husband might complain, as did the socially prominent free black Cato Gardner, that his wife "neglects her duty in my family." Ads by African American men were unique, however, in chastising their wives for "idling [their] time" or "refus[ing] to labour or do any Thing to support" themselves.[45] This semantic difference reflected African American women's continuing obligation to labor in households other than their own, and another way in which the privileges of marriage did not extend to free blacks. An African American wife's failure to "do any Thing to support" herself could give authorities an excuse to bind her husband into service to pay the costs of her maintenance. A husband's marital responsibilities could thus compromise his individual freedom even as they defined it. His wife was not a slave, but neither was the husband a "competent" householder fully able to dispose of his dependents' labor.[46]

Debates about marriage and racial hierarchy also surfaced in the 1780s and 1790s in the regions where America extended little or no revolutionary "liberality" to slaves. Pero Conrad, a free man of color in Delaware, found that new respect for slaves' marriages left him with the worst of both worlds. His wife Abbe was "the property of Adam Williamson," but Conrard had nevertheless become liable for her debts.[47]

In 1785, as the New York legislature debated a gradual emancipation law modeled after Pennsylvania's, papers in both states printed a vicious parody of black male aspirations to status as householders and citizens. The anonymous author pretended to have mistakenly received letters intended for his "Negro Quak"—a play both on Quok Walker and on the Quaker activists who bore primary responsibility for the legislation. The contributor sarcastically professed "exquisite pleasure" at the "laudable ambition" and "spirit of liberty" expressed in the "letter," and he was sure these would delight "every person who has been instrumental in affecting the emancipation of the poor Africans." The parody pioneered racist uses of dialect and proslavery arguments that would become staples of nineteenth-century debates. The "grate neus," that "de legeslatermen hab mak de blak peplee fre" filled "Quakee's" correspondent Cuffee and his family with joy, though it made his "masser be berry cros." It did not matter, however, because Cuffee would soon be as "gud man as he." Cuffee's son would marry his master's daughter and become a political leader. Cuffee's wife Dina, moreover, was wantonly eager for sex now that she did not fear that her children would be slaves. He broke off the letter because "Dina sa I mus cum bed, she no care how many fre mans she hab nou." After the New York legislature came just shy of the two-thirds majority needed to pass the manumission law, the fictional couple decided that they would make "no mo young nega."[48]

The racism of this proslavery parody was not far removed from that of the earnest pro-divorce pamphleteer. Indeed, the parody was *more* honest in acknowledging that even "simple" slaves felt a "dread from future consequences" in their marriages, even as it played on fearful white fantasies about the barely restrained nature of slaves' sexual desire. The connection shows how easily the Scottish Enlightenment arguments that the pamphleteer thought supported divorce could be inverted. The "Essay on Marriage" framed marriage reform and emancipation as signs of social progress. Defenders of slavery would use identical evidence to build a new defense of "tradition."

INDISSOLUBLE MARRIAGE AND THE DEFENSE OF SLAVERY

The ease with which progressive efforts to link divorce and emancipation could be inverted into a defense of slavery and indissoluble, hierarchical marriage help explain why American liberality with regard to divorce, as with emancipation, remained more limited in the slaveholding South than in other regions. Southern elites were far more cautious than leaders elsewhere about adopting provisions for divorce in the wake of revolution. This was *not* because of lack of interest or debate. Prior to the *Blair* divorce case discussed earlier in this chapter, Virginia newspapers tracked news of English marital scandals and parliamentary divorce actions more assiduously than any others in the colonies. In 1769 and 1770 alone, they repeated some two dozen stories about English elopements and divorces. They noted rumors that Parliament was about to consider new general regulations for divorce, and informed readers that "divorces are become so common among the great" that it had become fashionable to place bets on which noblewoman would cuckold her husband first. Shortly before the Blairs' unfortunate marriage in 1771, Virginia papers reported an ecclesiastical divorce case grounded on the husband's impotence, assuring readers that "the depositions furnished great entertainment to the gentlemen of the long robe."[49] When the Virginia planters and gentry who read the paper found their own leadership consumed by the Blairs' similar scandal, the potential for trouble outweighed the amusement such cases provided.

Jefferson's enlightened arguments did not win out in Virginia in 1772; neither did they succeed after independence, when the prospect of legalizing divorce was again raised and repeatedly rejected. South Carolinian authorities adamantly refused to grant divorce on any grounds until after the Civil War. Other former southern colonies "legitimized" divorce in the decades following the revolution only by granting a few private bills of divorce under extraordinary circumstances. If they were no longer "divorceless," neither did they formally authorize divorce until well into the nineteenth century.[50]

Southern reluctance to alter an official stance of divorcelessness, as well as the initial exceptions to the policy, were intimately connected with the region's investment in slavery. The first divorces awarded in Maryland and Virginia went to husbands who accused their wives of interracial adultery. And particularly in the nineteenth century, authorities explained opposition to divorce in terms of the need to preserve the inviolability of household government and to secure the power of husbands and masters alike.[51]

The logic of our Philadelphia pamphleteer tempts readers to think of this pattern as an exception to a liberal "American" norm. Like his Scottish Enlightenment contemporaries and later generations who adopted their social theories, he portrayed slavery and other forms of domestic patriarchy as fundamentally incompatible with "modern" national identity. When nineteenth-century Southern leaders justified opposition to divorce and support for slavery as parallel planks in an effort to conserve ancient and "natural" patriarchal norms, however, they were simply inverting this Scottish Enlightenment story. Their account of patriarchal "tradition" was as much a "modern" and revolutionary construct as the pamphleteer's account of social progress. Both versions of this conjectural history, moreover, were demonstrably false. Slavery was not only compatible with modern institutions, but—as the source of colonial capital and of the staple crops that sustained the growth of British industry in the early nineteenth century—it was fundamental to them. Divorce, like slavery, had an ancient history as a patriarchal prerogative. It could be used to uphold household hierarchies even in a liberal age.

Divorce as a Woman's Remedy: Revolutionary Expectations and the "First Families" of the United States

Revolutionary state legislatures made no pretense of intending divorce to be a "woman's remedy," and the divorce legislation they passed was inspired predominantly by male petitioners. The notion that it alleviated the burdens imposed by women's subordination in marriage emerged from sentimental arguments like those of our anonymous 1788 pamphleteer, and from later, postrevolutionary legal trends in which increasing numbers of women took advantage of new divorce laws. Casting divorce as a "woman's remedy" became a way to resolve the tension between sentimental rhetoric that framed masculine power as a form of protection and the frank abuse of patriarchal power normalized by Blackstone's account of coverture and the ascendance of the common law.

Our anonymous Philadelphia pamphleteer modeled the strategic use of the logic of sensibility—and the protection of women—in his arguments for divorce reform. He opened his "Essay on Marriage" with the claim that a *woman's* suicide inspired his call for legal change. Yet his professed concern for feminine distress, like his opportunistic invocation of antislavery sentiment, provided moral cover for controversial demands. The work quickly turned its attention from female victims to universal, and implicitly masculine, claims: "A strong sympathetic feeling for the weakness and distresses of *human* nature" induced the author to seek relief for other "wretched" souls who might be tempted to "plunge themselves into another world to avoid the miseries of this" one. The author compared marriage to slavery; he did not compare *wives* to slaves. If his motive was sympathy for female misery, he nonetheless appealed to his audience as "men." Expectations of female subordination were not among his many itemized causes of marital infelicity. Nor were women's economic and political dependence a consideration in his vague proposals for policy.[52]

The "Essay on Marriage," like revolutionary-era divorce legislation, did not fundamentally challenge a legal order that allowed all men to be tyrants if they could. Yet the essay and the real-world case that likely inspired it demonstrate how sentimental culture made it difficult to discuss marriage without reference to female welfare. Desperate women used sentimental scripts to claim divorce as a remedy in ways that defied legislative intent. Persistent expectations about divorce as a "woman's remedy" owe more to the sentimental framing of divorce stories than to revolutionary changes in legal practice.

SENSIBILITY AND PATRIARCHY:
THE CASE OF ANN SHIPPEN LIVINGSTON

No case better exemplifies the tension between sentimental expectations and enduring patriarchal norms than that of Anne Shippen Livingston, a prominent member of the circles of "sensible" young people educated in revolutionary Philadelphia. Like the author of the "Essay on Marriage," she spent more time than was good for her imbibing the heady mix of sentimental fiction, Scottish stadial theory, and radical politics found in Robert Bell's bookshop. She also corresponded at length on such topics with her uncle Arthur Lee (companion to the unfortunate James Blair during their education abroad in the 1760s). Anne had been courted by George Washington's nephew, by a noble French diplomat, and by Henry Beekman Livingston, a revolutionary war officer and heir to a New York manor and one of the largest fortunes in North America. Anne favored the Frenchman; her father favored Livingston. As he saw it, both suitors were sensible and handsome, but only Livingston had already secured his fortune and "a Bird in hand is worth 2 in a Bush." Their 1781 marriage collapsed within six months, apparently because Henry refused to forgo the pleasures of keeping mistresses, while at the same time remaining intensely jealous of Anne's sensible friendships with his erstwhile rivals. Anne learned too late about the sexual exploits of Robert Bell's coterie.[53]

Like other women bedeviled by their husband's tyranny, Anne turned first to networks of family and friends for support. She took refuge in her parents' home in Philadelphia and periodically attempted to reconcile with her husband until 1785, when he declared the separation final. She then sought a legal separation agreement, but negotiations appear to have collapsed.[54] In 1789, she began, but did not finish, an attempt to obtain a divorce in New York. Two years later, her jurisdiction-shopping husband divorced her in Connecticut. Anne failed to obtain divorce on her terms, but not, as some historians have claimed, because she had no legal grounds. Her husband reputedly had numerous adulterous relationships and illegitimate children. The underlying problems were rooted in her allies' comparative lack of resources and her concern for the fate of her daughter. Her husband was erratic, violent, and unpopular, but unlike Sir Edward Scott (from chapter 2) or Dr. James Blair, he was not a "weak man." Henry Livingston used his power to damage those who defied him.[55]

Anne Shippen chronicled her troubled marriage in a journal that blurred the distinctions between literary fictions of sensibility and lived experience. She did not destroy herself on account of her "infelicity" in love and marriage, but instead plunged herself into the world of books. In her letters and diary, the stories she discovered there intermingled with her own. She sobbed like a child over the suicide of Goethe's lovelorn Young Werther. She found herself "much affected at a little annecdote . . . of a young Lady who was sacrificed to the avarice & ambition of her parents to a man she hated—& her death was the natural consequence of her misery." The heroine of this story "had a soul form'd for friendship—she found it not at home, her elegance of mind prevented her seeking it abroad; & she died a meloncholy victim to the Tyranny of her friends & the tenderness of her heart." The "annecdote" came directly from Frances Brooke's *History of Emily Montague*, which Anne had been transcribing liberally over the previous weeks without noting the source. She copied Brooke's translation of Madame de Maintenon's advice to women, and declared the ideas very much in line with hers. Anne also included, as if it were her own, the first-person commentary on Maintenon that Brooke had placed in the mouth of her fictional hero: "I cannot agree with her that Women are only born to suffer & to obey—that men are generally tyrannical I will own, but such as know how to be happy, willingly give up the harsh title of master for the more tender & endearing one of Friend. Equality is the soul of friendship: marriage, to give delight, must join *two minds*, not devote a slave to the will of an imperious Lord." This was the same passage that Abigail Adams marshaled as her own in her famous 1776 letter admonishing John to "Remember the Ladies."[56]

Anne's writing cast her family and husband as characters out of sentimental fiction even more overtly than did newspaper advertisements by aggrieved wives. Throughout her journal, Anne referred to her parents as Lord and Lady Worthy—titles that might have been drawn from the novels of Eliza Haywood or Daniel Defoe. Her husband, an unreformed rake, she named Lord B., evoking the rake of Richardson's *Pamela*. Anne depicted herself as a distressed and virtuous heroine, a "wretched slave—doom'd to be the wife of a Tyrant that I hate." Her social circumstances lent themselves to such novelistic devices.[57]

Anne's painful divorce story appears in multiple histories as a parable of disappointed revolutionary expectations.[58] It is better understood as evidence of the fluctuating significance of coverture. The revolutionary "promise" of divorce was primarily as a remedy for men who found that new legal emphasis on masculine possessory rights brought unexpected liabilities. The sentimental critique of "tyranny" in marriage emerged as an ameliorative, feminine counterpart to the same set of conundrums. The trope of "virtue in distress" served many purposes, including those of women who found divorce their best option. By the nineteenth century, the sentimental rhetoric that began appearing in women's newspaper challenges to their husbands during the 1760s had also become a staple of their legal petitions in the courts. While such rhetoric could be used to turn the law to new ends, the shift had its roots in revolutionary legal constraints rather than in revolutionary promises.

There are nonetheless important and unrecognized continuities between Anne's divorce story and those of earlier and of later periods. Anne's story demonstrates the extent to which revolutionary politics—and enlightened circles of sensible sociability—remained family affairs. Her legal choices were shaped by dynastic familial concerns that made the case fundamentally similar to the seventeenth-century case of Catherine and Edward Scott (chapter 2). And although the historian Michael Grossberg uses the Livingston case as a contrasting foil for his fine study of the nineteenth-century trials of Ellen Sears d'Hauteville, similarities here also rival the differences.[59]

As in the Scott and d'Hauteville cases, family fortunes and dynastic ambitions shaped Anne's strategies, though they did not always serve her individual desires. The social and political prominence of the Shippen and Livingston families meant that a public trial could too easily turn the case into a political test that ill served the parties. Catherine Scott had managed to "shift" a similar situation well enough, despite being cast as a symbol of Royalist sexual decadence. Anne Shippen Livingston, in contrast, sought self-consciously to embody republican virtue. These symbolic terms won her much sympathy but gave her fewer concrete options.

Manby v. Scott as it was revivified by William Blackstone, moreover, gave Henry Livingston *more* powers than Edward Scott had tried to claim in his seventeenth-century litigation. Henry's hostility appears to have been driven by spite, and also (as was the case for men across class lines) by problems of debt and credit. His debts made him particularly jealous of the financial claims that Anne, and especially their young daughter, had on what he thought of as "his" estate. The child and her inheritance became sticking points; concern for her welfare prevented Anne from taking legal risks she might have ventured if she had only herself to consider. Children—or at least their inheritance claims—were a major underlying factor in marital disputes that pushed legal remedies to their limits across the period of this book; yet, prior to the late eighteenth century, they were rarely discussed in legal conflicts between couples. Legal authorities seem to have preferred to let the legal complexities that children created be worked out behind the scenes. It was not in the interest of couples who wanted a separation to suggest that it would leave children adrift. Child custody as a presumed possessory right of parents—particularly of fathers—was another Blackstonean invention.[60]

The Livingston case (like the nineteenth-century d'Hauteville case) was distinctive in the extent to which concern about the welfare, education, and possession of a child became an explicit part of the debate. Anne, faced with failure as a wife, crafted an alternative identity for herself as a sensible, virtuous, and adoring mother. Henry used this affection against her and insisted that she turn the child over to his own mother, Margaret Beekman Livingston, for whom the girl Peggy was named. Henry initially told his family that this was because Anne's willful disobedience to him made her unfit to educate the child. Within a few years, however, Margaret Livingston sided with Anne's efforts to keep the little girl out of Henry's power. Concern that Henry's sense of masculine entitlement would deprive all the women in his family of their own rights created female solidarity.

Henry's mother was a wealthy woman who understood herself and her granddaughter to have property rights in the family estates. Margaret had been ably managing the affairs of Clermont Manor since her husband's death in 1775. She had rebuilt the mansion and buildings destroyed by British troops during the revolution. She went to law to enforce the obligation of tenants to pay their rents, even as the aristocratic foundations of the family's wealth came under fire. Henry's assertion of common-law masculine privileges angered and frightened her. She believed he sought custody of Peggy only so that he might supplement his own wealth with that held in trust for the child. Once he had that, she thought, "he will never care a straw where she is"— unless Peggy could be used as a pawn to extort concessions regarding the portions of the family estate that the elder Margaret still controlled. As she aged, Margaret found it harder to face down her son's "turbulent temper," and feared that she would not be able to prevent him from taking Peggy by force.[61]

Her leverage against his claims came at least in part from racial privilege. Like Margaret Bannerman and Jane Tennant (chapter 7), the Livingston women obtained and defined their own power through the control of enslaved people. During the revolution, reported one of her daughters, Margaret faced down "visits from robbers" without "one white man in the house" for protection. The racial caveat here suggests that there was at least one *black* man aiding the Livingston women as they rebuilt their family "Chateau." During much of the 1780s, the aging Margaret had charge of little Peggy's education and estate. The small child's daily needs, however, were attended at least in part by "My Dinah," whom Margaret assured the girl's mother, was "very careful & tender of her." Such reassurance might have been necessary because Anne had resolved in her own writing about her daughter's education that she would "never let her converse with servants."[62]

If Peggy went to live with her father, however, she would have far too much contact with servants, slaves, and the "miserable, undeserving objects" upon whom Henry seemed intent on "throwing . . . away" the property of his "lawful wife & heir." For this reason, no one in the Livingston family believed Henry's claims that he genuinely wanted to take charge of the girl's education. The "whole family were in the greatest distress" when he carried Peggy to his house during one fit of temper, although it may have been for the best that there was "no Woman" there save his illegitimate "daughter Hariot." Margaret regained custody after "Gentlemen" of the family brought moral pressure to bear. They concurred with the family matriarch that "it was Impossible to permit a child of one of the first families in the United States to be in a family without a white woman in it." The unspoken concern here was not simply that women of color performed the domestic labor in Henry's "family," but that they were also the "miserable, undeserving objects" of his extramarital affections. His other, unlawful children blurred the color line. Relationships of this sort were an open secret among the "first families of the United States," and the desire to keep them from becoming fodder for more public conversations explains, at least in part, why the "Gentlemen" of those families were unwilling to test Anne's case in court.[63]

The list of gentlemen who provided Margaret and Anne with moral and extralegal (possibly even illegal) assistance includes a "Who's Who" of second-tier American political founders. Her father William Shippen and her eventual legal advisors Aaron Burr, Jared Ingersoll, and Tench Coxe, were all "sensible men."[64] They were also committed to a Blackstonean understanding of the law that made them think that Henry Livingston's conduct was legally—if not socially—"proper." Anne's staunchest supporter, her eccentric uncle Arthur Lee, had a somewhat more flexible understanding of the law, perhaps because he had learned Mansfield's and Blackstone's rules by watching the jurists in action when he studied law in England during the 1770s, before joining John Adams as a representative of American interests in France. Lee might well have authored the anonymous essay on marriage and divorce that frames this chapter. His numerous political pamphlets and his letters to Anne are filled with textual references to the same sensible and Enlightened reading list cited by the pro-divorce essayist, and he had a fraught relationship with antislavery that might explain the pamphlet's subtle challenges to Quaker activists.[65]

When Anne asked Arthur Lee for advice about obtaining a divorce in New York, he advised her that unless her father were willing to pursue her case for her in person, she would have little hope. Perhaps recalling the political dynamics of the Blair case, he recommended that she do her utmost to "Interest the Ladies," particularly the wives of the state attorney general and other legal authorities who would have to handle the affair; if they secured sympathy for her "none but a butcher of a Judge . . . will venture to decide against humanity & you."[66] Anne did interest the ladies, and she did win the sympathy of men with legal power.

Political contingencies and concern with family status nevertheless gave more weight to patriarchal prerogatives. Chancellor Robert Livingston Jr., the judge who by the terms of New York's 1787 divorce statute had to arrange and preside over the adultery trial by which Ann's divorce could be obtained, had good reason to avoid facing such an overt decision. Just a few months before Anne began her quest for a divorce, he had helped secure New York's ratification of the new US Constitution. His arguments attached his family's fortunes and the Federalist cause to vigorous claims about superior virtue that made elite families into a natural and necessary ruling class. Margaret Beekman Livingston was Chancellor Livingston's mother. Henry was his younger brother. Anne was his sister-in-law, and Peggy his niece.[67] A trial in which he prosecuted his own brother for adultery—especially interracial adultery— was neither in the family's nor the Federalists' interests.

This coterie of Federalist men did not want to formally challenge Henry Beekman Livingston in the courts, not least because he threatened to sue all who interfered with his "Right" to his wife and child. Behind the scenes, usually in anonymous and undocumented ways, they interfered a great deal. Chancellor Livingston did not hear Anne's suit for divorce, but neither would he hear his brother's, which could have seemed plausible to outsiders. Anne's social circle judged her innocent. She had nonetheless maintained an affectionate—and suspicious—correspondence with her onetime French suitor. Her decision to pursue a full divorce followed on the news (worthy of an Eliza Haywood novel) that her lover had been recently widowed. After Henry found his attempts at legal action thwarted in New York, he shopped for a more favorable forum in Connecticut. He threatened to sue his mother for custody of Peggy in the federal courts. Margaret sent the girl into hiding in the houses of various male allies, and Tench Coxe then whisked her away incognito to Anne in Philadelphia. Margaret Livingston hoped that Anne could use Philadelphia's courts to make her own custody claim as a *feme sole* or secure the girl's independence in her own right as a citizen of Pennsylvania.[68] New York laws, her son the chancellor had decided, would not permit such things. Anne probably could have obtained a divorce in Pennsylvania, but only by placing Peggy at considerable risk. She did not pursue the option. While she remained in legal limbo, her French lover remarried a daughter of the famous writer and diplomat Hector St. John de Crèvecoeur.

Peggy shuttled back and forth between her grandmother and an aunt in New York and Anne in Philadelphia for several more years. At sixteen, she opted to surrender her claims to the Livingston fortune in order to live with her mother year-round. As Henry had anticipated, Margaret Beekman Livingston made up for this sacrifice out of her own estate, and on her death in 1800, she left Peggy well off. Anne and Peggy remained together for the rest of their long lives, leaving a muted record of deep, Scotch-inflected sentimental piety. The early twentieth-century editor of Anne's journal and correspondence ended her own novelistic account of these novelistic lives in a manner befitting Frances Brooke. For a "soul form'd for Friendship," monastic piety meant being "buried alive" by "unnatural" religious fanaticism. The seventeenth-century aristocrats Madame de Maintenon and Margaret Cavendish, on the other hand, would have approved. Recall that Cavendish advised, "Where there is a Hazard in the Choice, and a Security in not Choosing," it was best to remain "Mistress of your self." A "Single Life" was the "Safest Way." The Livingston women's contemporary, Jane Austen, concurred. It was "poverty only which makes celibacy contemptible to a generous public!," her fictional heiress Emma explained to a fictional Harriet, an illegitimate child whose lack of patrimony made marriage both necessary and hard to secure. Poor single women were pitiable and burdensome. "A single woman of good fortune," however, was "always respectable and may be as sensible and pleasant as anybody else!"[69]

Neither Anne nor her legal advisors framed divorce as a revolutionary promise to women. Her pursuit of this legal remedy instead responded to revolutionary understanding of coverture that emphasized masculine power (as well as masculine legal liability) and correspondingly undermined claims on family property by women of both good and meager "fortune." The problem of female poverty explains how, at least in some jurisdictions, divorce came to be depicted as a "woman's remedy" by the early nineteenth century. Women seized on this legal option in disproportionate numbers in states where desertion was grounds for full divorce. In such divorce petitions, fear for familial property in the face of the claims of husbands' creditors or the whims of men with an exaggerated sense of their own rights generally overshadowed any expectations about the merits of female independence.

MARITAL POLITICS AND ENSLAVED RUNAWAYS
IN THE WASHINGTON FAMILY:
THE CASE OF ONA JUDGE STAINES

A final story about a woman raised, if not educated, in the same social circles as the Blair, Shippen, and Livingston women offers a counternarrative to sentimental plots that minimize the power structures underpinning sensible sociability. Ona Judge Staines might have been a sister to either Anne or Peggy Livingston. For Ona, however, the marital privileges that secured "good fortune" for aristocratic white women meant misfortune and slavery. And where elite white women like the Livingstons might turn to divorce as a remedy for the revolutionary era's legal emphasis on universal masculine possessory rights, Ona followed in the footsteps of women of color who used husband's rights under coverture against the claims of masters. Sentimental arguments won Ona allies, but marriage to a free man protected Ona and her daughters from being returned to slavery.

Ona was the child of the favored enslaved seamstress of Martha Custis Washington and, reputedly, an English tailor indentured at Mount Vernon. She might also have had white relations; in the Custis household, as in most great planter families, at least some of the slaves were siblings of the family's legitimate heirs. Ona's light skin and sensible demeanor led Martha Washington to select her as a personal attendant after Washington became president, when the first family took up residence first in New York and then in Philadelphia. Ona's youth—she was perhaps fifteen or sixteen—was also a factor, because it allowed the Washingtons to circumvent Pennsylvania's laws requiring the registration and eventual manumission of any adult slaves brought into the state for more than six months. Ona would have been an observer at many of the same social gatherings at which the Livingstons were guests; she also developed her own networks within the city's black community, and even attended the theater with others from the skilled cadre of Mount Vernon slaves in the President's Philadelphia mansion. Like Elizabeth Freeman in Massachusetts, she minded the conversations as she waited at the table. When George Washington informed his family of his plans to retire in 1796 and to send the household back to Virginia, Ona packed to go elsewhere. She slipped away one May evening while the family lingered over dinner.[70]

A few days later, a notice placed in the *Pennsylvania Gazette* by the household steward advertised her as having "Absconded . . . with no provocation" and offered a reward for her return. The advertisement's deviation from the formulaic "run away" acknowledged the politically delicate situation created in 1790s Philadelphia by the president and his wife's desire to recover a "slender and delicately formed" girl whom they had been keeping on terms that violated Pennsylvania law. Shifts in the idiom of runaway ads were also symptomatic of more general uncertainties about the meaning of different forms of social dependency in the new republic. Massachusetts former slaves were now advertised as having eloped, and were punished—like wives—with discrediting. White servants were advertised much less frequently, and with notices like one from 1787 Philadelphia, in which an Irish lad had "Walked" (not "run away") after some "rascally associates . . . encouraged him to elope." In South Carolina, a white mistress promised her "Eloped Negro" Peter, a man of about thirty who "reads very well," that he "would be forgiven" if he returned of his own accord. Her notice echoed those of abusive husbands, whose coerced promises of kindness reflected legal imperatives rather than remorse. In this case, the female advertiser's softened threats register as an admission that her own independence depended on the goodwill and labor of the black men in her household.[71]

George Washington did not place the advertisement for Ona Judge himself. When she departed, he was being pressed about the issue of slavery from many sides, and overt pursuit would have invited controversy at odds with his efforts to place himself above the fray. Nevertheless, Washington and Martha wanted Ona back very badly, and they exploited their political networks, rather than the national press, to search for her. When the daughter of a New Hampshire senator recognized Ona on the street in the tiny seaport town of Portsmouth, Washington acted quickly. His correspondence in this case would fit easily into an eighteenth-century epistolary novel, though it was not quite so attentive to fictional plots and characters as that of Anne Shippen Livingston. Had he been thinking explicitly in such terms, Washington would have cast himself as Lord Worthy. Ona, on the other hand, would have found him a Richardsonian villain. In life as in fiction, the thin line between these roles placed power at odds with virtue.

Samuel Richardson's seductive rakes used elopement stories as a ruse to prevent their virtuous female victims from escaping their power. The amoral Lovelace assumed the patronizing guise of respectable masculinity to persuade bystanders that Clarissa was a temperamental wayward wife, whose honor would be preserved if he could quietly carry her back to his home. Ona Judge, George Washington informed his Secretary of War Oliver Wolcott, was "simple and inoffensive herself." Her escape, over land and sea, could only have been possible with considerable aid. The Washingtons told a conveniently face-saving story about a deranged Frenchman who must have seduced the girl. There was no room in this narrative for Ona's agency or for principled, internal American opposition to slavery, but rather proof of the president's wisdom in distrusting French revolutionary radicals. "If enquiries are made openly," Washington cautioned his cabinet secretary, Ona's "Seducer . . . would take the alarm, and adopt instant measures (if he is not tired of her) to secrete or remove her." The "safest and least expensive" course of action would be for them to move secretly themselves. Washington instructed his minister to "seize" Ona and throw her on a boat that would depart immediately for Philadelphia, or better yet, Alexandria, Virginia, where there would be little chance of her making another escape. If the provisions in the 1793 Fugitive Slave Act requiring that runaways be positively identified before a judge before they were carried off had to be observed, the women in the senator's household could help. Washington was not much concerned about such niceties.[72]

To the president's frustration and embarrassment, John Whipple, the New Hampshire customs official to whom Wolcott delegated the task of capturing

Ona, had not learned aristocratic lessons about the dangers of conversing with servants. He "cautiously" interrogated the girl, and learned that she "had not been decoyed away" but rather drawn by "a thirst for compleat freedom which she was informed would take place" when she arrived in Massachusetts or New Hampshire. Whipple found Ona reverent and affectionate toward the "President and his Lady," and more than willing to return and serve them faithfully for the rest of their lives, if she could be freed after their deaths. But Ona would rather "suffer death than . . . be given or sold to any other person." Whipple claimed that he had persuaded Ona to return "without compulsion" on the promise that he would help her obtain freedom on these terms. A delay in the departure of the boat gave "bad advisors" (or rather more honest ones) a chance to dissuade her, and she was now in hiding. As Whipple saw it, the president had two options. He could provide a legally binding promise of emancipation and secure Ona's willing return. Or he could overtly send an agent of his household to follow the "legal mode of proceeding" outlined in the Fugitive Slave Act and "authorized by the Constitution of the United States." It was neither legal nor politically wise for him to use the mechanisms of federal power for these personal ends.[73]

Although it was cloaked in deferential language, this was a gutsy stance for someone whose job depended on federal patronage. Whipple justified his action with "sensible" concern for Ona's virtue in distress (a role the Washingtons themselves had given her) and for the domestic happiness of Washington and his wife, to which an unwilling servant would not contribute. But, as in the Livingston marital dispute, such sentimental rhetoric was thin cover for the political import of a supposedly "private" affair. Whipple's own political choices were not enviable. He invoked the wrath of his patrons by bungling the president's request. The alternative would have been local dishonor; if the affair became a public spectacle, he would be living proof of the pretense of federalist claims to virtue, and of the corrupting influence of expansive, aristocratic national power.

George Washington was outraged. "To enter into such a compromise with her, as she suggested to you," he chastised Whipple, "is totally inadmissible, for reasons that must strike at first view. . . . However well disposed I might be to gradual abolition, or even to an entire emancipation of that People," Washington continued, "it would neither be politic or just to reward unfaithfulness with a premature preference; and thereby discontent before hand the minds of all her fellow-servants who by their steady attachments are far more deserving than herself of favor." In language that sounded personal but which reflected the legal concerns we have seen in elopement notices and runaway ads, Washington promised forgiveness if Ona would "return to her former service without obliging me to use compulsory means to effect it." He deflected the potential dishonor of using compulsion against the weak onto the women concerned: his wife Martha and Ona herself. Ona, the story went, and been "brought up and treated more like a child than a Servant," and her "ingratitude . . . ought not to escape with impunity." If Ona came back willingly, Washington promised, "she will meet with the same treatment from me that all the rest of her family (which is very numerous) shall receive." If she would not, Whipple was still to throw her on a boat, albeit as legally and discreetly as possible. Washington did "not mean . . . that such violent measures should be used as would excite a mob or riot . . . or even uneasy Sensations in the Minds of well disposed Citizens." It was "of infinite more importance" that he set a good example, for which lofty purpose he would "forego her Services altogether." Nonetheless, he still expected compliance and "the less is said beforehand, and the more celerity is used in the act of shipping her when an opportunity presents, the better chance Mrs. Washington (who is desirous of receiving her again) will have to be gratified."[74]

Washington dismissed "an entire emancipation" as not "in itself practicable at this moment." This assertion remains a foundation stone of US national history. So also is the related notion that "that People"—the enslaved people of color whom Washington (and the US Constitution) refused to name—and all women were reflexively and automatically excluded from the borders of national belonging.[75] It is true that the abolition of slavery and significant changes in women's legal status were impolitic in this period of new national beginnings. Ona Judge's and Anne Livingston's stories remind us of the need to be very careful, however, about translating such statements into assumptions about what was and was not possible. "It was impossible," asserted Margaret Beekman Livingston, for "a child of the first families of the United States" to be raised by black women (or a single white father). This was a lie. Such household arrangements, Livingston well knew, were not only possible, but in her family's case a real and immediate prospect. It was "totally inadmissible," declared George Washington, that Joseph Whipple should listen to Ona Judge and do as she suggested. But Whipple heard and conveyed Ona's message to the Washingtons, even if he did not fully understand it. Martha Washington's desire for her return was never "gratified."

If the Washingtons had "brought up and treated" Ona "more like a child than a Servant," she was a child they taught to work, not to read. Ona nonetheless would have grasped the promises in Washington's messages better than did her would-be benefactor. Ona's "very numerous" and much missed family were legally destined to pass to Martha Dandridge Custis Washington's grandchildren, regardless of what George Washington intended for his own enslaved workforce. Ona's provocation for leaving the Washington household was Martha's promise to her granddaughter Eliza Custis that Ona would be a wedding present. "However well disposed" George Washington might be toward various emancipation schemes, the Custis women knew that their good fortune rested on patrimony in slaves. Enslaved women knew what it meant to be dependent on the fortune-seeking men who married their mistresses for that patrimony.

The other Custis-Washington granddaughter, Martha, had married in 1795 and received sixty-one Mount Vernon slaves as her inherited marriage portion. In 1796, the fate of this human dowry troubled both Ona and George Washington. Washington grounded his self-conception as a benevolent patriarch *both* on his provision for the marriages of these white dependents, who became his legal responsibility after their father died young, and also on his respect for the marriages of his slaves. He sold people only to enforce discipline, not for profit, and he avoided breaking up families. Martha Custis Peter's husband had no such qualms, and he thought his new family interests best served by maximizing profit. Immediately after he assumed control of Martha's estate, he not only began to sell people without respect for their families, but to pull out adolescent girls for separate sale. Unprotected by kin, they fetched higher prices as domestic concubines and "breeders" of a new enslaved population. Eliza Custis announced her own engagement in 1796, surprising her family with a love match to a much older Englishman who had made a fortune in India. His financial speculations and three illegitimate mixed-race children made the Washingtons nervous enough to take extra steps to protect Eliza's separate property, even as they offered their congratulations. Ona Judge's younger sister was among the eighty people that nonetheless passed into his power soon after Ona made her escape.[76]

George Washington deemed emancipation impractical but also necessary because of such family politics. Washington had been famously silent on slavery as a political question, and his failure to support Quaker antislavery lobbying at the Constitutional Convention and first national Congress helped put the matter "to sleep . . . until 1808" when the constitutional prohibition on federal action against the slave trade would expire. He deeply resented those who asserted that slavery automatically corrupted the principles of slaveholders. If the deception required to manage what he referred to as the "trifling" matter of Ona Judge did not prove the point for him, the behavior of his granddaughters' husbands seems to have. In 1796 Washington secretly began laying plans for the "example" he would set with regard to slavery. Having rejected the political solution of an "entire Emancipation," he found it legally difficult to free the more than three hundred people he thought of as "his" and who had made him one of the wealthiest men in the United States. Most of these people were not his "by right," but belonged to the estates that Martha had inherited from her father and first husband. Washington was legally required to pass this fortune on through the Custis lineage, but in the meanwhile he built his own fortune through the use of it. Slave labor provided his direct sources of income and secured the credit that financed his own profitable speculation in huge tracts of western land. Washington's financial interest in these lands drove his political choices before and after the revolution. He now hoped to sell them to protect the Dandridge and Custis slaves from the Custis heirs, and to fulfill his own image of himself as a moral patriarch who protected the marriages and families of all his dependents, including his slaves.[77]

Washington could have managed such a scheme, but it required compromises. Had he been willing to make less from his land claims than he thought them worth, cash would have been easier to come by. He could also have chosen to be a bit less generous with the extended network of white Washington family members who fell under his patronage. The Custis heirs and their spouses would have to play along. There were wealthy eighteenth-century families that went this route. The Quaker Fishers of Philadelphia, for instance, took the antislavery minister John Woolman's teaching on intergenerational debts seriously. They not only freed their own slaves in 1776, but also tracked down and purchased the freedom of all those descended from slaves that had been sold out of the family. Washington's family was not so motivated, and they considered his plan a poor use of resources. The business-minded among them knew that the credit that sustained gentility required mobile capital, even more than before the revolution, and that when creditors came calling, selling one's dependents was the surest way to maintain independence. The value of Washington's western land, moreover, depended on the availability of laborers to work it. In the 1790s and early 1800s, Virginia's wealthy white families provided for their own children by turning the children of their slaves into the state's largest export. The will Washington completed shortly before his death in 1799 provided that the 124 people "in which he had a right" would be freed on Martha's death; Martha speeded up the manumission process out of fear that they otherwise would be tempted to murder her. Their families, however, passed to Martha's heirs. George's nephew Bushrod Washington—Nancy Shippen's onetime suitor and now Supreme Court justice—took over Mount Vernon. He freed no one and auctioned fifty people to deter those who would take their own freedom.[78]

Ona Judge was not among them, although she technically remained a Custis slave until she died in 1848. A different Washington nephew came calling for her in New Hampshire two years after her escape. He found her married to a mariner named Jack Staines and nursing an infant daughter. Ona and Jack had gone to great lengths to marry legally, and had circumvented reluctant Portsmouth officials by traveling to a neighboring town for the certificate and ceremony; they had announced their union on the same page of the *New-Hampshire Gazette* that reported George Washington's "Farewell Address."[79] Washington's slavecatcher failed, again, to persuade her to return. He then made plans to claim her by stealth, and gave legal notice to the senator (now state governor) who had initially told Washington of Ona's whereabouts. The seizure of the wife and child of a free man gave the governor political, if not personal, qualms, and on his warning Ona went into hiding until the nephew left the state. After George Washington's death she was no longer pursued. She nevertheless kept her whereabouts quiet until her own children were dead and her own age and poverty made her a liability to potential masters rather than an asset. Her life in New Hampshire as one of a community of fewer than a hundred people of color was, she admitted to nineteenth-century abolitionists, harder than life as Martha Washington's favored attendant. Her husband died when her children were small, and the state did not let her keep them. Like Anne Shippen Livingston's Peggy, Ona's daughters returned to her when they were able. They lived out their lives together in a mutually supporting and pious household of black women who were poor, but who did not see themselves as "buried alive" by misfortune. By 1845, Ona had learned to read, become "wise unto salvation," and had no regrets about her own choices: "I am free, and have, I trust been made a child of God by the means."[80]

"Down the Stream of Time Unnoticed": Family Secrets, Family Stories, and Legal Change

In 1790 an English newspaper reported, and American newspapers repeated, the "Law Intelligence" that the English courts had finally settled questions about the "Liability of Husbands for Debts of their Wives." As in 1663, when *Manby v. Scott* claimed to settle the same issues, such pronouncements were not true. They grew out of the desire for certainty in the face of instability. The case to which they referred entered the law reports as precedent, but its substance recycled *Manby*'s ambiguities yet again. Judicial discretion and the desire to keep marital disputes under local law prevailed as practical "rules." Questions about masters' liabilities for emancipated slaves remained similarly unresolved.[81] George Washington's example of handling such matters locally and privately followed the imperfect and incomplete norm; such individual solutions tended to be more concerned with "freeing" masters from entanglement with what Washington termed "that species of property" than with the human needs of the formerly enslaved.[82] A century and a half after the United States finally effected an "entire Emancipation," the nation still finds it difficult to openly assess its obligations to people who were never allowed to accumulate patrimony.

Contrary to the optimistic and misleading claims in the 1788 "Essay on Marriage," American revolutionary idealism did not undo the "infelicity" caused by historical hierarchies. America did not willingly bestow her "liberality" on enslaved people, and in the absence of serious changes in the terms of female dependence, divorce did not provide much of a remedy for female distress. The essay was most astute in its assessment of the limits of law as a tool for reform. While the author encouraged his unhappy readers to "apply decently to the legislature for redress," he made his legal agenda subsidiary to a social one and dared his readers to emulate antislavery activists and make direct and visceral assaults on prevailing public opinion. Without people who were willing to risk their reputations and their public lives, and to share their stories of suffering and relief, "every thing goes on in its former course, and glides down the stream of time unnoticed." His call for those of "rank and character" to lead by example was remarkably prescient about the direction reform would actually take.

The seventeenth-century jurists in *Manby v. Scott* had voiced exaggerated fears of what would happen should reports of judicial sympathy for a disobedient wife "come abroad to all women." Eighteenth-century authorities were no less anxious about preserving the patriarchal "honor" and patrimony of household heads, "both great and small," and they had more reason to fear the spread of news.[83] They sought to contain it with sarcasm and with prescription. "Timothy Foresight," a "disconsolate" and "humble" Englishman, bemoaned the supposed impact of the revolution on marriage in a satire circulated on both sides of the Atlantic. He had been informed that "the New-States have among other alterations and reformations of the church-service, ordered the formidable word *obey* to be struck out of the marriage ceremony, giving as a reason that in a free country there should be neither male or female slaves!" He predicted that without preventative legal measures, his "fair country-women" would emigrate "if they are not put on equality with the damsels on the other side of the Atlantic." "Should the ladies take themselves off in a huff," the bachelor writer and his "rusty brethren may go whistle for their bed fellows. . . . If we want women, we shall want wives we shall want children." England would soon be worried about the decline rather than the increase of its population.[84]

The Pennsylvania physician and political founder Benjamin Rush took a more earnest approach. Among his many prescriptions for the health of the new nation, he recommended that the country's proliferating newspapers be made more "innocent, useful, and entertaining." America "was 3000 miles from Europe," he argued, and there was no reason for editors to keep filling their papers "with anecdotes of British vice and follies. What have the citizens of the United States to do with the duels, the elopements, the crim. Cons, the kept mistresses, the murders, the suicides . . . of the people of Great Britain? Such stuff, when circulated through our country, by means of a News-Paper, is calculated to destroy that delicacy in the mind, which is one of the safeguards of the virtue of a young country." He might well have had the anonymous essayist and Anne Shippen Livingston in mind when he advised that "if any of the above named vices should ever be committed in the United States, the less that is said about it the better."[85]

Timothy Foresight's parody made marriage reform—and particularly attempts to limit the powers of husbands—so absurd as to be unthinkable. But if so, why write about them? George Washington, Benjamin Rush, and the "sensible" men in Nancy Shippen Livingston's circle preferred not to. In domestic dramas, sentimental scripts left them with few good roles. Revolutionary legal culture gave husbands and masters expansive rights. The culture of sensibility pushed them to exercise them quietly.[86] Notwithstanding the anxieties of public men, people of "rank and character in the world" did begin separating and marrying again with greater frequency. Elite families became increasingly cautious about advertising such "examples," even as they kept records in case later generations chose to challenge their legacies. Marital reform and emancipation resembled each other in that they were driven not by elite benevolence, but by stories spread abroad. Our pamphleteer knew, as Virginia Woolf would later put it, that stories "continue each other, in spite of our habit of judging them separately."[87]

Epilogue:
"The Rigour of the Old Rule"

The creation of this book has spanned a historical cycle akin to the ones it describes. I began researching runaways in the late 1990s, and my earliest write-ups interpreted ads as evidence of "the limits of patriarchal authority." The field of women's history was shifting away from stories of progressive liberation from "total subjugation" to narratives of backlash and efforts to recover women's complex experiences under patriarchal systems. In US culture at large, President Bill Clinton's much-publicized sexual misconduct raised doubts about whether newfound cultural consciousness about sexual harassment had had any practical effect. I served briefly in the unfortunately titled capacity of student "Sexual Assault Sexual Harassment" advisor, as my graduate institution took baby steps toward improving its response to survivors. I was repeatedly struck by the similarities between contemporary women and early modern women who wanted to regain dignity by telling their stories, in spite of limited expectations for justice. However, I was unsure how to reconcile that sense of fundamental continuity with historians' imperative to study change over time, until the historian Judith Bennett named it "patriarchal equilibrium." There was change over the period covered by this book and even more in the following centuries. One can draw lines that look like "upward" progress, as well as lines that look like "downward" decline. But fundamental transformation of the relative power of women and men remains debatable, and thus I emphasize revolutionary circles rather than lines. This seemed a depressing framework for the "hope and change" Obama years, when personal circumstances left the manuscript just short of completion and the concept of patriarchy fell out of favor in historical scholarship.[1]

Analysis of continuities that defy gender and racial progress seem newly appropriate in the age of #MeToo and President Trump. This book has made

several arguments specific to the period it covers: It outlines the political contingencies that shaped seventeenth- and eighteenth-century English
and colonial divorce laws, and the reification and hardening of patriarchal
household order to support colonial slavery and eighteenth-century credit
relations. It demonstrates that expanding patriarchal responsibility—at least
as much as "tyrannical" oppression—fueled ordinary men's grievances in the
eighteenth-century political revolutions. Its most important contributions
are its focus on continuities in practices of local justice that belie variation in
formalized, written legal rules, and its documentation of the recurring trope
of an imagined "ancient patriarchy" in efforts to justify patriarchal legal innovations and silence "domestic" grievances.

The desire to impose order on the present by inventing patriarchal order in the past is a long-standing historical phenomenon. We build our own
histories on those of past actors who engaged in similarly strategic story-
telling, sometimes with irony (as with the seventeenth-century justices in
Manby v. Scott and nineteenth-century figures like Elizabeth Cady Stanton),
sometimes without (Sir William Blackstone). Narratives of progress are not
necessarily wrong, and they can be inspiring. But progressive stories can be
turned against the progress they claim to honor and become a way to belittle
and dismiss present injustices. We justly celebrate the formal end of slavery,
but still need to acknowledge that former slaveholders went to extraordinary
lengths to preserve and reinstitute racialized servitude in new legal guises.
Runaway slave ads disappeared with emancipation, but the slave patrols of
the nineteenth century merged into institutions that too often equated the
enforcement of law with the enforcement of white supremacy. Southern
newspapers noted in 1867 that the woodcuts used to illustrate advertisements
of male and female runaway slaves could be repurposed, with a "row of cuts
of the female fugitives to celebrate the defeat of woman suffrage, and of the
males to celebrate the like defeat of 'n[——]r suffrage.'"[2] We are still wrestling
with the legacy of racial slavery, and with conservative defenses of social hierarchy that misrepresent and falsely conflate the concerns and interests of
formerly dependent groups.

The legacy of coverture is even more confusing. Pronouncements about
the demise of coverture started in the mid-nineteenth century, as states began
to pass legislation allowing married women to own property. But the doctrine of marital unity and debate about women's contractual abilities never
had a decisive legal end. Neither did newspaper advertisements of eloping
wives, which persisted until the 1980s. Common-law possessory rights that
were novel in the eighteenth century and controversial in the nineteenth remain part of domestic law in the postcolonial world. "Restitution of conjugal

rights" was eliminated in England in the late nineteenth century, but it remains a frequently used and contested part of marriage law in India. North
Carolina and five other states still entertain civil suits for "alienation of affections" (partner to "criminal conversation") in cases of adultery, prompting
amazed coverage in the national press whenever there is a large award for
damages. Even if the Equal Rights Amendment is finally ratified, the legacy
of slavery and of empire will remain in battles over equity in marriage and
divorce that continue to be fought state by state and case by case.[3]

Elizabeth Cady Stanton's Legal Education

A brief survey of the nineteenth-century fate of *Manby v. Scott* can help us
understand how successive generations told histories that facilitated these
continuities. *Manby* resurfaced in the writings of major legal theorists, in
judicial decisions allowing debt peonage for former slaves, and indirectly
in Elizabeth Cady Stanton's feminist and abolitionist conversion narratives.
Stanton defined her personal history—and the history of women's activism more generally—through revolutionary ruptures. She effaced many of
the connections between nineteenth-century activism and much older traditions of grievance and redress. Her memoir allows us to revisit *Manby v.
Scott* as she would have encountered it in her father's law office in the 1820s,
when, as she later told it, she first tried to change women's legal status in marriage by defacing the law books. Though they are not so well remembered as
Blackstone, Stanton, or Henry Sumner Maine, early nineteenth-century legal
theorists also defined modernity through and against household relations of
dependence. They repeated themes and arguments documented across this
book, all the while insisting on the novelty of their own benevolence toward
persons "disabled in the law."[4] The inclination to locate the "bad old days"
of rigid patriarchy in a nebulous, distant past was—and remains—a time-
honored way of avoiding unresolved tensions between Americans' celebration
of independence and the reality of social dependence.

Stanton's stories of feminist awakening were anchored by early encounters with marriage law and legal texts. As a girl, she haunted the office of her
father, a distinguished New York judge and congressman. When her father's
law students noted her particular concern with the "tears and complaints
of women" who sought his advice, they made a game of "reading to me all
the worst laws they could find, over which," Stanton recalled, "I would laugh
and cry by turns." Stanton responded to these taunts with a girlish resolve to
change the "odious" laws by "cutting every one of them out of the books." Her
memoir traced her later career to the discovery that taking a knife to the texts

would not provide a remedy. Ann Wood, we saw in chapter 6, took a knife to the legal treatise *Baron and Feme.* Her purpose was to stake her ownership in laws that were manifestly unequal, but which, until the late eighteenth-century, nonetheless allowed many women of property to "shift [their legal disabilities] well enough." Stanton, famously, went far beyond Wood and other women of earlier generations by rewriting both marriage law and the historical narratives that still shape the way we interpret it.[5]

The Declaration of Sentiments that Stanton drafted for the 1848 Seneca Falls women's rights convention has become the iconic counterpart to the Declaration of Independence, and Stanton and her longtime collaborator Susan B. Anthony have assumed the mantle of feminist "founders." Stanton cultivated such parallels, and with them the notion that her own career marked a definitive, revolutionary break from an unrelentingly patriarchal past. The first paragraphs in the Declaration of Sentiments mirrored the Declaration of Independence almost exactly, with a few key exceptions. It was self-evident, Stanton declared, that "all men *and women*" were created equal. And where the revolutionary document criticized "the history of the present King of Great Britain" as having as its "direct object the establishment of absolute tyranny," Stanton took issue with the entire "history of mankind." She reinforced the point by opening and closing the Seneca Falls convention with readings from Blackstone's *Commentaries* to give "proof of woman's servitude to man."[6] Stanton's political speeches and writing readily conflated this "servitude" with slavery, and routinely declared that wives were *like* slaves. She bears much responsibility for the persistence of parallels between marriage and slavery, and emancipation and divorce, within feminist stories of social progress. Even more assertively than the Scottish Enlightenment theorists, whose accounts of the progress of civilization she borrowed, Stanton defined modernity by redefining marriage.

Stanton's arguments emerged from a life history that continued the stories this book has told about seventeenth- and eighteenth-century legal developments, intellectual and economic trends, and even specific familial conflicts. Stanton could casually assert that wives were *like* slaves because from her infancy it had been clear that she was *not* a slave. Even in her youth there were many who thought it a matter of common sense that women's powers equaled those of men, though that equality might also entail difference. Elizabeth's "queenly" mother was a Livingston who educated her in the ways of mistresses who expected power over slaves and servants. (As a relative and age-mate of Peggy Shippen Livingston, the unfortunate child of divorce whom we met in chapter 8, Margaret Livingston Cady might also have passed along this scandalous family story.)[7] Young Elizabeth learned about empathy and injustice from Peter Teabout, an enslaved man whom the Cady family did not free because New York's gradual emancipation did not require it; local practice and legal loopholes trumped seemingly major statutory change. Teabout supervised the Cady's children's adventures into the local community, courts, and jail, and let them wait and listen with him at Judge Cady's table (much like Elizabeth Freeman had in chapter 7).[8] Daniel Cady grieved that Elizabeth was not a boy, but he nonetheless paid for her to learn Greek and radical Scottish Enlightenment ideas from an elderly Glasgow-trained minister.[9] And finally, Elizabeth learned of women's misfortunes from abused wives, runaway slave women, and law students who passed through her father's house and law practice. As an adult, Stanton alternated between admirable, principled advocacy of universal rights for all women and people of color, and insensitivity to the ways in which her political priorities and universal claims reflected the privileges of her race and class.[10]

What set Stanton apart from earlier critics of patriarchal power was neither her extension of natural rights rhetoric to the cause of women, nor her analogies between wives and slaves. As we have seen, both rhetorical moves had a very long history.[11] Rather, Stanton was distinguished by her free and devastating humor. She dismissed her opponents with the same sort of satire that men of previous generations had used to make women's claims to power seem absurd. Even the "Declaration of Sentiments," which was a serious document about serious grievances, displayed subtle wit. Its title simultaneously acknowledged that sentimental culture gave women power and declared that this was not enough in a world that privileged legal rights. Stanton had the legal training to recognize that the "Declaration of Independence" followed the forms of a petition in equity. She also learned firsthand how attenuated women's equitable remedies had become in the early nineteenth-century United States, both by observing the "tears and complaints" of the women in her father's law office and through the education she shared with the law students who "not only improved their opportunities by reading Blackstone" and his American counterparts "Kent and Story, but also by making love to the Judge's daughters."[12]

Like the eighteenth-century compiler of *The Lady's Law*, the young men in Judge Cady's office found the "old Laws and Customs relating to Women . . . very merry." While some used those "odious laws" to humiliate Elizabeth, others brought them up to demonstrate their sympathy. Their teasing went hand in hand with courtship. They read Elizabeth the "admirable satire . . . on the old common law" in Shakespeare's *Taming of the Shrew* and the promise of Milton's Eve to Adam: "God thy law, thou mine." The point, however, was to show their erudition and enlightenment. They understood this as satire and wanted to impress upon the judge's daughters that they were sensible men who did not live by such old-fashioned ideas. This dynamic was evident in Stanton's story of how she learned the rules of coverture—another tale with multiple versions. As told in Stanton's 1890s memoir, it inclines the reader toward tears. One Christmas the young Elizabeth took her presents of a coral necklace and bracelets to the law office to show her admirers. One of the men of whom Stanton was most fond praised them and then informed her that, "if in due time you should be my wife, those ornaments would be mine; I could take them and lock them up, and you could never wear them except with my permission. I could even exchange them for a box of cigars, and you could watch them evaporate in smoke." Yet in a different, earlier telling, there was laughter as the young man took the ornamental chains and put them on himself. In earlier eras, a young man could not be so confident in his right to send his wife's patrimony up in smoke. But even today, women are expected to laugh with men at "jokes" that similarly demonstrate masculine power and rest on the presumption that "good" men will not abuse it.[13]

Manby v. Scott in the Nineteenth Century

This generation of lawyers ridiculed old laws, but they also gave them unprecedented power. If Stanton had succeeded in taking a knife to the "odious laws" in her father's books, the point would have cut through multiple versions of *Manby v. Scott*. In the nineteenth-century legal texts that stocked the shelves of her father's law office, *Manby* gained yet another lease on life. It was only in the nineteenth century that the full record of debates in the case became accessible beyond the select group of English lawyers who had access to the manuscript opinions of seventeenth-century jurists. The triumph of a legal culture intent on finding historical and textual answers that would liberate society from the "scourge of vague jurisprudence" multiplied the evidence of ambiguity. An idealistic young English lawyer justified his 1823 edition of Sir Orlando Bridgeman's manuscript opinions (with *Manby* prominent among them) on the grounds that "vast interests . . . both in the old and new worlds" were soon to "be determined upon principles drawn from English sources," and in consequence "the importance of knowing the true foundations of them cannot be overrated." "The period of . . . Bridgeman's experience" and of *Manby* had been "the most important era for settling the law," but it possessed "the least accurate . . . reporters."[14]

The writer and his cohort encountered what we now think of as a postmodern problem; the quest for historically "true foundations" only rendered them more shaky and uncertain. Contemporary historians take pride in skepticism of such foundational claims. Our own efforts to tell the history of marriage and domestic law, however, remain thoroughly entangled by the historical myths and the bad legal jokes with which nineteenth-century lawyers covered their own uncertainty. In its nineteenth-century guises, *Manby* unsettles competing historiographic narratives about marriage, patriarchy, and the law. From the Scottish Enlightenment in the eighteenth century through Lawrence Stone in the twentieth, historians of modernization told a story in which skepticism about household hierarchy and husbands' patriarchal power marched hand in hand with the rise of political liberalism. More recent scholarship, in contrast, has inverted this narrative, describing the late eighteenth and early nineteenth centuries as a period in which the legal retrenchment—or even expansion—of household patriarchy sustained the revolutionary claims to equality among white men.[15] Michael Grossberg's classic account of the rise of nineteenth-century "judicial patriarchy" can be made compatible with either story. So too can *Manby*, and therein lies the analytical difficulty.

In contrast with their seventeenth-century predecessors, no nineteenth-century commentators used *Manby* to defend patriarchal absolutism either in the home or in the state. That in itself can be seen as a sign of liberal modernity. Saxe Banister, the enthusiastic editor of Orlando Bridgeman's manuscripts, was also an enthusiastic reformer and opponent of slavery. His interest in Bridgeman (and in *Manby*) as a source of the "true foundations" of English common law derived less from a naive faith in the power of past authorities, than from the ambiguities Bridgeman's complex and contradictory legal reflections introduced into nineteenth-century debates.[16]

The South Carolina politician and scientist Thomas Cooper's interpretation of *Manby* straddled both revolutionary and proslavery sentiments. Cooper began his career as a revolutionary opponent of tyranny and the slave trade and ended it as an advocate of state's rights and slavery. Cooper came to the United States from England in the 1790s, together with Joseph Priestley and other radical supporters of the French Revolution. He obtained a judicial appointment in Pennsylvania through his friendship with Thomas Jefferson, but in 1811 he was forced from the bench when members of his own party challenged his "arbitrary conduct." In the midst of the controversy, he published the first American edition of *Justinian's Institutes*; his English translation and commentary on the Latin text used classical authority to buttress his own increasingly conservative political and social views. Christianity had not rendered classical laws regarding slavery irrelevant to modern circumstances, but it had "greatly tended to ameliorate the situation of women in society, and thereby to civilize society itself." He claimed that Christian concern for women and respect for the jurisdiction of the established courts (rather than frustration with those who challenged his authority on the bench) led him to reject both Justinian's rules and the Pennsylvania legislature's proceedings with regard to divorce. He pronounced legislative divorce proceedings "great public evils" that could be at the same time "irresistibly ludicrous." It was his somber opinion that Judge Hyde's opinion in *Manby*, "notwithstanding some harsh observations," embraced "the soundest principles" regarding marriage and the roles of husband and wife. *Manby* surpassed Justinian, and also early nineteenth-century practice in England and Pennsylvania, as an expression of "the law of England, the precepts of Christianity, . . . the dictates of natural reason and civilized expedience . . . [and] the general spirit of the laws throughout" the new United States.[17]

In the 1820s and 1830s, Judge David McCord worked together with Cooper to foment the South Carolina Nullification Crisis and to create an authoritative printed compilation of South Carolina's state laws. McCord did not, however, agree with Cooper's assessment of Hyde's opinion in *Manby*. When McCord invoked *Manby*'s rhetoric about the choice of a wayward wife to "submit or starve" in 1826, it was in a complicated legal jest about the relationship between law and equity. *Manby*, he observed, was a "curious" artifact that would "not only instruct the lawyer, but afford much amusement to the general reader." Contrary to one feminist historian's reading of his commentary, he was not attempting to shore up patriarchal absolutism in households or the state, but rather ridiculing a colleague who put too much store in the "venerable and noble" common law. It is easy to miss the joke, and opportunistic nineteenth-century husbands and their lawyers deliberately chose to overlook it. When it suited their needs, ordinary men were only too happy to make use of a precedent that aligned the powers of husbands with those of kings.[18]

Manby no longer worked as a defense of political absolutism (if it ever really had). It nevertheless remained "good law," according to Tapping Reeve, the prominent New England jurist who had helped Elizabeth Freeman challenge slavery in Massachusetts in the 1780s, and whose 1816 rewrite of *Baron and Feme* defined American marriage law for most of the nineteenth century. A different treatise that defined the *Rights, Duties and Liabilities of Husband and Wife: At Law and in Equity* in England for most of the nineteenth century also used *Manby* as a basic rule, although it followed it with forty pages of exceptions.[19]

New York Chancellor James Kent supplied a particularly nuanced reading of *Manby* in his *Commentaries on American Law*. Blackstone's *Commentaries* had used *Manby* but erased its historical context, citing it as evidence of a softening of England's laws toward women begun during the "politer reign of Charles the second." Kent argued instead that the views of the prevailing justices in *Manby* embodied the "rigour of the old rule." Enlightened moderns had "relaxed" these strict precepts, and the *dissenting* views in *Manby* were now common practice. "A principle of duty and justice" bound a husband to provide necessaries for his wife, when she was not at fault. When one reads Kent's fine print, his example better serves historians who emphasize the reification of household patriarchy than those who echo his liberal narrative about the progressive decline of patriarchal "rigour."[20] What suffers most, amidst all these conflicting opinions, are certainties about distinctions between "old" and "new" rules.

Nineteenth-century jurists sometimes proclaimed their enlightened sensibilities and laughed at husbands who insisted on their patriarchal power. Or, still proclaiming their modern sympathies, judicial patriarchs like Elizabeth Cady Stanton's father might wring their hands and insist that rigorous old rules left them unable to alleviate an aggrieved wife's tears. As in the seventeenth century, judges' abstract pronouncements about rules delineating husbands' authority and wives' submission frequently obscured the extent to which local networks of kin, community, and faith still determined legal outcomes.[21]

Manby remained unsettled in the late nineteenth century, despite theoretical pronouncements to the contrary, and changes in statute and constitutional law might have led to its demise. In his 1861 *Ancient Law*, the English jurist Henry Sumner Maine made the contested status of women and of slaves the key evidence for his influential claim that "movement from Status to Contract" defined the historical development of modern "progressive societies." As the United States began a civil war over exactly this issue, Maine prematurely pronounced the battles already won: "The status of the Slave has disappeared—it has been superseded by the contractual relation of the servant to his master. The status of the Female under Tutelage, if the tutelage be understood of persons other than her husband, has also ceased to exist." Maine viewed the "complete legal subjection" of wives under the English common law, at least "where it is untouched by equity or Statutes" as a last compelling example and final vestige of ancient patriarchy. He condemned William Blackstone's accounts of history and of law, but like Stanton nonetheless followed Blackstone's lead. Like Blackstone, Maine depicted equity as a newer, more progressive—although decidedly imperfect—remedy for ancient patriarchal norms. But in his own "modern" moment, he declared both legal traditions obsolete. Britain had "largely modified" the old rules by legislation (by which he probably meant the act reforming divorce and marriage law that

England passed in 1857), and historical "movement" was such that remaining traces of the old order were bound to pass away. Maine's ideas passed into common knowledge after *Ancient Law* became an international best seller, and they provided the theoretical foundation for multiple modern academic disciplines.[22]

Elizabeth Cady Stanton spent the last decades of the nineteenth century battling parts of this narrative. Stanton, like Maine and most of her white contemporaries, too readily embraced the ideas that the struggles of people of color ended with the demise of slavery. In her personal history and her histories of the movement for women's suffrage, she framed the battles of the antislavery movement as past precedents for the next phase of revolutionary progress: the extension to "Woman" of the political rights the Fourteenth Amendment to the US Constitution had extended to all "male citizens," but not the female sex. She did not acknowledge the distracting and dismaying fact that, as she wrote her memoir in the 1890s, the amendment's hard-won guarantee of "equal protection of the laws" was not being enforced in much of the United States. For many people of color, it became a dead letter through jurisdictional deferrals like those we saw in *Manby* during the seventeenth century, and histories that, like Stanton's and Maine's, relegated the injustices of slavery to the distant past. As activists pushed for the ratification of the constitutional amendment that granted voting rights to women in 1920, however, state jurists were still debating *Manby*'s legacy not only in marriage law, but in disputes about debt servitude and whether black sharecroppers could be compelled by contract to "work or starve."[23] Stories continue each other. Revolutions run in circles, not in straight lines.

The legacy of these old debates remains very much alive in contemporary conflicts over marriage. Indeed, the most traditional thing about the current defense of "traditional" marriage is the way in which it invents a monolithic past. Such appeals to timeless household order disguise the intensity of past conflicts over the meaning of marriage as a right, a privilege, and a fundamental social institution. As in those past conflicts, both the champions and the opponents of "modernity" blur the lines between law and farce, and prompt us to "laugh and cry by turns."

Acknowledgments

This book has taken an unusually long time to write, even for an academic undertaking. I have benefited from extraordinary individual and institutional generosity throughout this process, for which these acknowledgments are bound to be inadequate. I begin by thanking Robert Devens, Ellen Hartigan-O'Conner, and the late Jan Lewis for shepherding this project through approval by the University of Chicago Press, and Tim Mennel, Stephen Mihm, and the other editors of the American Beginnings series for their support and patience in bringing it to completion. Many, many colleagues have graciously provided feedback on different pieces and versions of the manuscript over the years, starting with my graduate advisors Laurel Thatcher Ulrich, David D. Hall, and Cornelia Hughes Dayton, and their students (now scholars in their own right). A shout-out in particular to Sarah M. S. Pearsall, Eliza C. Clark, and Michelle Morris for continuing to read as the project expanded, and to Amy Speckart for keeping an eye out for cover art. Karin Wulf, Chris Grasso, and participants and readers for the *WMQ*/EMSI workshop on Women in Early America and the OIEAHC/University of Texas at Austin conference Centering Families in Atlantic History provided invaluable help with the structure of the final chapters; so too did the Rocky Mountain Seminar in Early American History. Indiana University's Eighteenth-Century Studies Workshop and Early Americanist Reading Groups inspired the book's final reframing; thanks especially to Sarah Knott, Kon Dierks, Rebecca Spang, Amrita Myers, Khalil Muhammed, Matt Gutterl, Christina Snyder, Judith Allen, Wendy Gamber, and Michael Grossberg for their stimulating conversation and editorial suggestions, and to Penelope Anderson, Cynthia Herrup, Gregg Roeber, Richard Ross, and participants in the Newberry Library conference New Perspectives on Legal Pluralism in the Early Modern Atlantic, who provided much-needed reassurance as I expanded my research into seventeenth- and eighteenth-century English legal history.

Research for this book began early in the digital era, before we could entertain the illusion that "everything" is online; the proliferation of digital resources delayed its completion, as I double-checked and expanded on work begun with paper documents stored in numerous archives. This undertaking was possible only because of the preservation work done by the following institutions and their dedicated teams of archivists: Indiana University Libraries; Harvard University Libraries; Harvard University Law Library Special Collections; Massachusetts Historical Society; Massachusetts State Archives; New England Historical and Genealogical Society; New Hampshire State Archives; New Hampshire Historical Society; Rhode Island Historical Society; New Jersey State Archives; Burlington County (NJ) Historical Society; Princeton University Library Special Collections; Historical Society of Pennsylvania; Library Company of Philadelphia; Archives of the Evangelical and Reformed Historical Society of the UCC; Chester County Archives; Bucks County Archives; Lancaster County Archives; Philadelphia City Archives; Pennsylvania State Archives; Haverford College Special Collections; Swarthmore College Quaker Collections; Colonial Williamsburg Research Center and John D. Rockefeller Jr. Library; Library of Virginia; Virginia Museum of History and Culture; Library of Congress; Folger Shakespeare Library; North Carolina State Archives; Wilson Library at the University of North Carolina at Chapel Hill; Guilford College Special Collections; British Library; National Archives of the United Kingdom; Library of the Society of Friends, Friends House, London; National Archives of Scotland; National Library of Scotland.

Travel to the numerous archives was made possible through the generosity of Harvard University, Indiana University's New Frontiers Research Grants and Institute for Advanced Study, Mellon Foundation grants administered by the Massachusetts Historical Society, the Library Company of Philadelphia and Historical Society of Pennsylvania, the American Historical Association Kraus Grant, and the Woodrow Wilson Dissertation Grant in Women's Studies.

Finally, for the past decade I have been grappling with physical challenges that complicated and delayed the final revision of the manuscript, but also brought me many kind assistants. Kerilyn Harkaway-Krieger, Diane Fruchtman, and Gretchen Knapp provided invaluable editorial help; Kalani Craig of IDAH and Tassie Gniady and David Kloster of the CyberDH Team in UITS Research Technologies have helped preserve my aging research database and digest my findings into publishable form. I offer a general salute to the dozens of dedicated medical professionals who have kept me alive and somewhat functional, and specifically to Shannon Adams, without whom I may never have found appropriate care. Mary Favret and Andrew Miller's scholarly and moral support and frequent hospitality have been sustaining, as have Tanja and Mark Bisesi's encouragement to follow unconventional paths. Kara Wright, James Lawrence, Adine Kernberg Varah, Ellen Schur, and my amazing group of college friends have listened to my medical and historical misadventures for far too long, while giving me faith that new stories are always possible.

The study of families in collapse has made me all the more grateful that I have a family that rallies "in sickness" and when life turns "for worse." Budd Stalnaker and Marcia Stalnaker made it possible for Aaron and me to juggle work and family. Bryan, Phyllis, and Eric Sword have modeled resilience and confidence that things will get better, even when they do not go as planned. Tom Shirk and Felipe Lara have shown that the unplanned is sometimes wonderful. Elena and Rowan Stalnaker make it all joyful and worthwhile.

Aaron Stalnaker, without your patience, kindness, and love, this book and my life would not be possible. Words cannot express my gratitude.

Abbreviations and Source Notes

BCHS: Bucks County Historical Society, Doylestown, Pennsylvania

Burton Diary: *Diary of Thomas Burton Esq: Volume 1, July 1653–April 1657*, ed. John Towill Rutt (London: H. Colburn, 1828), *British History Online*, http://www.british-history.ac.uk/burton-diaries/vol1

CCA: Chester County Archives, West Chester, Pennsylvania

CHLA: *The Cambridge History of Law in America*, ed. Michael Grossberg and Christopher Tomlins (Cambridge: Cambridge University Press, 2007)

ER: *The English Reports: Decisions of All English Cases from 1220 to 1865*, 178 vols. (Edinburgh: W. Green & Son; London: Stevens & Sons, 1900–1932)

Hening: *The Statutes at Large; Being a Collection of All the Laws of Virginia, from the First Session of the Legislature*, and supplements, 1st and 2nd eds., 13 vols., ed. William W. Hening (Richmond, VA, New York, and Philadelphia, 1818–23; Vol. 2: 2nd ed., New York: printed for the editor by R & W & G. Bartow, 1823; Vol. 3: 2nd ed., printed for the editor by Thomas DeSilver, Philadelphia, 1823; Vol. 6: 1st ed., Richmond, VA: printed for the editor at the Franklin Press, 1819)

HSP: Historical Society of Pennsylvania, Philadelphia

LION: Literature Online, Proquest Information and Learning Company, 1996–2002

MAC: Massachusetts Archives Collections, Massachusetts State Archives, Boston

MHS: Massachusetts Historical Society, Boston

NEHGR: *New England Historical and Genealogical Register*, New England Historic Genealogical Society, Boston

NEHGS: New England Historic Genealogical Society, Boston

ODNB: *Oxford Dictionary of National Biography* (Oxford: Oxford University Press, 2004); online ed., January 2008

OIEAHC: Omohundro Institute of Early American History and Culture, Wil-
              liamsburg, Virginia
Suffolk Files: Suffolk Court Files Collections (original and microfilm), Massachu-
              setts State Archives, Boston

Newspaper Citations, Searching Digitized Early
Modern Texts, and Language

The newspaper advertisements used in this project were located both by reading the
surviving original papers and by browsing microfilmed and digitized papers as they
became available. Citations are issue/date only, because eighteenth-century colonial
papers usually were not paginated and contained only four pages per issue.

Note that word searches of digitized historical papers will fail a substantial portion of the time due to problems with optical character recognition, especially if the
letter *s* or *f* is included. Seventeenth- and eighteenth-century writers were seldom
punctilious about writing mechanics, and idiosyncratic spelling and punctuation can
also affect searches.

Throughout this book, I have preserved the language, spelling, and grammar as
written in primary sources, except where alterations were necessary for clarity.

Notes

Introduction

1. Eunice Davis, *New-Hampshire Gazette*, August 8, 1762.

2. Chanel Miller, *Know My Name: A Memoir* (New York: Viking, 2019); Judith Bennett, *History Matters: Patriarchy and the Challenge of Feminism* (Philadelphia: University of Pennsylvania Press, 2007), 77–81.

3. As the historian Lara Putnam has observed, microhistory conducted on a macro scale reveals that "populations we assumed to be insular, and whose events we therefore explained in terms of local dynamics" are "above-water fragments of . . . submarine unities." Putnam, "To Study the Fragments/Whole: Microhistory and the Atlantic World," *Journal of Social History* 39, no. 3 (2006): 615–30, quotation on 617.

4. Bennett, *History Matters*, 54–81.

5. William Blackstone, *Commentaries on the Laws of England*, 4 vols. (Oxford: Clarendon Press, 1765), 1:430, 443–45. Holly Brewer offers a particularly useful critique of Blackstone's historical claims and historians' ahistorical uses of them in "The Transformation of Domestic Law," in *CHLA*, 288–323; see also Hendrik Hartog, *Man and Wife in America: A History* (Cambridge, MA: Harvard University Press, 2002), 118–35; Henrik Hartog, "Coverture and Dignity: A Comment," *Law & Social Inquiry* 41, no. 4 (2016): 833–40; and Kathleen S. Sullivan, *Constitutional Context: Women and Rights Discourse in Nineteenth-Century America* (Baltimore: Johns Hopkins University Press, 2007). For Mary Ritter Beard's classic critique of Blackstone and his American legacy, see *Woman as Force in History: A Study in Traditions and Realities* (New York: Macmillan, 1946).

6. On Scottish Enlightenment stadial theory, see Sylvana Tomaselli, "Civilization, Patriotism, and Enlightened Histories of Women," in *Women, Gender and Enlightenment*, ed. Barbara Taylor and Sarah Knott (Houndsmills, UK: Palgrave Macmillan, 2005), 75–96; Silvia Sebastiani, "Race, Women and Progress in the Late Scottish Enlightenment," in *Women, Gender and Enlightenment*, 117–35; Carole Shammas, *A History of Household Government in America* (Charlottesville: University of Virginia Press, 2002), 7–10; Paul Bowles, "John Millar, The Four-Stages Theory, and Women's Position in Society," *History of Political Economy* 16, no. 4 (1984), 619–38; and Frank Palmeri, "Conjectural History and the Origins of Sociology," *Studies in Eighteenth Century Culture* 37 (2008): 1–21.

7. Gordon S. Wood, *The Radicalism of the American Revolution* (New York: Vintage Books, 1993), 147; Lynn Hunt, *Inventing Human Rights: A History* (New York: W. W. Norton, 2007),

62–64; Norma Basch, *Framing American Divorce: From the Revolutionary Generation to the Victorians* (Berkeley: University of California Press, 1999), 30. In the instance of divorce, such assertions draw on a scholarly literature that was, in Nara Milanich's words, "born under the sign of modernization." Nara Milanich, "Whither Family History? A Road Map from Latin America," *American Historical Review* 112, no. 2 (2007): 439–58, quotation on 446. This characterization is particularly true of classic histories of divorce by Lawrence Stone and Roderick Phillips. Stone's grand narrative in *The Family, Sex and Marriage in England* was arguably the last gasp of eighteenth-century Scottish Enlightenment theories of civilization. Studies of nineteenth-century American marriage and divorce by Hendrik Hartog, Norma Basch, Nancy F. Cott, Linda K. Kerber, and Michael Grossberg tell much subtler stories, in which challenges to household patriarchy run hand in hand with its reification. See Stone, *Road to Divorce: England 1530–1987* (Oxford: Oxford University Press, 1990); Stone, *The Family, Sex and Marriage in England, 1500–1800* (New York: Harper and Row 1977); Phillips, *Putting Asunder: A History of Divorce in Western Society* (Cambridge: Cambridge University Press, 1988); Hartog, *Man and Wife in America*; Basch, *Framing American Divorce*; Cott, *Public Vows: A History of Marriage and the Nation* (Cambridge, MA: Harvard University Press, 2000); Kerber, *No Constitutional Right to Be Ladies* (New York: Hill and Wang, 1999); and Grossberg, *A Judgment for Solomon: The d'Hauteville Case and Legal Experience in Antebellum America* (New York: Cambridge University Press, 1996). See also Rosemarie Zagarri, *Revolutionary Backlash: Women and Politics in the Early American Republic* (Philadelphia: University of Pennsylvania Press, 2007).

8. Hunt, *Inventing Human Rights*, 63; "Address to the Legislature of New York on Women's Rights, February 14, 1854," in Ellen Carol DuBois, ed. *The Elizabeth Cady Stanton–Susan B. Anthony Reader* (Boston: Northeastern University Press, 1992): 48; Henry Sumner Maine, *Ancient Law: Its Connection with the Early History of Society, and Its Relation to Modern Ideas* (New York, 1864), 163–65. Maine's *Ancient Law* helped transform eighteenth-century stage-driven theories of history into the accounts of modernization undergirding the twentieth-century social sciences. See Shammas, *A History of Household Government*, 1–23; Ann Taylor Allen, "Feminism, Social Science, and the Meanings of Modernity: The Debate on the Origin of the Family in Europe and the United States, 1860–1914," *American Historical Review* 104, no. 4 (October 1999): 1085–113; Paul Kockelman, "From Status to Contract Revisited: Value, Temporality, Circulation and Subjectivity," *Anthropological Theory* 7, no. 2 (June 2007): 151–76; Amy Dru Stanley, *From Bondage to Contract : Wage Labor, Marriage, and the Market in the Age of Slave Emancipation* (Cambridge; New York: Cambridge University Press, 1998); Laura F. Edwards, "Status without Rights: African Americans and the Tangled History of Law and Governance in the Nineteenth-Century U.S. South," *American Historical Review* 112, no. 2 (April 2007): 365–93; and Laura F. Edwards, *The People and Their Peace: Legal Culture and the Transformation of Inequality in the Post-Revolutionary South* (Chapel Hill: University of North Carolina Press, 2009). On connections between the Scottish Enlightenment and nineteenth-century German social theory, see Fania Oz-Salzberger, *Translating the Enlightenment: Scottish Civic Discourse in Eighteenth-Century Germany* (Oxford: Clarendon Press, 1995).

9. Virginia Woolf, *A Room of One's Own* (1929; Orlando: Houghton Mifflin Harcourt, 2005), 42–45.

10. Stone, *The Road to Divorce*, 13; Ken Burns, dir., *Not for Ourselves Alone: The Story of Elizabeth Cady Stanton and Susan B. Anthony*, Florentine Films and WETA, 1999, part 1.

11. Woolf, *A Room of One's Own*, 45; Francis Fukuyama, *Identity: The Demand for Dignity and the Politics of Resentment* (New York: Farrar, Straus and Giroux, 2018); Mark Lilla,

"The End of Identity Liberalism," *New York Times*, November 18, 2016, http://www.nytimes .com/2016/11/20/opinion/sunday/the-end-of-identity-liberalism.html; David Waldstreicher, "The Hidden Stakes of the 1619 Controversy," *Boston Review*, January 23, 2020, https://bostonreview .net/race-politics/david-waldstreicher-hidden-stakes-1619-controversy. On literature detailing "exceptions" to coverture, see Brewer, "Transformation of Domestic Law." On pluralism and variability as norms rather than exceptions in colonial legal culture, see Mary Bilder, *The Trans- atlantic Constitution: Colonial Legal Culture and the Empire* (Cambridge, MA: Harvard University Press, 2004); and Lauren A. Benton, *Law and Colonial Cultures: Legal Regimes in World History, 1400–1900* (Cambridge: Cambridge University Press, 2002). On the problem of agency in early modern women's history, see Allyson M. Poska, "The Case for Agentic Gender Norms for Women in Early Modern Europe," *Gender & History* 30, no. 2 (July 1, 2018): 354–65.

12. On the culture-defining fear of slave revolts, see Jill Lepore, *These Truths: A History of the United States* (New York: W. W. Norton, 2018).

13. For critique of presumptions about linear change and the historian's imperative to demonstrate transformation, see Judith M. Bennett, *History Matters*; and Margot C. Finn, *The Character of Credit: Personal Debt in English Culture, 1740–1914* (Cambridge: Cambridge University Press, 2003). Where scholarship on divorce emphasizes transformation, the transatlantic scholarly literature on domestic violence struggles to explain these frustrating continuities. In studies that range from seventeenth-century England to present-day America, Reva Siegel, Joanne Bailey, Elizabeth Foyster, and Frances Dolan have demonstrated the power of transformative rhetoric to mask—and to preserve—fundamental, coercive structures within marriage and household government. See Siegel, "'The Rule of Love': Wife Beating as Prerogative and Privacy," *Yale Law Journal* 105, no. 8 (June 1996): 2117–07; Bailey, *Unquiet Lives: Marriage and Marriage Breakdown in England, 1660–1800* (Cambridge: Cambridge University Press, 2003); Foyster, *Marital Violence: An English Family History, 1660–1875* (Cambridge: Cambridge University Press, 2005); and Dolan, *Marriage and Violence: The Early Modern Legacy* (Philadelphia: University of Pennsylvania Press, 2008). For efforts to integrate these concerns, see K. J. Kesselring and Tim Stretton, eds., *Married Women and the Law: Coverture in England and the Common Law World*, (Montreal: McGill-Queen's University Press, 2013), esp. 264–72.

14. John H. Baker, *An Introduction to English Legal History* (London: Butterworths, 1990), esp. 112–28; John H. Baker, *Collected Papers on English Legal History* (Cambridge: Cambridge University Press, 2013).

15. R. B. Outhwaite, *The Rise and Fall of the English Ecclesiastical Courts, 1500–1860* (Cambridge: Cambridge University Press, 2006).

16. Mary Bilder, "Salamanders and Sons of God: The Culture of Appeal in Early New England," in *The Many Legalities of Early America*, ed. Christopher L. Tomlins and Bruce H. Mann (Chapel Hill: University of North Carolina Press, 2001), 47–77.

17. On "narrative vindication" in early modern England, see Laura Gowing, *Domestic Dangers: Women, Words, and Sex in Early Modern London* (Oxford: Clarendon Press, 1996), 43, 196. For similar patterns in localized law in eighteenth-century England and the nineteenth-century United States, see Bailey, *Unquiet Lives*; and Edwards, *The People and Their Peace*.

18. For an overview and bibliography of the early history of British newspapers, see "British Library Newspapers: Early History of the English Newspaper," http://access.gale.com/gdc/docu ments/Burney%20Early%20Newspaper%20History.pdf. On colonial newspapers, see Charles E. Clark, *The Public Prints: The Newspaper in Anglo-American Culture, 1665–1740* (New York: Oxford University Press, 1994).

19. James Burgh, *Political Disquisitions; or, An Enquiry into Public Errors, Defects, and Abuses* (London: E. and C. Dilly, 1774), 1:37; paraphrased in "To the FREEMEN of PENNSYLVANIA," *Pennsylvania Gazette*, January 26, 1785.

20. "Petition for freedom to Massachusetts Governor Thomas Gage, His Majesty's Council, and the House of Representatives, 25 May 1774," Jeremy Belknap Papers, MHS https://www .masshist.org/database/viewer.php?item_id=549&img_step=1&mode=transcript#page1; "Negro Petitions for Freedom," *Collections of the Massachusetts Historical Society*, series 5, vol. 3 (Boston: MHS, 1877), 433; Herbert Aptheker, ed., *A Documentary History of the Negro People in the United States*, 7 vols. (New York: Citadel Press, 1967), 1:9, 6, discussed in Thomas J. Davis, "Emancipation Rhetoric, Natural Rights, and Revolutionary New England: A Note on Four Black Petitions in Massachusetts, 1773–1777," *New England Quarterly* 62, no. 2 (June 1989): 248–63; Eric Foner, *The Story of American Freedom* (New York: W. W. Norton, 1998), 34, 41; Sarah M. S. Pearsall, *Atlantic Families: Lives and Letters in the Later Eighteenth Century* (Oxford: Oxford University Press, 2008), 116–17. Legal historians know that seemingly trivial or technical disputes about legal jurisdiction hide greater stakes; the American Revolution had roots in conflicts over jurisdiction: over "home rule" and "who should rule at home." Bilder, *The Transatlantic Constitution*, 4–5; Bilder, "English Settlement and Local Governance," in *CHLA*, 63–103; Lauren A. Benton, *Law and Colonial Cultures: Legal Regimes in World History, 1400–1900* (Cambridge: Cambridge University Press, 2002); Lauren A. Benton, *A Search for Sovereignty: Law and Geography in European Empires, 1400–1900* (Cambridge: Cambridge University Press, 2010); Daniel Hulsebosch, *Constituting Empire: New York and the Transformation of Constitutionalism in the Atlantic World, 1664–1830* (Chapel Hill: University of North Carolina Press, 2005); Eliga H. Gould, *The Persistence of Empire: British Political Culture in the Age of the American Revolution* (Chapel Hill: University of North Carolina Press for the OIEAHC, 2000); Richard J. Ross, "Puritan Godly Discipline in Comparative Perspective: Legal Pluralism and the Sources of Intensity," *American Historical Review* 113, no. 4 (October 1, 2008): 975–1002; Finn, *Character of Credit*; Bruce H. Mann, *Republic of Debtors: Bankruptcy in the Age of American Independence* (Cambridge, MA: Harvard University Press, 2002); Sarah M. S. Pearsall, *Polygamy: An Early American History* (New Haven, CT: Yale University Press, 2019).

21. "Declaration of Sentiments," reprinted in Kathryn Kish Sklar, *Women's Rights Emerges within the Anti-Slavery Movement, 1830–1870: A Brief History with Documents* (Boston: Bedford/ St. Martin's, 2000), 175–79.

Chapter One

1. These introductory chapters differ methodologically from later ones in their focus on single case studies. The legal legacy of the Scotts' case warrants this approach; the Lawson dispute serves as a complementary example that reconnects New England stories aggregated by other scholars with their wider transatlantic context. Colonial Americans left very few indications of judicial reasoning in their court records; cases like the Lawsons' demonstrate what the parties thought would be persuasive. For our most accessible records, historians of early American law and society are indebted to nineteenth-century archivists, who organized, preserved, and reprinted documents with the aim of promoting a distinctive tradition of American, as opposed to English, law. Work with published records is challenging; systematic examination of surviving unpublished legal sources even more so. Studies of such material tend to focus on a single colony or even county. See Cornelia Hughes Dayton, *Women before the Bar: Gender, Law & Society*

in Connecticut, 1639–1789 (Chapel Hill: University of North Carolina Press for the OIEAHC, 1995); Michelle Morris, *Under Household Government: Sex and Family in Puritan Massachusetts* (Cambridge, MA: Harvard University Press, 2013); Lyle Koehler, *A Search for Power: The "Weaker Sex" in Seventeenth-Century New England* (Urbana: University of Illinois Press, 1980); Mary Beth Norton, *Founding Mothers & Fathers: Gendered Power and the Forming of American Society* (New York: Alfred A. Knopf, 1996); Holly Brewer, *By Birth or Consent* (Chapel Hill: University of North Carolina Press for the OIEAHC, 2007); and Mary Bilder, *The Transatlantic Constitution: Colonial Legal Culture and the Empire* (Cambridge, MA: Harvard University Press, 2004).

2. Colonial legal papers from the Lawson dispute are located in Suffolk Files, case no. 913 (the case is in volume 9, pages 113–18, of the bound Suffolk Files Collection, with multiple court papers pasted to each page; item pages are included only where legible on microfilm); MAC, vol. 9 (Domestic Relations), 58–59; "Christopher Lawson, Petition to the Court of Assistants at Boston (2/1/1668/69)," *Proceedings of the Massachusetts Historical Society*, 107 vols. (Boston: MHS, 1912), 46:479–84. Many thanks to Michelle Morris for calling the case to my attention and sharing her transcriptions and insights.

3. Michael P. Winship, *The Times and Trials of Anne Hutchinson: Puritans Divided* (Lawrence: University Press of Kansas, 2005); Michael P. Winship, *Making Heretics: Militant Protestantism and Free Grace in Massachusetts* (Princeton, NJ: Princeton University Press, 2002).

4. Stephen F. Peckham, "Richard Scott and his wife Catherine Marbury, and some of their Descendants," *NEHGR* 60 (1942): 169.

5. On Christopher Lawson's identity and movements, see Richard LeBaron Bowen, "The Mother of Christopher Helme," *NEHGR* 98 (1944); Richard LeBaron Bowen, "Richard Scott of Providence, Rhode Island," *NEHGR* 96 (1942): 3–12; Douglas Richardson, *Plantagenet Ancestry: A Study in Colonial and Medieval Families* (Baltimore: Genealogical Publishing, 2004); Nathaniel Shurtleff, ed., *Records of the Governor and Company of the Massachusetts Bay in New England: 1674–1686*, 5 vols. (Boston: W. White, 1854), 5:399–403; John Wentworth, *The Wentworth Genealogy* (Boston: A. Mudge & Son, 1870), 76; *A Volume Relating to the Early History of Boston Containing the Aspinwall Notarial Records from 1644–1651* (Boston: Municipal Printing Office, 1903), 24, 31, 113, 124, 152, 172, 212, 235, 329; Bush Sargent Jr., ed., *The Correspondence of John Cotton* (Chapel Hill: University of North Carolina Press, 2001), 398n5; Emerson W. Baker, "'A Scratch with a Bear's Paw': Anglo-Indian Land Deeds in Early Maine," *Ethnohistory* 36, no. 3 (1989): 235–56.

6. Neal Allen, ed., *Province and Court Records of Maine* (Portland: Maine Historical Society, 1991), 1: 243–44, https://catalog.hathitrust.org/Record/000536106.

7. Koehler, *A Search for Power*, appendix 1; John Noble and John Francis Cronin, eds., *Records of the Court of Assistants of the Colony of the Massachusetts Bay, 1630–1692*, 3 vols. (Boston: County of Suffolk, 1901–28).

8. William Trask, ed., *Suffolk Deeds*, 14 vols. (Boston: 1885), 3:172; Shurtleff, ed., *Records of Massachusetts Bay: 1661–1674*, vol. 4, part 2, 380; Richard Cooke, power of attorney to Elizabeth Lawson, January 16, 1668/9, Suffolk Files, no. 913.

9. Suffolk Files, no. 913; MAC, 9:58–59; "Christopher Lawson, Petition to the Court of Assistants (2/1/1668/69)," 479–84; *Christopher Lawson and Elizabeth his wife v. Anthony Rawlins and Elizabeth Shrimpton widow* (1670), C10/78/74, and *Roger Lawson v. Christopher Lawson and Elizabeth his wife and Lawrence Swainson* (1678), C10/132/80, "Court of Chancery: Six Clerks Office: Pleadings before 1714," Whittington, National Archives of the United Kingdom, Kew.

10. Roderick Phillips, *Putting Asunder: A History of Divorce in Western Society* (Cambridge: Cambridge University Press, 1988), 71–84, 105–16.

11. For a list of known seventeenth-century divorce suits, see Koehler, *A Search for Power*, appendix 1; for analysis, see Dayton, *Women before the Bar*, 105–30.

12. R. B. Outhwaite, *The Rise and Fall of the English Ecclesiastical Courts, 1500–1860* (Cambridge: Cambridge University Press, 2006).

13. Outhwaite, *English Ecclesiastical Courts*, 78.

14. "Marriages and Married Persons" and *Body of Liberties* (1641), items 80 and 94, in William H. Whitmore, ed., *The Colonial Laws of Massachusetts: Reprinted from the Edition of 1672, with the Supplements through 1686: Containing Also, a Bibliographical Preface and Introduction, Treating of All the Printed Laws from 1649 to 1686: Together with the Body of Liberties of 1641, and the Records of the Court of Assistants, 1641–1644* (Boston: Rockwell and Churchill, 1890), 101–2, 50–51, 54–55, http://archive.org/details/coloniallawsofma1890mass.

15. Phillips, *Putting Asunder*, 40–133.

16. Elizabeth Lawson, deposition [1], Suffolk Files, no. 913, 9:117. Elizabeth entered three separate, undated depositions; contextual evidence, including her reported age, her rebuttal of specific charges, and the identity of the recording magistrate suggest that these were originally taken between 1657 and 1662, at earlier stages in the Lawson conflict.

17. John Sunderland Sr., deposition, Suffolk Files, no. 913.

18. Charles Donahue, *Law, Marriage, and Society in the Later Middle Ages* (Cambridge: Cambridge University Press, 2007), 45–46.

19. Phillips, *Putting Asunder*, 71–77.

20. Naomi Tadmor, "The Concept of the Household-Family in Eighteenth-Century England," *Past and Present* 151, no. 1 (May 1996): 111–40.

21. Amy M. Froide, *Never Married: Singlewomen in Early Modern England* (Oxford: Oxford University Press, 2005).

22. John R. Gillis, *For Better, for Worse: British Marriages, 1600 to the Present* (New York: Oxford University Press, 1985), 101–2.

23. Bequests from two different uncles suggest that she would have had better prospects if not for laws that favored male heirs. See "Will of Henry James, Yeoman of Filton, Gloucestershire," June 29, 1639, PROB 11/180/551; and "Will of Thomas James, Yeoman of Filton, Gloucestershire," June 29, 1639, PROB 11/180/539, National Archives of the United Kingdom, Kew.

24. Margaret E. Newell, *Brethren by Nature: New England Indians, Colonists, and the Origins of American Slavery* (Ithaca, NY: Cornell University Press, 2015), esp. 57, 72–81.

25. Failure to make official record of a marriage ceremony was not unusual in colonial America, although the Lawsons' marriage does stand out because its exact date appears neither in surviving records of marriages nor in their legal attempts at divorce.

26. Margaret R. Hunt, "Wives and Marital 'Rights' in the Court of Exchequer in the Early Eighteenth Century," in *Londinopolis: Essays in the Cultural and Social History of Early Modern London*, ed. Mark S. R. Jenner and Paul Griffiths, Politics, Culture, and Society in Early Modern Britain (Manchester: Manchester University Press, distributed by St. Martin's Press, 2000), 107–29, quotation on 121; Timothy Stretton, *Women Waging Law in Elizabethan England* (Cambridge: Cambridge University Press, 1998), 21–38, 129–54.

27. Nathaneal Norcrosse to John Cotton, Exeter 5th month, 1647, in Sargent, *Correspondence of John Cotton*, 398.

28. Laurel Ulrich, *Good Wives: Image and Reality in the Lives of Women in Northern New England, 1650–1750* (New York, 1991); Laurel Ulrich, *A Midwife's Tale: The Life of Martha Ballard, Based on Her Diary, 1785–1812* (New York, 1990).

29. Susan H. Moore, *Pilgrims: New World Settlers and the Call of Home* (New Haven, CT: Yale University Press, 2007), 66–71, 100–102. On desertion, see Morris, "Under Household Government," 111–15; and Phillips, *Putting Asunder*, 46–56.

30. Christopher to Elizabeth Lawson, July 20, 1651, Kennebec, transcribed in Boston County Court Records in 1663 and again in 1668, Suffolk Files, no. 913, 9:114.

31. Sargent, *Correspondence of John Cotton*, 397–99.

32. Moore, *Pilgrims*, 66–71, 100–102, quotation on 102; Whitmore, *Colonial Laws of Massachusetts* (1890).

33. "Christopher Lawson, Petition to the Court of Assistants (2/1/1668/69)," 480. On powers of attorney, see Linda Sturtz, "'As Though I My Self Was Pr[e]sent': Virginia Women with Power of Attorney," in *The Many Legalities of Early America*, ed. Christopher L. Tomlins and Bruce H. Mann (Chapel Hill: University of North Carolina Press, 2000), 250–71; Linda Sturtz, *Within Her Power: Propertied Women in Colonial Virginia* (New York: Routledge, 2002); and Norton, *Founding Mothers & Fathers*, 84–86.

34. Gillis, *For Better, for Worse*, 102; Phyllis Mack, *Visionary Women: Ecstatic Prophecy in Seventeenth-Century England* (Berkeley: University of California Press, 1992). On radical sixteenth-century reformers' views on polygamy and divorce, see Phillips, *Putting Asunder*, 66–70.

35. "August 1653: An Act touching Marriages and the Registring thereof; and also touching Births and Burials," *Acts and Ordinances of the Interregnum, 1642–1660* (London: 1911), 715–18, http://www.british-history.ac.uk/report.aspx?compid=56495&strquery=marriage.

36. "Will of Henry James," PROB 11/180/551; "Will of Thomas James" PROB 11/180/539; Andrew R. Warmington, *Civil War, Interregnum and Restoration in Gloucestershire, 1640–1672* (Rochester, NY: Boydell & Brewer, 1997), 117.

37. Catie Gill, "Dyer, Mary (d. 1660)," *ODNB*; Peckham, "Richard Scott and his wife Catherine Marbury"; Mack, *Visionary Women*, 255–59.

38. Christopher Lawson to Elizabeth Lawson, Kennebach, July 20, 1651, copy in Suffolk Files, no. 913, 9:114.

39. Christopher Lawson to Elizabeth Lawson, Kennebach, July 20, 1651, Suffolk Files, no. 913, 9:114; 1 Corinthians 7:9, 3, 20, 24, 15.

40. Christopher Lawson to Elizabeth Lawson, Kennebach, July 20, 1651, Suffolk Files, no. 913, 9:114.

41. John Cutting, deposition before Richard Bellingham, deputy governor, January 9, 1757[8], Suffolk Files, no. 913.

42. John Cutting, deposition before Richard Bellingham, deputy governor, January 9, 1757[8], Suffolk Files, no. 913; *Body of Liberties* (1641), item 80, in Whitmore, *Colonial Laws of Massachusetts* (1890), 50–51. Like the early seventeenth-century prescriptive writers William Gouge and William Whately, Massachusetts authorities still thought wives might need "correction"; the issue was husbands' propensity to abuse this power. On early modern debates about domestic violence, see Frances E. Dolan, *Marriage and Violence: The Early Modern Legacy* (Philadelphia: University of Pennsylvania Press, 2008), 54; Elizabeth A. Foyster, *Marital Violence: An English Family History, 1660–1875* (Cambridge University Press, 2005); Laura Gowing, *Domestic Dangers: Women, Words, and Sex in Early Modern London* (Oxford: Clarendon Press, 1996); Keith Wrightson, "The Politics of the Parish in Early Modern England," in *The Experience of Authority in Early Modern England*, ed. Paul Griffiths, Adam Fox, and Steve Hindle (New York: St. Martin's Press, 1996), 13–16; and Kathleen M. Davies, "The Sacred Condition of Equality: How Original Were Puritan Doctrines of Marriage?," *Social History* 2, no. 5 (May 1977): 563–80.

43. "Christopher Lawson, Petition to the Court of Assistants (2/1/1668/69)," 482–84.

44. Elizabeth Lawson, deposition [1 and 2], Suffolk Files, no. 913, 9:117–18; "Christopher Lawson, Petition to the Court of Assistants (2/1/1668/69)," 481. Massachusetts authorities are known to have ordered seventeen couples to cohabit between 1660 and 1700. Morris, *Under Household Government*, 78.

45. Elizabeth Lawson, deposition [3], Suffolk Files, no. 913, 9:118.

46. "John Chamberlyn of Boston to Trustees of Elizabeth Lawson, July 1658," in Trask, *Suffolk Deeds*, 3:171–72; Oliver Ayer Roberts, *History of the Military Company of the Massachusetts, Now Called, the Ancient and Honorable Artillery Company of Massachusetts: 1637–1888* (Boston: A. Mudge & Son, 1895), 129, 175.

47. Christopher Lawson to Elizabeth Lawson, Kennebach, July 20, 1651, Suffolk Files, no. 913, 9:114; Morris, *Under Household Government*, 8, 40–41, 234–37; Walter Eliot Thwing, *Thwing: A Genealogical, Biographical and Historical Account of the Family* (Boston: D. Clapp & son, 1883), 18; "Records of Boston," *NEHGR* 2 (1848): 274; Abstract of Middlesex Court Files, MS 596, R. Stanton Avery Special Collections, NEHGS 1:134.

48. "Christopher Lawson, Petition to the Court of Assistants (2/1/1668/69)," 482–84; Christopher Lawson, petition to General Court of Assistants in Boston, October 11, 1670, MAC, 9:59.

49. In the summer of 1668, a panel of judges and a small military force displaced competing governments along the Kennebec River; they likely had orders regarding Christopher's outstanding obligations. Christopher had been a constable for the losing side in this controversy. *Maine Province and Court Records*, 1: 243–45. On Maine's contests over sovereignty, see Norton, *Founding Mothers and Fathers*, 308–12.

50. "Testimony of Robt Patteshall," [February 1668/9], Suffolk Files, no. 913.

51. Cutting, deposition, Suffolk Files, no. 913; Elizabeth Lawson, deposition [1], Suffolk Files, no. 913, 9:117; "Christopher Lawson, Petition to the Court of Assistants (2/1/1668/69)," 482–84.

52. Bellingham had also been governor in 1641, when the colony adopted the *Body of Liberties*, with its protection for battered wives and its provision that "Adultery with a maried or espoused wife" was a crime for which both "the Adulterer and Adulteresse shall surely be put to death." His first term as governor lasted only one year thanks to a hasty, self-officiated marriage to a woman thirty years his junior; the union was scandalous because pair married secretly in order to avoid challenges based on his bride's rumored espousal to another. Richard S. Dunn and Laetitia Yeandle, eds., *The Journal of John Winthrop, 1630–1649* (Cambridge, MA: Harvard University Press, 1996), 193–94; James Kendall Hosmer, ed., *Winthrop's Journal: "History of New England," 1630–1649* (New York: Scribner, 1908), 43–44, http://archive.org/details /winthropsjournal02wint.

53. Jacob Bailey Moore, *Lives of the Governors of New Plymouth and Massachusetts Bay* (New York: Gates & Stedman, 1848), https://books.google.com/books?id=0ssDAAAAYAAJ.

54. "Richard Cooke, Power of Attorney to Elizabeth Lawson, 16th January, 1668/9," and "Att a County Court held at Boston the 26: of January: 1668," Suffolk Files, no. 913; "Christopher Lawson, Petition to the Court of Assistants (2/1/1668/69)," 483.

55. "Christopher Lawson, Petition to the Court of Assistants (2/1/1668/69)," 484; Christopher Lawson, petition to General Court of Assistants in Boston, October 11, 1670, MAC, 9:59. On "due benevolence," see Morris, *Under Household Government*, 73–74; Belden C. Lane, "Two Schools of Desire: Nature and Marriage in Seventeenth-Century Puritanism," *Church History* 69, no. 2 (2000): 372–402; William Whately, *A Bride-Bush, or A Wedding Sermon* [. . .] (London: William Iaggard,

for Nicholas Bourne, 1617); and William Gouge, *Of Domesticall Duties: Eight Treatises* [. . .] (London: George Miller for Edward Brewster, 1634).

56. Elizabeth entered three separate, undated depositions; contextual evidence, including her reported age, her rebuttal of specific charges, and the identity of the recording magistrate suggest that these were originally taken between 1657 and 1662, at earlier stages in the Lawson conflict.

57. Cutting, deposition, Suffolk Files, no. 913. This might have been Capt. John Cutting, who owned and sailed the ship *Providence* (which had ferried numerous Puritans to New England), or a member of his family. The title *Mr.* was reserved for men of relatively high status and was not a courtesy given to Christopher in the court records.

58. On the 1644 adultery trial, see Dunn and Yeandle, *Journal of John Winthrop*, 246–47; and Hosmer, *Winthrop's Journal*, 161–63.

59. Morris, *Under Household Government*, 124–27, quotations on 124.

60. Sharon Block, *Rape and Sexual Power in Early America* (Chapel Hill: University of North Carolina Press for the OIEAHC, 2006).

61. John Winthrop's commentary on the deeply disturbing case of child abuse that prompted these disparate sentences also supported Elizabeth Lawson's charges of fornication, as "a man and woman taken . . . in bed together" were presumed to have had intercourse, regardless of their protests. Dunn and Yeandle, *Journal of John Winthrop*, 193–95, discussed in Laurel Thatcher Ulrich, "John Winthrop's City of Women," *Massachusetts Historical Review* 3 (2001): 19–48; Christopher Lawson, petition to General Court of Assistants in Boston, October 11, 1670, MAC, 9:59.

62. Elizabeth Lawson, deposition [1], Suffolk Files, no. 913, 9:117; Dayton, *Women before the Bar*; Cynthia B. Herrup, *A House in Gross Disorder: Sex, Law, and the 2nd Earl of Castlehaven* (Oxford: Oxford University Press, 1999), 41–47, 115–32. Cheap printed accounts of the Castlehaven trial were circulating during Elizabeth's years in England.

63. Wendy Anne Warren, "'The Cause of Her Grief': The Rape of a Slave in Early New England," *Journal of American History* 93, no. 4 (March 2007): 1031–49; John Winthrop, "Reasons for the Plantation in New England, ca. 1628," *Winthrop Papers* (Boston: MHS, 1929–1992), 2:138–45, https://www.winthropsociety.com/doc_reasons.php.

64. Margaret Ellen Newell, *Brethren by Nature: New England Indians, Colonists, and the Origins of American Slavery* (Ithaca, NY: Cornell University Press, 2015), 53–56.

65. Quotations by Christopher Levett (1628), Thomas Lechford (1642), and Gov. Edward Winslow in Michael L. Fickes, "'They Could Not Endure That Yoke': The Captivity of Pequot Women and Children after the War of 1637," *New England Quarterly* 73, no. 1 (2000): 66; Baker, "'A Scratch with a Bear's Paw,'" 242; William Wood, *New Englands Prospect: A True, Lively, and Experimentall Description of That Part of America, Commonly Called New England: Discovering the State of That Countrie, Both as It Stands to Our New-Come English Planters; and to the Old Native Inhabitants* (London: By Tho. Cotes for Iohn Bellamie, 1634), http://www.gutenberg.org/ebooks/47082. On the trope of the "squaw drudge," see David D. Smits, "The 'Squaw Drudge': A Prime Index of Savagism," *Ethnohistory* 29, no. 4 (1982): 281–306; and Sarah M. S. Pearsall, "'Having Many Wives' in Two American Rebellions: The Politics of Households and the Radically Conservative," *American Historical Review* 118, no. 4 (October 2013): 1001–28.

66. Baker, "'A Scratch with a Bear's Paw,'" 242; Ann Marie Plane, *Colonial Intimacies: Indian Marriage in Early New England* (Ithaca, NY: Cornell University Press, 2000); Sarah M. S. Pearsall, "Native American Men—and Women—at Home in Plural Marriages in Seventeenth-Century New France," *Gender & History* 27, no. 3 (November 2015): 591–610.

67. Plane, *Colonial Intimacies*, 1–13, 77–78, 178–79.

68. Hosmer, *Winthrop's Journal*, 47–48, 304–5, 316–17; *Maine Province and Court Records*, 1:xlvii–xlviii.

69. John Josselyn, *An Account of Two Voyages to New-England* [. . .], The second addition (London: Printed for G. Widdowes, 1675), 28.

70. Elizabeth Lawson, deposition [3], Suffolk Files, no. 913, 9:118.

71. Thomas Edgar and John Doddridge, *The Lawes Resolutions of Womens Rights* [. . .] (London, 1632), 59.

72. David Zaret, *Origins of Democratic Culture* (Princeton, NJ: Princeton University Press, 1999), 88.

73. "Richard Cooke, Power of Attorney to Elizabeth Lawson, 16th January, 1668/9," and "Att a County Court held at Boston the 26: of January: 1668," Suffolk Files, no. 913; "Christopher Lawson, Petition to the Court of Assistants (2/1/1668/69)," 483.

74. Trask, *Suffolk Deeds*, 11:110–11.

75. See *Christopher Lawson and Elizabeth his wife v. Anthony Rawlins and Elizabeth Shrimpton widow* (1670), C10/78/74; and *Roger Lawson v. Christopher Lawson and Elizabeth his wife and Lawrence Swainson* (1678), C10/132/80.

76. Bilder, *The Transatlantic Constitution*, 4–5.

Chapter Two

1. *Manby v. Scott* survived in manuscript notes by Justices Robert Hyde (Hide) and Orlando Bridgeman (Bridgman), and by the lawyer Joseph Keble, which then trickled into publication in multiple and sometimes conflicting law reports between 1682 and 1824. Subsequent references to these reports here include both the legal reference format cited in eighteenth- and nineteenth-century sources and, in parentheses, volume and page information from the more accessible twentieth-century compilation *English Reports* (*ER*). These multiple case reports obscure the frequency with which *Manby* appears as a precedent because legal citation does not make it obvious that they all refer to the same case.

2. Bridgman O 272, 236 (124 *ER* 585, 565).

3. Bridgman O 235 (124 *ER* 564). On the rhetorical strategy of disguising radical change as continuity, see Harold Joseph Berman, *Law and Revolution, II: The Impact of the Protestant Reformations on the Western Legal Tradition* (Cambridge, MA: Harvard University Press, 2003), 229.

4. James Kent, *Commentaries on American Law*, 4 vols. (New York: O. Halsted, 1826), 2:124.

5. Florene S. Memegalos, *George Goring (1608–1657): Caroline Courtier and Royalist General* (Aldershot, UK: Ashgate Publishing, 2007), 3–28, 96, 115.

6. On aristocratic marriage portions, see Lawrence Stone, *The Family, Sex and Marriage in England, 1500–1800* (New York: Harper & Row, 1977), 330, 381; Memegalos, *George Goring*, 30–31.

7. Memegalos, *George Goring*, 31–39.

8. Catherine Scott to Edward Scott, June 28, 1637, in James Renat Scott, *Memorials of the Family of Scott, of Scot's-hall, in the County of Kent* [. . .] (London: J. R. Scott, 1876), xxxvi. The sticking point appears to have involved resources to remain in her control while her husband was still alive, rather than just the jointure that would follow (in lieu of dower) after his death. On jointure and seisin, see Susan Staves, *Married Women's Separate Property in England, 1660–1833* (Cambridge, MA: Harvard University Press, 1990).

9. Memegalos, *George Goring*, 28–42; Lord Goring to Sir Edward Scott, September 5, 1632; Lord Keeper Coventry to Sir Edward Scott, December 1, 1636; Lady Katherine Scott (mother-in-law of Catherine Goring Scott) to Lady Knatchbull, December 3, 1636, in Scott, *Memorials of the Family of Scott*, xxxv–xxxvi.

10. Mary Goring to Sir Edward Scott, undated, in Scott, *Memorials of the Family of Scott*, xxxviii. In this letter, Catherine Scott's mother thanks Catherine's father-in-law for the care he gave her "poor daughter" during childbirth. Details date it before March 1642, contrary to the nineteenth-century editor's suggestion that it was written in 1643.

11. Memegalos, *George Goring*, 113–38.

12. *Oxford English Dictionary*, online ed., s.v. "Cavalier, n. and Adj."

13. Lawrence Stone, *Road to Divorce: England 1530–1987* (Oxford: Oxford University Press, 1990); Stone, *The Family, Sex and Marriage*; John R. Gillis, *For Better, for Worse: British Marriages, 1600 to the Present* (New York: Oxford University Press, 1985); Roderick Phillips, *Putting Asunder: A History of Divorce in Western Society* (Cambridge: Cambridge University Press, 1988), 113–16; Tim Stretton, "Marriage, Separation and the Common Law in England, 1540–1660," in *The Family in Early Modern England*, ed. Helen Berry and Elizabeth Foyster (Cambridge: Cambridge University Press, 2007), 18–39. For seventeenth-century prescriptive writings that managed to preserve pro-divorce arguments while toeing an official anti-divorce line, see Thomas Edgar and John Doddridge, *The Lawes Resolutions of Womens Rights* [. . .] (London: 1632), 57–68; and Jacqueline Eales, "Whately, William (1583–1639)," *ODNB*.

14. Burton Diary, December 22, 1656.

15. The most accessible reference for the timing of Milton's divorce debate is Thomas Luxon, "Milton: Doctrine and Discipline of Divorce—Notes," Milton Reading Room, n.d., https://www .dartmouth.edu/~milton/reading_room/ddd/introduction/text.shtml. Massachusetts had earlier ended one bigamous marriage in 1639, but this action would have passed muster under canon law. Christopher Lawson was charged with enforcing alimony in one of the 1644 divorce cases. For the timing of Massachusetts divorce cases, see John Noble and John Francis Cronin, eds., *Records of the Court of Assistants of the Colony of the Massachusetts Bay, 1630–1692*, vol. 2, part 1, 1630–1641 (Boston: County of Suffolk, 1904), 89, 138–39; Lyle Koehler, *A Search for Power: The "Weaker Sex" in Seventeenth-Century New England* (Urbana: University of Illinois Press, 1980), appendix 1.

16. R. B. Outhwaite, *The Rise and Fall of the English Ecclesiastical Courts, 1500–1860* (Cambridge: Cambridge University Press, 2006), 78.

17. "Archbishop Parker's Table of Kindred and Affinity, 1563," in Will Coster, *Family and Kinship in England, 1450–1800* (New York: Routledge, 2015), 120–21.

18. Martin Ingram, *Church Courts, Sex and Marriage in England, 1570–1640* (Cambridge University Press, 1990), 153; Bernard Capp, *England's Culture Wars: Puritan Reformation and Its Enemies in the Interregnum, 1649–1660* (Oxford: Oxford University Press, 2012), 132–44. The question of marital oversight in the absence of the church courts surfaced again in 1651, in response to the petition of an heiress who had been kidnapped and forced into marriage by a fortune hunter. Parliament opened the door to marital dissolution by appointing a commission to consider an annulment and to establish procedures for future cases. "May 1650: An Act for Suppressing the Detestable Sins of Incest, Adultery and Fornication," and "January 1651: An Act Enabling the Lords Commissioners for Custody of the Great Seal of England, to issue Commissions of Delegates in Cases of pretended Marriages," in *Acts and Ordinances of the Interregnum, 1642–1660*, ed. C. H. Firth and R. S. Rait (London: His Majesty's

Stationery Office, 1911), 387–89, 496–97, British History Online, http://www.british-history.ac.uk/no -series/acts-ordinances-interregnum/pp387-389; http://www.british-history.ac.uk/no-series/acts -ordinances-interregnum/pp496-497a.

19. "August 1653: An Act Touching Marriages and the Registring thereof; and also touching Births and Burials," in Firth and Rait, *Acts and Ordinances of the Interregnum*, 715–18, http:// www.british-history.ac.uk/no-series/acts-ordinances-interregnum/pp715-718.

20. Stone, *Road to Divorce*, 308–9; Phillips, *Putting Asunder*, 131–33.

21. Burton Diary, January 10, 1656/57, and December 22, 1656, 197–367; Phillips, *Putting Asunder*, 132.

22. Ruth Spalding, *Contemporaries of Bulstrode Whitelocke, 1605–1675: Biographies, Illustrated by Letters and Other Documents* (Oxford: Published for the British Academy by Oxford University Press, 1990), 313; Burton Diary, January 10, 1656/57, n2, and January 17, 1656/57, n1; J. T. Cliffe, *The World of the Country House in Seventeenth-Century England* (New Haven, CT: Yale University Press, 1999), 77; Patrick Morrah, *Prince Rupert of the Rhine* (London: Constable, 1976), 407.

23. Burton Diary, January 10, 1656/57; Barry Coward, *The Cromwellian Protectorate* (Manchester, UK: Manchester University Press, 2002); Frances Dolan, *Whores of Babylon: Catholicism, Gender, and Seventeenth-Century Print Culture* (Ithaca, NY: Cornell University Press, 1999), 98.

24. Dolan, *Whores of Babylon*, 98.

25. Dolan, 98; Memegalos, *George Goring*, 357; Burton Diary, January 10, 1656/57; *Diary and Correspondence of John Evelyn, F.R.S.* (London: Henry G. Bohn, 1862), 1:397.

26. Burton Diary, January 3, 1656/57.

27. Mrs. Catherine Scott to the Lady Mary Scott, January 20, 1641/2, in Scott, *Memorials of the Family of Scott*, xxxv–xxxvi. Lady Mary Scott was Edward's stepmother, who began mediating Catherine and Edward's marital dispute when she was still Lady Knatchbull, using family connections that also link her, by association, to the Royalists and to the Jesuits that Edward pointedly despised. Mary Knatchbull Scott was related by marriage to the Knatchbull women whose quest for Jesuit spiritual advisors led them to found Benedictine convents for English women in Ghent, Belgium, and who played an important role in Royalist cause throughout the Civil Wars. Dolan, *Whores of Babylon*; Caroline M. K. Bowden, "Knatchbull, Elizabeth (1584– 1629)," *ODNB*; Caroline M. K. Bowden, "Knatchbull, Mary (1610–1696)," *ODNB*; Nicholas Keene, "Knatchbull, Sir Norton, First Baronet (1602–1685)," *ODNB*.

28. "A letter dated February 12, 1646 [1647], from the siege at Nettlestead, by Henry Line," in Scott, *Memorials of the Family of Scott*, xxxix.

29. Barbara Donagan, "Goring, George, First Earl of Norwich (1585–1663)," *ODNB*.

30. Memeglos, *George Goring*, 115, 156. The transfer of family property to trusts for female relations long served to protect it from hostile governments and eager creditors. Hendrik Hartog, *Man and Wife in America: A History* (Cambridge, MA: Harvard University Press, 2000); Linda K. Kerber, *No Constitutional Right to be Ladies: Women and the Obligations of Citizenship* (New York: Hill and Wang, 1998).

31. *Diary and Correspondence of John Evelyn*, 260, 271. Catherine's father had just been released from prison following his trial for his role in the Kentish rising, and she might have been carrying the messages that again placed her father in trouble with Parliament for corresponding "with the enemies overseas" in 1650. Her "incognito" traveling companion was the younger brother of the man who had been a spy and messenger for Charles I, but who had been captured

and imprisoned shortly before the king's execution earlier in 1749. Donagan, "Goring, George," *ODNB*; Bernard Capp and Anita McConnell, "Slingsby, Sir Robert, Baronet (1611–1661)," *ODNB*.

32. Burton Diary, December 22, 1756. The dates of her suit are unclear, and not evident in surviving record. The lord chief justice was most likely John Glynne, who was in the process of returning his allegiance to the Crown. Keith Lindley, "Glynne, Sir John (1603–1666)," *ODNB*.

33. Burton Diary, December 22, 1656, and January 10, 1656/57.

34. Burton Diary, January 3, 1656/57.

35. Burton Diary, December 22, 1656.

36. Burton Diary, January 10, 1656/57.

37. For instance, under the terms of the 1650 act that made adultery a capital offense, sex with a woman whose husband had been absent three years was *not* a felony. "May 1650: An Act for suppressing the detestable sins of Incest, Adultery and Fornication," in Firth and Rait, *Acts and Ordinances of the Interregnum*, 387–89.

38. Michael Sparke, *The Narrative History of King James, for the First Fourteen Years* [. . .] (London: Printed for Michael Sparke, 1651); David Lindley, *The Trials of Frances Howard: Fact and Fiction at the Court of King James* (London: Routledge, 1993); Johanna Rickman, *Love, Lust, and License in Early Modern England: Illicit Sex and the Nobility* (Aldershot, UK: Ashgate, 2008).

39. It is not clear from the testimony whether "Col. Howard, brother to the Earl of Suffolk" was Col. Thomas Howard or his brother Lt. Col. Robert Howard, who were both younger brothers of the Earl of Suffolk and who fought under Prince Rupert at the Battle of Naseby. Other siblings included Katherine Stuart, née Howard, and George Stuart, both of whom served as Royalist spies. "Testimony of Ann Wheeler (Sat. January 17, 1656)," in "Diary Of Parliament, by Thomas Burton, M. P. for Westmoreland, in the Parliaments of Oliver and Richard Cromwell, from 3d December 1656 to 22d April, 1659. [The Autograph Manuscript, from Which the Edition Was Published by J. T. Rutt, 4 Vols. 8vo., 1828]," British Library Archives and Manuscripts, add_15859–008; Malcolm Wanklyn, *Decisive Battles of the English Civil War* (Barnsley, South Yorkshire, UK: Pen and Sword, 2006); Geoffrey Smith, *Royalist Agents, Conspirators and Spies: Their Role in the British Civil Wars, 1640–1660* (Farnham, UK: Routledge, 2011), 48, 105.

40. "Testimony of Major Riswick (January 10, 1656)," in "Diary Of Parliament, by Thomas Burton."

41. Paul D. Halliday, "Twisden, Sir Thomas, First Baronet (1602–1683)," *ODNB*.

42. On paid testimony, see Lawrence Stone, *Broken Lives: Separation and Divorce in England, 1660–1857* (Oxford: Oxford University Press, 1993), 6–8. On Dr. Hinton, see Gordon Goodwin and Michael Bevan, "Hinton, Sir John (1603?–1682), Physician," *ODNB*.

43. Burton Diary, January 19, 1656/57.

44. Burton Diary, January 19, 1656/57.

45. Leopold Damrosch, *The Sorrows of the Quaker Jesus: James Nayler and the Puritan Crackdown on the Free Spirit* (Cambridge, MA: Harvard University Press, 1996), 192.

46. Burton Diary, December 18, 1656.

47. Burton Diary, December 18, 1656.

48. Burton Diary, December 18, 1656.

49. Burton Diary, December 22 and December 27, 1656.

50. Laura Gowing, *Domestic Dangers: Women, Words, and Sex in Early Modern London* (Oxford: Clarendon Press, 1996), 43, 196.

51. Burton Diary, January 19, 1657.

52. Charles II became notorious for his mistresses, some of whom he appointed to be ladies-in-waiting to his Portuguese Catholic queen, Catherine. Charles considered divorce starting around 1667, after the queen proved unable to carry a child to term. He later reversed his position and stood by Catherine when former Protestant allies sought to force a divorce on him after James II, his brother and heir, converted to Catholicism in the 1770s. S. M. Wynne, "Catherine [Catherine of Braganza, Catarina Henriqueta de Bragança] (1638–1705), Queen of England, Scotland, and Ireland, Consort of Charles II," *ODNB*.

53. Halliday, "Twisden, Sir Thomas," *ODNB*; D. E. C. Yale, "Finch, Heneage, First Earl of Nottingham (1621–1682)," *ODNB*.

54. Published reports in *Manby* identify Bridgeman as chief baron of the Exchequer, a position he acquired in 1660 for the trial of the regicides; he seems simultaneously to have held the post of chief justice of the Court of Common Pleas, with some overlap with Robert Hyde, author of one of the other surviving opinions in *Manby* and cousin to Edward Hyde, Lord Clarendon. Bridgeman was an ally of Clarendon's, and thus part of the faction that kept the Gorings from returning to favor after the Restoration. Clarendon penned the foundational history of the English Civil Wars that condemned the Goring men to centuries of infamy and obscurity, and later sources made it appear that Clarendon himself was the author of Robert Hyde's opinion in *Manby*. Bridgeman became Keeper of the Great Seal upon Clarendon's fall from power in 1667. Memegalos, *George Goring*, 1–4; Howard Nenner, "Bridgeman, Sir Orlando, First Baronet (1609–1674), Judge," *ODNB*; Wilfrid Prest, "Hyde, Sir Robert (1595/6–1665), Barrister and Politician," *ODNB*; Paul Seaward, "Hyde, Edward, First Earl of Clarendon (1609–1674), Politician and Historian," *ODNB*.

55. *Manby v. Scott*, 1 Keble 206, 441, 361 (83 *ER* 902, 1042–43, 995).

56. Bridgman O 235 (124 *ER* 564); Hyde 1 Modern 129 (86 *ER* 786).

57. Mary Nyquist, "Hobbes, Slavery, and Despotical Rule," *Representations* (May 2009): 1–33; Glenn Burgess, "Filmer, Sir Robert (1588?–1653)," *ODNB*. Manuscript copies of Filmer's *Patriarcha* had been circulating in Royalist circles since the 1630s, though the text was not published until 1680. Filmer's friend and publisher Sir Roger Twysden was the elder brother of Sir Thomas Twysden, Catherine Scott's legal defender and purported lover.

58. 1 Modern 130 (86 *ER* 784–85).

59. 1 Modern 130 (86 *ER* 784–85).

60. 1 Modern 130 (86 *ER* 784).

61. 1 Keble 446 (83 *ER* 1045); Bridgman O 258 (124 *ER* 577).

62. Bridgman O 235 (124 *ER* 564).

63. Bridgeman O 236 (124 *ER* 565); Hyde 1-Modern 142 (86 *ER* 791).

64. 1 Keble 365 (83 *ER* 997).

65. On Sir Orlando Bridgeman and Robert Hyde, see note 54 above.

66. John Evelyn, diary entry, July 16, 1663, *Diary and Correspondence of John Evelyn, F.R.S.* (1862), 397; Samuel Pepys, diary entry, July 30, 1663, *The Diary of Samuel Pepys*, http://www.pepys diary.com/archive/1663/07/30/; Margaret Cavendish, "Letter CLXXIV," *CCXI sociable letters written by the thrice noble, illustrious, and excellent princess, the Lady Marchioness of Newcastle* (London: William Wilson, 1664), 364.

67. Hartog, *Man and Wife*, 3–4; Berman, *Law and Revolution, II*, 251.

68. 1 Siderfin Reports 119 (82 *ER* 1006).

69. *Christopher Lawson and Elizabeth his wife v. Anthony Rawlins and Elizabeth Shrimpton widow, Middlesex*, bill and two answers, 1670, C10/178/74, "Court of Chancery: Six Clerks Office: Pleadings before 1714," Whittington, National Archives of the United Kingdom, Kew.

70. *Christopher Lawson and Elizabeth his wife v. Anthony Rawlins and Elizabeth Shrimpton widow* (1670), C10/78/74; *Roger Lawson v. Christopher Lawson and Elizabeth his wife and Lawrence Swainson* (1678), C10/132/80, "Court of Chancery: Six Clerks Office: Pleadings before 1714," Whittington, National Archives of the United Kingdom, Kew.

71. Michelle Morris, *Under Household Government: Sex and Family in Puritan Massachusetts* (Cambridge, MA: Harvard University Press, 2013), 269n106; Phillips, *Putting Asunder*, 141–53.

72. David Zaret, *Origins of Democratic Culture: Printing, Petitions and the Public Sphere in Early-Modern England* (Princeton, NJ: Princeton University Press, 1999), 210–14; Holly Brewer, *By Birth or Consent: Children, Law, and the Anglo-American Revolution in Authority* (Chapel Hill: University of North Carolina Press for the OIEAHC, 2005), 169–70; Burton Diary, January 12, 1656/57; Richard J. Ross, "The Commoning of the Common Law: The Renaissance Debate over Printing English Law, 1520–1640," *University of Pennsylvania Law Review* 146, no. 2 (January 1998): 323–461.

73. See Anthony Colquitt, *Modern Reports, or, Select Cases Adjudged in the Courts of Kings Bench, Chancery, Common-Pleas, and Exchequer since the Restauration of His Majesty King Charles II Collected by a Careful Hand.* (London: Printed for T. Basset, J. Wright, R. Chiswell, and S. Heyrick, 1682). Only seven earlier publications had claimed "modernity," the first in the 1650s.

74. Dissenting justices in *Manby* included Thomas Twysden, brother of Locke's Whig ally Roger Twysden, and Thomas Tyrrel, a relation of Locke's ally James Tyrell.

75. Keith Wrightson, "The Politics of the Parish in Early Modern England," in *The Experience of Authority in Early Modern England*, ed. Paul Griffiths, Adam Fox, and Steve Hindle (New York: St. Martin's Press, 1996), 10–11.

76. 1 Modern 124–125 (86 *ER* 782); 1 Keble 441–2 (83 *ER* 1042).

Chapter Three

1. *Pennsylvania Gazette*, June 16, 1748.

2. Mary Sarah Bilder, "English Settlement and Local Governance," in *CHLA*, 63–103; John Smolenski, *Friends and Strangers: The Making of a Creole Culture in Colonial Pennsylvania* (Philadelphia: University of Pennsylvania Press, 2010), 55–57; David Zaret, *Origins of Democratic Culture: Printing, Petitions and the Public Sphere in Early Modern England* (Princeton, NJ: Princeton University Press, 1999); Adrian Johns, *The Nature of the Book: Print and Knowledge in the Making* (Chicago: University of Chicago Press, 1998); 1 *Siderfin Reports* 119 (82 *ER* 1006); 1 Modern 130 (86 *ER* 784–85).

3. Holly Brewer, "The Transformation of Domestic Law," *CHLA*, 288–323; Holly Brewer, *By Birth or Consent: Children, Law and the Anglo-American Revolution in Authority* (Chapel Hill: University of North Carolina Press for the OIEAHC, 2005); Carole Shammas, *A History of Household Government in America* (Charlottesville: University Press of Virginia, 2002); Douglas Hay and Paul Craven, eds., *Masters, Servants, and Magistrates in Britain and the Empire, 1562–1955* (Chapel Hill: University of North Carolina Press, 2004).

4. Marcus Kuhl, *Pennsylvania Gazette*, May 19, 1748; June 9, 1748; July 13, 1749; November 2, 1749; Joseph Nicholson, *Pennsylvania Gazette*, November 17, 1757. On ads' uses as sources, see David Waldstreicher, "Reading the Runaways: Self-Fashioning, Print Culture and Confidence in Slavery in the Eighteenth Century Mid-Atlantic," *William and Mary Quarterly* 54, no. 2 (1999): 243–72; Eric Slauter, *The State as a Work of Art: The Cultural Origins of the Constitution* (Chicago: University of Chicago Press, 2009), 169–213; Shane White, *Somewhat More Independent: The End of Slavery in New York City, 1770–1810* (Athens: University of Georgia Press,

1991), 114–20; and Sharon Block, *Colonial Complexions: Race and Bodies in Eighteenth-Century America* (Philadelphia: University of Pennsylvania Press, 2018).

5. Marcus Kuhl, *Pennsylvania Gazette*, May 19, 1748; June 9, 1748; July 13, 1749; November 2, 1749; Joseph Nicholson, *Pennsylvania Gazette*, November 17, 1757.

6. Marcus Kuhl, *Pennsylvania Gazette*, May 19, 1748; June 9, 1748.

7. Marcus Kuhl, *Pennsylvania Gazette*, July 13, 1749, November 2, 1749.

8. Joseph Nicholson, *Pennsylvania Gazette*, November 17, 1757.

9. Most advertised runaways (75–80 percent) were men in their twenties; disproportionate numbers were "hired out." On runaway demographics and summary of classic literature on runaways, see John Hope Franklin and Loren Schweninger, *Runaway Slaves: Rebels on the Plantation* (New York: Oxford University Press, 1999), 134–45, 210–13; Billy G. Smith, "Runaway Slaves in the Mid-Atlantic Region during the Revolutionary Era," in *The Transforming Hand of Revolution: Reconsidering the American Revolution as a Social Movement*, ed. Ronald Hoffman and Peter J. Albert (Charlottesville: University Press of Virginia, 1995), 199–230; Billy G. Smith, "Black Women Who Stole Themselves in Early America," in *Inequality in Early America*, ed. Carla Pestana and Sharon Salinger (Hanover, NH: University Press of New England, 1999), 134–59. On British runaway slave ads, see Susan Dwyer Amussen, *Caribbean Exchanges: Slavery and the Transformation of English Society, 1640–1700* (Chapel Hill: University of North Carolina Press, 2007); and Gretchen Gerzina, *Black London: Life before Emancipation* (New Brunswick, NJ: Rutgers University Press, 1995).

10. On the misleading nature of "the dichotomous bright line between freedom and coercion, found in American constitutional jurisprudence and enshrined in a long sociological literature," and the "plural" character of colonial cultures of work, see Hay and Craven, *Masters, Servants, and Magistrates*, 28; Christopher Tomlins, "Early British America, 1585–1830, Freedom Bound," in Hay and Craven, *Masters, Servants, and Magistrates*, 150; and Tomlins, "Law, Population, Labor," *CHLA*, 1:211–52, esp. 242.

11. *Body of Liberties* (1641), items 80 and 85, in William H. Whitmore, ed., *The Colonial Laws of Massachusetts: Reprinted from the Edition of 1672, with the Supplements through 1686: Containing Also, a Bibliographical Preface and Introduction, Treating of All the Printed Laws from 1649 to 1686: Together with the Body of Liberties of 1641, and the Records of the Court of Assistants, 1641–1644* (Boston: Rockwell and Churchill, 1890), 50–51, http://archive.org/details /coloniallawsofma1890mass.

12. Richard Nichols cited in Alfred L. Brophy, "Law and Indentured Servitude in Mid-Eighteenth Century Pennsylvania," *Willamette Law Review* 28 (1991): 76–77.

13. "Acts respecting Masters, Servants and Labourers," *The Charters and General Laws of the Colony and Province of Massachusetts Bay* [. . .] (Boston: T. B. Wait, 1814), 155–57; Gail McKnight Beckman, ed. *The Statutes at Large of Pennsylvania in the Time of William Penn* (New York: Vantage Press, 1976), 97–98.The Duke's Laws were more generous to abused servants than were those in Virginia, where a servant whose master had misused him or her was to be sold, not freed. "An Act Concerning Servants and Slaves" (1705), Hening, 3:448–49;

14. Robert C. Ritchie, "Nicolls, Richard (1624–1672)," *ODNB*.

15. Beckman, *The Statutes at Large of Pennsylvania*, 97; "An Act for the better Regulating of Negroes" (1727), *Laws of the Province of Pennsylvania* (Philadelphia: Andrew Bradford, 1728), 323; "Act for the Regulating of Free Negroes, &c" (1701), *Charters and General Laws* [. . .] *of Massachusetts* [. . .] (1814), 386–87.

16. Kathleen M. Brown, *Good Wives, Nasty Wenches, and Anxious Patriarchs: Gender, Race, and Power in Colonial Virginia* (Chapel Hill: University of North Carolina Press for the OIEAHC, 1996); "An Act Concerning Servants and Slaves" (1705), Hening, 3:448–49. On similar statutory developments and the centrality of runaway regulation to defining slavery in seventeenth-century English Barbados, see Amussen, *Caribbean Exchanges*, 129–35.

17. "An Act Concerning Servants and Slaves" (1705), Hening, 3:447–62, quotations on 448–49.

18. "An Act for the better Regulating of Negroes" (1727), *Laws of Pennsylvania* (1728), 323.

19. Marcus Kuhl, *Pennsylvania Gazette*, June 16 and May 19, 1748.

20. For examples of colonial freedom suits, see Sally Hadden, "The Fragmented Laws of Slavery in the Colonial and Revolutionary Eras," in *CHLA*, 1:253–87; T. H. Breen, *"Myne Owne Ground": Race and Freedom on Virginia's Eastern Shore, 1640–1676* (New York: Oxford University Press, 1980); and Emily Blanck, *Tyrannicide: Forging an American Law of Slavery in Revolutionary South Carolina and Massachusetts* (Athens, GA: University of Georgia Press, 2014).

21. Hay and Craven, *Masters, Servants, and Magistrates*, 5–6.

22. These cases are intertwined, with Brown serving as a witness to their master's abuse of McWilliams's child. The precise connections and chronology are uncertain because it is not clear whether the clerk was using the Julian calendar (with March 25 marking the new year) or the Gregorian. "The Humble Petition of Mary McWilliams, March Term 1749 [1750?]," Bucks County Miscellaneous Court Papers, no. 96, and "The Petition of Margaret Brown of Wrightstown, March 1749 [1750?]," Bucks County Miscellaneous Court Papers, no. 98, BCHS.

23. Inconsistent calendar use in these records makes it unclear whether Brown's petition led to her 1749 indenture or was prompted by it. "Petition of John Leadley of Wrightstown, Court of Quarter Sessions and Newtown, Bucks County, June 15, 1749," indentures of Margaret Brown to John Ladely/Leadlie, December 17, 1743, and November 18, 1749; "The Petition of Margaret Brown of Wrightstown, March 1749 [1750?]," Bucks County Miscellaneous Court Papers, nos. 97–100, BCHS; John Leadlie, advertisements for Margaret Brown, *Pennsylvania Gazette*, January 21, 1746, and June 1, 1749.

24. "An Act to Prevent the tumultuous Meetings, and other Irregularities of Negroes and other Slaves" (1723), *Archives of Maryland*, 75:342–44. The act was altered slightly in 1737 (40:92–95) and 1751 (46:618–21); "An Act Concerning Servants and Slaves" (1705), Hening, 3:460–62; "An Act to encourage the Takers up of run-away Slaves, that shall be taken up by any Person and brought in from the Back-Woods," (1725), *Archives of Maryland*, 36:583–86, http://www.mdarchives.state.md.us.

25. Marcus Kuhl, *Pennsylvania Gazette*, June 16, 1748.

26. Marcus Kuhl, *Pennsylvania Gazette*, June 16, 1748.

27. "An Act for the better Regulating of Negroes" (1727), *Laws of Pennsylvania* (1728), 324; "An Act to encourage the Takers up of run-away Slaves (1725)," *Archives of Maryland*, 36:583–86; "An Act Concerning Servants and Slaves" (1705), Hening, 3:454.

28. Kuhl was clearly not inclined to free Scipio—an expensive proposition because masters were required to indemnify their communities against the cost of supporting freed slaves. "An Act for the better Regulating of Negroes" (1727), *Laws of Pennsylvania* (1728), 322–24.

29. Generalizations about servant and wife ads based on a survey of the digitized Seventeenth and Eighteenth Century Burney Newspapers Collection, https://www.gale.com/c/17th-and-18th-century-burney-newspapers-collection. For runaway ads as evidence of slavery in Britain, see the Runaway Slaves in Britain database, https://www.runaways.gla.ac.uk/.

30. Daniel Defoe, *The Fortunes and Misfortunes of the Famous Moll Flanders* (London: John Brotherton, 1722), 138–39; emphasis in the original.

31. For consent and anti-"clandestine marriage" laws, see "Acts Respecting Marriages and Married Persons" and "Act for the Orderly Consummating of Marriages" (1697), *Laws of Massachusetts Bay* (1814), 151–52, 242–43; "An Act for the preventing of Clandestine Marriages (1702)," *Laws of Pennsylvania* (1728), 28–29; "An Act Concerning Marriages," Hening, 3:443–4; Rhode Island's act "Touching Manstealers" cited in Mary Beth Norton, *Founding Mothers & Fathers: Gendered Power and the Forming of American Society* (New York: Alfred A. Knopf, 1996), 65, see also 62–72, 101–5; George Elliott Howard, *A History of Matrimonial Institutions Chiefly in England and the United States*, vol. 2 (Chicago: University of Chicago Press, 1904), chapter 3, esp. 228. On state efforts to regulate marriage in the nineteenth century, see Nancy F. Cott, *Public Vows: A History of Marriage and the Nation* (Cambridge, MA: Harvard University Press, 2000); and Norma Basch, *Framing American Divorce: From the Revolutionary Generation to the Victorians* (Berkeley: University of California Press, 1999). Colonial statutes requiring government certification of marriages and outlawing "clandestine marriages" antedated by as much as a century Britain's controversial 1753 Marriage Act. On Britain's 1753 act, see Rebecca Probert, *Marriage Law and Practice in the Long Eighteenth Century: A Reassessment*, Cambridge Studies in English Legal History (Cambridge: Cambridge University Press, 2009); see also chap. 4.

32. The central concerns of these laws were the right to dependents' labor and the control of family property. Parental control of children received the greatest emphasis in the early laws. By the early eighteenth century, the rhetoric demanding parental consent had eased in Massachusetts and Pennsylvania, but the revised laws expanded masters' authority by extending the consent requirement to servants. In Pennsylvania and Virginia, marrying without an owner's consent would add an additional year to a servant's allotted period of indenture. A free person marrying a servant faced a stiff fine, the alternative to which was to "well and faithfully serve" his or her spouse's "master . . . one whole year"; the official performing the ceremony was also rendered liable for masters' losses. In Virginia, a minister could be fined the staggering sum of ten thousand pounds of tobacco—ten times the amount levied against the servant's spouse. The restrictions on white servants appear trifling when compared with the penalties for interracial intimacy; laws particularly targeted black men and white women, serving to unify the interests of white men across the lines of status by making "patriarchal authority . . . a privilege of race as well as sex." "An Act for the Better Preventing of Spurious and Mixt Issue" (1705), *The Acts and Resolves* [. . .] *of the Province of the Massachusetts Bay*, Published Colonial Records of the American Colonies, 27 vols. (Boston: Wright and Potter, 1869), 1: 578–79. "An Act for the better Regulating of Negroes" (1727), *Laws of Pennsylvania* (1728), 323–24; "An Act Concerning Servants and Slaves" (1705), Hening, 3:453–54; Brown, *Good Wives, Nasty Wenches*, 198.

33. "An Act Concerning Feme-Sole Traders" (1719), *Laws of Pennsylvania* (1728), 167–69. For useful reframing of anachronistic debates about whether feme sole trader laws and provisions concerning dower promoted or curtailed female independence, see especially Serena Zabin and Ellen Hartigan-O'Connor. Zabin notes, "Coverture reveals not the ways in which women's participation in the market was limited but the ways in which it was channeled." On balance, earlier analyses suggest that colonial-era legal changes with regard to married women's property rights were driven by concern with preservation of family property, including property in slaves, and preventing white women from becoming public charges. Zabin, *Dangerous Economies: Status and Commerce in Imperial New York* (Philadelphia: University of Pennsylvania Press, 2009), 35; Hartigan-O'Connor, *The Ties That Buy: Women and Commerce in Revolutionary America*

(Philadelphia: University of Pennsylvania Press, 2009); Marylynn Salmon, *Women and the Law of Property in Early America* (Chapel Hill: University of North Carolina Press, 1986); Susan Staves, *Married Women's Separate Property in England, 1660–1833* (Cambridge, MA: Harvard University Press, 1990); Mary Beth Norton, "The Evolution of White Women's Experience in Early America," *American Historical Review* 89, no. 3 (1984): 593–619; Joan Gundersen and Gwen Gampel, "Married Women's Legal Status in Eighteenth-Century New York and Virginia," *William and Mary Quarterly* 39, no. 1 (1982): 114–33; Linda L. Sturtz, *Within Her Power: Propertied Women in Colonial Virginia* (New York: Routledge, 2002).

34. "Against trading with servants" (1661), Hening, 2:118–19; "An Act against receiving of Stolen Goods" (1698), *Charters and General Laws of Massachusetts* (1814), 313; "An Act for the better Regulation of Servants in this Province and Territories" (1702) and "An Act for the better Regulating of Negroes" (1727), *Laws of Pennsylvania* (1728), 11, 323. These statutes reflect servants' and slaves' persistent commercial activities rather than their incapacity. Even with the law in force, masters still occasionally felt the need to remind the community of it in newspaper advertisements: "Molatto Bess, who used to go about selling Cakes" in Philadelphia used her employment to borrow money and take up "Goods upon Trust in her Master's Name." *Pennsylvania Gazette,* March 5, 1745. And the "negroes belonging to the estate of Mr. William Lee" of Virginia carried on considerable trade in fruit and vegetables, much to the dismay of their overseer. *Virginia Gazette* (Rind), July 21, 1774. The attempt to limit "huckstering" by slaves and servants was a repetitive legislative theme in the Caribbean and Carolinas as well. Hadden, "Fragmented Laws of Slavery," 262–63, 267.

35. "An Act Concerning Feme-Sole Traders" (1719), *Laws of Pennsylvania* (1728), 167.

36. Defoe, *Moll Flanders,* 164.

37. The 1738 edition of the leading eighteenth-century reference on marriage law, *Baron and Feme,* supplied readers with a model of the pleas entered in cases where a husband sought to bar his wife's dower on grounds of elopement. The forms required specific allegations (and rebuttals) of her adultery with a named third party. The definition of elopement as adulterous desertion was also consistent across Giles Jacob's popular reference works, including the third edition of *Every Man His Own Lawyer* owned by the Library Company of Philadelphia in the 1740s. *Baron and Feme: A Treatise of Law and Equity, Concerning Husbands and Wives* (London: E. and R. Nutt, and R. Gosling (assigns of E. Sayer, Esq.) for T. Waller, 1738), 117; [Giles Jacob], *Every Man His Own Lawyer* [. . .], 3rd ed. ([London]: 1740), 329; Jacob, *The Common Law Common-Placed* [. . .] (London, 1726), 184; Jacob, *The Student's Companion* [. . .] (London, 1734), 61; Jacob, *New Law-Dictionary* [. . .], 6th ed. ([London]:1750), [272]; *A Treatise of Feme Coverts: or The Lady's Law* [. . .] ([London], 1732), 175–76; Thomas Edgar and John Doddridge, *The Lawes Resolutions of Womens Rights* [. . .] (London, 1632), 144–45.

38. *Manby v. Scott,* 1 Keble 206 (83 *ER* 902); Defoe, *Moll Flanders,* 95.

39. *Etherington v. Parrot,* 1 Salkeld 118 (20 *ER* 110–11).

40. *Moore v. Moore,* West Temp Hardwicke 35 (25 *ER* 809). Susan Staves argues that the contrast between *Manby v. Scott* and *Moore v. Moore* "conveniently illustrates the displacement of an older view of the marital relation in which the husband's authority has a religious and hierarchical justification by a newer view more dependent on the rhetoric and logic of contract," which had the potential to subvert patriarchy but was instead used to reinforce it. Staves, *Married Women's Separate Property in England,* 164–67.

41. Moreover, a husband who pursued his wife and "lies with her, tho' but for a night" would again be liable for her debts. The prohibition against newspaper notices of wives was repeated

320 NOTES TO PAGES 94-97

in every edition of Giles Jacob's *Every Man His Own Lawyer*, ranging from the first (1736, 331) through the tenth (1788) London editions, including a seventh edition published in New York in 1768 and an eleventh Dublin edition in 1791. The passage also appeared in Jacob's *New Law-Dictionary*, [272], and *The Common Law Common-Placed*, 184.

42. Peter Henry Dorsius, *Pennsylvania Gazette*, June 9, 1748.

43. Amussen, *Caribbean Exchanges*, 221–25.

44. *London Printers Lamentations* cited in Adrian Johns, *The Nature of the Book: Print and Knowledge in the Making* (Chicago: University of Chicago Press, 1998), 72; Berkeley cited in David D. Hall, *Cultures of Print: Essays in the History of the Book* (Amherst: University of Massachusetts Press, 1996), 99; James Runcieman Sutherland, *The Restoration Newspaper and Its Development* (Cambridge: Cambridge University Press, 2004), 94–98.

45. Helen Berry, *Gender, Society, and Print Culture in Late Stuart England: The Cultural World of the Athenian Mercury* (Aldershot, UK: Ashgate, 2003), esp. 85; E. J. Clery, *The Feminization Debate in Eighteenth-Century England: Literature, Commerce and Luxury* (Houndsmills, UK: Palgrave Macmillan, 2004), 26–50; "Quest. 1," *Athenian Gazette or Casuistical Mercury* (London), issue 29, July 5, 1692; William Hockmore, *Post Boy* (London, England), issue 410, December 18, 1697; John Bode, *Post Man and the Historical Account* (London, England), issue 459, May 5, 1698; John Bodt, *Flying Post or The Post Master* (London, England), issue 466, May 5, 1698; Godfrey Lee, *Flying Post*, issue 716, December 9, 1699. Dunton also entertained the public with an extensive printed account of his own marital difficulties. John Dunton, *The Case Is Alter'd: Or, Dunton's Re-Marriage to the Same Wife: Being the First Instance of That Nature That Has Been in England: To Which Is Added, the Tender Letters That Pass'd Between This New Bride and Bridegroom: the History of Their Courtship* (London: A. Baldwin, 1701); *The Life and Errors of John Dunton, Late Citizen of London* (London: S. Malthus, 1705).

46. Edward Ward, *The Pleasures of a Single Life, or, The Miseries of Matrimony: Occasionally Writ Upon the Many Divorces Lately Granted by Parliament* (London: J. Nutt, 1701); Lawrence Stone, *The Road to Divorce* (Oxford: Oxford University Press, 1990), 313–22; Lawrence Stone, case studies in *Uncertain Unions and Broken Lives: Marriage and Divorce in England, 1660–1857* (Oxford: Oxford University Press, 1995); Roderick Phillips, *Putting Asunder: A History of Divorce in Western Society* (Cambridge: Cambridge University Press, 1988), 227–28.

47. *Lungworthy v. Hockmore*, discussed in the 1698 report on *Tod v. Stokes*, 12 Modern 244 (88 ER 1294). Holt's judgment appears to have made it into print only once before the 1790s: Charles Viner, *A General Abridgment of Law and Equity* [. . .] (Aldershot, UK, 1748), 174; *English Reports* took it from one of several new editions of Viner published between 1790 and 1795; it can also be found in John Impey, *The Modern Pleader* [. . .] (London: printed for the author, by His Majesty's law-printers, and sold by Joseph Butterworth, 1794), 249.

48. *Baron and Feme: A Treatise of the Common Law concerning Husbands and Wives* [. . .] (London, 1700), 4–5 of unpaginated preface "To the Reader," and 216.

49. Stone, *Road to Divorce*, 320; Thomas R. Meehan, "'Not made out of Levity': Evolution of Divorce in Early Pennsylvania," *Pennsylvania Magazine of History and Biography* 92, no. 4 (1968): 441–64, esp. 442; Phillips, *Putting Asunder*, 142–43.

50. R. B. Outhwaite, *Clandestine Marriage in England, 1500–1850* (Rio Grande, Ohio: Hambledon Press, 1995), 1–19. As Norma Basch has observed in the instance of the nineteenth-century United States: "To make divorce legitimate was to make all other dissolutions illegitimate." *Framing American Divorce*, 320.

51. *Manby v. Scott*, 1 Keble 361 (83 *ER* 995). As we saw in chapter 1, the specific legal disabilities effected by coverture varied according to the legal tradition being applied. Continental civil law acknowledged the separate personhood and interests of married women, at least with regard to questions of property. Britain's courts of chancery used canon law to mediate some of the more stringent restrictions placed on women by the common law. The American colonies for the most part did not have a well-developed separate system of chancery courts, and consequently sometimes admitted principles of equity in common-law courts. Mary Bilder, "Salamanders and Sons of God: The Culture of Appeal in Early New England," in *The Many Legalities of Early America*, ed. Christopher L. Tomlins and Bruce H Mann (Chapel Hill: University of North Carolina Press, 2001), 47–77; Salmon, *Women and the Law of Property*, 58–71; Norton, *Founding Mothers & Fathers*, 83–89.

52. John Jackson, *Boston Gazette*, January 14, 1725; John Jackson (reprint), Jeremiah Clement, *Boston Gazette*, January 18, 1725; John Jackson, *Boston Gazette*, April 5, 1725; Miles Roberts, *Pennsylvania Gazette*, August 13, 1730; William Hutchinson, *American Weekly Mercury*, September 24, 1730; Benjamin Ashton, *Pennsylvania Gazette*, January 12, 1731; Ann Ashton, *Pennsylvania Gazette*, January 26, 1731; Margaret and William Vincent, *New-Hampshire Gazette*, March 16 and March 23, 1759; William and Bulah Holt, *New-Hampshire Gazette*, May 2, 1760; Patrick and Elizabeth Markham, *New-Hampshire Gazette*, May 30, June 13, June 27, 1760; John and Eunice Davis, *New-Hampshire Gazette*, August 29, 1760, July 30, August 6, 1762; Robert and Elizabeth Hastey, *New-Hampshire Gazette*, November 6 and November 27, 1761. Later chapters discuss most of these cases in more detail.

53. Caroline M. Peters, "Derrick Hogeland," *Biographical Dictionary of Pennsylvania Legislators*, ed. Craig Horle (Philadelphia: University of Pennsylvania Press, 1997), 2:504–6. This was not the only time Derrick Hogeland seems to have been attacked, via his children, in the press. In 1756 one of his sons was advertised as a deserter in the *Gazette*, and Derrick was again targeted by name. In the next issue Derrick took out a rebuttal, with testimony on his son's behalf from the chief justice of the province, William Allen. *Pennsylvania Gazette*, April 8 and April 15, 1756.

54. "Reformed Dutch Church, Churchville, Bucks County, PA: Baptisms 1737–1780; Marriages 1738–1772," reprinted in *Pennsylvania Genealogical Magazine* 20, no. 2 (1956).

55. Kirsten Sword, "Wayward Wives, Runaway Slaves and the Limits of Patriarchal Authority in Early America" (PhD diss., Harvard University, 2002), 259, table E.1, "Outcomes of Legal Cases Related to Husbands' Advertisements."

56. William J. Hinke, *Rev. Peter Henry Dorsius: A Paper Presented . . . at a meeting of the Bucks County Historical Society at Doylestown, Pa., January 19, 1918*, BCHS Papers, 1918, 5:1–16, HSP; Howard G. Hageman, *Two Centuries Plus: The Story of New Brunswick Seminary* (Grand Rapids, MI: Wm. B. Eerdmans, 1984), 1–6.

57. Hinke, *Rev. Peter Henry Dorsius*, 15–16; John P. Boehm, William J. Hinke and James I. Good, eds., *Minutes and Letters of the Coetus of the German Reformed Congregations in Pennsylvania, 1747–1792. Together with Three Preliminary Reports of Rev. John Philip Boehm, 1734–1744* (Philadelphia: Reformed Church Publication Board, 1903); Derrick Hogeland, Bucks County Estate File 1571 (microfilm), BCHS.

58. *Oxford English Dictionary*, online ed., s.v. "publish"; "An Act for the preventing of Clandestine Marriages (1702)," *Laws of Pennsylvania* (1728), 28–29 (the procedures in Massachusetts and Virginia were similar); "An Act Concerning Servants and Slaves" (1705), Hening, 3:462; Thomas Baker, *Boston News-Letter*, November 10, 1768. On the importance of oral ceremonies in

constructing legal authority in eighteenth century Virginia, see Rhys Isaac, *The Transformation of Virginia, 1740-1790* (Chapel Hill: University of North Carolina Press for the OIEAHC, 1982), 91-94.

59. Charles E. Clark, *The Public Prints: The Newspaper in Anglo-American Culture, 1665-1740* (New York: Oxford University Press, 1994), 78-79.

60. See the *American Weekly Mercury*, January 2, 1722.

61. *Boston News-Letter*, April 24, 1704.

62. John M'Comb, *American Weekly Mercury*, March 24, 1720; *Boston News-Letter*, October 9, 1704.

63. John Snider, *Pennsylvania Gazette*, May 28, 1730.

64. John Taylor, *American Weekly Mercury*, December 4, 1732.

65. *Boston News-Letter*, April 22, 1706; Waldstreicher, "Reading the Runaways," 243-72.

66. *Weekly Jamaica Courant*, Kingston, 14 surviving issues, 1718-1730, Film NB 243, Harvard University Libraries.

67. "An act for the better government of Servants and Slaves" (1753), Hening, 6:364-66.

68. The *Pennsylvania Gazette* distributed between 1,500 and 2,000 copies of each weekly issue, and served subscribers from Virginia, Maryland, Delaware, and New Jersey, in addition to Philadelphia and its surrounding counties. The *American Weekly Mercury*, the *Gazette*'s predecessor and chief competitor until the 1740s, sought a similar geographic range, but probably retained a much smaller subscriber base. The historian Charles E. Clark estimates that a more typical circulation would have been about 600. This smaller figure was almost certainly applicable to the numerous Boston papers, where fierce competition prevented any one printer from dominating the market. (When these papers are taken together, Boston had the greatest density per capita.) The *Virginia Gazette*, in contrast, was the only paper in Virginia, and its weekly run had grown to roughly 960 by 1751. It served Williamsburg (population roughly 2,000) and also far-flung outlying areas. Clark and Wetherell calculate that before 1749, during Franklin's tenure, ads concerning labor made up 31.5 percent of the *Gazette*'s advertising content, slightly edging out goods for sale at 29.5 percent. Under David Hall, ads for labor slid back to 19.2 percent, nearly tying with ads for real estate at 20.3 percent. See Clark, *The Public Prints*, 206; and Charles E. Clark and Charles Wetherell, "The Measure of Maturity: *The Pennsylvania Gazette*, 1728-1765," *William and Mary Quarterly* 46, no. 2 (1989), 299. Using a different approach, David Waldstreicher determined that ads concerning unfree labor made up 18-26.5 percent of paid notices in the *Pennsylvania Gazette* between 1729 and 1755. Waldstreicher, "Reading the Runaways," 250. Philadelphia's population at this time, to give some perspective, was between ten thousand and fifteen thousand. Estimates from Billy G. Smith, "Death and Life in a Colonial Immigrant City: A Demographic Analysis of Philadelphia," *Journal of Economic History* 37, no. 4 (1977), 863-89; and Susan E. Klepp, *Philadelphia in Transition: A Demographic History of the City and Its Occupational Groups, 1720-1830* (New York: Garland Publishing, 1989), 336.

69. Samuel Allinson, *Pennsylvania Gazette*, December 7, 1774. Tens of thousands of runaway ads appeared in the eighteenth-century press, but this is the only published challenge to one about a person of color. Allinson was a Quaker antislavery activist and prominent lawyer; the runaway in this case remained safely in hiding.

70. *Boston Gazette*, June 28 and July 5, 1748. The wife in this case was a member of the prominent Waldo family.

71. Thomas Jacob, *Pennsylvania Gazette*, July 21, 1748 (his original notice appeared May 7, 1747); William Beard, *Boston Gazette*, November 1, 1748; Jacob Snider, *Pennsylvania Gazette*, June 23, 1748; John Boyden, *Pennsylvania Gazette*, July 28, 1748.

72. Nathaniel Woods, *Boston Gazette*, December 27, 1748.

73. John Rue, *American Weekly Mercury*, September 1, 1748; Lydia Rue, *American Weekly Mercury*, September 22, 1748.

74. See, for example, Benjamin Stewart Jr.'s combination and imitation of ads taken out by Samuel Osborn and John Murphy, *Boston News-Letter*, July 24 and August 14, 1755, April 30, 1756; Timothy Cavanaugh, *Pennsylvania Gazette*, September 18 and October 16, 1766; Thomas Russell, *Virginia Gazette* (Purdie and Dixon), November 6 and November 20, 1766; and Eleazar Coleman, *New-Hampshire Gazette*, April 3 and April 10, 1761.

75. The historian Lawrence Friedman has pronounced the tension between "uniformity and diversity" to be "one of the great, and constant, themes of American law." Friedman, *A History of American Law* (New York: Simon & Schuster, 2005), 5.

Chapter Four

1. William Blackstone, *Commentaries on the Laws of England*, 4 vols. (Oxford: Clarendon Press, 1765), 1:433.

2. Stephen Taylor, "Gibson, Edmund (bap. 1669, d. 1748)," *ODNB*.

3. See Lawrence Stone, *The Road to Divorce* (Oxford: Oxford University Press, 1990), 145, figure 6.1, "Recorded Wife Sales," 247; figure 9.1, "Recorded Criminal Conversation Actions 1680–1849," 325; figure 10.1, "Parliamentary Divorce Petitions and Acts 1700–1857."

4. Mary Bilder, *The Transatlantic Constitution: Colonial Legal Culture and the Empire* (Cambridge, MA: Harvard University Press, 2004), 4.

5. For description and images, see James Oldham, *English Common Law in the Age of Mansfield* (Chapel Hill: University of North Carolina Press, 2004), 14, 43–46; and Clive Emsley, Tim Hitchcock, and Robert Shoemaker, "Historical Background—history of the Old Bailey Courthouse," *Old Bailey Proceedings Online*, version 7.0, October 21, 2019, http://www.oldbaileyonline.org.

6. John H. Baker, *The Common Law Tradition: Lawyers, Books, and the Law* (London: Hambledon Press, 2000), 259; James Oldham, *The Mansfield Manuscripts and the Growth of English Law in the Eighteenth Century* (Chapel Hill: University of North Carolina Press, 1992), 119–21.

7. "The Womens Petition, to the Right Honorable, his Excellency, the most noble and victorious Lord General Cromwell [. . .]," ([London], 1651); Christopher W. Brooks, *Lawyers, Litigation, and English Society since 1450* (London: Hambledon Press, 1998); Margot C. Finn, *The Character of Credit: Personal Debt in English Culture, 1740–1914* (Cambridge: Cambridge University Press, 2003), 197–201, 234–35; Donna T. Andrew, "The Press and Public Apologies in Eighteenth-Century London," in *Law, Crime, and English Society, 1660–1830*, ed. Norma Landau (Cambridge: Cambridge University Press, 2002), 208–29.

8. When authorities acted, they most often compelled misbehaving husbands to admit and swear to amend their errors before witnesses. Scattered references indicate that this was a significant punishment, but its effectiveness is difficult to gauge because it only became a matter of public record when it failed. More severe and less common were formal recognizances, in which a husband secured his promises of good behavior with a bond. Criminal indictment was rarer still, pursued when the threat to public order justified the expense of prosecution. Prosecution might be dropped or delayed indefinitely in the event of settlement that obtained public order. In the colonies, cases in which the parties simply vanish from the local records were more common than those in which the offending couple took their disorder elsewhere.

Similarly, the "tedious and expensive" process of obtaining a divorce might be started with the aim of persuading a reluctant spouse of the merits of private negotiations and abandoned once an agreement was reached. Cases from previous chapters alluded to these kinds of negotiations and to arrangements for separation from bed and board; they left public records only because these earlier settlements failed. Notably, "wife sale" as a means of separation is missing from the fragmentary local records of seventeenth-century marital disputes; if it happened, it was not recorded as part of the legal repertoire. On the distinction between the "low" law of summary jurisdiction and criminal courts in relation to labor, see Douglas Hay and Paul Craven, eds., *Masters, Servants, and Magistrates in Britain and the Empire, 1562–1955* (Chapel Hill: University of North Carolina Press, 2004), 57. On localized justice and connections to the wider literature on the "common peace," see Laura F. Edwards, *The People and Their Peace: Legal Culture and the Transformation of Inequality in the Post-Revolutionary South* (Chapel Hill: University of North Carolina Press, 2009). On legal proceedings in English marital disputes, see Joanne Bailey, *Unquiet Lives: Marriage and Marriage Breakdown in England, 1660–1800* (Cambridge: Cambridge University Press, 2003), 30–52.

9. Mary Bilder, "Salamanders and Sons of God: The Culture of Appeal in Early New England," in *The Many Legalities of Early America*, ed. Christopher L. Tomlins and Bruce H. Mann (Chapel Hill: University of North Carolina Press, 2001), 47–77. On Blackstone's distorting effect on historians understanding of equity, see Peter Hoffer, *The Law's Conscience: Equitable Constitutionalism in America* (Chapel Hill: University of North Carolina Press, 1990); Edwards, *The People and their Peace*, 245; and Thomas Edgar and John Doddridge, *The Lawes Resolutions of Womens Rights* [. . .] (London, 1632), 6.

10. For an instance of the same court simultaneously wearing equitable and common-law hats, see the 1735 Virginia General Court case *Myhil v. Myhil*, which used equitable arguments to overturn the well-established common-law legal fiction that declared a child legitimate so long as both spouses remained within the king's jurisdiction, even if the married couple had no contact. Discussed in David Konig, "Legal Fictions and the Rules of Law: The Jeffersonian Critique of Common-Law Adjudication," in *The Many Legalities of Early America*, 97–117, esp. 109–10. For colonial jurisprudence more generally, see Holly Brewer, *By Birth or Consent: Children, Law, and the Anglo-American Revolution in Authority* (Chapel Hill: University of North Carolina Press, 2007); Terri Snyder, *Brabbling Women: Disorderly Speech and the Law in Early Virginia* (Ithaca, NY: Cornell University Press, 2003); Linda Sturtz, *Within Her Power: Propertied Women in Colonial Virginia* (New York: Routledge, 2002); Mary Beth Norton, *Founding Mothers & Fathers: Gendered Power and the Forming of American Society* (New York: Alfred A. Knopf, 1996); and Cornelia Hughes Dayton, *Women before the Bar: Gender, Law & Society in Connecticut, 1639–1789* (Chapel Hill: University of North Carolina Press for the OIEAHC, 1995).

11. *Flying Post*, London, March 1, 1729, cited in Paula R. Backscheider, "Defoe, Daniel (1660?–1731)," *ONDB*; Taylor, "Gibson, Edmund," *ODNB*.

12. John Smolenski, *Friends and Strangers: The Making of a Creole Culture in Colonial Pennsylvania* (Philadelphia: University of Pennsylvania Press, 2010); Taylor, "Gibson, Edmund," *ODNB*; Edmund Gibson, *Codex Juris Ecclesiastici Anglicani: Or, The Statutes, Constitutions, Canons, Rubricks and Articles, of the Church of England* [. . .], 2 vols. (London: J. Baskett, 1713).

13. Philip C. Yorke, *The Life and Correspondence of Philip Yorke, Earl of Hardwicke, Lord High Chancellor of Great Britain*, 3 vols. (Cambridge: Cambridge University Press, 1913), 1:89–90; William Gerald McLoughlin, *New England Dissent, 1630–1833: The Baptists and the Separation*

of Church and State, 2 vols. (Cambridge, MA: Harvard University Press, 1971), 1:165–243; Bilder, *The Transatlantic Constitution*, 87–90, 105.

14. Travis Glasson, "'Baptism doth not bestow Freedom': Missionary Anglicanism, Slavery, and the Yorke-Talbot Opinion, 1701–30," *William and Mary Quarterly* 67, no. 2 (April 2010): 279–318; Travis Glasson, *Mastering Christianity: Missionary Anglicanism and Slavery in the Atlantic World* (New York: Oxford University Press, 2012); David Brion Davis, *The Problem of Slavery in the Age of Revolution, 1770–1823* (Ithaca, NY: Cornell University Press, 1975), 479. On historians' debt to eighteenth-century antislavery agendas, see Kirsten Sword, "Remembering Dinah Nevil: Strategic Deceptions in Eighteenth-Century Antislavery," *Journal of American History*, September 2010.

15. On evangelical antislavery ambitions, see Glasson, "'Baptism doth not bestow Freedom'"; and Edwin S. Gaustad, *George Berkeley in America* (New Haven, CT: Yale University Press, 1979).

16. John Jackson, *Boston News-Letter*, January 14 and April 5, 1725; *Dorothy Jackson v. John Jackson* (April 26, 1725), Mss. Records of the Court of General Sessions of Suffolk, 3:330, Massachusetts Supreme Judicial Court Records, Massachusetts State Archives; *Catherine Cobb v. Elijah Cobb* (1767), Suffolk Files, no. 129748, 99–101; *Anne Gardner v. David Gardner*, Suffolk Files (1783), no. 129813, 168–70; Elizabeth A. Foyster, *Marital Violence: An English Family History, 1660–1875* (Cambridge: Cambridge University Press, 2005), 1. On lack of privacy, see Nancy F. Cott, "Eighteenth-Century Family and Social Life Revealed in Massachusetts Divorce Records," *Journal of Social History* 10, no. 1 (Autumn 1976): 20–43, esp. 23. The divorce case of Catherine and Elijah Cobb, for example, contained testimony by thirty-four people who had witnessed their quarrels over the years. The exceptional violence of their relationship was not in doubt, but the community differed in opinion as to whether Catherine warranted relief because she was prone to "provoke" her husband by complaining about him in front of others. Anne Gardner complained that her husband's violence and threats had made her friends and family afraid to associate with her, lest they also become his victims. Elizabeth Blair Clark, "The Inward Fire: A History of Marital Cruelty in the Northeastern United States, 1800–1860" (PhD diss., Harvard University, 2006); Elizabeth Blair Clark, "She begged me to take her in: Searching for Relief from a Violent Home in Eighteenth Century Massachusetts: The Case of Katherine Cobb," unpublished MS, courtesy of the author.

17. John Jackson, *Boston News-Letter*, January 14 and April 5, 1725; *Jackson v. Jackson*, General Sessions of Suffolk (April 26, 1725); George Elliott Howard, *A History of Matrimonial Institutions Chiefly in England and the United States*, 3 vols. (Chicago: University of Chicago Press, 1904), 2:340–41; John Jackson, case no. 5299, Suffolk County Probate, 13:424–29.

18. John Jackson, case no. 5299, Suffolk County Probate, 13:424–29, 25:51, 26:96; Glasson, "'Baptism doth not bestow Freedom'"; Bilder, *The Transatlantic Constitution*, 88. The lawyer Robert Auchmuty had an intimate knowledge of the vagaries of marriage law. In 1722, the Massachusetts General Court prosecuted him for living with a woman without following the forms prescribed by Massachusetts marriage laws. He pleaded the validity of alternate forms of private marriage by mutual consent on his own behalf, and a few years later in the case of a client who had been impregnated and then abandoned after a private exchange of promises to marry. Yet he had also built his legal reputation through his sophisticated pleading on behalf of a man accused of abandoning a different woman, here using technicalities stemming from women's disabled status in law to invalidate the woman's testimony. Ann Marie Plane, *Colonial Intimacies: Indian Marriage in Early New England* (Ithaca, NY: Cornell University Press, 2000), 135, 228n26; David H.

Flaherty, "Criminal Practice in Provincial Massachusetts," in *Law in Colonial Massachusetts, 1630–1800: A Conference Held 6 and 7 November 1981*, ed. Daniel R. Coquillette (Boston and Charlottesville, VA: University of Virginia Press for the Colonial Society of Massachusetts, 1984), 191–242, esp. 198–99, 210–11.

19. Samuel Sewall, *The Selling of Joseph: A Memorial* (Boston: Bartholomew Green, and John Allen, 1700).

20. See "Nathaniel Wheeler," "Nathaniel Wheeler, Jr.," and "Susanna Wheatley" entries in the Thwing Index, MHS.

21. Jean R. Soderlund, *Quakers & Slavery: A Divided Spirit* (Princeton, NJ: Princeton University Press, 1985), 23; David Waldstreicher, *Runaway America: Benjamin Franklin, Slavery, and the American Revolution* (New York: Hill and Wang, 2004).

22. Anne Ashton, *Pennsylvania Gazette*, January 26, 1731; Benjamin Ashton, *Pennsylvania Gazette*, January 12, 1731.

23. "Indictment of Elizabeth Ashton for fornication, March Term 1726/27," doc. 68B; "Indictment of Elizabeth wife of Benjamin Ashton Dickup for bigamy," doc. 86; "Indictment of William Wells for bigamy," doc. 66B; all in Bucks County Criminal Papers 1697–1786, BCHS. As with similar cases in England, it is not clear that the severe prescribed punishments were carried out. Pennsylvania's statutory punishment for bigamy was thirty-nine lashes, life imprisonment at hard labor, and the voiding of the second marriage; the English handbook *Baron and Feme* claimed that bigamy remained a capital offense in Britain. *The Laws of the Province of Pennsylvania* [. . .] (Philadelphia: Andrew Bradford, 1714), 37–41; *Baron and Feme: A Treatise of the Common Law concerning Husbands and Wives* [. . .], 1st ed. (London, 1700); Bailey, *Unquiet Lives*.

24. Stone, *Road to Divorce*, 206–9.

25. *The Laws of the Province of Pennsylvania*, 37–41; Benjamin Ashton, Philadelphia Wills, no. 290 (microfilm), 319, HSP.

26. Petition of Anna Maria Boehm Miller, Philadelphia and Montgomery County Papers, collection 144E, box 6, HSP; also transcribed in Martin Duberman, "Male Impotence in Colonial Pennsylvania," *Signs* 4 (1978): 395–401; Gibson, *Codex Juris Ecclesiastici Anglicani*, 535–36; William J. Hinke, *Life and Letters of the Rev. John Philip Boehm, Founder of the Reformed Church in Pennsylvania, 1683–1749* (Philadelphia: Publication and Sunday School Board of the Reformed Church in the United States, 1916), 149–50, http://www.archive.org/details/lifeletter sofrevooboeh; Kevin L. Sterner, "Founding Father: The Ministry of John Philip Boehm," *Der Reggeboge* 52, no. 1 (2018): 3–19; Merril D. Smith, *Breaking the Bonds: Marital Discord in Pennsylvania, 1730–1830* (New York: New York University Press, 1991), 16, 79–82.

27. *Pennsylvania Gazette*, July 29, 1731; David E. Sterner, "The Genealogical Legacy of Rev. John Philip Boehm," *Der Reggeboge* 52, no. 1 (2018): 21–28.

28. Calhoun Winton, "Keimer, Samuel (1689–1742)," *ODNB*. Samuel Keimer's solo printing ventures included serialized extracts of some of the earliest Protestant antislavery writing and Daniel Defoe's somewhat livelier advice books on courtship and domestic affairs. Paula R. Backscheider, "Defoe, Daniel (1660?–1731)," *ODNB*.

29. Waldstreicher, *Runaway America*, 55–83; Benjamin Franklin, *The Autobiography of Benjamin Franklin: With Related Documents*, ed. Louis Masur, 2nd ed. (Bedford/St. Martin's, 2003), esp. 10.

30. Glasson, "'Baptism doth not bestow Freedom'"; McLoughlin, *New England Dissent*, 1:225–39; Taylor, "Gibson, Edmund," *ODNB*.

31. Stone, *Road to Divorce*, 253–54; Oldham, *English Common Law in the Age of Mansfield*, 5.

32. *The Lady's Law: Or, a Treatise of Feme Coverts: Containing All the Laws and Statutes Relating to Women* [. . .] ([London]: 1732), v–viii.

33. Hendrik Hartog, *Man and Wife in America: A History* (Cambridge, MA: 2002), 139–40; Stone, *Road to Divorce*, 26, 44; Oldham, *English Common Law in the Age of Mansfield*, 334–41.

34. Deborah M. Valenze, *The Social Life of Money in the English Past* (Cambridge: Cambridge University Press, 2006), 223–59, esp. 248, 251. The 1745 English case of *Winsmore v. Greenbank* became the decisive precedent regarding the enticement of a "wife to continue absent" from her husband. While ostensibly about a man's right to "the comfort and society" of his wife, the suit was motivated primarily by the husband's loss of access to her separate estate of thirty thousand pounds. The ruling declared such concerns irrelevant, and evidence of the wife's agency in the separation inadmissible (as it was in criminal conversation). A wife's reasons for absenting herself theoretically had no bearing on a husband's right to sue those who kept him from possessing her. Well into the nineteenth century, thanks in large part to Blackstone's reification of the principle, *Winsmore v. Greenbank* was used to defend cases in which the loss of a wife's "comfort," "assistance," and even "service" were at issue. Such arguments drew on old patriarchal ideals, certainly, but both their framing and their frequency made them new legal phenomena in the mid-eighteenth century. *Winsmore v. Greenbank*, Willes 577 (125 ER, 1330).

35. Dunton's connections to better-known radicals and religious reformers of the late seventeenth and eighteenth centuries are remarkable. Dunton traveled between old and New England from the 1680s to the early 1700s and printed the English edition of Samuel Sewall's antislavery pamphlet *The Selling of Joseph*. Dunton's partner in the publication of advice in the *Athenian Mercury* was Samuel Wesley, a schoolmate of Defoe's who became a committed Anglican, a friend of Bishop Gibson, and the father of the Methodist founders John and Charles Wesley. Dunton's first wife Joanna Ainsley was the sister of Susanna Wesley, whose own evangelical leanings and ministry inspired her sons. Joanna Dunton's competence kept John in business, and her death led him into debt as well as political and marital misfortune. Dunton's own writing and marital (as well as extramarital) behavior would have fueled the ire of both Sewall and Bishop Gibson.

36. *Athenian Gazette or Casuistical Mercury*, no. 29 (London, England), July 5, 1692.

37. For an overview of wife sale and its lack of legal sanction in England, see Samuel Pyeatt Menefee, *Wives for Sale: An Ethnographic Study of British Popular Divorce* (Oxford: Basil Blackwell, 1981); Edward Coke, *The Second Part of the Institutes of the Lawes of England* (London, 1642); and Edward Coke, *A Book of Entries Containing Perfect and Approved Presidents of Counts, Declarations, Informations, Pleints, Indictments, Barres, Replications, Rejoynders, Pleadings, Processes, Continuances, Essoines, Issues, Defaults, Departure in Despight of the Court, Demurrers, Trials, Judgements, Executions, and All Other Matters and Proceedings (in Effect) Concerning the Practick Part of the Laws of England* (London, 1671). For the papers of the late eighteenth-century colonial lawyer, see [Miers Fisher], bill of sale for a wife, William Hudson to William Soards, 1767, box 15, call no. (phi) 2094, series 1, Miers Fisher Papers, 1761–1831, HSP.

38. Hendrik Hartog, *Man and Wife in America: A History* (Cambridge, MA: 2002), 139–40; Stone, *Road to Divorce*, 26, 44; Oldham, *English Common Law in the Age of Mansfield*, 334–41. Versions of criminal conversation (*crim con*) existed earlier, but it was rare. It became the subject of titillating pamphlet literature through its connection with one of the first successful petitions for parliamentary divorce in the 1690s. By the 1740s, a series of well-publicized sensational trials helped generate demand, but it became relatively common only in the 1770s, after it became a prerequisite for parliamentary divorce. Accepting it as "ancient" overlooks the

lessons of Hartog's work on the malleable legal arguments about timeless masculine honor in the nineteenth-century United States and much of Stone's own evidence. Stone, *Road to Divorce*, 244–54; Hartog, *Man and Wife in America*, 96–99, 136–142, 346n1; Hendrik Hartog, "Lawyering, Husbands' Rights, and 'the Unwritten Law' in Nineteenth-Century America," *Journal of American History* 84, no. 1 (June 1997): 67–96.

39. Valenze, *The Social Life of Money*, 251.

40. Brewer, *By Birth or Consent*, 121–37; R. B. Outhwaite, *Clandestine Marriage in England, 1500–1850* (Rio Grande, OH: Hambledon Press, 1995); Eve Tavor Bannet, *The Domestic Revolution: Enlightenment Feminisms and the Novel* (Baltimore: Johns Hopkins University Press, 2000), 94–124.

41. Such reasoning also lent itself to broader support for divorce. Ryder cited in Outhwaite, *Clandestine Marriage in England*, 87.

42. Peter D. G. Thomas, "Yorke, Philip, First Earl of Hardwicke (1690–1764)," *ODNB*; *A Letter to the Public: Containing the Substance of* [. . .] *in the Late Debates upon* [. . .] *the Act of Parliament, for the Better Preventing of Clandestine Marriages* (London: Printed for C. Marsh, 1753), 7; Hardwicke cited in David Lieberman, *The Province of Legislation Determined* (Cambridge: Cambridge University Press, 2002), 15. Historians remain divided over whether the legal changes in the act had significant social consequences. Lawrence Stone echoes the supporters of the act who depicted it as a long-overdue effort to rationalize an irrational system. Gillis and Trumbach see it as driving a wedge between the emerging middle class and a lower sort who resisted moralists and retained customary practices of informal marriage and divorce. Outhwaite argues that such claims are overblown and impossible to prove. Bannett has convincingly positioned the act as a pivotal cultural moment that changed the stakes in courtship for women. Probert's more recent "reassessment" concludes that the act simply codified mainstream practices and effected little change. None of these writers considers the debates about the act as anything other than an English phenomenon, even though the critics they cite are disproportionately Scots. Stone, *Road to Divorce*; John R. Gillis, *For Better, for Worse: British Marriages, 1600 to the Present* (New York: Oxford University Press, 1985); Randolph Trumbach, *The Rise of the Egalitarian Family: Aristocratic Kinship and Domestic Relations in Eighteenth-Century England* (New York: Academic Press, 1978); Randolph Trumbach, "Review: Is There a Modern Sexual Culture in the West; Or, Did England Never Change between 1500 and 1900?," *Journal of the History of Sexuality* 1, no. 2 (October 1990): 296–309; Outhwaite, *Clandestine Marriage in England*; Eve Tavor Bannet, *The Domestic Revolution* (Boston: Johns Hopkins University Press, 2000); Rebecca Probert, *Marriage Law and Practice in the Long Eighteenth Century: A Reassessment*, Cambridge Studies in English Legal History (Cambridge: Cambridge University Press, 2009).

43. Stone, *Road to Divorce*, 122–28. The applicability of the act in the colonies was ambiguous. Outhwaite claims that the final version did not extend to marriages conducted overseas, but I have not seen that reference. *Clandestine Marriage in England*, 85–86. An exemption for the colonies and marriages contracted overseas was not mentioned in a photocopy of the bill from Sheila Lambert, ed., *House of Commons Sessional Papers of the Eighteenth Century*, vol. 9, George II Bills 1748–1754 (Wilmington, DE: Scholarly Resources, 1975).

44. In the late 1740s, Hardwicke exercised brutal judgment on the Scottish peers who participated in the Jacobite uprising of 1745 and secured legislative measures suppressing clan identity that helped turn kilt wearing and clan tartans into a paradigmatic example of "invented tradition." Stone, *Road to Divorce*, 122n5; Thomas, "Yorke, Philip"; David Lieberman, "The Legal Needs of a Commercial Society: the Jurisprudence of Lord Kames," in *Wealth and Virtue:*

The Shaping of Political Economy in the Scottish Enlightenment, ed. Michael Ignatieff and Istvan Hont (Cambridge: Cambridge University Press, 1985), 203–34; Eric J. Hobsbawm and Terence O. Ranger, *The Invention of Tradition* (Cambridge: Cambridge University Press, 1992), 20–21.

45. David Hume, *Essays, Moral and Political* (Edinburgh: A. Millar and A. Kincaid, 1748), 247–60. Franklin was working on the topic of population as early as 1751, but the economic questions about slavery and the arguments about the colonists' place within the empire may have come later. Robert Wallace, *A Dissertation on the Numbers of Mankind in Antient and Modern Times . . . and Some Remarks on Mr. Hume's Political Discourse* (Edinburgh: G. Hamilton and J. Balfour, 1753); Benjamin Franklin, "Observations Concerning the Increase of Mankind," in [William Clarke], *Observations On the late and present Conduct of the French, with Regard to their Encroachments upon the British Colonies in North America. . . . To which is added, wrote by another Hand; Observations concerning the Increase of Mankind, Peopling of Countries, &c.* (Boston: S. Kneeland, 1755); B. Barnett Cochran, "Wallace, Robert (1697–1771)," *ODNB*.

46. A. G. Roeber, *Hopes for Better Spouses: Protestant Marriage and Church Renewal in Early Modern Europe, India, and North America* (Grand Rapids, MI: Eerdmans, 2013), 101–2; Stone, *Road to Divorce*, 122n5.

47. A long excursus in Boyd's 1787 treatise on the administration of local justice in Scotland drew particularly explicit links between these jurisdictional politics and Scottish Enlightenment developmental social theories. John Erskine, *The Principles of the Law of Scotland* (Edinburgh: 1754), 64, 260; George Wallace, *A System of the Principles of the Law of Scotland Vol. I* (London and Edinburgh, 1760), 174; Robert Boyd, *The Office, Powers, and Jurisdiction, of His Majesty's Justices of the Peace, and Commissioners of Supply* (Edinburgh: 1787), 377–408.

48. William Cobbett, *Cobbett's Parliamentary History of England* (London: R. Bagshaw, 1806), 89; Rebecca Larson, *Daughters of Light: Quaker Women Preaching and Prophesying in the Colonies and Abroad, 1700–1775* (Chapel Hill: University of North Carolina Press, 2000), 198–230; Barry Levy, *Quakers and the American Family: British Settlement in the Delaware Valley* (New York: Oxford University Press, 1988), 232, 251–62.

49. On the fundamental place of domestic ideals in Quaker politics and by extension in American culture, see Levy, *Quakers and the American Family*, quotation on 71. On Quaker marriage discipline, see Larson, *Daughters of Light*, 133–71; and Phyllis Mack, *Visionary Women: Ecstatic Prophecy in Seventeenth-Century England* (Berkeley: University of California Press, 1992).

50. Outhwaite, *Clandestine Marriage in England*, 85; McLoughlin, *New England Dissent*, 1:190–99.

51. Larson, *Daughters of Light*, 198–230; Levy, *Quakers and the American Family*, 232, 251–62; Jack D Marietta, *The Reformation of American Quakerism, 1748–1783* (Philadelphia: University of Pennsylvania Press, 1984), 3–72; Benjamin H. Newcomb, "Dickinson, John (1732–1808)," *ODNB*.

52. John Woolman, *The Journal and Major Essays of John Woolman*, ed. Phillips P. Moulton (Richmond, IN: Friends United Press, 1989). The mid-eighteenth-century reformation of Quakerism intensified the group's sectarianism, leading historians to overlook connections people like Benezet had to international religious and political radicalism. Benezet grew up among religious refugees in London in the 1720s; his family associated with the same circles as the printer Samuel Keimer and appear to have been the London agents for the secular (but Quaker-loving) philosopher Voltaire. The Benezet family arrived in Philadelphia in the pivotal year of 1729, and subsequently hosted and befriended many of the radical religious figures who passed through the city, including John Wesley, Count Zinzendorf, and George Whitefield. Jean R.

Soderlund, *Quakers & Slavery: A Divided Spirit* (Princeton, NJ: Princeton University Press, 1985), 173–87; Levy, *Quakers and the American Family*, 251–62; Maurice Jackson, *Let This Voice Be Heard: Anthony Benezet, Father of Atlantic Abolitionism* (Philadelphia: University of Pennsylvania Press, 2009), 2–9. For a sample of Benezet's activities, see *Philadelphia Yearly Meeting for Sufferings Minutes* (1771–1775), microfilm, Swarthmore College Quaker Collection, Swarthmore, Pennsylvania.

   53. Nancy F. Cott, "Divorce and the Changing Status of Women in Eighteenth-Century Massachusetts," *William and Mary Quarterly* 33, no. 4 (October 1976): 586–614; Phillips, *Putting Asunder*, 150–51.

   54. Thomas Hutchinson, *The History of the Colony of Massachusets-Bay* (London, 1760), 444–45; William Pencak, "Hutchinson, Thomas (1711–1780)," *ODNB*.

   55. Hutchinson, *The History of the Colony of Massachusets-Bay*, 444–45. On Josselyn and Maverick, see chap. 1; see also Wendy Anne Warren, "'The Cause of Her Grief': The Rape of a Slave in Early New England," *Journal of American History* 93, no. 4 (March 2007): 1031–49; Wendy Anne Warren, *New England Bound: Slavery and Colonization in Early America* (New York: Liveright Publishing Corporation, 2016); Emily Blanck, *Tyrannicide: Forging an American Law of Slavery in Revolutionary South Carolina and Massachusetts* (Athens, GA: University of Georgia Press, 2014), esp. 38–45; William Piersen, *Black Yankees: The Development of an Afro-American Subculture in Eighteenth-Century New England* (Amherst: University of Massachusetts Press, 1988); and Jared Ross Hardesty, *Unfreedom: Slavery and Dependence in Eighteenth-Century Boston* (New York: New York University Press, 2016).

   56. Holly Brewer offers a useful critique of historians' ahistorical uses of Blackstone in "The Transformation of Domestic Law," *CHLA*; see also Hartog, *Man and Wife in America*, 118–35. My argument here in some ways recapitulates Mary Beard's classic critique of Blackstone. The specific equitable remedies Beard cited as counterbalancing Blackstone's assertions about women's legal disempowerment were, as her critics noted, the province of the elite. But at the local level throughout the empire, officials seemed far less concerned about the jurisdictional lines dividing English common law and equity than were metropolitan accounts of those divisions. Mary Ritter Beard, *Woman as Force in History: A Study in Traditions and Realities* (New York: Macmillan, 1946), 78–95, 122–44.

   57. William Blackstone to Sir Roger Newdigate, July 3, 1753, in *The Letters of Sir William Blackstone*, 28–30. On the development of contract law driven by desire to circumvent women's legal claims to separate property, see Susan Staves, *Married Women's Separate Property in England, 1660–1833* (Cambridge, MA: Harvard University Press, 1990). A remarkable letter written in January 1746, when Blackstone was a twenty-three-year-old law student, encompasses his frustration with marriage law and the problem of Scottish rebellion, and lays out his vision for rebuilding the common law. Blackstone to Seymour Richmond, January 1746 and December 7. 1751, in *The Letters of Sir William Blackstone: 1744–1780* (London: Selden Society, 2006), 3–4, 21.

   58. Brooks, *Lawyers, Litigation, and English Society*; Finn, *The Character of Credit*; Blackstone to Seymour Richmond, January 1746, 4.

   59. Blackstone, *Commentaries* (1765), 1:61–62.

   60. Kames cited in Lieberman, "The Legal Needs of a Commercial Society," 229; Blackstone, *Commentaries* (1765), 1:61–62. Blackstone specifically attacked Kames in volume 3. See Lieberman, *The Province of Legislation Determined*, 145, 173.

   61. Blackstone, *Commentaries* (1765), 1:3–26.

62. Of sixty-six sources cited, Coke's *Commentaries on Littleton* accounts for twelve, *Manby* for at least seven; no other case accounts for more than two or three references. Unlike earlier treatises, Blackstone did not trumpet the connection to *Manby*, and scholars have not noticed it because citation of multiple case reports obscures the common source.

63. Hartog, *Man and Wife in America*. Margot Finn reminds us that Blackstone's arguments came from a position of jurisdictional weakness rather than strength, though this point was frequently lost later generations of American jurists, reformers, and historians. Finn, *The Character of Credit*, 197–235.

64. Bridgman O 235 (124 *ER* 564); Blackstone, *Commentaries* (1765), 1:433.

65. William Gouge, *Of Domesticall Duties* (London: George Miller for Edward Brewster, 1634); Defoe, *The Family Instructor* (London, 1715); Gibson, *Family-Devotion: Or, A Plain Exhortation to Morning and Evening Prayer in Families* (Dublin, 1721); William Blackstone, *An Analysis of the Laws of England* (Oxford, 1756), 24; Blackstone, *Commentaries* (1765), 1:123, 410–13.

66. For an example of the historical schema underlying Blackstone and also of the role of Quakers in making it available, see George Wallace's 1760 *A System of the Principles of the Law of Scotland*. Barrister George Wallace, son of the lawyer-turned-historian and population theorist Robert Wallace, built Montesquieu and Frances Hutcheson's abstract critique of slavery into a direct critique of English policy. Anthony Benezet gave Wallace's work a wide and multilingual readership by almost immediately reproducing substantial parts in his antislavery compilations. Jackson, *Let This Voice Be Heard*, 58–60, 142, 172. For an example of Benezet's ability to keep antislavery statements in print (regardless of their original authors' intentions), see George Wallace, *From the United States Chronicle, Thursday, February 19, 1784: In This Paper Last Week a Clear Confutation of the Original Claim to the Right of Slavery Was Given, by Judge Blackstone,—the Subject Is Now Concluded with the Sentiments of That Ingenious Lawyer and Excellent Writer George Wallis* [i.e., Wallace] *as Published in His "System of the Laws of Scotland* (Providence: Bennett Wheeler, 1784).

67. Blackstone, *Commentaries* (1765), 1:417.

68. Blackstone, *Commentaries* (1765), 1:412; William Blackstone to Sir Roger Newdigate, July 3, 1753, in *The Letters of Sir William Blackstone*, 29. For Blackstone's acknowledgment of activists' role in his revision of the discussion of slavery in *Commentaries*, see William Blackstone to Granville Sharp, Bath, October 11, 1768, and Lincolns Inn Fields, February 20, 1769, in "Granville Sharp Letter Book," n.d., Library Company of Philadelphia, Philadelphia, Pennsylvania.

69. Blackstone, *Commentaries* (1765), 1:123; Holt's decisions reprinted in Helen Tunnicliff Catterall, ed., *Judicial Cases Concerning American Slavery and the Negro*, 5 vols. (New York: Negro Universities Press, 1968), 1:11–12. On Benezet's propaganda machine, see Kirsten Sword, "Remembering Dinah Nevil: Strategic Deceptions in Eighteenth-Century Antislavery," *Journal of American History* 97, no. 2 (September 2010): 315–43; and Jackson, *Let This Voice Be Heard*, 58–60, 142, 172. On the importance of the 1730 compromises in 1765, see William Knox, *The Claim of the Colonies to an Exemption from Internal Taxes Imposed by Authority of Parliament, Examined* (London, 1765), discussed in Claire Priest, "Creating an American Property Law: Alienability and Its Limits in American History," *Harvard Law Review* 120, no. 2 (December 2006), 385–459, esp. 55–56. Blackstone's declarations and Benezet's propaganda forced Knox to make a carefully recalibrated defense of the morality of colonial slavery, predicated on the extension of greater imperial authority in the colonies. William Knox, *Three Tracts Respecting the Conversion and Instruction of the Free Indians, and Negroe Slaves in the Colonies Addressed to the Venerable*

Society for Propagation of the Gospel in Foreign Parts (London, 1768); Christopher Leslie Brown, *Moral Capital: Foundations of British Abolitionism* (University of North Carolina Press for the OIEAHC, 2006), 226–27; Leland J. Bellot, "Knox, William (1732–1810)," *ODNB*. On Blackstone's and Mansfield's efforts to contain the jurisdictional consequences of antislavery rhetoric, see Oldham, *English Common Law in the Age of Mansfield*, 312–23, esp. 316–17.

70. Bilder, "English Settlement and Local Governance," 103.

71. John Adams to Jedediah Morse, December 2, 1815, cited in Arthur Lyon Cross, *The Anglican Episcopate and the American Colonies* (New York: Longmans, Green, 1902), 269; Adams's letter and also Francis Alison's to Ezra Stiles, August 7, 1766, cited in Patricia U. Bonomi, *Under the Cope of Heaven: Religion, Society, and Politics in Colonial America* (New York: Oxford University Press, 1986), 200.

72. Paradoxically, Blackstone used his attacks on equity to claim for common-law judges the judicial discretion he denounced as "arbitrary" in other jurisdictions. Lord Mansfield was more directly criticized for using his equitable training to substantively modify common-law rules governing commercial transactions. Thomas Jefferson would later blame Mansfield for introducing and Blackstone for disseminating a "sly poison" that undermined popular sovereignty and thorough legal reform. Oldham, *English Common Law in the Age of Mansfield*, 102–6; Konig, "Legal Fictions and the Rule(s) of Law," 106.

73. Finn, *The Character of Credit*, 197–235.

74. Waldstreicher, *Runaway America*, 55–83; *Autobiography of Benjamin Franklin*.

75. Bishop Gibson and his followers, in contrast, had used the terms of the Union to argue against colonial religious independence from the Anglican Church. McLoughlin, *New England Dissent*, 165–224.

76. Franklin cited in Richard B. Sher, "An 'Agreeable and Instructive Society': Benjamin Franklin and Scotland," in *Sociability and Society in Eighteenth-Century Scotland*, ed. John Alfred Dwyer and Richard B. Sher (Edinburgh: Mercat Press, 1993), 181–93, esp. 190.

Chapter Five

1. Philip Wood, *Pennsylvania Gazette*, January 19, 1774.

2. Defoe cited in Toby Ditz, "Shipwrecked; or, Masculinity Imperiled: Mercantile Representations of Failure and the Gendered Self in Eighteenth-Century Philadelphia," *Journal of American History* 81, no. 1 (1994): 67. On the gendered meanings of credit, see excellent work by Sarah M. S. Pearsall, *Atlantic Families: Lives and Letters in the Later Eighteenth Century* (Oxford: Oxford University Press, 2008); Margot C. Finn, *The Character of Credit: Personal Debt in English Culture, 1740–1914* (Cambridge: Cambridge University Press, 2003); Alexandra Shepard, "Poverty, Labour and the Language of Social Description in Early Modern England," *Past and Present* 201, no. 1 (November 1, 2008): 51–95; and Alexandra Shepard, "Manhood, Credit and Patriarchy in Early Modern England," *Past and Present* 167, no. 1 (November 1, 2000): 75–106.

3. Sarah Knott, *Sensibility and the American Revolution* (University of North Carolina Press for the OIEAHC, 2009); Pearsall, *Atlantic Families*, 80–110.

4. On the "law's shadow" and the nineteenth-century reification of the common law in America, see Michael Grossberg, *A Judgment for Solomon: The d'Hauteville Case and Legal Experience in Antebellum America* (Cambridge: Cambridge University Press, 1996), 2, chap. 3, 6, 7, epilogue; and Hendrik Hartog, *Man and Wife in America: A History* (Cambridge, MA: Harvard University Press, 2000), 118–22.

5. On untenable analytic "divisions between market values and family values," see esp. Pears-all, *Atlantic Families*, 113, and also literature on women's commercial activities and domestic disputes: Finn, *The Character of Credit*; Ellen Hartigan-O'Connor, *The Ties That Buy: Women and Commerce in Revolutionary America* (Philadelphia: University of Pennsylvania Press, 2009); Serena R. Zabin, *Dangerous Economies: Status and Commerce in Imperial New York* (Philadel-phia: University of Pennsylvania Press, 2009); Linda L. Sturtz, *Within Her Power: Propertied Women in Colonial Virginia* (New York: Routledge, 2002); Margaret R. Hunt, *The Middling Sort: Commerce, Gender, and the Family in England, 1680–1780* (Berkeley: University of California Press, 1996); Joanne Bailey, *Unquiet Lives: Marriage and Marriage Breakdown in England, 1660–1800* (Cambridge: Cambridge University Press, 2003); Elizabeth A. Foyster, *Marital Violence: An English Family History, 1660–1875* (Cambridge: Cambridge University Press, 2005); Mary Beth Sievens, *Stray Wives: Marital Conflict in Early National New England* (New York: New York University Press, 2005).

6. Charles E. Clark, *The Public Prints: The Newspaper in Anglo-American Culture, 1665–1740* (New York: Oxford University Press, 1994); Charles E. Clark and Charles Wetherell, "The Measure of Maturity: *The Pennsylvania Gazette*, 1728–1765," *William and Mary Quarterly* XLVI, no. 2 (1989): 279–303; Bruce H. Mann, *Republic of Debtors: Bankruptcy in the Age of American In-dependence* (Cambridge, MA: Harvard University Press, 2002), 36; Craig Muldrew, *The Economy of Obligation: The Culture of Credit and Social Relations in Early Modernå England* (New York: St. Martin's Press, 1998); Finn, *The Character of Credit*.

7. I am indebted to James N. Green, associate librarian of the Library Company of Philadel-phia, for this interpretation of Franklin's bequests; the ledger in which Franklin listed his debts contains hundreds of accounts, "most of them decades old and most of them for a few shillings for ads in the Gazette." Green, email to author, November 30, 2001.

8. Mann, *Republic of Debtors*, 12–13.

9. On colonists' simultaneous reliance on and distrust of lawyers, the demand-driven ex-pansion of the legal system, and widespread litigious behavior, see Peter Charles Hoffer, *Law and People in Colonial America* (Baltimore: Johns Hopkins University Press, 1998), 44–46, 81; and Cornelia Hughes Dayton, *Women before the Bar: Gender, Law, and Society in Connecticut, 1639–1789* (Chapel Hill, NC: University of North Carolina Press for the OIEAHC, 1995), 91. While most American lawyers trained in the colonies, a striking number of colonial legal educators were Scots-born and/or educated. James A. Henretta, "Magistrates, Common Lawyers, Legisla-tors: The Three Legal Systems of Early America," in *CHLA*, 555–592, esp. 578. On the influx of Scottish-trained lawyers and on Americans studying law in Glasgow, Edinburgh, and by 1760s with Blackstone, see *The Letters of Sir William Blackstone: 1744–1780*, ed. Wilfrid Prest (London: Selden Society, 2006); Alan L Karras, *Sojourners in the Sun: Scottish Migrants in Jamaica and the Chesapeake, 1740–1800* (Ithaca, NY: Cornell University Press, 1992); and Bruce Mann, "The Transformation of Law and Economy in Early America," in *CHLA*.

10. Kirsten Sword, "Wayward Wives, Runaway Slaves and the Limits of Patriarchal Author-ity in Early America" (Harvard University, 2002), appendix C, 253–56.

11. Daniel Vickers, *Farmers & Fishermen: Two Centuries of Work in Essex County Massachu-setts, 1630–1850* (Chapel Hill: University of North Carolina Press for the OIEAHC, 1994): 15–20; Alexandra Shepard, "Poverty, Labour and the Language of Social Description in Early Modern England," *Past and Present* 201, no. 1 (November 1, 2008): 51–95.

12. Hinsdale served as a town selectman in 1748 and again in 1771 and 1772. He served in the Massachusetts House of Representatives in 1771, 1772, and 1775. John A. Schutz, *Legislators of*

the Massachusetts General Court, 1691–1780: A Biographical Dictionary (Boston: Northeastern University Press, 1997), 251.

13. Timothy Cavenaugh, *Pennsylvania Gazette*, September 18, 1766, and August 17, 1774; F. Edward Wright, ed., *Tax List of Chester County, 1768* (Westminster, Maryland: Family Line Publications, 1989), 65.

14. Georg Simon Tampler and Johann Andreas Seuling advertised only in Philadelphia's German-language papers. *Pennsylvanische Staatsbote*, February 18 and July 21, 1772; other difficulties with language can be inferred from the garbled English spelling of German and Irish names. See, for example, Charles McGlaucklen/McGlauchlen, *Boston Gazette*, August 24, 1742; John McGlaughlin, mariner, *Boston Gazette*, September 3, 1772.

15. One-third of those whose ads place them in the vicinity of tax collectors in years with surviving tax lists do not appear on them. If one expands the window of advertisement years or narrows the criteria used for identifying advertisers, the proportion missing climbs to near 70 percent. Because tax lists are our only approximation of census data before 1790, it is difficult to determine whether these figures are abnormally high or simply the ordinary margin of error one might expect from imperfect sources. On systematic undercounting of the poor, disenfranchised, and mariners, see Karin Wulf, "Assessing Gender: Taxation and the Evaluation of Economic Viability in Late Colonial Philadelphia," *Pennsylvania Magazine of History and Biography* CXXI, no. 3 (1997), 201–35; Gary Nash, "Urban Wealth and Poverty in Pre-Revolutionary America," *Journal of Interdisciplinary History* 6, no. 4 (1976), 545–84; Billy G. Smith, *The "Lower Sort": Philadelphia's Laboring People, 1750–1800* (Ithaca, NY: Cornell University Press, 1990), 213–15.

16. Uriah Snow, *Boston News-Letter*, October 3, 1771; Uriah Snow warned from Boston, May 22, 1769, Suffolk Files, no. 89009; Cornelia H. Dayton and Sharon V. Salinger, *Robert Love's Warnings: Searching for Strangers in Colonial Boston* (Philadelphia: University of Pennsylvania Press, 2014); Ruth Wallis Herndon, *Unwelcome Americans: Living on the Margin in Early New England* (Philadelphia: University of Pennsylvania Press, 2001), 1–21; Nash, "Urban Wealth and Poverty," 562–65.

17. John Taylor, *Pennsylvania Gazette*, December 13, 1770; Peter J. Coleman, *Debtors and Creditors in America: Insolvency, Imprisonment for Debt, and Bankruptcy, 1607–1900* (Madison: University of Wisconsin Press, 1974), 41, 141–43; Laurel Thatcher Ulrich, *A Midwife's Tale: The Life of Martha Ballard, Based on Her Diary, 1785–1812* (New York: Vintage Books, 1990), 264–269; Christine Daniels, "'Without any Limitacon of Time': Debt Servitude in Colonial America," *Labor History* 36, no. 2 (1995), 232–50; Vickers, *Farmers & Fishermen*, 202–3, 270–73; and Daniel Vickers, "Nantucket Whalemen in the Deep-Sea Fishery: The Changing Anatomy of an Early American Labor Force," *Journal of American History* 72, no. 2 (1985), 277–96.

18. Samuel Oldham, *Boston News-Letter*, April 20, 1769; George Beck, *Pennsylvania Gazette*, November 5, 1767; Ebenezer Smith, *Boston News-Letter*, May 15, 1740; Georg Simon Tampler, *Pennsylvanische Staatsbote*, February 18, 1772; Benjamin Crawfourd, *Pennsylvania Gazette*, May 21, 1767; wording for Crawfourd from James Dockham, *New-Hampshire Gazette*, February 13, 1793. See also John Hood, *Pennsylvania Gazette*, October 20, 1768. On the strategic uses of similar claims in eighteenth-century England, see Bailey, *Unquiet Lives*, 75–76.

19. Mary Willington, *Boston Evening-Post*, July 12, 1762, 3.

20. Timothy Cavenaugh, *Pennsylvania Gazette*, September 18, 1766 and August 17, 1774; Wright, ed. *Tax List of Chester County, 1768*, 65; Jack Marietta et al., "Tax List of Chester County, 1775," datafile, CCA.

21. Sword, "Wayward Wives," appendix C.

22. Moses Lyon, *Boston News-Letter*, May 4, 1767; Vinkler Jones, *Virginia Gazette* (Purdie and Dixon), April 1, 1773; Samuel Blaker, *Pennsylvania Gazette*, September 20, 1770.

23. Richard B. Sher, *The Enlightenment & the Book: Scottish Authors & Their Publishers in Eighteenth-Century Britain, Ireland, & America* (Chicago: University of Chicago Press, 2006), 518–23.

24. John Taylor, *Pennsylvania Gazette*, December 13, 1770. On "deputy husbands," see Laurel Thatcher Ulrich, *Good Wives: Image and Reality in the Lives of Women in Northern New England, 1650–1750* (New York: Vintage Books, 1991), 35–50. On early American women's working lives, see chap. 1; Ulrich, *A Midwife's Tale*; Laurel Thatcher Ulrich, *The Age of Homespun: Objects and Stories in the Creation of an American Myth* (New York: Alfred A. Knopf 2001); Joan M. Jensen, *Loosening the Bonds: Mid-Atlantic Farm Women, 1750–1850* (New Haven, CT: Yale University Press, 1986); Hartigan-O'Connor, *The Ties That Buy*; Zabin, *Dangerous Economies*; and Sturtz, *Within Her Power.*

25. Moses Lyon, *Boston News-Letter*, May 4, 1767. In colonial Virginia, powers of attorney primarily "served the distinctive interest of commercially active" and "relatively prosperous families." Mary Beth Norton has documented a few instances in which seventeenth-century courts refused to uphold transactions in which a wife acted without formal permission. Like ads discrediting wives, such court cases testify to the willingness of laypeople (at least, in small matters) to accept a wife as the representative of a couple's joint interests. Linda Sturtz, " 'As Though I My Self Was Pr[e]sent': Virginia Women with Power of Attorney," in *The Many Legalities of Early America*, Christopher L. Tomlins and Bruce H. Mann eds. (Chapel Hill: University of North Carolina Press, 2000), 250–71; Sturtz, *Within Her Power*; Norton, *Founding Mothers & Fathers: Gendered Power and the Forming of American Society* (New York: Alfred A. Knopf, 1996), 84–86.

26. Quotations from Vinkler Jones, *Virginia Gazette* (Purdie and Dixon), April 1, 1773. On female extravagance, see Bailey, *Unquiet Lives*, 75; Finn, *The Character of Credit*, 25–63; Daniel Defoe, *Moll Flanders* (Toronto: Dover Publications, 1996), 41–42.

27. John Berrow, *Virginia Gazette*, December 5, 1751; David Carslack, *Pennsylvania Gazette*, November 20, 1776.

28. A total of 159 advertisers in my colonial sample accused their wives of some sort of theft, but very few specified what was taken. Eighteen indicated that household goods or furniture were the issue; nine mentioned clothing. John Connor, *Pennsylvania Gazette*, April 17, 1782; Lawrence Sandman, *Pennsylvania Gazette*, August 27, 1777. John McClelland, in the *Pennsylvania Gazette*, October 31, 1765, announced a mutually agreed separation with his wife in which she had taken "with her all her Apparel, and such Furniture as she brought to me since our Marriage." Newspapers occasionally ran stories of women who married in their shifts (undergarments) as a symbolic, extralegal way of indicating that they brought none of the financial assets or obligations of their first marriages with them to their new husbands. *Pennsylvania Gazette*, February 27, 1734, picked up by *Boston Gazette*, April 1, 1734; *New-Hampshire Gazette*, March 7, 1760. On women's personal property, see Ulrich, *The Age of Homespun*, 108–41; Toby Ditz, *Property and Kinship: Inheritance in Early Connecticut, 1750–1820* (Princeton, NJ: Princeton University Press, 1986), 126; and Marylynn Salmon, *Women and the Law of Property in Early America* (Chapel Hill: University of North Carolina Press, 1986).

29. Samuel Blaker, *Pennsylvania Gazette*, September 20, 1770, and October 11, 1775.

30. Samuel Blaker, *Pennsylvania Gazette*, October 11, 1775; Samuel Blaker, will and inventory, Bucks County Probate Records, BCHS; emphasis mine.

31. Samuel Blaker, will and inventory, Bucks County Probate Records, BCHS; Catherine Blaker and Andrew McMicken, *Pennsylvania Gazette*, July 17, 1782.

32. Zabdiel Fitch, *Boston News-Letter*, October 5, 1769; John Jaquet, *Pennsylvania Gazette*, August 27, 1783.

33. Sarah Wiggin, *New-Hampshire Gazette*, September 2, 1768; Thomas Elliot, *Virginia Gazette*, October 15, 1772; John Stickney, *Boston Evening-Post*, March 10, 1760; Edward Jones, *Pennsylvania Gazette*, October 13, 1743 and June 28, 1744.

34. Sword, "Wayward Wives," research database and appendix E. The proportions in the sample of English ads pulled from the digital Burney collection are similar, as are those in Bailey, *Unquiet Lives*, 217, appendix 20.

35. Sword, "Wayward Wives," appendix E. Similarly, less than 10 percent of English ads made such charges explicit.

36. The proliferation of husbands' postings and wives' rebuttals tells us more about shifts in legal consciousness than about changing sexual culture; greater legal literacy allowed effective manipulation of formal rules but did not indicate compliance with them, contrary to interpretations that see advertisers' allusions to adultery as evidence of female sexual rebellion. Clare A. Lyons, *Sex among the Rabble: An Intimate History of Gender & Power in the Age of Revolution, Philadelphia, 1730–1830* (Chapel Hill: University of North Carolina Press for the OIEAHC, 2006).

37. Thomas Jacob, *Pennsylvania Gazette*, July 21, 1748.

38. John McGlaughlin, *Boston News-Letter*, September 3, 1772.

39. The patterns in English elopement notices were similar. This language evoked wifely disobedience and a husband's fear of public disgrace, but stopped short of explicit references to "criminal" sexual conduct. Sexual allusions in ads overlapped imperfectly with the vocabulary from Puritan sermons that Richard Godbeer has analyzed in *Sexual Revolution in Early America* (Baltimore: Johns Hopkins University Press, 2002), chaps. 3 and 5.

40. William Pyle, *Pennsylvania Gazette*, August 29, 1771; Charles Prosser, *New-York Gazette*, April 19, 1762.

41. Martha Reamy, *Early Church Records of Chester County Pennsylvania* (Westminster, MD: Willow Bend Books, 1999), 3:57; William Pyle, *Pennsylvania Gazette*, September 29, 1757; Chester County Court of Quarter Sessions, docket 6, 1742–59:299–300 and file papers for March court, 1758, CCA.

42. William Pyle, *Pennsylvania Gazette*, May 12, 1773; Chester County Court of Quarter Sessions, papers, August 1773. See also Merril D. Smith, *Breaking the Bonds: Marital Discord in Pennsylvania, 1730–1830* (New York: New York University Press, 1991), 165–66.

43. William Blackstone, *Commentaries on the Laws of England* (Philadelphia: Robert Bell, 1771). On the publishing history of this edition, see Sher, *The Enlightenment & the Book*, 518–23.

44. Daniel Wismar, *Pennsylvania Gazette*, December 15, 1763.

45. In their superb studies of the legal culture of nineteenth-century American marriage, Hendrik Hartog and Norma Basch describe a nineteenth-century world in which couples "looked to the law" for remedies to their marital conflicts because "courts were where one did such things." When we examine marital separations through the lens postings of wayward wives, however, it becomes clear that at least until 1790—and probably for quite some time afterward— the courts were the arena of last resort. Hartog, *Man and Wife in America*, 1, 6; Basch, *Framing American Divorce: From the Revolutionary Generation to the Victorians* (Berkeley: University of California Press, 1999). On the continuing importance of "friends" and extralegal mediation in the nineteenth century, see Mary Beth Sievens, *Stray Wives: Marital Conflict in Early National New England* (New York: New York University Press, 2005); and Laura F. Edwards, *The People*

and Their Peace: Legal Culture and the Transformation of Inequality in the Post-Revolutionary South (Chapel Hill: University of North Carolina Press, 2009).

46. John Hope Franklin and Loren Schweninger, *Runaway Slaves: Rebels on the Plantation* (New York: Oxford University Press, 1999), 100–107; Daniel E. Meaders, *Dead or Alive: Fugitive Slaves and White Indentured Servants before 1830* (New York and London: Garland Publishing, 1993); Gerald W. Mullin, *Flight and Rebellion: Slave Resistance in Eighteenth-Century Virginia* (New York: Oxford University Press, 1972), 55–58; Philip D. Morgan, "Colonial South Carolina Runaways: Their Significance for Slave Culture," *Slavery and Abolition* 6, no. 3 (1985), 57–78.

47. Chester County Court of Quarter Sessions, papers, August 1773; Smith, *Breaking the Bond*, 165–66.

48. Hendrik Hartog, "Marital Exits and Marital Expectations in Nineteenth Century America," *Georgetown Law Journal* 80 (1991), 110.

49. At minimum, 7 percent of advertised couples were permanently reunited. When wives who separated and returned "sundry" times are also counted, the combined rate of temporary and permanent reconciliation rises to roughly 15 percent. These figures at first seem similar to the proportion of newspaper disputes that ended in divorce, but differences in the sources render the comparison superficial. Negotiations that led to a couple's reconciliation usually left formal records only when they broke down, creating gaps in the records that lead to undercounts relative to divorce, where missing data is less of a factor.

50. Sievens, *Stray Wives*, 87–89.

51. John Ross, *American Weekly Mercury*, October 15, 1741; Edward Day, *Pennsylvania Gazette*, December 11, 1760; Obadiah Cookson, *Boston Gazette*, June 28, 1748; John Holbrook, *Boston Gazette*, September 17, 1754. Cookson's advertisement had prompted the editors of the *Boston Gazette* to require that future wife ads come to press with certification from a magistrate, as discussed in chapter 3.

52. Abigail Hubbard, *Connecticut Courant*, September 4, 1775.

53. Mark Keith, *Boston News-Letter*, June 30, 1763; comparison of elopement and runaway ads based on Sword, "Wayward Wives" database, and runaway ads in "The Geography of Slavery in Virginia," http://www2.vcdh.virginia.edu/gos/explore.html; Bailey, *Unquiet Lives*, 55.

54. Philip Wood, *Pennsylvania Gazettte*, January 19, 1774; David Rice, *New-Hampshire Gazette*, July 15, 1768; Peter Heyett, *Pennsylvania Gazette*, July 11, 1765.

55. Sixteen ads concerning wives offered some sort of reward. All except three were from the middle colonies, and four were in German-language papers. Massachusetts had two, one of which is a probably a parody, and the other by a husband of German origin. German-language advertisements did not adhere to a firm linguistic distinction between "running away" (*weglaufen*) as an activity for servants and "eloping" as an activity for wives. Although this might suggest comparably less respect within the German community for the distinctive status of wives, advertisements also indicate that married women retained more independent control of economic resources than did Anglo-American women. Advertisements in which wives discredit husbands account for 6 percent of all the discreditings in the German-language press, but only 1 percent of those in the English-language press. At least half of such ads in the English press were taken out by women who were clearly of German origin.

56. The exception is intriguing as evidence of the wife's role in the establishment of a household's economic credit and of sexual reputation as important to men: "Whereas Sarah the wife of John Bazin, eloped from his home by the Enticement of some ill minded Persons, he being

absent from Home, and carried away almost all his Linen, Money, Bonds and Notes of Hand, and sundry other Things, to his great Ruin and Damage, who was obliged to hire a Woman to take care of his House, which may cause unthinking People to give them a bad Name: These are therefore to forewarn all Persons whatsoever to harbour, entertain or Credit her, upon the Penalty of being prosecuted according to Law, and not to trust or credit her on any Account whatsoever; declaring, that I will not pay any Debts she shall contract after this Time and also if any Person conveys her Home, and the Things above mentioned, or part of them, they shall have Ten Pounds in Cash, Old Tenor, paid by John Bazin." *Boston Evening-Post*, December 27, 1742. See also Alexandra Shepard, *Meanings of Manhood in Early Modern England* (Oxford: Oxford University Press, 2003).

57. John Brown, *Pennsylvania Gazettte*, October 20, 1768.

58. Nicholas Sournas, *Virginia Gazette*, October 31, 1751.

59. Samuel Huggins, *Pennsylvania Gazette*, August 10, 1785, August 20, 1794, and October 1, 1794. The second elopement did prompt Huggins to seek a divorce, though his decision to do so came in 1794, after the liberalization of New Jersey's divorce laws.

60. For analysis of patterns in adultery prosecution in New England, see Dayton, *Women before the Bar*, 164–73.

61. William Holt, *New-Hampshire Gazette*, May 2, 1760.

62. See chap. 2 and 3; see also examples in Laura Gowing, *Domestic Dangers: Women, Words, and Sex in Early Modern London* (Oxford: Clarendon Press, 1996), 253–58; and Pearsall, *Atlantic Families*, 220–21.

63. Bruce H. Mann, *Neighbors and Strangers: Law and Community in Early Connecticut* (Chapel Hill: University of North Carolina Press, 1987), chap. 1, esp. 18, 23.

64. Dennis Donovan and Jacob Andrews Woodward, *The History of the Town of Lyndeborough, New Hampshire, 1735–1905* (Tufts College Press, H. W. Whittemore, 1906), 773–74.

65. Elizabeth Markham, *New-Hampshire Gazette*, June 13, 1760.

66. Patrick Markham, *New-Hampshire Gazette*, June 27, 1760.

67. *Samuel Hogg v. Patrick Markham*, court file 28369, New Hampshire State Archives.

68. The figure includes eleven divorce cases, mostly from Massachusetts, which I include because they did not differ much from separate maintenance suits in other colonies. The women involved were sometimes awarded "full divorce" with alimony, but they generally weren't seeking it.

69. See the discussion of localized law in chapter 4. On inconclusive marital litigation in England, see Bailey, *Unquiet Lives*, 30–60.

70. *New-Hampshire Gazette*, June 27, 1766, 1, col. 3.

Chapter Six

1. *Baron and Feme: A Treatise of Law and Equity, Concerning Husbands and Wives* (London: 1738). On the reification of the common law, see chap. 4, 7–8, and epilogue; see also Hendrik Hartog, *Man and Wife in America: A History* (Cambridge, MA: Harvard University Press, 2000), 118–22. For the phrase "In Justice to my Character," used for the chapter title, see Katherine Kirkpatrick, rebuttal of John Kirkpatrick, *Pennsylvania Gazette*, August 11, 1768.

2. The 1785 Act Concerning Divorce was a paradigmatic example of the problems with interpreting postrevolutionary American divorce laws as "revolutionary"; see chap. 8.

3. *Baron and Feme* was offered for sale several times in the *Pennsylvania Gazette* during the 1760s, so a copy could have found its way into her hands. Dates advertised for sale: October 29, 1761, December 2, 1762, April 28, 1763, December 13, 1764, June 27, 1765, January 23, 1766, March 27, 1782.

4. Ann and Philip Wood appear to have moved to Bucks County, Pennsylvania, sometime after their marriage and the births of their children, and it has consequently been impossible to trace her kin and life before her union with Phillip. She was not mentioned in Philip's will and seems to have predeceased him. Neither does she appear in any surviving land, church, or probate records from Bucks County.

5. Ann Wood, *Pennsylvania Gazette*, February 9, 1774.

6. On the law's shadow, see chap. 5, note 4.

7. John Elwell, *Pennsylvania Gazette*, November 2, 1772. Such retractions were themselves evidence that not all wives who might have turned to the press did so; only one of these public apologies was spurred by a wife's rebuttal.

8. It also corresponds to an influx of Scottish-trained lawyers and with Americans studying law in Glasgow, Edinburgh and by the 1760s, with Blackstone; see chap. 5, note 9. On booksellers, see Richard B. Sher, *The Enlightenment & the Book: Scottish Authors & Their Publishers in Eighteenth-Century Britain, Ireland, & America* (Chicago: University of Chicago Press, 2006); and Ruth H. Bloch, "Changing Conceptions of Sexuality and Romance in Eighteenth-Century America," *William and Mary Quarterly* 60, no. 1 (2003): 13–42.

9. Clare A. Lyons, *Sex among the Rabble: An Intimate History of Gender & Power in the Age of Revolution, Philadelphia, 1730–1830* (Chapel Hill: University of North Carolina Press for the OIEAHC, 2006), 175; Joanne Bailey, *Unquiet Lives: Marriage and Marriage Breakdown in England, 1660–1800* (Cambridge: Cambridge University Press, 2003), 56–60, 201.

10. Bailey, *Unquiet Lives*, 56–59, 149–66, 174–78, 213, 217.

11. One of the earlier disputes involved a New Hampshire couple who turned to the Massachusetts papers because their own colony did not yet have a newspaper; Sarah Dwyer, *Boston Post-Boy*, December 12, 1753; Loyalty and American Liberty, *Pennsylvania Packet*, November 22, 1773; reprinted in the *Boston Weekly News-Letter*, January 13, 1774; discussed in chapter 7, table 5.2, figure 5.2, table 6.1, and figure 6.2.

12. Elizabeth Markham, *New-Hampshire Gazette*, June 13, 1760.

13. At least nine of the twenty-seven (33 percent) advertisements in which wives took the initiative in denouncing their husbands were placed by Pennsylvania women who either used the German-language press or who had distinctively German names. Only a handful of English-language ads inverted the form in the same manner. See chap. 5, note 55. On German colonists' negotiation of English marriage practices, see A. G. Roeber, *Hopes for Better Spouses: Protestant Marriage and Church Renewal in Early Modern Europe, India, and North America* (Grand Rapids, MI: William B. Eerdmans, 2013), chap. 6.

14. See, for example, Charity Welch, petition, *New-Hampshire Gazette*, July 23, 1781.

15. *Baron and Feme* (1738), 9; Cornelia Hughes Dayton, *Women before the Bar: Gender, Law & Society in Connecticut, 1639–1789* (Chapel Hill: University of North Carolina Press for the OIEAHC, 1995), 136–37. By the nineteenth century, in contrast, legal authorities were more vocal in their condemnations of domestic violence. This expansion of the role of formal legal authorities went hand in hand with an understanding of domestic privacy that made neighbors reluctant to intervene, and arguably left women with fewer resources. Bailey, *Unquiet Lives*; Elizabeth

A. Foyster, *Marital Violence: An English Family History, 1660–1875* (Cambridge: Cambridge University Press, 2005).

16. *Baron and Feme* (1738), 259, 434.

17. Sword, "Wayward Wives," 261, appendix E, table 6, "Legal Claims in Wives' Rebuttals (Inclusive)."

18. Dayton, *Women before the Bar*, 136.

19. Moreover, half of the sixteen deserting wives in Dayton's study had been previously married. They brought to their new relationships "the example of the previous husband to measure against the experiences of the second." As widows, they had experience independently managing their households and a claim to their first husbands' estates. These deserting wives were also from communities at a distance from their husbands' homes, giving them places to which they could return and be judged according to their own reputations rather than the scandals attached to their marriages. Dayton, *Women before the Bar*, 146.

20. Louise Leddel, *Pennsylvania Gazette*, January 23, 1753; Lydia Anderson, *Pennsylvania Gazette*, October 7, 1763; Mary Dicks, *Pennsylvania Gazette*, January 21, 1762; Jane Tennant, *Pennsylvania Gazette*, January 15, 1767; Margaret Bannerman, *Virginia Gazette* (Purdie and Dixon), January 12, 1768, July 17, 1768, May 25, 1769; Mary Meyer, *Pennsylvanische Staatsbote*, August 17, 1773; Sword, "Wayward Wives," 258, appendix D, table 3, "Economic Distribution of Wives Placing Newspaper Advertisements," and 261, appendix E, table 7, "Percentage of Wives' Direct Responses Indicating That Dispute Involved Control of Property."

21. Sophia Conner, *Pennsylvania Gazette*, February 26, 1767.

22. Dayton, *Women before the Bar*, 149–54, esp. n84.

23. Elizabeth Dunlap, *American Weekly Mercury*, June 17–24, 1742, and *Pennsylvania Gazette*, June 17, 1742.

24. Priscilla Butler, *New-Hampshire Gazette*, August 15, 1765; *Baron and Feme* (1738), 259.

25. Precillia Howard, *Boston Post-Boy*, January 11, 1773; *Precilla Howard v. Simon Howard*, February 18, 1773, Suffolk Files, no. 129771, Massachusetts Divorces, vol. 794, p. 54, MAC. On equity and debt litigation in Massachusetts, see David Konig, "Regionalism in Early American Law," in *CHLA*, 144–77, esp. 175. Unlike Priscilla Butler in New Hampshire or Ann Wood in Pennsylvania, Precillia Howard threatened legal action as well as moral condemnation her advertisement, apparently because she hoped that Massachusetts divorce laws would provide equitable remedies not available in her local courts. In this instance, a husband's advertisement pushed the wife to pursue legal solutions. The Massachusetts governing council heard and dismissed her case in February 1773, judging her not to have sufficient evidence of Simeon's life-threatening cruelty. The political context examined in the remaining chapters might have contributed to the court's conservativism.

26. "Mittimus a Phillip Woods," doc. 2779, Bucks County Criminal Papers 1697–1786, BCHS.

27. Psalm 109:1–2, 5, King James Version.

28. Psalm 109:6–7, 9–13, 16–17, King James Version.

29. Rachel Terry, *Boston Gazette*, August 18, 1747.

30. Barbara Arndorff, *Pennsylvania Gazette*, February 14, 1771.

31. John Arndorff, *Pennsylvania Gazette*, February 21, 1771. John attempted to discredit Barbara again in 1777; she responded by advertising him as a runaway and an adulterer. We don't know her fate, but he apparently settled with his new partner in Virginia, leaving his estate to the children of this second relationship in 1798. John Arndorff, *Pennsylvania Gazette*, April 16, 1777; Barbara Ornduff, *Pennsylvania Gazette*, April 23, 1777. Genealogical data available at https://

www.wikitree.com/wiki/Orndorff-50. Lawyerly reference to the "very superstitious Dutch" refers to a case in which a man accused of murdering his mother-in-law defended himself by claiming (earnestly) that she was a witch. Jaspar Yeates, Miscellaneous Trial Notes, June 1779, *Respublica v. Frederick Flake, Herr Flake & Elizabeth his wife*, Jacob Flake and John Flake, folder 2, Misc. Legal Papers 1777–1781, Yeates Family Papers, 1718–1876, HSP.

32. Sara McDougall and Sarah Pearsall, "Introduction: Marriage's Global Past," *Gender & History* 29, no. 3 (October 2017): 505–28; Sarah Pearsall, "'Having Many Wives' in Two American Rebellions: The Politics of Households and the Radically Conservative," *American Historical Review* 118, no. 4 (October 2013): 1001–28; Sarah Pearsall, *Polygamy: An Early American History* (New Haven, CT: Yale University Press, 2019).

33. Samuel Richardson, *Pamela*, 1st ed. (London, 1741–42), 2:140.

34. Psalm 102:8, 11; Samuel Richardson, *Clarissa*, 3rd ed., 8 vols. (London, 1751), 7:153–54.

35. They began to appear in divorce proceedings during this period as well.

36. Richardson, *Clarissa*, 7:56–57.

37. These descriptions of men were used by numerous wives and dozens of times by Richardson. Wives could not directly describe themselves in the language Richardson used to glorify his heroine without compromising their claims to modesty; instead they cited the "good opinion" of their neighbors and their own forbearance in giving the reader only as much information about their grievances as was necessary for self-protection.

38. Ann Weaver, *Pennsylvania Gazette*, September 20, 1780; Edith Brooks, *Pennsylvania Packet*, April 14, 1785; Elisabeth Zieganhan, *Pennsylvanische Staatsbote*, April 23, 1777; Rachel Gardette, *Independent Chronicle*, December 19, 1782.

39. Richardson, *Clarissa*, 5:27, 72; Samuel Richardson, *Sir Charles Grandison*, 7 vols. (London, 1754), 1:228–36; Richardson, *Pamela*.

40. During much of her career, Haywood (1693?–1756) produced four books a year, in addition to a range of other writings. Today she is known chiefly as the writer and editor of *The Female Spectator*, the first English periodical written by and for women. Her first novel, *Love in Excess* (1719), was one of the three most popular fictional works published prior to Richardson's *Pamela* (1740)—a distinction it shared with Defoe's *Robinson Crusoe* and Swift's *Gulliver's Travels*. She responded to *Pamela* both with work that imitated it and with a parody, *The Anti-Pamela*. She also appeared on and wrote for the stage. Christine Blouch, "Eliza Haywood," in *Selected Works of Eliza Haywood I: Miscellaneous Writings, 1725–1743*, ed. Alexander Pettit (London: Pickering & Chatto, 2000), xxi–lxxxii.

41. Eliza Fowler Haywood, *The Fortunate Foundling* (1744), chap. XV.

42. Eliza Haywood, *Betsy Thoughtless*, 4 vols. (1751), 4:60, 52, 57, 237, 226, 238.

43. Richardson, *Pamela*, 1:19; Richardson, *Clarissa*, 5:61; Richardson, *Sir Charles Grandison*, 1:230.

44. For differing accounts of sensibility, novels, and female power, see G. J. Barker-Benfield, *The Culture of Sensibility: Sex and Society in Eighteenth-Century Britain* (Chicago: University of Chicago Press, 1992), xxvi; Adela Pinch, "Emotion and History: A Review Article," *Comparative Studies in Society and History* 37, no. 1 (1995): 100–109; Lynn Hunt, *Inventing Human Rights: A History* (New York: W. W. Norton, 2007), 40–41; Sarah Pearsall, *Atlantic Families: Lives and Letters in the Later Eighteenth Century* (Oxford: Oxford University Press, 2008), 87; and Sarah Knott, *Sensibility and the American Revolution* (Chapel Hill: University of North Carolina Press for the OIEAHC, 2009).

45. Sarah Wiggin, *New-Hampshire Gazette*, September 2, 1768. Birth records for Tuften Wiggin's children have not been traced, but the death of one of his children was recorded in 1742, the (probable) year of Sarah Darling Wiggin's birth. Tuften Wiggin also lost three children

within a few weeks of one another in 1754, and his first wife died in 1757. "Deaths in Stratham, New Hampshire," *NEHGR* 30 (October 1876): 428, *NEHGR* 48 (January 1894): 28, 29, *NEHGR* 73 (January 1919): 64, 66, 73. Wiggin's 1776 will listed four children of uncertain ages and mentioned others who had already received their shares of his estate. Rockingham County Probate Records, microfilm, NEHGS. One of these daughters, also named Sarah Wiggin, was prosecuted for fornication and bastardy in 1769, about a year after Tuften and Sarah's marital dispute; the baby died shortly after birth, and she was still single and in Tuften Wiggin's household in 1776. New Hampshire Provincial Court Records no. 028589, New Hampshire State Archives; "Deaths in Stratham, New Hampshire," *NEHGR* 48 (July 1894): 340.

46. Haywood, *Betsy Thoughtless*, 4:52–53; Sarah Wiggin, *New-Hampshire Gazette*, September 2, 1768.

47. Sarah Wiggin, *New-Hampshire Gazette*, September 2, 1768.

48. The divorces of the Scottish-immigrant booksellers Ann and William McAlpine and the radical printer Isaiah Thomas—all purveyors of sentimental and Scottish Enlightenment ideas—were the first to employ the language of sensibility in Massachusetts. The 1773 divorce petition of Precillia Howard, on the other hand, did not replicate the expansive, sentimental tone of her advertisement and stuck to documented instances of physical violence. *Ann McAlpine v. William McAlpine*, agreement, August 17, 1763, Suffolk Files, no. 129139, vol. 793, 168–70; William McAlpine, "Imported [. . .]," *Boston Evening-Post*, June 21, 1762; *Isaiah Thomas v. Mary Dill Thomas*, Supreme Court Divorces, decree date May 27, 1777, Massachusetts Divorces, 1760–1786, 93, MAC; Precillia Howard, *Boston Post-Boy*, January 11, 1773; *Precilla Howard v. Simon Howard*, February 18, 1773, Suffolk Files, no. 129771, vol. 794:54.

49. Tuftin Wiggin, *New-Hampshire Gazette*, October 7, 1768; Tufton Wiggin, will, 1776, and inventory, 1779, microfilm, Rockingham County Probate Records, NEHGS; "Deaths in Stratham, New Hampshire," *NEHGR* 73 (January 1919): 71.

50. Philip Woods to Peter Woods, March 16, 1780, Bucks County Deeds, book 19, 194; Philip Wood, Bucks County Wills, no. 1779, 1782.

51. Patrick Markham, *New-Hampshire Gazette*, June 27, 1760.

52. Patrick Markham, *New-Hampshire Gazette*, June 27, 1760.

53. Richardson, *Clarissa*, 3:141, 349, 7:195.

54. For an example of the nineteenth-century reification masculine "possessory rights" and the way in which ascribing a wife's authorship to the "agency of others" undermined women's community support networks and liberalizing divorce laws, see the case of Isaac and Susan Danforth in Mary Beth Sievens, " 'The Wicked Agency of Others': Community, Law, and Marital Conflict in Vermont, 1790–1830," *Journal of the Early Republic* 21 (2001): 19–39; and Mary Beth Sievens, *Stray Wives: Marital Conflict in Early National New England* (New York: New York University Press, 2005), 74–85.

55. Rebecca Makkai, "The Power and Limitations of Victim-Impact Statements," *New Yorker*, June 8, 2016, https://www.newyorker.com/culture/culture-desk/the-power-and-limitations-of-victim -impact-statements; Chanel Miller, *Know My Name: A Memoir* (New York: Viking, 2019), 319–22.

56. Hunt, *Inventing Human Rights*, 35–69, quotations on pages 61, 62, 68.

Chapter Seven

1. *Pennsylvania Packet*, November 22, 1773; reprinted in the *Boston Weekly News-Letter*, January 13, 1774.

2. *Pennsylvania Packet*, November 22, 1773.

3. For a reading of the Liberty/Loyalty exchange as legitimating revolution, see Clare A. Lyons, *Sex among the Rabble: An Intimate History of Gender & Power in the Age of Revolution, Philadelphia, 1730–1830* (Chapel Hill: University of North Carolina Press for the OIEAHC, 2006), 237. On the *Boston Newsletter*'s politics, see Isaiah Thomas, *The History of Printing in America* (1874; New York: Burt Franklin, 1972), 1:145–47; and Alfred Young, *The Shoemaker and the Tea Party: Memory and the American Revolution* (Boston: Beacon Press, 1999).

4. On revolutionary analogies, see Jay Fliegelman, *Prodigals and Pilgrims: The American Revolution against Patriarchal Authority, 1750–1800* (Cambridge: Cambridge University Press, 1982); Eric Foner, *The Story of American Freedom* (New York: W. W. Norton, 1998), chap. 2; and Christopher Brown, *Moral Capital: Foundations of British Abolitionism* (Chapel Hill: University of North Carolina Press for the OIEAHC, 2006).

5. Richard B. Sher, "An 'Agreeable and Instructive Society': Benjamin Franklin and Scotland," in *Sociability and Society in Eighteenth-Century Scotland*, ed. John Alfred Dwyer and Richard B. Sher (Edinburgh: Mercat Press, 1993), 181–93; John Millar, *Observations Concerning the Distinction of Ranks in Society* (London: W. and J. Richardson, 1771), 242. Millar's observations about colonial hypocrisy capped one of the most influential formulations of the Scottish Enlightenment stadial theory, in which marriage and slavery became indices of modern civilization. See the introduction, note 6.

6. See chap. 8 for details of the Declaration's concrete relationship to the legal remedies sought in marital disputes.

7. "John Davis, Taylor," notice of new business location, *New-Hampshire Gazette*, May 13, 1763.

8. Between 1758 and 1763, John Davis was party to more than twenty actions for debt, both as plaintiff and defendant. New Hampshire, Rockingham County Superior Court Records Collection, New Hampshire State Archives; Davis, *New-Hampshire Gazette*, August 29, 1760, July 30, 1762, May 13, 1763; "Stolen out of the House late in the Occupation of John Davis," *New-Hampshire Gazette*, September 2, 1763; Davis, notice to creditors, *New-Hampshire Gazette*, September 9, 1763. On postwar credit crises and debtors' strategies for avoiding lawsuits, see Bruce Mann, *Republic of Debtors: Bankruptcy in the Age of American Independence* (Cambridge, MA: Harvard University Press, 2002), 53–55, 25–26.

9. John Davis, "Whereas my wife Eustace," *New-Hampshire Gazette*, August 29, 1760 (page 1, margin), and "Whereas my wife Eunice," *New-Hampshire Gazette*, July 30, 1762; *New-Hampshire Gazette*, January 2, 1761. On invitations to return and violence, see chap. 5. Eunice Davis left no record of attempted legal separation, suggesting that the abuse of which she complained was sufficiently severe to frighten John into protecting himself, but didn't force him to court. Eunice's innovative political reference might have masked her inability to document life-threatening cruelty.

10. *Williams v. Williams* (1619), cited in Laura Gowing, *Domestic Dangers: Women, Words, and Sex in Early Modern London* (Oxford: Clarendon Press, 1996), 226. For seventeenth-century New England cases, see chap. 1.

11. "Divorce Papers of Theophilus Morgan (1742/3)," cited in Cornelia Hughes Dayton, *Women before the Bar: Gender, Law & Society in Connecticut, 1639–1789* (Chapel Hill: University of North Carolina Press for the OIEAHC, 1995), 147–48; Theophilus Morgan, *New-England Weekly Journal* (Boston), October 2, 1739.

12. "Testimony of Thomas Cushman (May 7, 1767)," in *Cobb v. Cobb*, Suffolk Files, no. 12974; Elizabeth Markham, *New-Hampshire Gazette*, June 13, 1760; Elizabeth Badder, *Pennsylvania*

Gazette, June 16, 1768; Hannah Gardner, *Boston Gazette*, April 3, 1769; Hannah Merriman's allusion to grievances "not fit to write nor modesty allow mee to speak" discussed in Dayton, *Women before the Bar*, 141.

13. Laurel Thatcher Ulrich, *Well-Behaved Women Seldom Make History*, 1st ed. (New York: Alfred A. Knopf, 2007); Gerda Lerner, *The Creation of Feminist Consciousness: From the Middle Ages to Eighteen-Seventy* (New York: Oxford University Press, 1993).

14. Gouge cited in Frances Dolan, *Marriage and Violence: The Early Modern Legacy* (Philadelphia: University of Pennsylvania Press, 2008), 104.

15. Thomas Hutchinson, *The History of the Colony of Massachusets-Bay* [. . .] (Boston: Thomas & John Fleet, 1764), 444–45.

16. Dolan, *Marriage and Violence*, 104.

17. See chap. 4, note 55.

18. For evidence of the popular, pervasive understanding of sexual abuse as an element of slavery and an issue even for New England's "first families," see the slander suit *Otis v. Hinkley* (1744), Suffolk County Court Files, MAC. For a visual representation of men who "lodge with their negro Wenches by night" and whip them during the day, see the undated eighteenth-century painting *Virginian Luxuries*, depicting a white man beating an enslaved man in one frame and kissing an enslaved woman in another, reprinted in Kathleen M. Brown, *Good Wives, Nasty Wenches, and Anxious Patriarchs: Gender, Race and Power in Colonial Virginia* (Chapel Hill: University of North Carolina Press for the OIEAHC, 1996), 372.

19. Thomas left a contemptuous account of feeble attempts by his master, the Boston printer Zechariah Fowle (a relation to the printer of the *New-Hampshire Gazette*), to set to type a poem composed by "a barber's apprentice, illiterate, but as he fondly believed a favorite child of the muses," and transcribed by another semiliterate man whose writing included no punctuation. Isaiah Thomas, *The History of Printing in America*, 2nd ed., 2 vols. (New York: Burt Franklin, 1972), 1:xxiv.

20. Margaret Cavendish, "Letter CLXXIV," *CCXI sociable letters written by the thrice noble, illustrious, and excellent princess, the Lady Marchioness of Newcastle* (London: William Wilson, 1664), 364.

21. Cavendish, "Letter XVI," *CCXI sociable letters*, 26–28.

22. Cavendish, "Letter XVI," "Letter CCI," *CCXI sociable letters*, 28, 427.

23. Cavendish, "Letter CCI," 427.

24. See chap. 6; see also Dayton, *Women before the Bar*, 146–154.

25. Penelope Anderson, *Friendship's Shadows: Women's Friendship and the Politics of Betrayal in England, 1640–1705* (Edinburgh: Edinburgh University Press, 2012); Karen Offen, "How (and Why) the Analogy of Marriage and Slavery Provided the Springboard for Women's Rights Demands in France, 1640–1848," in *Women's Rights and Transatlantic Antislavery in the Era of Emancipation*, ed. Kathryn Kish Sklar and James Brewer Stewart (New Haven, CT: Yale University Press, 2007), 57–81; Joan E. DeJean, *Tender Geographies: Women and the Origins of the Novel in France* (New York: Columbia University Press, 1991); James Fitzmaurice, "Cavendish, Margaret, Duchess of Newcastle upon Tyne (1623?–1673)," *ODNB*.

26. Mary Jane Edwards, "Frances Brooke's *The History of Emily Montague*: A Biographical Context," *English Studies in Canada* 7, no. 2 (Summer 1981), 171–82; Mary Jane Edwards, "Brooke, Frances (*bap.* 1724, *d.* 1789)," *ODNB*.

27. Frances Brooke, *The History of Emily Montague*, 4 vols. (London: J. Dodsley, 1769), 2:206, 3:39–40.

28. Brooke, *Emily Montague*, 1:102, 65–67, 30–34, 116.

29. Brooke, 1:69; William T. Ojala and Jeanne A. Ojala, "Francoise d'Aubigne, Marquise de Maintenon," in *An Encyclopedia of Continental Women Writers*, ed. Katharina M. Wilson (Taylor & Francis, 1991), 756–58; Brooke, 2:194–95.

30. Abigail Adams to John Adams, March 31–April 5, 1776, Adams Family Papers Electronic Archive, MHS, https://www.masshist.org/digitaladams/archive/doc?id=L17760331aa; Elaine Forman Crane, "Abigail Adams, Gender Politics, and 'The History of Emily Montague: A Postscript,'" *William and Mary Quarterly* 64, no. 4 (October 2007): 839–44j; Elaine Forman Crane, "Political Dialogue and the Spring of Abigail's Discontent," *William and Mary Quarterly*, 56, no. 4 (October 1999): 745–74; Woody Holton, *Abigail Adams* (New York: Free Press, 2009); Sarah M. S. Pearsall, *Atlantic Families: Lives and Letters in the Later Eighteenth Century* (Oxford: Oxford University Press, 2008), 4–10.

31. I have not been able to determine Eunice Davis's fate, though her husband did not use the papers to "publicly retrieve" her character. Elizabeth Markham and her father engaged in a sharply contested legal battle with her husband, ultimately losing on appeal. Despite overwhelming evidence and her husband's own acknowledgment of "treating her like a slave" and with "severity," Catherine Cobb was denied a divorce from bed and board because many of her neighbors thought her behavior a bad example to other women. Theophilus Morgan won his divorce from Elizabeth. *Hogg v. Markham*, New Hampshire Provincial Court Records, file no. 028369, New Hampshire State Archives; *Cobb v. Cobb*, Suffolk Files, no. 12974; "Divorce Papers of Theophilus Morgan (1742/3)."

32. John Adams, diary entry, December 30, 1759, John Adams to Abigail Smith, September 30, 1764, Abigail Smith to John Adams, October 4, 1764, Adams Family Papers Electronic Archive; Holton, *Abigail Adams*, 14, 31–32.

33. "Divorce Papers of Theophilus Morgan (1742/3)."

34. Jane Tennent, *Pennsylvania Gazette*, January 15, 1767.

35. Margaret (Mary) Bannerman, *Virginia Gazette* (Purdie and Dixon), January 21, 1768; July 7, 1768; May 25, 1769.

36. William Buell Sprague, *Annals of the American Pulpit*, 9 vols. (New York: R. Carter and brothers, 1857), 3:26, 53.

37. Jane Tennent, *Pennsylvania Gazette*, January 15, 1767.

38. Margaret (Mary) Bannerman, *Virginia Gazette* (Purdie and Dixon), January 21, 1768; July 7, 1768; May 25, 1769.

39. *The King v. Jane Galbreath (assault and battery)*, Chester County Court of Quarter Sessions, file papers, October 1755, February 1756, May 1756; docket 6 (1752–1759), August 1756 session, 272–73, quotations in February 1756 bond for good behavior; *The King v. Jane Tennent (assault and battery)*, file papers, August 1767; *Henry McClellan v. Charles Tennent and his wife*, Chester County Common Pleas Narratives, August 1768 (filed Nov. 28, 1768), no. 44, all in CCA. Jane's violent temper might provide clues to the conflict over "her Negroe Wench." Jane apparently found it difficult to keep maidservants during her first marriage. Charles's intervention was a marital power play, but could also reflect dismay at her treatment of a enslaved person with less power to object to abuse. See runaway ads for Elizabeth Maddock and Mary Brown; Brown was a recent Irish immigrant, and presumably the female servant whose remaining five years of indented time Jane's first husband, John Galbreath, offered for sale shortly after posting Mary as a runaway. John Galbreath, *Pennsylvania Gazette*, July 12, 1759, September 13, 1759, October 4, 1759.

40. Benjamin Bannerman, *Virginia Gazette* (Purdie and Dixon), April 20, 1769.

41. Margaret Bannerman, *Virginia Gazette* (Purdie and Dixon), January 21, 1768; May 25, 1769; Jane Tennent, *Pennsylvania Gazette*, January 15, 1767.

42. Paul Kingston, will, March 4, 1764, proved March 1764, and John Streep, will, February 1, 1765, proved April 18, 1765, both in "Norfolk County Will Book I, 1755–1772," microfilm, Library of Virginia, Richmond, Virginia.

43. John Galbreath, will, April 12, 1766, proved April 1766, Philadelphia Wills, Philadelphia City Archives, Philadelphia, Pennsylvania; Sprague, *Annals of the American Pulpit*, 3:26, 53.

44. Sprague, *Annals of the American Pulpit*, 3:26, 53. Charles had assumed his boarding school positions only a few years before, shortly after his brothers' death and after leaving a ministerial post he had held for over twenty years because the church could not support him; the educational component of the Chester County appointment indicates that Alison almost certainly had a hand in it.

45. *The King v. Jane Tennent (assault and battery)*, August 1767, CCA.

46. *Henry McClellan v. Charles Tennent and his wife*, Chester County Common Pleas Narratives, August 1768 (filed Nov. 28, 1768), no. 44, CCA.

47. On arbitration see Bruce H. Mann, *Neighbors and Strangers: Law and Community in Early Connecticut* (Chapel Hill: University of North Carolina Carolina Press, 1987), 101–36.

48. Jane Tennent, will, November 1773, will no. 2800, Chester County Wills and Administrations, CCA.

49. Margaret placed the value of all her property nearer to three thousand pounds—fifteen hundred pounds in "paper currency," five hundred pounds in gold and silver, and a thousand pounds in real estate, slaves, and household effects. Mary Bannerman, "To the Publick," *Virginia Gazette* (Purdie and Dixon), July 7, 1768; Benjamin Bannerman, *Virginia Gazette* (Purdie and Dixon), April 20, 1769.

50. Susan Staves, *Married Women's Separate Property in England, 1660–1833* (Cambridge, MA: Harvard University Press, 1990), 174–75.

51. Benjamin Bannerman, *Virginia Gazette* (Purdie and Dixon), Williamsburg, April 20, 1769; Margaret Bannerman, *Virginia Gazette* (Purdie and Dixon), Williamsburg, May 25, 1769.

52. Benjamin Bannerman, *Virginia Gazette* (Purdie and Dixon), Williamsburg, April 20, 1769; Margaret Bannerman, *Virginia Gazette* (Purdie and Dixon), Williamsburg, May 25, 1769.

53. Lawrence Stone, *Road to Divorce: England 1530–1987* (Oxford: Oxford University Press, 1990), 160; Norma Basch, *Framing American Divorce: From the Revolutionary Generation to the Victorians* (Berkeley: University of California Press, 1999), 102–17.

54. Margaret's fate after 1770 is unclear. Benjamin Bannerman's colonial career included stints as a slave trader and a loyalist spy; after the war, he lived off the inheritance belonging to a new wife in England. If the "mulatto bastard" of Margaret's notices was Jacob, an enslaved "Barber, Drummer, Fifer and professed Hair Dresser" who was stolen "by the Rebels," but who eventually rejoined him in England, Bannerman received compensation for freeing his own child. His loyalist claim reinforces the impression that he was habitually deceptive. For example, he reduced the age and claimed an implausible income for a studhorse, when compared with his last advertisement of the animal in the *Virginia Gazette*. "An Estimate of Losses sustained [. . .] London, 25 June, 1787," Benjamin Bannerman, loyalist claim, microfilm, Virginia Colonial Records Project, Library of Virginia; *Virginia Gazette* (Dixon), March 14, 1777.

55. Fortunatus [Sharper] to Col. [James] Otis, undated correspondence, MS N-621, Otis Family Papers, MHS.

56. Court records for Barnstable County—home to Fortunatus, Benjamin Gifford, and the Otis family—burned in the early nineteenth century, and no legal records for this case appear to survive. Fortunatus Sharper was born in 1730. Oliver B. Brown, *Vital Records of Falmouth, Massachusetts to the year 1850* (Camden, Maine: Picton Press, 1776). Record of the 1745 pledge to free "Fortunatious Sharper" at the age of thirty-five transcribed from the records of the Sandwich Friends Monthly Meeting in Christine R. Brown, *The Genealogy of the Gifford Family from Massachusetts to Maine* (Knoxville, TN: Campbell Printing, 1981). It is not entirely clear from this record how Fortunatus came to be Gifford's "Negro man"; Gifford pledged the money to free him, but a man named John Hammond seems to have held the title. Fortunatus's query probably dates from between 1765, when he would have attained freedom, and 1778, when Col. Otis died. Otis did not take the title Colonel until about 1760, so it was no earlier than that. The query might have been prompted by James Jr.'s 1764 *The Rights of the British Colonies Asserted and Proved*, which attributed natural rights to blacks. On the Otises, see John J. Waters, *The Otis Family in Provincial and Revolutionary Massachusetts* (Chapel Hill: University of North Carolina Press, 1968).

57. Foner, *The Story of American Freedom*, 29–30; Linda K. Kerber, "*No Constitutional Right to be Ladies*": *Women and the Obligations of Citizenship* (New York: Hill and Wang, 1998), 9–10; Kate Davies, *Catharine Macaulay and Mercy Otis Warren: The Revolutionary Atlantic and the Politics of Gender* (Oxford: Oxford University Press, 2005).

58. Fortunatus [Sharper] to Col. [James] Otis, undated correspondence, MS N-621, Otis Family Papers, MHS.

59. John Fielding, *Extracts from Such of the Penal Laws* [. . .] (London: H. Woodfall and W. Strahan, for A. Millar, 1762), 143, cited in Travis Glasson, "'Baptism doth not bestow Freedom': Missionary Anglicanism, Slavery, and the Yorke-Talbot Opinion, 1701–30," *William and Mary Quarterly* 67, no. 2 (April 2010): 279–318, esp. 288.

60. William Blackstone, *Commentaries on the Laws of England*, 4 vols. (Oxford: Clarendon Press, 1768), 3:138–43; Gretchen Gerzina, *Black London: Life before Emancipation* (New Brunswick, NJ: Rutgers University Press, 1995), 56–58; Steven M. Wise, *Though the Heavens May Fall: The Landmark Trial That Led to the End of Human Slavery* (Cambridge, MA: Da Capo Press, 2005), 45–48.

61. Fielding, *Extracts from Such of the Penal Laws*, 143.

62. For an introduction to the literature on Anglo-imperial freedom suits and the importance of American actors in English cases, see Kirsten Sword, "Remembering Dinah Nevil: Strategic Deceptions in Eighteenth-Century Antislavery," *Journal of American History* 97, no. 2 (September 2010): 315–43. On New England suits, see Catherine Adams and Elizabeth Pleck, *Love of Freedom: Black Women in Colonial and Revolutionary New England* (Oxford: Oxford University Press, 2010), 127–57.

63. Slaves' importance as mobile capital in New England helped create communication networks throughout the region; young black men became itinerant conduits for information both through repeated sales and through service to imperial officials. Adams and Pleck, *Love of Freedom*, 109; T. H. Breen, "Making History: The Force of Public Opinion and the Last Years of Slavery in Revolutionary Massachusetts," in *Through a Glass Darkly: Reflections on Personal Identity in Early America*, ed. Ronald Hoffman, Mechal Sobel, and Fredrika J. Teute (Chapel Hill: University of North Carolina Press for the OIEAHC, 1997), 67–95; Sword, "Remembering Dinah Nevil."

NOTES TO PAGES 234-237

64. This does not seem to have been the sort of secretive break from one's local community that frustrated masters' efforts at recovery and prompted advertisements. The rural setting precluded the kind of hiding in plain sight done by runaway slaves in urban environments. To "pass as free," Flora would have had to run farther than she did. She and Exeter appear to have been bargaining for new standing in their home communities.

65. Testimony of Eliakim Pomeroy and Ebenezer Wyman, January 5, 1784, *Exeter v. Oliver Hanchett*, Suffolk Files, no. 158594.

66. *The Acts and Resolves* [. . .] of *the Province of the Massachusetts Bay*, Published Colonial Records of the American Colonies, 27 vols. (Boston: Wright and Potter, 1869), 1:578; Samuel Sewall, diary entry, cited in George Elliott Howard, *A History of Matrimonial Institutions* 3 vols. (Chicago: University of Chicago Press, 1904), 2:218; Gloria McCahon Whiting, "Power, Patriarchy, and Provision: African Families Negotiate Gender and Slavery in New England," *Journal of American History* 103, no. 3 (December 2016): 583–605.

67. Brown, *Good Wives, Nasty Wenches*, 120–35; Adams and Pleck, *Love of Liberty*, 103–25. See also chap. 3.

68. Testimony of the Reverend John Graham, February 7, 1784, *Exeter v. Hanchett*, Suffolk Files, no. 158594.

69. Rev. Samuel Phillips, "Form of a Negro Marriage," cited in Howard, *A History of Matrimonial Institutions*, 2, 225.

70. Phillips, "Form of a Negro Marriage," 225–26.

71. "Petition for freedom to Massachusetts Governor Thomas Gage, His Majesty's Council, and the House of Representatives, 25 May 1774," Jeremy Belknap Papers, MHS https://www .masshist.org/database/viewer.php?item_id=549&img_step=1&br=1&mode=transcript#page1; "Negro Petitions for Freedom," *Collections of the Massachusetts Historical Society*, series 5, vol. 3 (Boston: MHS, 1877), 433; Herbert Aptheker, ed, *A Documentary History of the Negro People in the United States*, 7 vols. (New York: Citadel Press, 1967), 1:9, 6, discussed in Thomas J. Davis, "Emancipation Rhetoric, Natural Rights, and Revolutionary New England: A Note on Four Black Petitions in Massachusetts, 1773–1777," *New England Quarterly* 62, no. 2 (June 1989): 248–63; Foner, *The Story of American Freedom*: 34, 41; Pearsall, *Atlantic Families*, 116–17.

72. Junius T. Hanchett, *The Hanchett Family* (Salem, MA: Higginson, 1997), 71–75; Benjamin Scott to Oliver Hanchett, bill of sale, May 14, 1781, *Exeter v. Hanchett*, Suffolk Files, no. 158594; Arthur Zilversmit, *The First Emancipation: The Abolition of Slavery in the North* (Chicago: University of Chicago Press, 1967), 109–124.

73. Elizabeth Freeman to Harriet Martineau, cited in Adams and Pleck, *Love of Freedom*, 147.

74. A lawyer's brief from the case noted, "The master has a right to separate Husband and wife," and asked, "Is it consistent with the law of nature to separate what God has joined and no man can put asunder." The "Walker case" involved six distinct decisions, with major Supreme Judicial Court verdicts in 1781 and 1783. Explanation of the courts' rulings does not exist for the 1781 cases, and their significance has to be inferred from other events. "Brief of Levi Lincoln for *Nathaniel Jennison v. Wm. Caldwell and Others*," *Collections of the MHS*, series 5, 3:441; *Walker v. Jennison*, Suffolk Files, no. 153101; *Jennison v. Caldwell*, Suffolk Files, no. 158693; *John Caldwell et al. v. Jennison*, Supreme Judicial Court Record Books, vol. 1781–82:179–80, 84. Partial transcriptions of these and other documents relevant to the case are reprinted in William O'Brian, "Did the Jennison Case Outlaw Slavery in Massachusetts?," *William and Mary Quarterly* 17, no. 2 (1960), 219–41. For interpretations, see Emily Blanck, "Seventeen Eighty-Three: The Turning Point in the Law of Slavery and Freedom in Massachusetts," *New England Quarterly* 75, no. 1

(2002), 24–51; Arthur Zilversmit, "Quok Walker, Mumbet and the Abolition of Slavery in Massachusetts," *William and Mary Quarterly* 25, no. 4 (1968), 614–624; Robert M. Spector, "The Quock Walker Cases (1781–1783)—Slavery, Its Abolition, and Negro Citizenship in Early Massachusetts," *Journal of Negro History* 53, no. 1 (1968), 12–32; Elaine MacEacheren, "Emancipation of Slavery in Massachusetts: A Reexamination, 1770–1790," *Journal of Negro History* 55, no. 4 (1970), 289–306; and A. Leon Higginbotham, *In the Matter of Color, Race & The American Legal Process: The Colonial Period* (Oxford: Oxford University Press, 1978), 91–99.

75. Copies of arrest warrant and court record from Suffield, Hartford County, Connecticut, October 29, 1781, in *Exeter v. Hanchett*, Suffolk Files, no. 158594.

76. Hanchett's indictment had named Exeter and another woman as Flora's confederates in the theft. Were Exeter and Flora free and white, it would have been standard to prosecute them jointly because husbands bore legal and financial liability for the actions of their wives. Hanchett's failure to identify them as husband and wife suggests discomfort with the legal ramifications of granting Exeter responsibility for Flora. In the final verdict—reached summarily on the same day as Hanchett's charge—Flora stood alone. Arrest warrant and court record from Suffield, Hartford County, Connecticut, October 29, 1781, in *Exeter v. Hanchett*, Suffolk Files, no. 158594.

77. *Exeter v. Hanchett*, Suffolk Files, no. 158594; *Salem and Rose Orne v. Elisha Haskett Derby*, Suffolk Files, no. 92575, vol. 527.

78. Gerzina, *Black London*, 77–78.

79. Such compensation did not guarantee that Flora—with or without her clothes—would be returned to him. Depending on how literally the legal authorities followed Blackstone, Exeter's right to "take away and hold" her might not have been enforceable. The form of the charge drew on three elements of Blackstone's account of private wrongs, one of which explicitly stated that suits of this type were to recover damages and "not the possession" of a man's wife. Specifically, for "abduction or taking away a man's wife" the remedy was obtained by "a writ of ravishment, or action of *trespass vi et armis, de uxora rapta et abducta*," through which the husband could "recover, not the possession of his wife, but damages for taking her away." (These writs were the earliest manifestations of legal punishment for rape, which by the eighteenth century was more routinely dealt with as a criminal, rather than a civil, matter.) A husband could also claim damages for the "beating" or "ill use" of his wife. He would ordinarily seek redress through an "action of trespass, *vi et armis*," taken out jointly "in the names of husband and wife." Salem and Rose Orne followed this form. When maltreatment deprived a husband "for any time of the company and assistance of his wife," he was entitled to "a separate remedy, by an action upon the case . . . *per quod consortium amisit*." Exeter followed this prescription. Reference to the loss of "service," made explicitly in *Orne v. Derby* and in the clerk's private notes on *Exeter v. Hanchett*, appeared in Blackstone only in discussion of wrongs done to masters through the loss or injury of their servants. Blackstone, *Commentaries* (1768), 3:138–43. On the history of the charges of ravishment and *rapta et abducta*, see Caroline Ford, "Private Lives and Public Order in Restoration France: The Seduction of Emily Loveday," *American Historical Review* 99, no. 1 (1994), 21–43, esp. 37–38; and Sharon Block, *Rape and Sexual Power in Early America* (Chapel Hill: University of North Carolina Press for the OIEAHC, 2006).

80. Gary B. Nash and Jean R. Soderlund, *Freedom by Degrees: Emancipation in Pennsylvania and Its Aftermath* (New York: Oxford University Press, 1991; Joanne Pope Melish, *Disowning Slavery: Gradual Emancipation and Race in New England, 1780–1860* (Cornell University Press, 2000); Zilversmit, *The First Emancipation*.

81. Comity, as a principle of federalism, developed first in English and then in American law through disputes over marriage and slavery. Blanck, "Seventeen Eighty-Three," 24–51; Emily Blanck, *Tyrannicide: Forging an American Law of Slavery in Revolutionary South Carolina and Massachusetts* (Athens: University of Georgia Press, 2014); Daniel Joseph Hulsebosch, *Constituting Empire: New York and the Transformation of Constitutionalism in the Atlantic World, 1664–1830* (Chapel Hill: University of North Carolina Press, 2005).

82. Amy Dru Stanley, *From Bondage to Contract: Wage Labor, Marriage, and the Market in the Age of Slave Emancipation* (Cambridge: Cambridge University Press, 1998), 1–59.

83. John Hooker, *Some Reminiscences of a Long Life* (Hartford, Connecticut: Belknap & Warfield, 1899), 31–34.

84. John Adams to Abigail Adams, April 14, 1776.

85. Cavendish, "Letter XVI," *CCXI sociable letters*, 26–28; John Adams to Abigail Adams, April 14, 1776.

86. Abigail Adams to Mercy Otis Warren, Braintree, April 27, 1776, and John Adams to James Sullivan, Philadelphia, May 26, 1776, in *The Feminist Papers: From Adams to De Beauvoir*, ed. Alice S. Rossi (Boston: Northeastern University Press, 1988), 12–15.

87. For an overview of these debates about citizenship, see Rosemarie Zagarri, *Revolutionary Backlash: Women and Politics in the Early American Republic* (Philadelphia: University of Pennsylvania Press, 2007), 26–46. The Pennsylvania essayist lifted this argument from the 1774 *Political Disquisitions* of the Scottish radical James Burgh, who in turn built on ideas with seventeenth-century Lockean roots. "To the FREEMEN of PENNSYLVANIA," *Pennsylvania Packet*, January 26, 1785; James Burgh, *Political Disquisitions; or, An Enquiry into Public Errors, Defects, and Abuses*, 3 vols. (London: E. and C. Dilly, 1774), 1:37.

Chapter Eight

1. There is no clear connection between this work and an antidivorce pamphlet that appeared in Connecticut in the same year. I suspect that both pamphlets had links to the Shippen-Livingston divorce case discussed in this chapter, prompted by the jurisdiction-shopping parties who sought—unsuccessfully—to have their allies influence state legislatures in their favor. These works were the *only* published arguments about divorce policy in any of the newly United States. *An Essay on Marriage; or, The Lawfulness of Divorce, in Certain Cases, Considered: Addressed to the Feelings of Mankind* (Philadelphia: Zachariah Poulson Jr., 1788), 28 (the copy in the Delaware Institute Free Library attributed to James Adams and dated 1783 is a ghost with publishing information that appears to be pasted from another work); Benjamin Trumbull, A.M., *Appeal to the Public, Respecting Divorce* (New Haven, CT: J. Meigs, 1788).

2. The expectation that divorce *ought* to represent radical, revolutionary change shapes historical scholarship, though focused studies are ambivalent about its practical significance. Gordon S. Wood, *The Radicalism of the American Revolution* (New York: Vintage Books, 1993), 147; Lynn Avery Hunt, *Inventing Human Rights: A History* (New York: W. W. Norton, 2007), 62–64; Marylynn Salmon, *Women and the Law of Property in Early America* (Chapel Hill: University of North Carolina Press, 1986); Marylynn Salmon, "Republican Sentiment, Economic Change, and the Property Rights of Women in American Law," in *Women in the Age of the American Revolution*, ed. Ronald Hoffman and Peter J. Albert (Charlottesville: University Press of Virginia, 1989), 447–75; Nancy F. Cott, "Divorce and the Changing Status of Women in Eighteenth-Century Massachusetts," *William and Mary Quarterly* 33, no. 4 (October 1976): 586–614; Linda K.

Kerber, *Women of the Republic: Intellect and Ideology in Revolutionary America* (New York: Norton, 1986), 158–84; Mary Beth Norton, *Liberty's Daughters: The Revolutionary Experience of American Women, 1750–1800* (Boston: Little, Brown, 1980), 47–50, 234; Carole Shammas, *A History of Household Government* (Charlottesville: University Press of Virginia, 2002), 58–62; Norma Basch, *Framing American Divorce: From the Revolutionary Generation to the Victorians* (Berkeley: University of California Press, 1999), quotation on 30.

3. *An Essay on Marriage*, 3.

4. Basch, *Framing American Divorce*, 23; Hendrik Hartog, *Man and Wife in America: A History* (Cambridge, MA: Harvard University Press, 2000): 1–2.

5. Basch, *Framing American Divorce*, 24.

6. See the case of Precillia Howard, chap. 5; see also Laura Edwards, *The People and Their Peace: Legal Culture and the Transformation of Inequality in the Post-Revolutionary South* (Chapel Hill: University of North Carolina Press, 2009), 169–86, esp. 179.

7. Kerber, *Women of the Republic*, 181; "An Act Concerning Divorce and Alimony," *The Statutes at Large of Pennsylvania from 1682 to 1801*, ed. James T. Mitchell and Henry Flanders (Harrisburg: Harrisburg Publishing, State Printer, 1906), 12:94–99.

8. On England, see Lawrence Stone, *Road to Divorce: England 1530–1987* (Oxford: Oxford University Press, 1990), 325–328, 432. On Scotland, see Leah Leneman, *Alienated Affections: The Scottish Experience of Divorce and Separation, 1684–1830* (Edinburgh: Edinburgh University Press, 1998), 14. On New England, see Nancy F. Cott, "Eighteenth-Century Family and Social Life Revealed in Massachusetts Divorce Records," *Journal of Social History* 10, no. 1 (Autumn 1976): 20–43; Cott, "Divorce and the Changing Status of Women"; and Cornelia Hughes Dayton, *Women before the Bar: Gender, Law, and Society in Connecticut, 1639–1789* (Chapel Hill: University of North Carolina Press for the OIEAHC, 1995).

9. Kimberly Smith Maynard, "Divorce in Nova Scotia, 1750–1890," in *Essays in the History of Canadian Law*, ed. Philip Girard and Jim Phillips, 9 vols. (Toronto: University of Toronto Press, 1990), 3:232–72; Roderick Phillips, *Putting Asunder: A History of Divorce in Western Society* (Cambridge: Cambridge University Press, 1988), 149–53; Sheldon Cohen, "The Broken Bond: Divorce in Providence County, 1749–1809," *Rhode Island History* 44 (1985): 67–79; Sheldon Cohen, "What Man Hath Put Asunder: Divorce in New Hampshire, 1681–1784," *Historical New Hampshire* 41 (1986): 118–41. Nova Scotia's legislation appears to reflect the influence of Massachusetts jurist Thomas Hutchinson, whose assertion of Massachusetts traditions against English pressure was discussed in chap. 4 and 7, together with Scottish military officers and the Protestant migrants from Germany, Switzerland, and France. Maynard, "Divorce in Nova Scotia," 3:232–72; Phillips, *Putting Asunder*, 149–53.

10. "Votes of Assembly," in Charles F. Hoban, ed., *Pennsylvania Archives, January 4, 1764–October 19, 1770*, series 8 (Harrisburg, 1935), 7:5840–41. For the Boehm Miller case, see chap. 4.

11. John Goggin, *Pennsylvania Gazette*, January 12, 1764.

12. "Votes of Assembly," in Hoban, *Pennsylvania Archives*, 7:5840–41.

13. Concern about local enforcement of the "common peace" could trump concerns about white women whose sexual relationships crossed the color line even in the nineteenth-century South. See Edwards, *The People and Their Peace*, 245–47; and Craig Horle, introduction to *Lawmaking and Legislators in Pennsylvania: A Biographical Dictionary*, vol. 3 (Philadelphia: University of Pennsylvania Press, 2005).

14. William Renwick Riddell, "Legislative Divorce in Colonial Pennsylvania," *The Pennsylvania Magazine of History and Biography* 57, no. 2 (1933): 175–80; W. L. Grant et al., eds., *Acts*

of the Privy Council of England: Colonial Series, 6 vols. (Hereford, UK: Printed for H.M.S.O., by Anthony Brothers, 1908), 5:365–66, manuscript pagination 251; W. P. Courtney and J.-M. Alter, "Jackson, Richard (1721/2–1787), Politician," *ODNB*.

15. The prohibition on divorces in Britain's colonies remained in effect until the mid-nineteenth century. Divorce proceedings in Massachusetts also appear to have been influenced by these jurisdictional debates. After Thomas Hutchinson readmitted the practice in 1760, Massachusetts passed two to three petitions per year, but became cautious in 1768 and heard no divorce petitions during the political turmoil of 1769. During the 1770–1773 interim between the Privy Council's approval and revocation of legislative divorces from Pennsylvania, Massachusetts suddenly heard nine petitions a year. Suffolk Files, Divorces; George Elliott Howard, *A History of Matrimonial Institutions*, 3 vols. (Chicago: University of Chicago Press, 1904), 2:332–48.

16. See chap. 1–2, 4.

17. Kirsten D. Sword, "Remembering Dinah Nevil, Strategic Deceptions in Eighteenth-Century Antislavery," *Journal of American History* 97, no. 2 (September 2010): 315–343; Van Gosse, "As a Nation, the English Are Our Friends: The Emergence of African American Politics in the British Atlantic World, 1772–1861," *American Historical Review* 113, no. 4 (October 1, 2008): 1003–28; Eliga H. Gould, "Zones of Law, Zones of Violence: The Legal Geography of the British Atlantic, circa 1772," *William and Mary Quarterly* 60 (July 2003): 471–510; George VanCleve, Daniel J. Hulsebosch, and Ruth Paley's contributions in "Forum: Somerset Revisited," *Law and History Review*, 24 (Fall 2006); Christopher Leslie Brown, *Moral Capital: Foundations of British Abolitionism* (Chapel Hill: University of North Carolina Press for the OIEAHC, 2006), 91–98: Ruth Paley, "Somerset: Mansfield, Slavery and the Law in England, 1772–1830," in *Law, Crime, and English Society, 1660–1830*, ed. Norma Landau (Cambridge: Cambridge University Press, 2002), 165–84; David Waldstreicher, "The Wheatleyan Moment." *Early American Studies* 9, no. 3 (2011): 522–51; "Great Case of the Negroes," *London Evening Post*, Thursday, April 23, 1772.

18. James Parker to Charles Steuart, February 23, 1772, correspondence cited in Frank L. Dewey, "Thomas Jefferson and a Williamsburg Scandal: The Case of Blair V. Blair," *The Virginia Magazine of History and Biography* 89, no. 1 (January 1981): 44–63.

19. Dewey, "Thomas Jefferson and a Williamsburg Scandal," 45–47.

20. John Millar, *Observations Concerning the Distinction of Ranks in Society* (London: W. and J. Richardson, 1771), 242.

21. George Morrow, *A Cock and Bull for Kitty: Lord Dunmore and the Affair That Ruined the British Cause in Virginia* (Williamsburg: Telford Publications, 2010), 18, 23–25; John Eustace, "The Admirers of the Works of the Late Celebrated and Ingenious Ilr. Sterne," *Boston Chronicle*, February 12, 1770. No explanation for Kitty's parents prolonged separation survives, but it appears to have been a family pattern; a different medically trained Eustace had discredited his wife in New York and Philadelphia not long before. Charles Eustace elopement notices, *New-York Mercury*, July 31, 1758, and *Pennsylvania Gazette*, August 3, 1758; Charles Eustace, "Surgeon and Man Midwife," *Pennsylvania Packet*, October 11, 1773.

22. James Parker to Charles Steuart, May 1771, in Dewey, "Thomas Jefferson and a Williamsburg Scandal," 44.

23. Morrow, *A Cock and Bull for Kitty*, 26.

24. James Parker to Charles Steuart, June 12, 1772, in Dewey, "Thomas Jefferson and a Williamsburg Scandal," 45–46.

25. James Parker to Charles Steuart, May 25, 1772, in Dewey, "Thomas Jefferson and a Williamsburg Scandal," 45.

26. Jefferson's notes are reprinted in Frank L. Dewey, "Thomas Jefferson's Notes on Divorce," *William and Mary Quarterly* 39, no. 1 (January 1982): 212–23. For analysis of connections between the notes on divorce and Jefferson's framing of the Declaration of Independence, see Basch, *Framing American Divorce*, 22–30; Peter Hoffer, *The Law's Conscience: Equitable Constitutionalism in America* (Chapel Hill: University of North Carolina Press, 1990), 71–79; and Morrow, *A Cock and Bull for Kitty*, 13.

27. Dewey, "Thomas Jefferson and a Williamsburg Scandal," quotations on 57, 63; Morrow, *A Cock and Bull for Kitty*, 38–42.

28. Kirsten D. Sword, "Remembering Dinah Nevil, Strategic Deceptions in Eighteenth-Century Antislavery," *Journal of American History* 97, no. 2 (September 2010), 315–43. On Dunmore, see Simon Schama, *Rough Crossings: Britain, the Slaves, and the American Revolution* (New York: Ecco, 2006).

29. Morrow, *A Cock and Bull for Kitty*, 42–44, 50–58.

30. When his Irish wife and son arrived on his doorstep in 1774, he kept the boy but sent his wife away, choosing instead to live with a new family he had started in Philadelphia. Richard B. Sher, *The Enlightenment & the Book: Scottish Authors & Their Publishers in Eighteenth-Century Britain, Ireland, & America* (Chicago: University of Chicago Press, 2006), 515–31; Sarah Knott, *Sensibility and the American Revolution* (Chapel Hill: University of North Carolina Press for the OIEAHC, 2009), 29–62.

31. Robert Boyd, *The Office, Powers, and Jurisdiction, of His Majesty's Justices of the Peace, and Commissioners of Supply* (Edinburgh: 1787), 389, 395–96.

32. Lawmakers did not leave much direct testimony regarding their reasoning; the change occurred with relatively little debate. The fact that legislative divorces "employ a very considerable part of the time of the Legislature and of course consume a considerable part of the taxes which are paid every year by the people" was used as an argument in North Carolina's move to implement judicial divorce in the early nineteenth century. *Raleigh Register*, June 8, 1809, quoted in Phillips, *Putting Asunder*, 447; Thomas R. Meehan, " 'Not made out of Levity': Evolution of Divorce in Early Pennsylvania," *Pennsylvania Magazine of History and Biography* 92, no. 4 (1968): 446; Stone, *Road to Divorce*, 325–39, 432.

33. "An Act for Regulating Marriage and Divorce" (February session, 1785; March 16, 1786), *The Acts and Laws of the Commonwealth of Massachusetts, 1785* (Boston: Wright & Potter, State Printers, 1890), 564–67; Cott, "Divorce and the Changing Status of Women in Eighteenth-Century Massachusetts," 586–614; Dayton, *Women before the Bar*, 135, table 6; Kirsten Sword, "Wayward Wives, Runaway Slaves and the Limits of Patriarchal Authority in Early America" (PhD diss., Harvard University, 2002), 261, appendix E, table 5, "Legal Claims in Wives' Advertisements Compared with Women's Divorce Petitions"; "An Act directing the mode of trial, and allowing of divorces in cases of adultery" (March 30, 1787), *Laws of the State of New York Passed at the Sessions of the Legislature Held in the Years 1785, 1786, 1787, and 1788*, 5 vols. (Albany: Weed Parsons, 1886), 2:494–95; Basch, *Framing American Divorce*, 40.

34. On colonial and English bankruptcy law, and on the distinctiveness of Pennsylvania's 1785 act, see Bruce Mann, *Republic of Debtors: Bankruptcy in the Age of American Independence* (Cambridge, MA: Harvard University Press, 2002), 46–47, 175–82. On divorce in Scotland, see Leneman, *Alienated Affections*.

35. Sword, "Remembering Dinah Nevil," 315–42. For the disputed runaway slave claimed by Baldwin Wake, the brother-in-law of North Carolina and New York Governor William Tryon, see Wake, *Pennsylvania Gazette*, September 28, November 2, and November 23, 1774; Samuel

Allinson, *Pennsylvania Gazette*, October 26, November 16, and December 7, 1774; Charles Henry Hart, "Letters from William Franklin to William Strahan," *Pennsylvania Magazine of History and Biography* 35 (1911), 456–59; and Paul David Nelson, "Tryon, William (1729–1788)," *ODNB*.

36. The suicide story originated with Benezet's much-circulated final letters to American activists in England, and was entrenched in a 1787 history of the Society that became the basis for later founding narratives. *An Essay on Marriage*, 2; "Anthony Benezet to John Pemberton, Philadelphia ye 10th 8th mo. 1783," in *Friend Anthony Benezet*, ed. George Brookes (Philadelphia: University of Pennsylvania Press, 1937), 397; Sword, "Remembering Dinah Nevil," 315–42.

37. *An Essay on Marriage*, 28.

38. Roger Bruns, ed., *Am I Not a Man and a Brother: The Antislavery Crusade of Revolutionary America, 1688–1788* (New York: Chelsea House, 1977), 215, 218–19; Benjamin Rush, *An Address to the Inhabitants of the British Settlements, on the Slavery of the Negroes in America to Which Is Added, a Vindication of the Address, in Answer to a Pamphlet Entitled, "Slavery Not Forbidden in Scripture; or, A Defence of the West India Planters"* (Philadelphia: John Dunlap, 1773), 8.

39. *An Essay on Marriage*, 26–27.

40. *An Essay on Marriage*, 15–16. Similar strategies were employed by the abused wife Elizabeth Markham (chap. 7) and the writers Frances Brooke and Thomas Paine.

41. See chap. 3, 4, and 7.

42. Cited in John D. Cushing, "The Cushing Court and the Abolition of Slavery in Massachusetts: More Notes on the 'Quock Walker Case,'" *American Journal of Legal History* 5, no. 2 (April 1961): 118–44, esp. 126–27; see also Jennison's petition to the House of Representatives, June 18, 1782 (Journal of the House of Representatives, vol. 3, 99), cited in George H. Moore, *Notes on the History of Slavery in Massachusetts* (New York: D. Appleton, 1866), 219.

43. James Penniman, *Independent Chronicle* (Boston), April 29, 1784; Christopher Dyer, *Independent Chronicle*, April 3, 1783.

44. For estimates of Massachusetts's black population in the eighteenth century, see William D. Pierson, *Black Yankees: The Development of an Afro-American Subculture in Eighteenth-Century New England* (Amherst: University of Massachusetts Press, 1988), chap. 2. In the mid-1760s, a free black man named Scipio Purnam did post his wife Lucy locally in Salem without using the newspapers. *Purnam v. Purnam*, Suffolk Files, Divorces, no. 129751; Cornelia Hughes Dayton, "The Peregrinations of Lucy Pernam, or 'Black Luce' and the Law in Eighteenth-Century Massachusetts," presented at the OIEAHC conference *Microhistory: Advantages and Limitations for the Study of Early American History*, 1999, Storrs, Connecticut, cited with permission. Catherine Adams and Elizabeth Pleck elaborate on Dayton's research and on Sword, "Wayward Wives, Runaway Slaves," in Adams and Pleck, *Love of Freedom: Black Women in Colonial and Revolutionary New England* (Oxford: Oxford University Press, 2010), 53–61, 118–25.

45. Cato Gardner, *Independent Chronicle* (Boston), January 17, 1781; Boston Paul, *Independent Chronicle*, December 26, 1782. On Cato Gardner and other advertisers' role in Boston's black community, see Adams and Pleck, *Love of Freedom*, 121–23; and Chernoh Momodu Sesay, "Freemasons of Color: Prince Hall, Revolutionary Black Boston, and the Origins of Black Freemasonry, 1770–1807" (PhD diss., Northwestern University, 2006).

46. Free black women in late eighteenth-century Boston worked as domestics and laundresses, as was the pattern elsewhere. Adams and Pleck, *Love of Freedom*, 41; Margot Minardi, "A Rugged Maze: The Emancipation of Belinda and Chloe Spear" (undergraduate honors thesis, Harvard College, 2000); Gary B. Nash, *Forging Freedom: The Formation of Philadelphia's Black Community, 1720–1840* (Cambridge, MA: Harvard University Press, 1988); Shane White,

Somewhat More Independent: The End of Slavery in New York City, 1770–1810 (Athens: University of Georgia Press, 1991); Billy Smith, "Black Women who Stole Themselves in Eighteenth-Century America," in *Inequality in Early America*, ed. Carla Gardina Pestana and Sharon V. Salinger (Hanover, NH: University Press of New England, 1999), 134–59.

47. Pero Conrard, *Delaware Gazette*, February 20, 1790.

48. "From a late New York Paper," *Pennsylvania Packet*, March 9, 1785, and March 31, 1785.

49. *Virginia Gazette* (Dixon), June 15, 1769; *Virginia Gazette* (Purdie and Dixon), March 8, 1770, and April 11, 1771.

50. Virginia's legislature explicitly rejected proposals for a general divorce law in 1790 and 1804. Thomas E. Buckley, *The Great Catastrophe of My Life: Divorce in the Old Dominion* (Chapel Hill: University of North Carolina Press, 2002).

51. Richard H. Chused, *Private Acts in Public Places: A Social History of Divorce in the Formative Era of American Family Law* (Philadelphia: University of Pennsylvania Press, 1994), 1; Joshua D. Rothman, " 'To Be Freed from Thate Curs and Let at Liberty': Interracial Adultery and Divorce in Antebellum Virginia," *Virginia Magazine of History and Biography* 106, no. 4 (1998): 443–81; Stephanie McCurry, *Masters of Small Worlds: Yeoman Households, Gender Relations, and the Political Culture of the Antebellum South Carolina Low Country* (Oxford: Oxford University Press, 1995), 85–91; Salmon, *Women and the Law of Property*, 79.

52. *An Essay on Marriage*, 1–2; emphasis mine. He did assert that "no distinction of preference in favour of either sex ought to be made when nature has made none," an egalitarian statement in which "natural" distinctions still justified inequality. Ibid., 26.

53. William Shippen to Thomas Lee Shippen, Philadelphia, January 27, 1781, in *Nancy Shippen, Her Journal Book: The International Romance of a Young Lady of Fashion in Colonial Philadelphia with Letters to Her and about Her*, ed. and comp. Ethel Armes (Philadelphia: J. B. Lippincott, 1935), 101, 111–29.

54. *Nancy Shippen, Her Journal Book*, 227–28, 234.

55. For claims about Anne's lack of legal ground, see Norton, *Liberty's Daughters*, 48–49; and Knott, *Sensibility and the American Revolution*, 139.

56. *Nancy Shippen, Her Journal Book*, 185, 143–47; Brooke, *Emily Montague*, 3:125; Elaine Forman Crane, "Political Dialogue and the Spring of Abigail's Discontent," *William and Mary Quarterly* 56, no. 4 (October 1999): 745–74; Elaine Forman Crane, "Abigail Adams, Gender Politics, and The History of Emily Montague: A Postscript," *William and Mary Quarterly* 64, no. 4 (October 2007): 839–44.

57. *Nancy Shippen, Her Journal Book*, 233. For superb analysis of Shippen Livingston's use of the literary names and the trope of virtue in distress, see Knott, *Sensibility and the American Revolution*, 133–40.

58. Norton, *Liberty's Daughters*, 48–49; Kerber, *Women of the Republic*, 184.

59. Michael Grossberg, *A Judgment for Solomon: The d'Hauteville Case and Legal Experience in Antebellum America* (New York: Cambridge University Press, 1996).

60. Holly Brewer, *By Birth or Consent: Children, Law, and the Anglo-American Revolution in Authority* (Chapel Hill: University of North Carolina Press for the OIEAHC, 2005), 250–64, 340, 356, 364.

61. Cynthia Kierner, *Traders and Gentlefolk: The Livingstons of New York, 1675–1790* (Ithaca, NY: Cornell University Press, 1992), 102–3, 126–27, 218–42; Margaret Livingston to Anne Shippen Livingston, December 5, 1789, in *Nancy Shippen, Her Journal Book*, 270.

62. Margaret Livingston to Anne Shippen Livingston, 1786, in *Nancy Shippen, Her Journal Book*, 246, 148.

63. "Margaret Beekman Livingston to Anne Hume Shippen Livingston, 1790?" and "October 29, 1790," *Nancy Shippen, Her Journal Book*, 234, 284, 312. On the most famous of those open secrets, see Annette Gordon-Reed, *The Hemingses of Monticello: An American Family* (New York: W. W. Norton, 2008).

64. *Nancy Shippen, Her Journal Book*, 270.

65. The 1788 "Essay on Marriage" and Lee's letters to Nancy both invoke Edward Young's *Night Thoughts*, a quintessential example of eighteenth-century sentimental ideals. Lee's most lasting claim to fame has been an antislavery essay published in the *Virginia Gazette* in 1767, at the behest of Benezet's coadjutors, which Quaker activists kept in circulation long after Lee wished it forgotten. Paul C. Nagel, *The Lees of Virginia: Seven Generations of an American Family* (Oxford: Oxford University Press, 2007); *Nancy Shippen, Her Journal Book*, 273; "Essay on Marriage," 23; Bruns, *Am I Not a Man and a Brother*, 107–11.

66. "Arthur Lee to Anne Livingston," *Nancy Shippen, Her Journal Book*, 273.

67. Kierner, *Traders and Gentlefolk*, 102–3, 126–27, 218–42.

68. "Margaret Beekman Livingston to Anne Shippen Livingston, October 29, 1790," *Nancy Shippen, Her Journal Book*, 286–89.

69. *Nancy Shippen, Her Journal Book*, 300; Brooke, *Emily Montague*, 1:65–67, 30–34; Cavendish, "Letter CCI," *CCXI sociable letters*, 427; Jane Austen, *Emma*, 2 vols. (New York: Little, Brown, 1902), 1:112–13.

70. On Elizabeth Freeman, see chap. 7; and Adams and Pleck, *Love of Freedom*, 147. On Ona Judge Staines, see Evelyn Gerson, "A Thirst for Complete Freedom: Why Fugitive Slave Oney Judge Staines Never Returned to Her Master, President George Washington" (master's thesis, Harvard University, June 2000); and Erica Armstrong Dunbar, *Never Caught: The Washingtons' Relentless Pursuit of Their Runaway Slave, Ona Judge* (New York: 37 Ink/Atria, 2017). I have deferred to Dunbar's spelling of Ona Judge's name, which frequently appears in the records as "Oney."

71. Frederick Kitt advertisement for Oney Judge, *Pennsylvania Gazette*, May 24, 1796; George Tudor advertisement for Henry Henson, *Independent Gazeteer* (Philadelphia), July 9, 1787; Henrietta Wragg advertisement for Peter, *State Gazette of South-Carolina*, July 11, 1785; F. Pinckney's advertisement of the "Eloped" cook Sambo in the *Columbian Herald or the Patriotic Courier of North-America*, July 27, 1785.

72. George Washington to Oliver Wolcott, September 1, 1796, and George Washington to Joseph Whipple, November 28, 1796, in Fritz Hirschfeld, *George Washington and Slavery: A Documentary Portrayal* (Columbia: University of Missouri Press, 1997), 113–15. For political context, see Joseph J. Ellis, *Founding Brothers: The Revolutionary Generation* (New York: Alfred A. Knopf, 2000), 120–61.

73. Joseph Whipple to Oliver Wolcott, October 4, 1796, in Hirschfeld, *George Washington and Slavery*, 114–15.

74. George Washington to Oliver Wolcott, September 1, 1796, and George Washington to Joseph Whipple, November 28, 1796, in Hirschfeld, *George Washington and Slavery*, 113–15.

75. George Washington to Oliver Wolcott, September 1, 1796, in Hirschfeld, *George Washington and Slavery*, 113–14. On the possibility of revolutionary emancipation and on shifting legal frames for racial and gender exclusion, see Gary B. Nash, *The Forgotten Fifth: African Americans in the Age of Revolution* (Cambridge, MA: Harvard University Press, 2006); David

Waldstreicher, *Slavery's Constitution: From Revolution to Ratification* (New York: Hill and Wang, 2009); and Barbara Young Welke, *Law and the Borders of Belonging in the Long Nineteenth Century United States* (New York: Cambridge University Press, 2010).

    76. Rev. Benjamin Chase, letter to the editor, *Liberator*, January 1, 1847; Henry Wiencek, *An Imperfect God: George Washington, His Slaves, and the Creation of America* (New York: Farrar, Straus and Giroux, 2003), 336–38.

    77. Wiencek, *An Imperfect God*, 336–38; Joseph J. Ellis, *His Excellency: George Washington* (New York: Vintage Books, 2005), 202–3, 256–70.

    78. Ellis, *His Excellency: George Washington*, 256–70; Gary Nash and Jean Soderlund, *Freedom by Degrees: Emancipation in Pennsylvania and Its Aftermath* (New York: Oxford University Press, 1991), 90; Wiencek, *An Imperfect God*, 352.

    79. Dunbar, *Never Caught*, 158–60.

    80. "Washington's Runaway Slave," *Granite Freeman*, Concord, New Hampshire, May 22, 1845, reprinted as "Washington's Runaway Slave," *Liberator*, August 22, 1845. https://www.encyclopedia virginia.org/_Washington_s_Runaway_Slave_The_Liberator_August_22_1845; Benjamin Chase, "A Slave of George Washington!," *Liberator*, January 1, 1847. https://www.encyclopediavirginia .org/_A_Slave_of_George_Washington_by_Benjamin_Chase_The_Liberator_January_1_1847.

    81. "Law Intelligence: Liability of Husbands for Debts of their Wives," *News World* (London), July 29, 1790; "Law Intelligence from a Late London paper Liability of Husbands for Debts of their Wives," *Federal Gazette, and Philadelphia Evening Post*, November 13, 1790; reprinted in the *Carlisle Gazette, and the Western Repository of Knowledge*, December 1, 1790. Massachusetts legislature and courts were still squabbling over the problem of liability raised by Quok Walker's master (note 42 above) ten years later: "Where negroes have taken their freedom against the consent of their masters, and have since become paupers, there is yet a question respecting their support. Some say that their former masters ought to be at the expence. Others say that, as the public opinion emancipated them, they ought to come within the description of state paupers. Others say that they are within no description of town inhabitants, that towns could never warn them to depart, and that they could never gain a legal settlement. This dispute is not known in Boston, but it exists in many places in the country. Suits are pending on the question, but the judges do not seem to have formed any system of opinions on the subject; and, though a bill has been long before the legislature, nothing is yet agreed upon respecting it." James Sullivan to Jeremy Belnap, *Collections of the Massachusetts Historical Society*, series 5, 3:403.

    82. Washington to Benjamin Dulaney, July 15, 1799, Hirschfeld, *George Washington and Slavery*, 80; Dorothy Twohig, "'That Species of Property': Washington's Role in the Controversy over Slavery," *George Washington Reconsidered*, ed., Don Higginbotham, University Press of Virginia, 2001, https://washingtonpapers.org/resources/articles/species/.

    83. Hyde 1 Modern 142, 142 (86 *ER* 791).

    84. Timothy Foresight [pseud.], "From the Bristol Journal of March 18," *Boston Independent Chronicle*, June 15, 1786.

    85. Rush's advice to Mr. Brown on newspapers, *Berkshire Chronicle* (Pittsfield, Massachusetts), July 14, 1789.

    86. Henry Beekman Livingston might cut a more sympathetic figure for modern readers, if, as a family historian has claimed, he angered his white family by selling off the patrimonial lands in order to gather all his children, of "various hues," into his house and to redistribute that patrimony to his illegitimate and unfree children as well as his "lawful heir." Clare Brandt, *An American Aristocracy: The Livingstons* (Garden City, NY: Doubleday, 1986), 140.

87. Virginia Woolf, *A Room of One's Own*, ed. Susan Gubar (Orlando: Houghton Mifflin Harcourt, 2005), 79. Eliza Custis Law, the Custis-Washington granddaughter Ona Judge refused to serve, was one such example of elite separation and divorce. Shortly after Martha Washington's death, she obtained a legal separation from her husband with support from her family, and Ona Judge's younger sister and her children received their freedom from Eliza's estranged husband Thomas Law, whose idiosyncrasies included sympathy for families who crossed the color line. Delphy Judge, like Ona, had a white father. She had married William Costin, a leader in Washington DC's emerging free black community, who was reputed to be both the grandson and nephew of Martha Washington. Law's previous relationship with—and children by—an unknown Indian woman implied a predilection for concubinage that had probably been a factor in Ona Judge's decision to flee rather than become an intimate part of his household. Delphy Judge and William Costin instead made him their ally against the known predations of the white Custis family. Margaret Law Callcott, *Mistress of Riversdale: The Plantation Letters of Rosalie Stier Calvert, 1795–1821* (Baltimore: Johns Hopkins University Press, 1992), 241, 242n4; Allen Culling Clark, *Greenleaf and Law in the Federal City* (Washington, DC: Press of W. F. Roberts, 1901), 285–90. On power dynamics in the preservation of family letters and the silence of a cuckolded Jamaican patriarch, see Sarah M. S. Pearsall, *Atlantic Families: Lives and Letters in the Later Eighteenth Century* (Oxford: Oxford University Press, 2008), 11, 232–38. Another example of long-closed correspondence related to a late eighteenth-century divorce can be found in "Jasper Yeates Brinton Collection 1762–1916," series 1, John Steinmetz Personal Correspondence—Henry Steinmetz's Divorce, box 5, folders 7–8, HSP.

Epilogue

1. Merry Wiesner-Hanks, "Forum Introduction: Reconsidering Patriarchy in Early Modern Europe and the Middle East," *Gender & History* 30, no. 2 (July 1, 2018): 320–30.

2. Michelle Alexander, *The New Jim Crow: Mass Incarceration in the Age of Colorblindness* (New York: New Press, 2010); Sally E. Hadden, *Slave Patrols: Law and Violence in Virginia and the Carolinas* (Cambridge, MA: Harvard University Press, 2001); comment in the *Louisville Democrat, Richmond Whig*, Richmond, Virginia, November 15, 1867.

3. Hilary Sargent, "All's Fair in Love and Classified Ads: Three Centuries of Public Spouse Shaming," Boston.com, February 9, 2015, https://www.boston.com/culture/relation ships/2015/02/09/alls-fair-in-love-and-classified-ads-three-centuries-of-public-spouse -shaming; Joan Hoff, "American Women and the Lingering Implications of Coverture," *Social Science Journal* 44, no. 1 (January 1, 2007): 41–55; Kathleen S. Sullivan, *Constitutional Context: Women and Rights Discourse in Nineteenth-Century America* (Johns Hopkins University Press, 2007); Sylvia Vatuk, *Marriage and Its Discontents: Women, Islam and the Law in India* (New Delhi: Women Unlimited, an associate of Kali for Women, 2017), esp. 9–13; Isaac Stanley-Becker, "$8.8 Million 'Alienation of Affection' Penalty: Another Reason Not to Have an Affair in North Carolina," *Washington Post*, July 31, 2018, https://www.washingtonpost.com/news/morning -mix/wp/2018/07/31/8-8-million-alienation-of-affection-award-another-reason-not-to-have-an -affair-in-north-carolina/.

4. *Baron and Feme: A Treatise of Law and Equity concerning Husbands and Wives*, 3rd ed. ([London], 1738), 7.

5. Elizabeth Cady Stanton, *Eighty Years and More: Reminiscences, 1815–1897*, ed. Ellen Dubois and Ann Gordon (Boston: Northeastern University Press, 1993), 31; *The Lawes Resolutions of Womens Rights* (London: 1632), 6.

6. "Report of the Woman's Rights Convention" and "Declaration of Sentiments" reprinted in Kathryn Kish Sklar, *Women's Rights Emerges within the Anti-Slavery Movement, 1830–1870: A Brief History with Documents*, Bedford Series in History & Culture (Boston: Bedford/St. Martin's, 2000), 172–79.

7. Col. James Livingston, Margaret Livingston Cady's father (and Elizabeth's grandfather), was a first cousin of Margaret Beekman Livingston. Elizabeth's mother was an age-mate of Peggy Shippen Livingston who lived in the circles where Margaret Beekman Livingston held court; she probably knew the family secrets as well as the family stories. John Schuyler, "Minor Topics: Colonel James Livingston," and Maturin L. Delafield, "Minor Topics: Colonel Henry Beekman Livingston," ed. Martha Joanna Lamb, *Magazine of American History with Notes and Queries* 21 (1889), 71–74, 256–58.

8. Stanton, *Eighty Years and More*, 12–30; Laurel Thatcher Ulrich, *Well-Behaved Women Seldom Make History* (New York: Alfred A. Knopf, 2007), 138–42. Of Stanton's many biographers, Kathi Kern has made the most serious attempt to track the fragmentary details of Peter Teabout's life. Kern, *Mrs. Stanton's Bible* (Ithaca, NY Cornell University Press, 2001), 22–48.

9. Ann Gordon, afterword to Stanton, *Eighty Years and More*, 425. Stanton's last great revisionary project, *The Woman's Bible*, drew on not only her teacher Simon Hosack's spiritual legacy, but also on books he bequeathed to the young Elizabeth in his will: the Greek Testament and grammar he had used during his theological studies in Glasgow, and Thomas Scott's multivolume *Commentary in the Whole Bible*. Stanton, *Eighty Years and More*, 24; Kern, *Mrs. Stanton's Bible*, 78, 244n124, n128.

10. The "Declaration of Sentiments" reflected her ambivalence. In it, for instance, supposedly universal "woman" challenged the supposedly universal "mankind" for withholding "from her rights which are given the most ignorant and degraded men––both natives and foreigners." Where "ignorant and degraded" native-born and foreign women fit into this call for redress was not immediately clear. "Declaration of Sentiments" reprinted in Sklar, *Women's Rights Emerges*, 176–77. Stanton's memoir also effaces the connection between the general troubles of women with property and the specific grievances of her nurse Flora Cambell (whom she also does not identify as a servant). Kern, *Mrs. Stanton's Bible*, 236n63; Lois Banner, *Elizabeth Cady Stanton, a Radical for Woman's Rights* (Boston: Little, Brown, 1980). On Stanton and the runaway slave Harriet Powell, see Ulrich, *Well-Behaved Women*, 123–32.

11. The historian Nancy Cott observes that "it was hardly innovation to compare the wife to a slave. Since the emergence in England of political theories based on natural rights, some writers had seen the paradox of women's consenting 'freely' to give up their freedom, and had used the analogy to critical or ironic purpose." This book is the first to closely examine the eighteenth-century developments that laid the groundwork for nineteenth-century "convergence of proslavery and antislavery rhetorics on marriage." Cott, *Public Vows: A History of Marriage and the Nation* (Cambridge, MA: Harvard University Press, 2000), 64–65. For social historical and biographical accounts of the ways in which Stanton, like Thomas Jefferson, built on ideas that were already "common sense," see Lori Ginzberg, *Untidy Origins: A Story of Woman's Rights in Antebellum New York* (Chapel Hill: University of North Carolina Press, 2005); and Lori Ginzberg, *Elizabeth Cady Stanton: An American Life* (New York: Hill and Wang, 2009). On the relationship of marriage and slavery in the rhetoric of nineteenth-century antislavery and women's rights activists, as well as in the reasoning of their opponents, see Amy Dru Stanley, *From Bondage to Contract: Wage Labor, Marriage, and the Market in the Age of Slave Emancipation* (Cambridge: Cambridge University Press, 1998), esp. 17–35; Nancy Isenberg, *Sex and Citizenship*

in Antebellum America (Chapel Hill: University of North Carolina Press, 1998); Stephanie Mc-Curry, "The Two Faces of Republicanism: Gender and Proslavery Politics in Antebellum South Carolina," *Journal of American History* 78, no. 4 (1992), 1245–64; and Stephanie McCurry, *Masters of Small Worlds: Yeoman Households, Gender Relations, and the Political Culture of the Antebellum South Carolina Low Country* (New York: Oxford University Press, 1995).

12. Stanton, *Eighty Years and More*, 31, 26. She likely singled out James Kent and Joseph Story precisely because they were key nineteenth-century agents in the erosion of an understanding of equity that was useful for women. On Kent, Story, equity, and jurisdiction, see Daniel Hulsebosch, *Constituting Empire: New York and the Transformation of Constitutionalism in the Atlantic World, 1664–1830* (Chapel Hill: University of North Carolina Press, 2005), 277, 291–92.

13. *A Treatise of Feme Coverts: or, the Lady's Law*, vii; Stanton, *Eighty Years and More*, 34, 31; Kern, *Mrs. Stanton's Bible*, 236n65. Contemporary historians, Frances Dolan has noted, tend to miss the satirical treatment of law present *within* the *Taming of the Shrew*. Dolan, *Marriage and Violence: The Early Modern Legacy* (Philadelphia: University of Pennsylvania Press, 2008), 125.

14. Orlando Bridgeman and Saxe Bannister, *Reports of Judgments Delivered by Sir Orlando Bridgman, when Chief Justice of the Common Pleas, from Mich. 1660 to Trin. 1667* (London: Joseph Butterworth and Son, 1823), xii–ix. Bannister undertook this editorial project as he readied himself for assignment as attorney general of England's Australian colony of New South Wales. His term there was short, in part because he insisted that the freedoms of the old common law extended to Aborigines and convict laborers. Dean Wilson, "Bannister, Saxe (1790–1877)," *ODNB*.

15. McCurry, *Masters of Small Worlds*; Laura Edwards, *Gendered Strife & Confusion: The Political Culture of Reconstruction* (Urbana: University of Illinois Press, 1997); Laura Edwards, *The People and Their Peace: Legal Culture and the Transformation of Inequality in the Post-Revolutionary South* (Chapel Hill: University of North Carolina Press, 2009); Carole Shammas, *A History of Household Government in America* (Charlottesville: University of Virginia Press, 2002); Holly Brewer, "The Transformation of Domestic Law," in *CHLA*, 288–323.

16. Dean Wilson, "Bannister, Saxe (1790–1877)," *ODNB*; Zoë Laidlaw, "'Aunt Anna's Report': The Buxton Women and the Aborigines Select Committee, 1835–37," *Journal of Imperial & Commonwealth History* 32, no. 2 (May 2004): 1–28; Bridgeman and Bannister, *Reports of Judgments Delivered by Sir Orlando Bridgman*, 229–70.

17. Edwards, *The People and Their Peace*, 256–57; Stephen Newman, "Cooper, Thomas (1759–1839)," *ODNB*; Thomas Cooper, *The Institutes of Justinian: With Notes* (Philadelphia: P. Byrne, 1812), 433.

18. *John Lowden et. al. v. J. C. Moses*, in David McCord, *Reports of Cases Determined in the Court of Appeals of South Carolina* (Columbia, SC.: Doyle E. Sweeny, State Printer, 1826), 3:98–100, note A, https://babel.hathitrust.org/cgi/pt?id=mdp.35112102519677&view=1up&seq=118; McCurry, *Masters of Small Worlds*, 91; Edwards, *The People and Their Peace*.

19. Tapping Reeve, *The Law of Baron and Femme: Of Parent and Child, of Guardian and Ward, of Master and Servant, and of the Powers of Courts of Chancery* (New York: Oliver Steele, 1816), 80–81n1; James Clancy, *A Treatise of the Rights, Duties and Liabilities of Husband and Wife: At Law and in Equity* (London: Printed by A. Strahan for J. Butterworth, 1827), 22–48.

20. William Blackstone, *Commentaries on the Laws of England*, 4 vols. (Oxford: Clarendon Press, 1765), 433; James Kent, *Commentaries on American Law*, 4 vols. (New York: O. Halsted, 1826), 2:124.

21. Edwards, *The People and Their Peace*.

22. Maine's personal story also continues those told in this book. His father was a doctor trained in the Scottish universities, who deserted Maine and his mother during the 1820s. Maine thus had intimate knowledge from an early age of the differences between Scottish and English marriage law, of the pitfalls coverture contained for married women, and of "extraordinary ingenuity" that lawyers might use "to defeat ancient rules" relating to women. Henry Sumner Maine, *Ancient Law: Its Connection With the Early History of Society, and Its Relation to Modern Ideas* (New York: Charles Scribner, 1864), 148. Maine, like Blackstone, preferred intellectual inquiry to the "active" conflicts of the courts. And like antislavery and women's rights reformers, he understood that the press could be used to give meaning to legal actions that had little to do with the intentions of legal authorities. At Cambridge, he began a lifelong friendship with the influential jurist and journalist James Fitzjames Stephen, the (eventual) uncle of Virginia Woolf. Maine, *Ancient Law*, 163–64, 154, note on xxxix. For a succinct account of the details of the 1857 marriage reform act, see Lawrence Stone, *Road to Divorce: England 1530–1987* (Oxford: Oxford University Press, 1990), 368–82. For Maine's biography, see R. C. J. Cocks, "Maine, Sir Henry James Sumner (1822–1888)," *ODNB*. For his enduring relevance to social theories of modernity, see Paul Kockelman, "From Status to Contract Revisited: Value, Temporality, Circulation and Subjectivity," *Anthropological Theory* 7, no. 2 (June 1, 2007): 151–76. Jürgen Habermas unintentionally documents one trajectory of Marxist uses of the wives/slaves analogy in chapter 6 of his influential work *The Structural Transformation of the Public Sphere*, trans. Thomas Burger and Frederick Lawrence (Cambridge, MA: MIT Press, 1991). For a general overview of late nineteenth-century theorizing about household government, see Shammas, *A History of Household Government*; and Ann Taylor Allen, "Feminism, Social Science, and the Meanings of Modernity: The Debate on the Origin of the Family in Europe and the United States, 1860–1914," *American Historical Review* 104, no. 4 (October 1, 1999): 1085–113.

23. The language of submission versus starvation appeared in a 1920 case that did not cite *Manby* directly, but which displayed remarkable parallels. It declared that an employer could not be sued for "enticing," "harbouring," or hiring a sharecropper bound by contractual debt peonage to someone else. *Shaw v. Fisher*, February 23, 1920, 10378, Supreme Court of South Carolina 113 S.C. 287; 102 S.E. 325; 1920 S.C. LEXIS 58.

Index

Page numbers in italics refer to tables or figures.